T0319928

Fair Wages

In memory of my father

Picture on the cover by Sabrina Bosson
Cover design by Boroka Gergely
Copy editing and layout by James Patterson

Fair Wages

Strengthening Corporate Social Responsibility

Daniel Vaughan-Whitehead

Senior Adviser, Responsible for Wages Policies, ILO, Geneva

Professor, Sciences Po, Paris

Edward Elgar
Cheltenham, UK • Northampton, MA, USA

Published by
Edward Elgar Publishing Limited
The Lypiatts
15 Lansdown Road
Cheltenham
Glos GL50 2JA
UK

Edward Elgar Publishing, Inc.
William Pratt House
9 Dewey Court
Northampton
Massachusetts 01060
USA

A catalogue record for this book
is available from the British Library

Library of Congress Control Number: 2009941284

ISBN 978 1 84980 147 8 (cased)

Printed and bound by MPG Books Group, UK

Contents

List of Figures and Maps

FIGURES

MAPS

List of Tables and Boxes

TABLES

BOXES

Foreword

This is an exceptionally important and timely piece of work for the simple reason that it brings to our attention a global crisis – that of unfair wages. 'Crisis' is an overworked concept these days but the wage crisis is the Great White Shark preying just below the surface of our troubled economies. In the first chapter of this book, Daniel Vaughan-Whitehead shows that the wage crisis goes back at least a decade and that workers' wages did not keep pace with the economic growth that characterized the period up to the financial crisis in 2008. Wages declined as a share of GDP and of company profits, while wage inequality widened. This means that workers were getting poorer in a period of robust economic growth and wealth creation. The data presented in this book are troubling and have led me to conclude that we are faced with a situation that is unfair and unequal and will surely lead to conflict. Indeed, it already has. In 2006, workers in Bangladesh went on strike on a massive scale because they simply could not make ends meet on wages that had not been adjusted in over a dozen years. The government finally convened the Wage Board and the Board increased wages to US$23 per month, a level well below what many believe to be necessary for an acceptable standard of living. This is borne out by continuing wage protests and the Bangladeshi Wage Board is again discussing an adjustment to the minimum wage. This is not an isolated example – wage disputes are frequent in China as well, despite the fact that provincial authorities in the major industrial centres increase the minimum wage regularly.

There are many reasons for the global stagnation of wages compared to increases in profits, GDP and the cost of living, among them the decline in trade union density and collective bargaining, and an abundant supply of labour in key exporting companies. Even in countries where wage adjustments have been regular, however, wages have lagged. Why? I believe that part of the answer lies in the way we have looked at wages. Most calculations – by government agencies analysing the minimum wage or NGOs advocating a living wage – have been based on the basket of goods needed to reproduce workers and their families. This approach overlooks the fundamental issue of equity. Is the wage a fair return on the investment made by the worker in the firm? Does the wage reflect the contribution of the worker to the sales and profits of the company and to the growth of the economy? The statistics in this book show that, in most cases, the answer is 'no'. This is a fundamentally unfair and untenable situation and one that needs to be addressed urgently.

If we are to confront the issue of fairness in respect of wages, where do we begin? In this volume, Daniel Vaughan-Whitehead provides an excellent analytical framework and tool that can be applied at firm level, either by management as a way of assessing the firm's wage policy and practice; by workers in evaluating their wages; or by social auditors in determining legal and code compliance. I fully expect that the different dimensions of the fair wage proposed in this book will become standard features of company annual wage reviews and of social audits. We in the Fair Labor Association have already collaborated with Daniel on a number of field tests and have incorporated elements of the system in our independent auditing of factories. We have also cooperated in designing a self-assessment on fair wages that is available on our Assessment Portal. The results have been quite revealing and instructive to the enterprises that have used them and I believe that the fair wage concept developed by Daniel Vaughan-Whitehead will recast the way in which we all think about wages.

Auret van Heerden

President and CEO
Fair Labor Association

Preface

In recent years, Corporate Social Responsibility (CSR) has developed both rapidly and extensively. It has become an essential dimension and tool of good corporate governance which is increasingly recognized and even demanded by the different stakeholders. This has undoubtedly made it possible to tackle a number of important and urgent work-related issues, such as child labour, health and safety at work and other core working conditions.

In this book, it is proposed that the time has come to include wage issues in the CSR approach and to start developing a monitoring process in this area. Wages continue to represent the most essential working condition, as well as constituting employers' main production cost and, therefore, the object of permanent pressure.

'Fair wages' is a term traditionally used in Anglo-Saxon regulatory frameworks, as illustrated by the Fair Wage Resolution, back in nineteenth-century Scotland, or by fair wage or fair minimum wage resolutions in the United States and the United Kingdom. They referred originally to public policy on wage issues and were also very much related to the living wage approach. It is proposed here to develop a new concept of fair wages, which would refer mainly to enterprises' responsibility with regard to a number of complementary wage issues and would, therefore, not be limited to the living wage approach.

The present report legitimizes this proposal on the basis of an assessment of wage developments around the world, which depicts a number of worrying phenomena at the macroeconomic level, such as the general increase in low pay and working poor, a continuous rise in wage differentials and a decline in the wage share of economic growth, as well as a series of dysfunctional practices in wage fixing at local level, especially along the supply chain, including the non-payment of wages, lack of transparency of pay systems, discrimination, lack of social dialogue and so on.

This proposal provides a methodology that could make it possible: first, to provide an assessment of wage developments at company level; second, to start building a regular monitoring process in this area; and, third, to provide the necessary tools for assisting and advising managers on wage policy.

The main aim of this proposal is to become rapidly operational, while taking into account problems which may be faced in the process, which suggest that a progressive approach might be advisable in this particularly sensitive area.

Since this work started in 2006, it has had a favourable reception, with our suggestion of a Fair Wage approach receiving wide acceptance among CSR actors. With the help of the FLA, which was the first organization to be convinced of the usefulness of this new approach on wages, in 2008 we were able to implement, for the first time, a complete audit of all wage issues. We conducted it again in 2009. At the same time, a number of case studies on Fair Wages were carried out in the field, which enabled us to present the first set of findings on fair wage practices in different forums. This led to the setting up of the Fair Wage Network in October 2009 and will lead to the launching of a major Fair Wage Campaign in CSR in 2010. We hope that this book will help to enlarge this general movement, encouraging many more suppliers, brands and NGOs – including consumers – as well as trade unions and employers' organizations to join our network and progressively come to promote fairer wage practices along the supply chain. We hope that the inclusion of wages in CSR will help to improve working conditions, while helping individual companies – including major corporations – to improve their competitiveness, not only through low labour costs, but also through better wage practices and improved quality of goods, thereby helping to promote sustainable development.

Acknowledgements

This book would never have seen the light of day without the original request from the Fair Labour Association to extend the work they were doing on wage issues. I am particularly grateful to Auret van Heerden, President of the FLA, for his continuing support and confidence in this work, as well as for deciding to implement the Fair Wage approach on a large scale. The work proposed here is an original approach aimed at strengthening CSR actors' work on wages. It does not reflect the views of the International Labour Office, but those of the author alone. This book could also not have been achieved without the commitment and contributions of Lina Arbelaez, Sumathi Chandrashekaran, Lina Marmolejo and Jinghan Zhang and their field work in 2008 and also Lihui Jin, Caroline Lavoie, Lolita Sagitari and Natalie Unwin-Kuruneri for the case studies carried out in 2009. The continuous support of the MPA-SciencesPo was also essential and I am particularly grateful to its academic director, Professor Erhard Friedberg. I would also like to thank James Patterson for his copyediting and layout work, Boroka Gergely for the cover design and Sabrina Bosson for providing the picture of workers on the cover. My final thanks go to the FLA staff, especially Ines Kaempfer and Youli Gouli, but also to Eva Chen and Xiaolei Qian, whose support, high competence and motivation in the field were extremely valuable, and to Jorge Lopez, FLA executive director, for his support and enthusiasm in organizing the first Fair Wage Conference in October 2009 in Washington. I hope that what is proposed here will facilitate the tremendous work they are doing to improve labour standards along the supply chain.

Introduction

1. The General Context: Global Wage Trends

INTRODUCTION

In order to obtain a first insight into wage issues at enterprise level, it is essential to understand wage trends at macro level since they are the sum of micro behaviour – of managers and workers at enterprise level, but also of individual governments, consumers and other actors. We propose, therefore, a brief review of major wage developments around the world, in terms of real wages, the wage share, wage disparity and minimum wages during the last 15 years – between 1995 and 2009 – in particular, to better identify the possible effects of globalization on wages. In doing so, we shall try to distinguish, as far as possible, between the period before the crisis – that is, before 2008, which was characterized by rapid economic growth despite financial crises, notably in Asia and Latin America – and the current period, characterized by a deep financial crisis (starting in the second half of 2008) which has plunged most countries into a prolonged recession. For this purpose, we shall first present the trends observable between 1995 and 2007, followed by the most recent trends in the crisis, in 2008–2009. We shall also try to provide – from the existing literature – a first report on wage practices along the supply chain, in particular, by identifying all major wage-fixing problems identified so far among the suppliers and sub-contractors of the brands.

The wage trends in question are obviously very much interrelated. The progression of real wages shows how the purchasing power of wages evolves over time. Real wages can, however, have a direct effect on the wage share, which measures how economic growth is distributed between labour and capital. If the growth in average wages is slower than the growth in GDP per capita, then the wage share usually declines. If, on the contrary, average wages grow faster than GDP per capita, then the wage share is expected to increase. Wage differentials are also very much influenced by real wage progression by categories of workers, for instance between men and women or between those at the bottom and those at the top. A knowledge of minimum wage developments is also essential since generally they help to improve the wage situation of the most vulnerable workers – those on the lowest wage scale – and thus to reduce the number of working poor, narrowing the wage gap with those on the highest wage scale. Finally, with subcontracting and outsourcing becoming wide-spread alongside increased movements of capital in a global economy, wages along the supply chain also need to be better identified since they will influence macro developments, such as competitiveness and trade, foreign investment and labour migration, and thus also help to shape wage trends – such as real wages and the wage share – at macroeconomic level. These wage trends, which we propose to address, point towards a number of structural imbalances, which will also help us to understand some aspects of the current economic crisis.

1.1 IMBALANCES IN REAL WAGE INCREASES

The first trend we shall report on is real wages, calculated as nominal wages (average compensation or total compensation to all employees), discounted for inflation or the consumer price index (CPI).

Estimates of real wages based on wage data for 85 countries – representing 70 per cent of the world's population – provide a series of interesting results, which will be described next.

Increase in a Majority of Countries and Some Impressive Cases

First, a widespread catch-up process may be observed with regard to wages. Although significant differences in wage levels continue to prevail between developed and developing countries, real wages were found to have increased in a substantial number of developing countries. This is especially true of the countries which have significantly opened up their trade, so that degree of openness seems to play a role. As shown in Figure 1.1 on real wage increases over the period 1995–2007, the most impressive growth has been in Central Asia (with a more than 600 per cent increase in Azerbaijan, Georgia, Turkmenistan and Uzbekistan), but also in China (265 per cent, that is, nearly 12 per cent per year on average), as well as in other transition countries in Central and Eastern Europe, such as Estonia, Latvia and Lithuania (more than 100 per cent). Growth has also been sustained in some Asian countries, such as South Korea and Singapore (nearly 50 per cent). In Latin America, real wages increased by 15 per cent on average over the same period, but with higher increases in countries such as Honduras, Nicaragua and Mexico (nearly 30 per cent). In Africa, real wages also increased significantly in South Africa.

Real Wage Growth Rates Modest and Unbalanced by Region

At the same time, one major finding from our wage data analysis is that, despite strong economic growth and some real wage growth over the whole

Africa

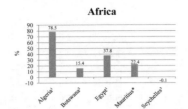

Notes: ¹ 1996–2004; ² 1997–2005; ³ 1995–2006; * 1995–2007.

Americas

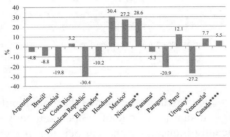

Notes: ¹ 1996–2006; ² 1995–2006; ³ 1996–2004; * 1998–2004; ** 1995–2004; *** 1996–2006; **** 1995–2007.

Asia and Pacific

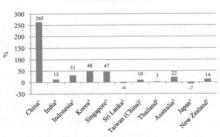

Notes: ¹ 1995–2007; ² 1995–2005; ³ 1995–2006.

CIS, Central Asia and Middle East

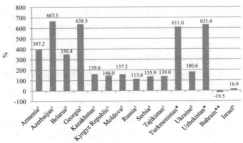

Notes: ¹ 1995–2006; ² 1995–2007; ³ 1997–2007; * 1995–2005; ** 1998–2006.

Source: ILO wage data base.

Figure 1.1 Real wage progression, 1995–2007 (cumulative % since 1995)

Europe

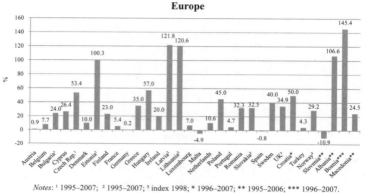

Notes: [1] 1995–2007; [2] 1995–2007; [3] index 1998; * 1996–2007; ** 1995–2006; *** 1996–2007.

Figure 1.1 (cont.)

period, the rate of wage growth has remained disappointingly low. While the global economy grew at an average rate of 3.3 per cent per year between 1995 and 2007 – significantly higher than the 2.9 per cent per year in the period 1980–94 – annual wage growth remained rather low, at less than 3 per cent, and at an average of 1.9 per cent per year over the most recent period, from 1999 to 2007.

Map 1.1 shows that annual real wage rates have remained low in most countries: nearly two-thirds of countries experienced annual real wage growth of less than 3 per cent.

Moreover, the figure masks wide variations by region and by country. In industrialized countries, wages increased by 1 per cent per year, while, in Latin America, growth was only 0.50 per cent and even less in African countries. Conversely, among the countries with annual real wage growth above 3 per cent, China experienced nearly 12 per cent growth per year and the CIS countries and non-EU Central Europe saw 14 per cent annual growth. Spectacular real wage growth since the mid-1990s thus seems to have been limited to transition economies from Central and Eastern Europe (Estonia, Latvia, Lithuania), Central Asia (Turkmenistan, Uzbekistan, Georgia and Azerbaijan) and Asia (China, Vietnam).

In their early transition years – the early 1990s – however, these same (CEE) countries experienced a sharp deterioration in real wages (more than 50 per cent in most of them), alongside serious economic contraction. This process halted in the mid-1990s and the rapid increase in real wages since then has acted as a sort of balancing process to recover pre-transition levels (Vaughan-Whitehead, 2003; 2010). China is the only country – possibly also Vietnam – which has experienced continuous real wage growth, with no decline in the early 1990s like the one witnessed in all Central and Eastern European countries.

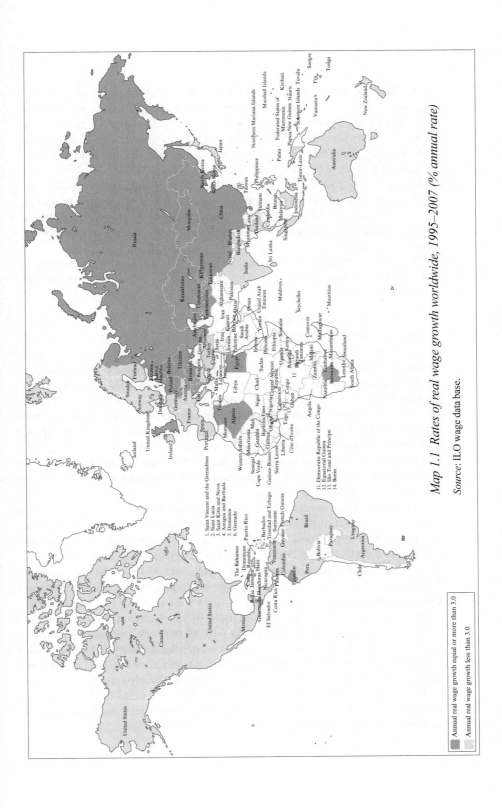

Map 1.1 Rates of real wage growth worldwide, 1995–2007 (% annual rate)

Source: ILO wage data base.

1. Saint Vincent and the Grenadines
2. Saint Lucia
3. Saint Kitts and Nevis
4. Antigua and Barbuda
5. Dominica
6. Grenada

11. Democratic Republic of the Congo
12. Equatorial Guinea
13. São Tomé and Principe
14. Benin

Annual real wage growth equal or more than 3.0

Annual real wage growth less than 3.0

While former EU-15 member countries do benefit from higher wage levels, they have generally experienced some wage moderation over the last ten years. Real wage figures confirm the fall – as in Spain – or slow progress (as in Austria, Germany, Portugal and France). Of the former EU-15 countries, only Sweden, the United Kingdom, Greece, Finland and Ireland have seen substantial real wage growth over the period.

Neighbouring countries, such as the Former Yugoslav Republic of Macedonia, continue to experience very moderate real wage growth – only 2.8 per cent between 1998 and 2007 – despite rapid GDP growth. Real wages also experienced a significant fall in Turkey following the 2001 crisis and have never fully recovered.

With the exception of some rapid increases in the transition countries, Europe has thus been characterized by general wage moderation over the last decade.

1.2 A FALLING WAGE SHARE

The wage share measures the share of total income or Gross Domestic Product (GDP) that goes to labour. Labour income is generally measured by 'compensation of employees', provided in most national accounts, which captures the income of salaried workers (thus excluding self-employed persons) that we then divide by GDP per number of total employees. In some countries, however, national accounts have tried to take the self-employed into account, since they also contribute to GDP growth. In this case, 'compensation of the self-employed' was added, on the assumption that self-employed persons earn, on average, the same as employees.

The global picture with regard to wage share is striking. In a large majority of countries (51 out of 85 or nearly three-quarters) wages have experienced a declining share in economic growth. The decline has occurred in all regions of the globe (ILO, 2008a, 2008b). The most dramatic falls have occurred in a number of transition economies in Central Asia and Central and Eastern Europe, such as Bulgaria (–16 percentage points), Kyrgyzstan (–13), Poland (–9), Slovenia (–8) and Hungary (–6), but also in a number of EU-15 countries, such as Austria (–8), Spain (–6), Ireland (–6) and Germany (–5). The wage share also declined in FYR Macedonia – by 14 per cent – between 1997 and 2005, in a context of rapid GDP growth averaging 5.3 per cent. It has also declined in Turkey, despite rapid economic growth after the 2001 crisis and also an increase in the share of wage earners in total employment.

In Europe, the wage share was found to have declined in 25 out of 30 countries studied. Moreover, the declines have been much more substantial than the (few) increases (Vaughan-Whitehead, 2010).

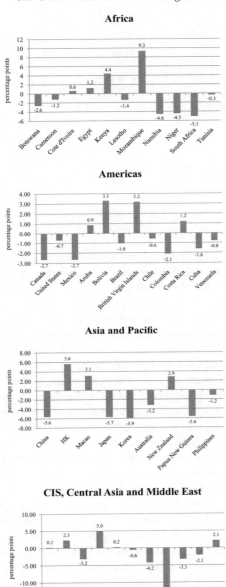

Source: ILO wage data base.

Figure 1.2 Evolution of wage share by country, 1995–2007 (percentage points)

Fair Wages

Europe

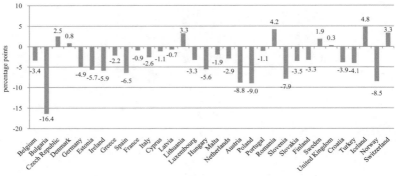

Figure 1.2 (cont.)

The fall was also marked in Canada and Mexico (–3 percentage points). Some Asian countries have also experienced significant falls, especially Japan, South Korea and China (–6). Similarly in Africa, where the countries most affected are South Africa, Namibia, Niger (–5) and Botswana (–2). There were some exceptions to this long-term and generally downward trend, including Romania, the Czech Republic and Sweden in Europe; Bolivia and Costa Rica in South America; Hong Kong, Macao and New Zealand in Asia and the Pacific; and Kenya and Mozambique in Africa.

However, if we look at its level rather than changes over time, we see that the wage share has increased where the wage share level was particularly low, as in Bulgaria (where total employees' compensation was between 32 and 42 per cent of GDP in the period 1995–2006) and the Czech Republic (32.3 per cent in 2006), and where workers have also benefited from real wage growth.

Interestingly, countries with the highest economic growth are no exceptions. Even in China, where we have seen that real wages increased significantly, this increase has not been proportionate to the impressive economic growth (more than 10 per cent per year), so that the wage share fell significantly. All in the forefront with regard to economic growth, the BRICs (Brazil, Russia, India and China) plus South Africa have experienced a fall in wage share, despite impressive real wage growth. As in China, the fall is also impressive in South Africa, with a drop of 5 percentage points since 1995, despite its rapid economic growth and real wage increases. Russia has also experienced a drop in the wage share despite real wage growth. In other words, a rapid real wage increase is not a sufficient condition for an increase in the wage share.

This means that real wages have not progressed as much as productivity, as confirmed by wage and productivity data. An analysis of countries for which data are available indicates that, for the period between 1995 and 2007, real

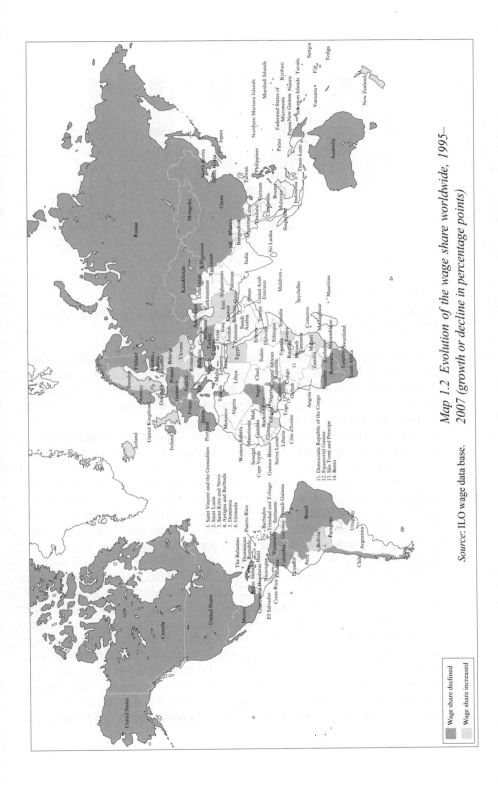

Map 1.2 *Evolution of the wage share worldwide, 1995–2007 (growth or decline in percentage points)*

Source: ILO wage data base.

1. Saint Vincent and the Grenadines
2. Saint Lucia
3. Saint Kitts and Nevis
4. Antigua and Barbuda
5. Dominica
6. Grenada

11. Democratic Republic of the Congo
12. Equatorial Guinea
13. São Tomé and Príncipe
14. Benin

Wage share declined

Wage share increased

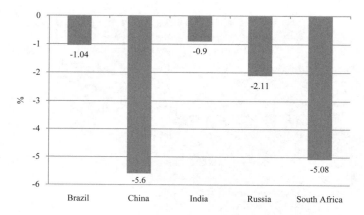

Source: National statistics.

Figure 1.3 The evolution of the wage share in the BRICs plus South Africa, 1995–2007 (percentage points)

wage growth remained behind productivity growth in a majority of countries (24 out of 32 countries). Elasticity of real wages to productivity (measured by GDP per capita) was found to be 0.75 – that is, less than 1 – indicating that real wages on average, over the whole period 1995–2007, lagged behind productivity growth: each additional 1 per cent increase in the annual growth of GDP per capita was associated, on average, with a 0.75 per cent increase in the annual growth of real wages (ILO, 2008a). This confirms the fall in the labour share of income.

All international organizations confirm this generalized and steady decline in the wage share – that is, in the labour share of income – over the past few decades (ADB, 2007; EC, 2007; ILO, 2008a, 2008b; IMF, 2007a, 2007b; OECD, 2007; World Bank, 2007). They also confirm that the decline in the wage share remains a dominant trend, even after controlling for cyclical fluctuations. The generalized fall in the wage share is thus a structural issue.

While there is a consensus on this declining trend, there are variations in the accompanying explanations. The IMF has posited the effect of technological progress, on the assumption that the progressive increase in technology would automatically devalorize labour's contribution and put more emphasis on capital and technology – although favouring skilled workers – an explanation that has also been put forward by the OECD (2007) and, rather prominently, by the EC (2007). The ILO has tried to explain the decreasing labour share in terms of industrial relations factors, such as the declining power of trade unions and the reduced scope of collective bargaining (ILO, 2008a, 2008b). The ILO has also highlighted that globalization may have played a part in the story. Over the past decade, the countries in which trade has grown as a percentage of GDP were also the countries with the most rapid decline in the wage share (ILO, 2008a). This would suggest that the intensification of competition – particularly the presence of large low-wage exporters in the market for labour-intensive products – has worked as a wage moderating factor. This is why we propose to address the wage share dimension in the operations of large corporations along the supply chain in the following chapters.

Interestingly, no real challenge to the technological explanation of wage share decline has been proposed. This is surprising since this explanation does not seem to take into account the basic functioning of wage fixing and wage trends at the microeconomic level – that is, their progressive increase in tandem with any increase in technology.

The explanation of the declining wage share in terms of higher technological content and capital intensity takes as its basic assumption that the fall is not due to declining total wage compensation (numerator) and thus to unfavourable income distribution for labour, but rather due to an increase in the denominator, that is, GDP divided by total employment. This would be caused by higher value added generated by more capital-intensive and technological processes, which would imply either creating more GDP with the same number of employees or creating the same level of GDP with a lower number of employees, automatically reducing the total wage share ratio. To some extent, this could be considered progress – due to more efficient production – rather than a problem (in terms of unequal growth distribution). However, this approach fails to consider that a more efficient production process due to higher technological content requires a better skilled and motivated labour force capable of adapting to more capital-intensive processes of this kind. This should, therefore, automatically involve an increase in total wage compensation per employee since either fewer employees have to create the same value added or the same number of employees have to create more value added. In order to reach these new standards, employees have to be better paid to be more adaptable and motivated, and also undergo training to acquire new skills, something that should normally be translated into higher wages.

In other words, even if technological improvements did explain the increase in the denominator, it should also be expected to increase the numerator, if we want the process to be truly efficient.

Technological content and capital intensity have increased in almost every country, but this should also have led to a progressive adjustment of average wages to reflect changes in the composition and skills of the labour force. Where this has not occurred, it might therefore be due to such factors as labour's declining negotiating power and the increasing dominance of the employers, especially in a context of high unemployment, restructuring and outsourcing.

The fact that the wage share seems to respond significantly to wage policy changes is another indication that wage institutions matter. For example, the wage share decline was halted in Brazil some time after the implementation of a very active minimum wage policy by President Lula. Uruguay presents similar trends. On the other hand, the dramatic fall in the wage share during early transition in most Central and Eastern European countries may have reflected the very restrictive wage policies implemented as part of their early reform strategies. This means that 'wage policy counts' and is likely to influence the wage share. Similarly, the disconnection between wage growth and productivity growth may also be due to the failure of certain pay systems to reward labour's contribution, an aspect that we shall examine further.

Whatever the explanation, this falling wage share has attracted much attention in global and national debates. It means that workers are not receiving a fair share of economic gains to the detriment of an increasing share for profits, an outcome that is not only difficult to accept on the social side – as witnessed by a number of campaigns on this issue launched by international and European trade unions and a number of political parties in many countries – but also on the economic side, since it reduces workers' purchasing power and thus their consumption. A number of economists have attracted attention to such adverse economic effects (Krueger, 1999; Luebker, 2007; Stiglitz, 2009). Because the marginal propensity to consume is higher for labour income than for capital income, an increase in the wage share would lead to a direct consumption boost, as shown by Stockhammer (2008) with regard to Europe, where a one percentage point increase in the wage share would increase GDP by 0.17 per cent.

For Stiglitz, this unequal redistribution of economic growth is the main and deepest cause of the current financial and economic crisis:

> The current crisis is due to the insufficiency of aggregate demand caused by the growing inequality ... The current crisis is due to lax monetary policy and weak regulations, but why was it so? A very simple answer – in the absence of lax monetary policy, there would have been insufficient aggregate demand in the United States and in the world. Because we have destabilized the economy by making wages more flexible rather than providing job security ... and because, over the last 30 years, there has been an increase in global inequality and we thought we could solve the problem because we told the people who had no money, keep spending as if you had money and they enjoyed it for a while, and so we had this massive debt credit finance bubble that enabled America to continue to spend. The system was based on American consumers spending beyond their means by borrowing and borrowing and borrowing and the bubble has broken. So we created a global economic system which was, in some sense, not sustainable. (Stiglitz, 2009)

There can be no question that monitoring of the wage share should continue in the future, in tandem with more permanent policy solutions to rebalance such an unequal distribution of growth. In this book, we shall propose how wage practices at enterprise level might contribute to such an objective.

1.3 INCREASED WAGE INEQUALITY

Within the labour share of wages, it was also important in our overview to identify how it was distributed between different categories of labour and to check whether there were any significant developments over time.

One key result that came out fairly clearly from the data was the increase in wage disparity (Figure 1.4), notably with an increasing wage gap between those at the bottom and those at the top of the wage scale.[1] While income disparity is generally measured by the Gini coefficient, which has also increased in recent decades (ILO, 2008b), wage disparity is better measured by calculating the highest wage decile – which is the wage level above which the top 10 per cent of workers are paid and commonly referred to as D9 – over the first wage decile (which is the wage level below which the bottom 10 per cent of workers are paid and commonly referred to as D1). This wage disparity ratio (D9/D1) was found to have increased in 70 per cent of the countries for which data are available. Although economic theory predicts that wage inequality is a sort of 'natural' by-product of early economic development and should thus be expected to increase more in developing countries – only to fall back once more at higher stages of economic development (Kuznets, 1955) – our findings show the rather robust result that wage inequality has increased in most countries, irrespective of their national income levels.

The increase in wage disparity is observable world-wide and in all regions (Map 1.3). The countries recording the largest increases in wage inequality are those hardest hit by past economic crises, such as South Korea and Thailand in Asia, and Argentina in South America. In Europe, the growth of wage disparity has been particularly rapid in the transition countries of Central and Eastern Europe, which experienced relatively low wage differentiation in the Communist era. They have all seen increased wage differentiation, particularly in Hungary and Estonia. In Poland, the ratio of the lowest wage decile to the highest also increased, from 3.33 in 1996 to 4.32 in 2006, and in the Czech Republic, from 2.45 in 1989 to 3.13 in 2006. The increase in wage inequality in Russia has also been dramatic, with a D9/D1 ratio of nearly 20.

The gap between low- and high-wage earners has also increased in several EU-15 countries in the last 15 years. This is the case in, for example, Austria

---

1. Since this was a clearly emerging trend we decided to scrutinize this source of wage disparity. Nevertheless, there are many other sources of wage disparity or wage inequality, based on differences of sex, level of education, age, ethnicity, migration status and formality. For more details on developments with regard to these different sources of wage disparity, see ILO (2008b).

Russian Federation (18.00)
Argentina (12.25)
Uruguay (12.06)
Armenia (12.01)
Thailand (9.27)
Latvia (5.97)
Lithuania (6.56)
Chile (8.24)
Bulgaria (5.30)
Georgia (17.13)
Poland (4.21)
Peru (7.17)
Hungary (4.56)
New Zealand (2.91)
Sri Lanka (4.97)
Germany (3.26)
Australia (3.34)
United Kingdom (7.28)
Slovenia (3.50)
United States (5.00)
Sweden (2.06)
Switzerland (2.65)
Canada (3.75)
Finland (2.55)
Czech Republic (3.11)
Denmark (2.69)
Norway (2.11)
Netherlands (2.91)
Panama (7.49)
Romania (4.76)
Costa Rica (7.53)
Japan (3.02)
Honduras (9.38)
Luxembourg (3.75)
Ecuador (6.86)
Ireland (3.78)
France (2.91)
Kazakhstan (6.17)
Greece (5.80)
Estonia (3.37)
Indonesia (15.50)
Austria (3.37)
Mexico (5.71)
Brazil (8.62)
Venezuela (4.56)
Paraguay (7.10)
Belgium (2.43)
Belarus (3.19)

Note: Latest available D9/D1 ratio indicated in parenthesis after country names.

Source: ILO wage data base.

Figure 1.4 Evolution of wage disparity (D9/D1) by country, 1995–2007 (percentage-point progression)

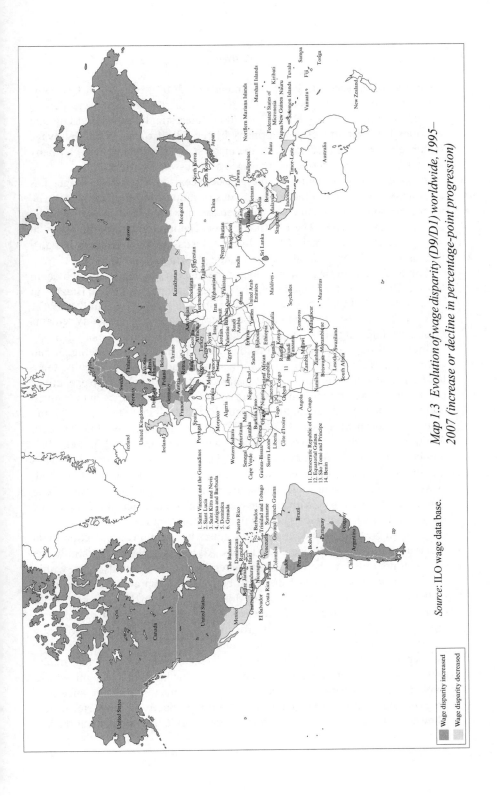

Source: ILO wage data base.

Map 1.3 Evolution of wage disparity (D9/D1) worldwide, 1995–2007 (increase or decline in percentage-point progression)

1. Saint Vincent and the Grenadines
2. Saint Lucia
3. Saint Kitts and Nevis
4. Antigua and Barbuda
5. Dominica
6. Grenada

11. Democratic Republic of the Congo
12. Equatorial Guinea
13. São Tomé and Príncipe
14. Benin

Wage disparity increased
Wage disparity decreased

(Guger and Marterbauer, 2007; Rechnungshof, 2007), but also in Germany, where the relative gap between the lowest and the highest wage deciles increased from 3.2 in 1996 to 3.7 in 2005. Interestingly, this increasing gap was mostly driven in western Germany by the fall of wages in the low-wage sector relative to the median, while the increase in the gap in eastern Germany was attributable more to the rising wages of high-wage earners.

Among developed countries, the gap between top and bottom wages has also increased rapidly in the United States (a ratio of top to bottom workers' wages of more than 4). In Asia, the increase has been high in the Republic of Korea and Thailand. The BRICs are no exception, with rapid increases in wage differentials in Brazil, China, India and Russia. Wage disparity has also increased significantly along with economic growth in South Africa.

Some of the countries which managed to reduce wage inequality include, in Europe, France and the United Kingdom. Wage disparity also fell in Brazil – in the second half of the period 2000–2007, with a fall from 8 to 6 of the D9/D1 ratio – and Indonesia, although in these latter two countries inequality remains at an alarmingly high level, together with India (D9/D1 ratio of more than 8).

Increased wage inequality can be due either to increases at the higher end of the wage scale or to a reduction at the lower end, or both. Recently, there has been a general campaign against the indecent wage levels of top executives (ILO, 2008b), which represent the main source of wage disparity in the United States and the United Kingdom: for example, in the United States in 2007, the chief executive officers (CEOs) of the 15 largest companies were found to earn 500 times more than the average worker, which is up from 360 in 2003. In a number of countries, the increasing wage gap is due rather to a deterioration in the lowest wages, as in Argentina, Chile, Germany and Thailand. In general, however, the increase in wage inequality in the majority of countries is due to a mixture of these types, with changes both at the bottom and at the top of the wage scale which combine to ratchet up wage polarization.

These increasing wage inequalities must be seen in conjunction with previous real wage and wage share trends. All together, these trends indicate, first, that not only has the wage share generally declined, but also that, within this lower wage share, wage disparity between the top and the bottom has increased, which means much less for those at the bottom. We also saw in our overview that even impressive increases in real wages were not sufficient to impede declining wage share and growing wage differentials, as shown by China and other rapidly growing economies.

Such increases in wage differentials present both economists and public policy with a number of complex issues. On the one hand, it is recognized that wage differentials between workers can be economically efficient since they are expected to reflect individual workers' skills, productivity and performance. They could thus be crucial in rewarding work effort, talent and innovation, key engines of economic growth. On the other hand, growing inequalities often not justified by differing individual performance have increased in recent years and their economic efficiency is being called into question. There have been instances in which wage and income inequality have reached excessive levels, posing a danger to social stability, besides considerations of economic efficiency. It has been shown that such inequality may lead to many economic costs, such as higher crime rates, higher expenditure on private and public security, and higher public health costs (UNDP, 2007; ILO, 2008b). Higher wage inequality may also deepen macroeconomic crises because low-income households have been shown to consume more in proportion to richer people, so that their reduced purchasing power could further aggravate the lack of demand, an aspect particularly important in the current economic crisis, which has been shown to be mainly a crisis of demand (Stiglitz, 2009).

Moreover, research findings seem to show that individual perceptions of happiness depend much more on how individuals compare their incomes with those of other people than on the absolute level of their income (Layard, 2006). Such inequality would thus also have high moral, social and political costs. In particular, the fact that workers at the bottom are, comparatively, getting less and less signals serious problems in the social sphere, since such an increasing wage gap is often associated with growing social exclusion and poverty, as we shall see in Section 1.4.[2]

1.4 LOW PAY AND WORKING POOR: INCREASING DESPITE MINIMUM WAGE DEVELOPMENT

Increase in Low Pay

There was an increase in the number of low-paid workers during the period under study (1995–2007), which, consequently, saw the emergence of the so-called 'working poor', that is, people in poverty despite having a job. It is important to highlight that a period of relative economic growth has been accompanied by an increased proportion of workers in poverty, thus showing that the unequal distribution of growth indicated by the wage share decline – together with increased wage inequality – is not neutral in terms of social outcomes. The phenomenon of working poverty affects as many as 200 million workers in South Asia and 150 million workers in Sub-Saharan Africa (ILO, 2005). There are also approximately 7–8 million working poor in the United States.

---

2. Ferreira and Ravallion (2008) and UNDP (2007) show the importance of reducing inequality to achieve a reduction in poverty.

The proportion of low-paid workers is defined as the proportion of workers who earn less than two-thirds of the median wage. Almost all countries on which data are available have been found to have experienced an increasing number of low-paid workers, including the United States, the Netherlands and Germany. There are exceptions, however, such as France and some Nordic countries. The low pay phenomenon is also observed in developing countries, where the low pay indicator – in the absence of reliable data on the median wage – is calculated by the relative poverty line of 1 US dollar per day. Statistics show that, since 1995, the proportion of workers earning less than 1 US dollar a day has increased. The picture is not totally bleak, however, with a relative decline since early 2000. At the same time, the proportion of workers around the world earning less than 2 US dollars per day has been increasing, from 1 billion to 2.6 billion since 2000 (ILO, 2005).

While the low pay indicator is indicative of poverty trends, a low-paid worker is not automatically among the working poor since he or she may live in a household in which several accumulated incomes raise it above the poverty threshold.

Nevertheless, the growth of low-paid workers has become a new concern for almost all governments, with particular policy initiatives in countries such as Brazil and Mexico.

This growing share of low-paid workers – alongside the falling wage share – has also led European trade unions to mobilize workers around these issues. The ETUC launched its campaign for 'fairer wages' in 2008, while the European public sector union EPSU has carried out a campaign against low pay in Europe, partly aimed at boosting minimum wages and collective bargaining policies.[3] Similarly, international trade unions have campaigned against low wages and increasing wage disparity (ITUC, 2008).

Rising food and commodity prices – particularly fuel prices – have further contributed to making the poorest worse off. Needless to say, food and fuel have no substitutes, so that their consumption cannot really be reduced in response to increasing prices. Households' purchasing power is thus directly affected, especially among low-income households which spend a larger proportion of their income on such goods. As an example, increasing food prices in India in 2007 caused the poorest urban households to experience an estimated fall in purchasing power of over 5 per cent, against a drop of only 2.2 per cent among the richest urban dwellers (ILO, 2008b). Food price increases also affect more workers in developing countries. It has been shown that, in advanced countries (such as Denmark, the Netherlands and Switzerland), food expenditure is less than 20 per cent of total expenditure, but more than 60 per

---

3. 'Pay campaign: On the offensive for fairer wages', ETUC (2008): http://www.etuc.org/a/4561; 'Tackling low pay – EPSU document', EPSU (2006): http://www.epsu.org/a/2027.

cent in many developing countries, with the ratio even exceeding 70 per cent in countries such as Armenia, Niger and Romania (ILO, 2008b). Clearly, for the sake of sustainable development an urgent response to the food crisis is called for on the wage policy front.

The Minimum Wage Revisited

The low pay phenomenon has helped to put the minimum wage at the top of policymakers' priorities (Vaughan-Whitehead, 2010). The minimum wage is seen as a potential solution to improve the situation of low-paid workers and so reduce their risk of falling into destitution.

Low-paid workers, for instance, were the main motivation for introducing the minimum wage in the United Kingdom and Ireland. Similarly, in Turkey, progressive improvement of the minimum wage has been seen as a way of addressing low pay and poverty issues. Tackling the working poor phenomenon is also a major concern underlying minimum wage discussions in Greece, especially in the context of a relatively undeveloped welfare policy. The new minimum wage policy in Bulgaria – with more regular adjustments – is also aimed at reducing the considerable number of low-paid workers.

In Germany, the political desire to expand the low-wage sector to boost employment in the early 2000s led to attention being diverted from a national minimum wage. More recently, however, the minimum wage has been a hot topic of debate, precisely to counter the adverse effects of the rapid increase in low-paid employment and the influence of greater wage dispersion on working poverty and inequality. The rapid increase in the number of low-paid workers seems to have been facilitated by the absence of a national minimum wage. By comparison, in 2006, 1.9 million employees in Germany were working for hourly wages of less than €5, much less than their counterparts in France and the United Kingdom, who benefited from hourly minimum wages of around €8 (Bosch and Weinkopf, 2008; Caroli and Gautié, 2008; Lloyd et al., 2008). Similarly, in the Netherlands, weak adjustments of the minimum wage coincided with an increase in the proportion of low-paid workers.

The emergence of working poverty as an issue all over the world has led to renewed interest in the minimum wage on the part of policy-makers. Countries as diverse as Sri Lanka and Rwanda are contemplating implementation of a national statutory minimum wage to address the low pay phenomenon. At the same time, it must be emphasized that the minimum wage is not a panacea for the problem of low pay, which also depends, for example, on the number of family members and their working status. This may partly explain why an active minimum wage policy has not been enough to curb the proportion of low-paid workers in a number of countries. Other policies are necessary in the area of social protection and taxation. While the minimum wage policy should certainly be complemented by other types of policies, it remains, nevertheless, an important tool for protecting the most vulnerable workers and limiting the growth of wage inequality, as the empirical evidence shows (ILO, 2008a).

1.5 WAGE PROBLEMS ALONG THE SUPPLY CHAIN

General Assessment: Wages Serve as the Residual Variable at Micro Level

Since wages are an essential component of labour costs but also, generally speaking, the last one to be paid in an employer's chain of payments – raw materials and administrative costs are given priority – they often represent a residual payment that the employer provides in accordance with whatever funds are left. In the current race to the bottom with regard to labour costs, and with contracting companies often accepting contracts offered by major brands that oblige them to operate below production costs, evidence reported so far indicates that wages seem to be the most adversely affected variable in global competition today. This has resulted in a series of local dysfunctions, such as the non- or only partial payment of wages, the failure to respect minimum wage legislation – with wages being reported well below the statutory minimum wage in a number of countries – or breaches of anti-discrimination laws (for instance, discrimination against migrant workers). In order to minimize the payment of social contributions, wages are also often paid informally – with 'under the table' cash payments – and there is a total lack of transparency in the use of certain pay systems, such as piece rates or other bonuses, including 'attendance' bonuses. There is also an absence of bargaining over wages, especially in subcontracting companies. In addition, an increased gap between executives/white-collar workers and blue-collar workers can be observed within enterprises, as we report with regard to China.

No Systematic Sources of Information on Wage Practices

No systematic evidence is available on wage practices along the supply chain. However, there have been some reports, compiled by NGOs and brands, as well as items of information provided by the media on wage problems among suppliers, that also refer to the role of the brands.

To take one example, a 2008 report by the NGO Human Rights Watch catalogued a variety of forms of deprivation suffered by the estimated 1 to 2 million migrant workers employed on construction sites before the Summer Olympics in Beijing. They included: a lack of safety equipment, crowded and unhygienic dormitories, no medical care, arbitrary fines by managers and unpaid wages.[4] Interviews with workers at nine different building sites revealed that more than half of them had not received wages from their employers each month, as required by Chinese law, and many had had to wait until the end of the year for pay which was, to add insult to injury, less than what they had been promised. In one case, about 160 workers hired for three months to build a multi-storey building were eventually paid an average wage of less than half of the daily official minimum wage. Before paying the workers, the employers made deductions for unspecified living expenses, such as food and shelter.

A number of articles in the press have confirmed that low wages and the non-payment – or delayed payment – of wages are the most important causes of labour disputes in China.[5] They also emphasize that, while average wage levels have increased steadily, so has the gap between wages in different employment sectors and regions. Many companies were also found to pay less than the official minimum wage, although the government's official minimum wage is already insufficient to support workers' basic needs. Excessive working hours for only low pay are also reported.[6] Furthermore, more than half of companies do not permit a trade union presence, which makes workers' interest representation extremely difficult, as illustrated by the case of a steel company in Shaanxi.[7] Discrimination against migrant workers, including with regard to wages and benefits, is also reported, although migrant workers are starting to win compensation awards in the courts for injuries, non-payment of wages or occupational disease.[8]

At the same time, there are examples of companies in which wages have been pushed up and firms' margins have been squeezed because they are finding it increasingly difficult to obtain the workers they need.[9] This was one major finding of visits to 12 small clothing firms in Guangdong province in 2008 (Li and Edwards, 2008). These contradictory findings should serve as motivation to instigate a more structured and more systematic assessment of wage practices and wage trends along the supply chain.

---

4. 'China's migrant workers powerless', H. Sanderson, Associated Press, 12 March 2008.
5. 'Getting a decent wage and benefits: An uphill task for workers in China', *China Labour Magazine*, 10 February 2006. Available at: http://www.china-labour.org.hk/en/node/100206.
6. 'More work for less gain', *China Labour Magazine*, 28 January 2008. Available at: http://www.china-labour.org.hk/en/node/100196.
7. 'Solidarity from the sidelines: Union passivity allows a steel strike to escalate', *China Labour Magazine*, 10 February 2000.
8. 'Migrant workers start to win significant compensation awards in the courts', *China Labour Magazine*, November 2007; available at: http://www.china-labour.org.hk/en/node/50878. See also 'Company boss and the courts add insult to injury for migrant worker in Wuhan', December 2007; available at: http://www.clb.org.hk/en/node/51543.
9. 'Picky Chinese workers spell end of cheap labor', S. Rabinovitch, Reuters, 10 March 2008.

Bad Wage Practices Reported

The brands are often shamed for their behaviour, for instance, when they tried to influence Chinese authorities to adopt more flexible labour laws.

As an example, in 2007–2008, groups of multinationals lobbied for months – including threats to relocate their operations out of China – against new labour law provisions, such as the right to collective bargaining for wages and benefits, which workers previously had had to negotiate individually with their employers.[10] Moreover, suppliers of brands have multiplied the cases of bad practice or non-compliance on wages and working conditions, as shown in Table 1.1, which presents some examples from the early 2000s. Such wage problems among brand suppliers compelled local authorities to react. For example, the Guangdong province Labour and Social Bureau decided in 2005 to issue a list of 20 sweatshops, condemning their behaviour in their province.

The brands have, on occasion, admitted such problems and are, reportedly, trying to find remedies. Adidas has tried to check that its suppliers adhere to the firm's code of conduct, but problems remain, for example in Indonesia.[11] Nike admitted, in a report posted on its website, that it faces problems with sub-contractors in China, where around one in three pairs of Nike shoes are produced, involving contracts with 180 manufacturers, employing more than 210,000 workers. Falsification of documents, such as payroll records, generally to hide excessive overtime and inaccurate payment of wages, were reported, and wages in some places were found not to be tracking government-mandated wage rises.[12] It was also found that a majority of workers were not unionized. Nike's efforts to provide remedies to some wage problems, such as the non-payment of wages, should be noted, however. In 2005 and 2006, Nike 'secured' over 6.53 million yuan (USD 921,300) in back wages owed to workers in China. In 2007, Nike said it had recovered more than 500,000 yuan in back pay. Although these are certainly minor measures in comparison to the size of the phenomenon, it shows that, in some areas, there is already some sort of CSR on wage issues.

10. 'As unrest rises, China broadens workers' rights', J. Kahn and D. Barboza, *New York Times*, 30 June 2007. Available at http://www.nytimes.com/2007/06/30/world/asia/30china.html ?scp=1&sq=As+Unrest+Rises%2C+China+Broadens+Workers%92+Rights&st=nyt8.
    'Solidarity from the sidelines: Union passivity allows a steel strike to escalate', *China Labour Magazine*, 10 February 2000.
11. 'Adidas attacked for Asian "sweatshops"', *The Guardian*, 23 November 2000.
12. 'Nike report on factories in China', in *Washington Post*, 14 March 2008. Available at http://www.washingtonpost.com/wp-dyn/content/article/2008/03/04/AR2008031400950.html.

Table 1.1 Examples of wage problems among suppliers of brands

Suppliers and brands	City and year	Number of workers	Wages and related issues	Source
(Wal-Mart Stores Inc.)	Shenzen; Dongguan; Guangzhou 2006	NA	– Problems of low pay; many temporary workers were paid RMB 3 per hour – Problems of overdue payments; excessive overtime; no vacations; no insurance; problems of stress at work	Commonwealth Times, 21 March 2006 China Labor Watch May 2006
(Timberland)	Guandong province; City of Zhongshan	4,700	Overdue payments; low wages; excessive overtime; no paid vacations; no individual labour contracts; no insurance for workers; fast working rhythm; terrible accommodation and food conditions; little respect for human rights	China Labor Watch
Foreway Industrial China (Fotoball)	Guangdong province; City of Dongguan 2004	Peak season 2,100; low season 500–600	Minimum wage non-compliance; excessive overtime; no paid vacations; no insurance; work intensity too high; bad accommodation and food conditions	China Labor Watch; February 2004
(Reebok, Clerk)	Guangdong province; City of Dongguan 1999–2000	5,500–6,000	Non-payment of wages, and if paid, very low; excessive overtime; no paid vacations or no vacation at all; no insurance; high work intensity; bad accommodation and food conditions	China Labor Watch; from February 1999 to February 2000
(Nike; Reebok)	Guangdong province Early 2000	1,500'	Low pay; excessive overtime; no holidays or social insurance provided; high work intensity; no protection at work; bad accommodation and food conditions	China Labor Watch; January–February 2000
(Reebok)	Shenzen 1999	6,000	Overtime; no paid holidays; no individual labour contract and no insurance	China Labor Watch April 1999
(Farberware)	Shenzen 1999	3,500	Overtime; no individual labour contract; no insurance; bad accommodation	China Labor Watch December 1999
(Nike, Adidas, NB)	Dongguan Since 1999	NA	Excessive overtime; overdue wage payments; labour contracts only for one year; bad accommodation	China Labor Watch

Table 1.1 (cont.)

Suppliers and brands	City and year	Number of workers	Wages and related issues	Source
(Nike, Adidas; Reebok; Puma)	Guangdong province		Wage arrears; excessive overtime; no vacations; no individual labour contract; no insurance; stress at work; bad accommodation and food	
Tuntex Tainan Nikomas Gemiland (Adidas)	Indonesia, Jakarta 2000	NA	Forced overtime which exceeds legal limits; physical abuse; wages under the statutory minimum wage and under the poverty line; child labour Heavy wage cuts when workers make mistakes or are late to work; sexual harassment and verbal and physical abuse	Guardian (23 November 2000); Clean Clothes Campaign

Problems of Business Sustainability

There is thus a general recognition of the unsustainability of wage developments in relation to business operations in terms of wage share, wage disparity, low wages and pay systems. This situation is unsustainable also for companies, from a number of different angles.

The increased proportion of working poor, for instance, has been recognized as likely to reduce workers' motivation and productivity, which can undermine the long-term prospects of business activities. The potential negative effects on consumption of falling wage share and purchasing power has also been recognized. The effects of unfair wage developments could also be extremely large in terms of absenteeism, work stoppages and strikes. There are many recent examples of companies all over the world which had to close down following a serious conflict on wage issues with workers and their representatives.

For the employers – as for the shareholders – crucial progress could thus be made with regard to workers' motivation and productivity. The Fair Wage process proposed in this book could also provide them with an essential tool against unfair competition, a sort of 'fair wage label'.[13]

---

13. For Nike's report, see http://nikeresponsibility.com/pdfs/bw/Nike_FY05_06_CR_Report_BW.pdf.

1.6 WAGE PROBLEMS EXACERBATED BY THE CURRENT ECONOMIC CRISIS

The prospects are that income inequality will continue to rise as a result of the present economic slowdown and other recent developments, such as the financial crisis and the sharp rise in food prices. The latter has already disproportionately affected poorer households (ILO, 2008a and 2008b).

Previous crises have had direct and long-term effects on wages. In Argentina, when GDP per capita declined during the financial crisis in 2001–2003, wages fell by an average of 11 per cent per year. Moreover, they needed more time to recover – with a one- to two-year lag – than other indicators, such as GDP or employment. It is also important to note that the wage share has declined most in countries which have experienced a severe crisis, such as Argentina and Korea. It is thus to be expected that the current crisis will directly affect wages.

This is confirmed by the first findings we were able to obtain in relation to the current crisis (up to the end of first semester 2009).

Real Wage Decline

According to the available data on 50 countries up to the end of 2008, it appears that the growth of real wages declined, on average, from 4.7 per cent in 2007 to 1.5 per cent in 2008. However, a majority of countries were able to maintain positive – albeit declining in comparison to the previous year – wage growth in 2008. In fact, real wages were found to react with some time lag, since they generally continued their normal trend until the end of 2008 and started declining only from the first quarter of 2009, when not only real but also nominal wages declined (Figure 1.5). This lag is to be explained by the annual collective bargaining round (in some countries, every two years). Wages are adjusted in response to economic conditions in the next bargaining round. In contrast, as our description of wage trends during the crises that occurred between 1995 and 2007 shows, wages also need more time to recover from a crisis, sometimes recovering more than one year after economic growth and employment begin to improve. The same scenario is to be expected in the current crisis: even if there is an economic recovery in 2010–2011, wages will start to recover lost ground only one or two years later, that is, no earlier than 2012 on the best possible scenario.

The wage picture worsened considerably in the first semester of 2009: compared to the 2008 average, real wages experienced negative growth in nearly 55 per cent of the countries for which data are available. Even among the 45 per cent experiencing positive real wage growth, a majority saw only small rises in progression rates, well below those in 2008 (ILO, 2009). Among the countries which experienced higher wage growth in the first semester of

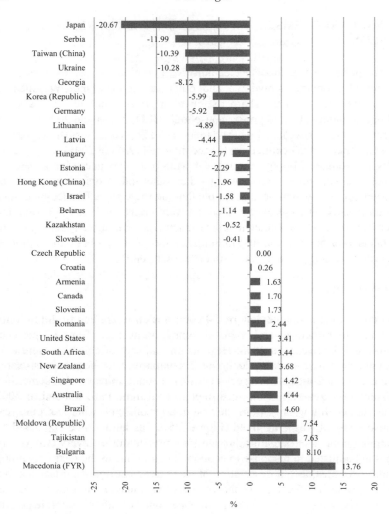

Source: ILO wage data base.

Figure 1.5 Real wages in 2008–2009 (annual % growth)

2009, Brazil should be noted – indicating the success of its income sustaining policy within the crisis – but also Macedonia, New Zealand and South Africa.

As shown in Figure 1.5, the fall has been most striking – more than 10 per cent – in Japan, but also in Serbia, Taiwan and Ukraine, while there was a decline of more than 5 per cent in Georgia, followed by Korea, Germany, Latvia, Lithuania, Hungary and Estonia. This fall in wages might also be due to

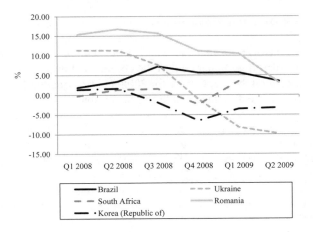

Source: ILO wage data base.

Figure 1.6 Real wages in selected countries, 2008–2009 (quarterly changes and comparison with same quarter in previous year)

a fall in the number of hours worked, which was also found to have decreased in a number of countries as a way of coping with the decline in production without generating too much unemployment.

For a better understanding of the dynamics of real wages during the crisis, in Figure 1.6 we present the evolution of real wages, quarter by quarter, in 2008–2009 in five countries, comparing each quarter to the same quarter in the previous year in order to take seasonal variations into account. The figure shows that real wages started to fall after the second quarter of 2008 in countries such as Ukraine, Romania and Korea, while they started their decline later – in the third quarter of 2008 – in Brazil and South Africa. However, the figure also shows that these two countries had managed – at least until June 2009 – to maintain real wage growth, despite the crisis.

Re-emergence of Non-payment of Wages

We should add that the fall in real wages was not the only sign of a wage crunch during the crisis. In a number of CIS countries, the problem of the non-payment of wages and wage arrears has once more reared its ugly head. In Ukraine, wage arrears have been doubling with the economic crisis in the first half of 2009, reaching UAH 1,559.026 million by 1 August 2009 (State Statistical Office). Significantly, this includes not only bankrupt enterprises but also economically active enterprises, which accounted for 64 per cent of total wage arrears in 2009, compared to 36 per cent the previous year.

Wage Share Not Declining Immediately

Interestingly, we also found that the wage share has not declined in 2008–2009, but has increased in 90 per cent of the countries (approximately 40) for which we have data on the wage share for 2008 and first quarter 2009 (Figure 1.7). This is due to the fact that, while the denominator – that is, GDP per

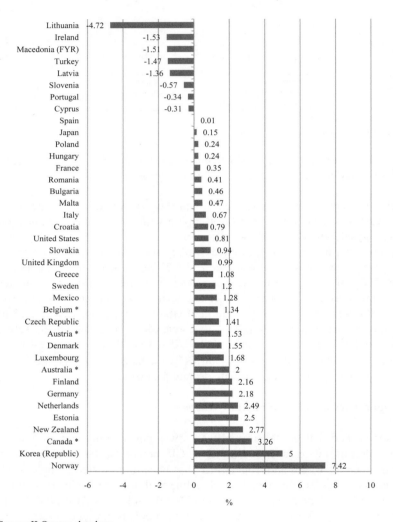

Source: ILO wage data base.

Figure 1.7 Wage share, 2008–2009

capita – has fallen, the numerator (total compensation) has so far declined less: as we have seen, wages took more time to adjust downward in 2008 and early 2009. Nevertheless, the reverse movement is to be expected at the end of the crisis, with economic growth and GDP expected to increase, while total compensation will continue to decline for some time. This combination may

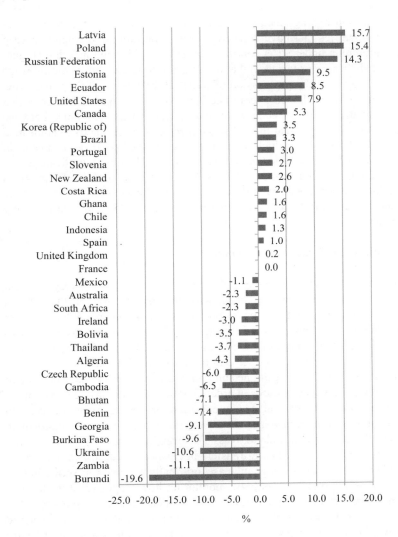

Source: ILO wage data base.

Figure 1.8 Minimum wages, progression in 2008

rapidly lead to a significant fall in the wage share in most countries, which must be closely monitored and be addressed robustly by both governments and enterprises themselves.

Growth in Wage Inequality Expected

A deterioration in wage inequality is also to be expected in the crisis, especially in countries that have decided to freeze the minimum wage and keep wage bargaining under strict control in order to avoid rising inflation (Figure 1.8). We shall see, for instance, that the decision to freeze the minimum wage in China may limit the progression of wages at the bottom of the wage scale, while companies will need to continue increasing the wages of higher skilled workers if they want to retain them. An increase in the difference between wages at the bottom and at the top was expected. This seems to be confirmed by our preliminary data, which show an increase in the D9/D1 ratio – that is, in the gap between the last and the first wage deciles. The most significant examples are the United States and the United Kingdom – two advanced economies which have been at the heart of the crisis – where the gap between those at the top and those at the bottom increased by 0.15 and 0.25 points, respectively (ILO, 2009).

Minimum Wage Responses Diversified

Minimum wage responses in the crisis were found to have been very different between countries, but coming under two principal categories (ILO, 2009). A number of countries, with a view to preserving employment, have decided to reduce labour costs through a minimum wage freeze or only marginal adjustments. Based on a sample of 86 countries, half (43) have allowed minimum wages to be eroded by inflation (see examples in Figure 1.8). This was the case in China, but also in Ireland, Ukraine and Zambia. The other half have decided to adjust minimum wages upwards in order to protect the purchasing power of the most vulnerable workers and sustain consumption and aggregate demand. In these countries, minimum wages have maintained their value in comparison to inflation, for example, in Poland, Russia or Brazil, where the government not only increased conditional cash transfers but also decided, in February 2009, to implement a minimum wage increase, originally planned for April 2009.

It will be important to continue monitoring how wages react in the next few months, especially when the much heralded economic recovery takes place. In any case, we can already question the impact that the above described downward trends in wages will have on the consumption of workers and their families, and thus on global aggregate demand, which is essential to initiate and sustain economic recovery.

CONCLUSIONS

General wage trends have provided us with a general context to help illustrate the importance of wage-fixing and wage practices at both macro and micro level, and have also emphasized the need to better investigate wage issues along the supply chain. Analysis of the main wage developments has led us to identify four major policy issues.

First, the reported wage trends in 1995–2007, a period of relative economic growth, are worrying. Not only has the progression of real wages been limited since 1995, but they have not been adjusted in accordance with the positive economic performance of world economies, with a worldwide continuous decline in the wage share and also a significant increase in wage disparity. At the same time, the empirical evidence collected so far indicates a series of wage problems along the supply chain – in terms of non-payment of wages and non-compliance with key wage regulations, including minimum wages – clearly imposing downward pressure on wages and thus directly contributing to adverse and worrying wage trends.

These wage trends clearly point to structural – and not only cyclical – problems in wage fixing and income distribution more generally; they may partly be the result of globalization and outsourcing, as shown by the numerous wage problems identified along the supply chain.

The second major finding from wage trends over the period 1995–2007 is that wages are seriously affected by periods of economic slowdown. The crises experienced in Asia in the early 1990s or South America – for example, in Argentina – have shown that wages need more time to catch up in the period of recovery and that they are, overall, much more affected by a crisis than other variables, such as employment or economic growth. Similarly, this means that the reported wage trends documented up until 2007 may be expected to get worse as a result of the current financial and economic crisis. First findings confirm that wages are starting to be seriously affected, with real wages and, in some cases, also nominal wages decreasing. Increasing wage differentials are also reported, especially as a direct consequence of restrictive government policy in terms of minimum wages and wage determination in general, aimed at reducing labour costs and limiting unemployment. The wage share is also expected to decrease along with the recovery – although with a lag – when wages will adjust more slowly to the acceleration of economic indicators.

The third policy lesson from global wage trends is that government action on wage policy seems insufficient, especially in the context of globalization and the general liberalization of trade, capital and labour movements, which render national policies less effective. This highlights the need for employers to take responsibility in the wage field to ensure that certain wage practices are respected, even without a mandatory national framework. It also points to the need for a general CSR movement on wages to ensure that companies cannot play one country against another in terms of wage policies or instigate a race to the bottom on wages and working conditions.

Finally, these wage trends clearly show the need to address wages in a multidimensional fashion. We saw in the case of China, for instance, but also in other major emerging economies, such as India and South Africa, that the impressive real wage increases over the past 15 years do not provide the full wage story. Increased workers' purchasing power has been accompanied by a continuously declining wage share – showing that workers are not receiving a fair share of economic growth – thereby increasing wage inequality and, in some cases, also the proportion of low-paid workers. Our report on wage trends also shows that any national action – for instance, to address low pay through the minimum wage – may be rather hopeless if not accompanied by better wage practices along the supply chain, which may manage to break the vicious circle of bad wage practices and also help to ensure that wages are not used systematically as the residual adjustment variable.

Part I

Towards a New Wage Policy:
The Fair Wage Approach

2. CSR Deficit on Wages

INTRODUCTION

Most people would agree that companies have some responsibility with regard to wages and could play an active role in promoting wage practices which are more in line with long-term, sustainable development. But although the CSR process highlights employers' responsibilities and roles with regard to working and employment practices, no concrete or comprehensive initiative seems yet to have been conceived to include wage issues.

In this context, wages could pay the price of CSR, in the sense that the cost of further improvements with regard to other working conditions may have a direct negative effect on wage levels and turn out to be something of a poisoned chalice for workers and their families. The fact that wages continue to be treated as a residual variable, especially in subcontracting companies, can only confirm this concern.

There is thus a clear and urgent need to integrate wage issues in CSR and to establish a monitoring process in this area.

The point of departure of the fair wage approach involves looking at what has been done so far by CSR actors and what they have taken up as relevant wage indicators. A number of initiatives will be presented here that non-governmental organizations, workers' and employers' representatives and national or local authorities have launched on wages issues.[1] However, it shall also be explained why these initiatives have taken a rather narrow approach.

2.1 NGO WAGE INITIATIVES FRAGMENTED

In recent times, a number of non-governmental organizations (NGOs) have added wage issues to their list of items to be measured along the supply chain.

NGO Initiatives on Wage Issues

The initiatives launched by NGOs on wages are diverse and can be distinguished by type of initiative – from informative to auditing – but also by scale –

---

1. The aim of this synthesis is to present major initiatives on wages by CSR actors but the list is not exhaustive.

international, regional, national/local – and, finally, by scope, in terms of wage issues covered. All these initiatives on wages are summarized in Table 2.1.

Many NGO initiatives provide information or policy advice on wages to the actors concerned. Others set a number of standards or guidelines on working conditions, including on wages. This can consist in highlighting international standards which already exist (for instance, International Labour Standards), or can lead to the elaboration of a specific code of conduct. The Social Accountability Standard, known as SA8000, is based on standards established by the International Labour Organization (ILO) and the United Nations Human Rights Covenants. The Ethical Trading Initiative (ETI) has created its own code of conduct – also derived from the core ILO conventions – with wages being one of the nine points (with a focus on the living wage) and with the aim of promoting good practice. The International Labour Rights Fund promotes universally acceptable living wage guidelines.

Some NGOs also provide some standard methodology on wages, such as the World of Good Development Organization, which has developed a fair wage guide, aimed at empowering artisans and buyers by giving them user-friendly access to information on wage levels. This is an advisory tool to help artisans to negotiate what they would consider a 'fair wage' with their employer.

Other NGOs also implement external monitoring on wages, such as the Fair Labour Association (FLA), the Worker Rights Consortium, the Fair Wear Foundation, Labour Behind the Label, with also certification in the case of Worldwide Responsible Apparel Production.

There are also joint initiatives between different NGOs, as exemplified by the Joint Initiative on Corporate Accountability and Workers' Rights (Jo-In), which brings together multiple stakeholders to seek out best practices for cooperation and coordination in order to improve workplace conditions across the world, including on improving wage practices, which was one area covered by the project, notably through the 'wage ladder', a sort of benchmarking system for charting factory progress in improving wages.

While these different initiatives may have a different geographical or sectoral coverage, they all aim at international and universal coverage.

Whatever the nature and the scope of the initiatives that these organizations have launched, it is striking to note, first, that they all felt the need to develop a number of indicators on wages. This is a sign that wages should definitely have a place within CSR.

Second, it must be also reported that initiatives on wages seem to have intensified over the past few years, undoubtedly in response to increasing abuses and concerns in this sensitive area, as reported in Chapter 1. We present below these different initiatives in more details, with a summary provided in Table 2.1. which distinguishes two elements in each of these initiatives: their main wage focus and their list of wage indicators.

Social Accountability International (SAI)

SAI promotes workers' rights by means of a voluntary approach. Its main instrument is the Social Accountability Standard, known as SA8000. This standard, published in 1997 and revised in 2001, is based on standards set by the International Labour Organization (ILO) and the United Nations Human Rights Conventions. It is a widely known standard related to the workplace and working conditions against which companies can measure their performance. The companies are monitored to assess their compliance in respect of a number of key factors, such as child labour, forced labour, health and safety, freedom of association and the right to collective bargaining, non-discrimination, discipline, working hours, management systems and compensation.

SA8000 stipulates that, in a company, 'wages paid for a standard working week must meet the legal and industry standards and be sufficient to meet the basic needs of workers and their families' and that there should be 'no disciplinary deductions'.[2] According to this definition, a living wage is the wage sufficient to provide a worker with basic needs, complemented by some discretionary income.

Ethical Trading Initiative (ETI)

ETI is a UK-based alliance of companies, NGOs and trade union organizations that was established in 1998 with the aim of promoting good practice through the implementation of its code of conduct.[3] Wages – with a clear focus on living wages – is one of the nine points of the ETI code of conduct, which is derived from the core conventions of the ILO. It strongly echoes the SA8000 code, stating that 'wages and benefits paid for a standard working week must meet, at a minimum, national legal standards or industry benchmark standards, whichever is higher. In any event, wages should always be enough to meet basic needs and to provide some discretionary income' (Steele, 2000). Its definition has been developed using a bottom-up approach: workers, NGOs and trade unions collectively investigate basic needs in a particular country, on the basis of which they bargain collectively with regard to their specific needs. In terms of the ETI, workers have a role in determining what the living wage is in their local context, so that free collective bargaining should become the most legitimate method of determining a living wage by local standards.

Worldwide Responsible Apparel Production (WRAP)

WRAP is a factory monitoring and certification programme created by the American Apparel and Footwear Association in 1999. It includes major US

---

2. See Social Accountability International website: http://www.sa-intl.org/.
3. See Ethical Trading Initiative website: http://www.ethicaltrade.org/.

apparel manufacturers that produce for the discount retail market, as well as associations in Latin America and the Caribbean, Asia and Africa.

Regarding compensation, WRAP's code of conduct asserts that '[m]anufacturers of sewn products will pay at least the minimum total compensation required by local law, including all mandated wages, allowances and benefits.'[4]

However, the standards set by WRAP have been criticised, above all because they do not follow the principles of the ILO conventions, which require more than mere obedience of local laws. As an example, Neil Kearney of the International Textile, Garment and Leather Workers Federation (ITGLWF) says that 'WRAP damages and does not uphold or enhance workers' rights because its standards undercut ILO Conventions, even on issues like child labor' (Maquila Solidarity Network, 2002). He notes, in particular, that WRAP fails to provide for a living wage and, more importantly perhaps, to set any limits on working hours where there is no legal specification.

International Labor Rights Fund

This organization advocates a living wage strategy geared towards international cooperation to develop universally acceptable living wage guidelines. It notes that, unlike other core workers' rights standards, there is no internationally accepted definition of a living wage. They advocate the inclusion of a living wage among core labour rights and the integration of living wage guidelines in a new ILO convention and in social clauses tied to enforcement mechanisms.[5]

Labor behind the Label (Clean Clothes Campaign)

Their non-profit auditing initiatives centre on the observation that 'a living wage should cover basic needs, include an additional discretionary income and cater for dependents'. Crucially, they specify that the wage should 'be enough to provide for the basic needs of workers and their families, to allow them to participate fully in society and live with dignity' and 'take into account the cost of living, social security benefits and the standard of living of others nearby'. Their operative principle concludes that the living wage 'should be based on a standard working week, before overtime, and apply after any deductions'.[6]

Fair Wear Foundation (FWF)

Founded in 1999, the FWF initiated its own monitoring process in 2003 through the use of external auditors who verify compliance with its code of

---

4. See Worldwide Responsible Apparel Production website: http://www.wrapapparel.org/modules.php?name=Content&pa=showpage&pid=3.
5. ILRF (1999). See also WWW.laborrights.org.
6. Based on the Wear Thin (2001) and Let's Clean Up Fashion (2006) reports, Clean Clothes Campaign, Labor behind the Label. Website: http://www.laborbehindthelabel.org/.

conduct along the production line. It advocates the payment of a living wage, closely following the ILO definition, stating that 'wages and benefits paid for a standard working week shall meet at least legal or industry minimum standards and always be sufficient to meet basic needs of workers and their families and to provide some discretionary income'.[7]

Fair Labor Association (FLA)

The FLA was established in 1998 by the Apparel Industry Partnership (AIP), which is a Forum initiated in the United States during the Clinton administration in order to address sweatshop abuse. The FLA conducts an external monitoring and verification programme in order to ensure that certain basic workplace standards are met.

The FLA workplace code of conduct mentions a few wage issues in its paragraph on 'Wages and benefits', stipulating that 'employers recognize that wages are essential to meeting employees' basic needs. Employers shall pay employees, as a floor, at least the minimum wage required by law or the prevailing industry wage, whichever is higher, and shall provide legally mandated benefits.'[8]

In addition, the FLA has been part of the path-breaking Joint Initiative on Corporate Accountability and Workers' Rights (Jo-In), which brings together multiple stakeholders to seek out best practices for cooperation and coordination in order to improve workplace conditions across the world. Improvement in wage practices was one area covered by the project. The Jo-In project promoted by the FLA has developed a benchmarking system for charting factory progress in improving wages in respect of the so-called 'wage ladder'. While the pilot project implemented in the garment industry in Turkey focuses mainly on the living wage, it also mentions other wage dimensions, such as 'distribution of income between factory owners and workers', 'productivity', 'trade union negotiations' (document *Wage ladder in Jo-In to date*), 'wage standards' (p. 3 of *Explanatory note*), 'minimum wage', the 'prevailing industry wage', 'the negotiated wage', 'fringe benefits' (pp. 1 and 2 of *Appendix A – Wage ladder*) and 'wage distribution' (p. 1 of *Wage ladder draft*) (Jo-In project, 2008).

Worker Rights Consortium (WRC)

The same wage indicators are applied by the Worker Rights Consortium, created in 1999, which has developed a code of conduct primarily to ensure

---

7. Fair Wear Foundation. 2008. The Fair Wear Code of Labor Practices for labor conditions in the garment sector. Available at: http://www.fairwear.nl/images%20site/File/Bibliotheek/Voor%20 bedrijven/FWF-Gedragscode-EN.pdf.
8. Fair Labor Association. The FLA Workplace Code of Conduct. Available at: http://www.fairla-bor.org/conduct.

that factories that produce clothing and other goods bearing university logos respect the basic rights of workers.[9] The code of conduct insists on the need for wages 'to provide for essential needs and establish a dignified living wage for workers and their families' and highlights the 'living wage' function. A living wage is regarded as a take-home or net wage, earned during a country's legal maximum working week. A living wage provides for the basic needs (housing, energy, nutrition, clothing, health care, education, potable water, childcare, transportation and savings) of an average family unit of employees in the garment manufacturing sector.[10]

The WRC also emphasizes the need for companies to comply with all 'laws and regulations', a definition that thus includes important wage regulations, such as the minimum wage. Along with the FLA, it also takes into account the need for wages to ensure these basic functions within a certain number of working hours, defined as 48 hours by the WRC and 48 hours plus 12 overtime hours by the FLA.

World of Good Development Organization
Committed to strengthening fair trade standards in the handicraft sector, the World of Good Development Organization has also developed a fair wage guide, which is aimed at empowering artisans and buyers by giving them user-friendly access to wage information. Through free access to the web or the organization, artisans can check what wages should be paid, according to their respective location and position, local prices and costs, while also reflecting international wage standards, such as minimum wages or international poverty lines.

The originality of this approach lies in directly helping artisans to fix what they would consider a 'fair wage' in their field – providing them with the arguments needed to negotiate for higher wages – and thus to play more of an advisory than a monitoring role. This approach also makes it possible to cover artisans in the informal sector. It clearly integrates wage issues among basic fair trade principles, notably by cooperating with the fair trade movement and with the ultimate aim of creating a product label for crafts.

Other community or specialized organizations
A number of other organizations aimed at specific – for instance, religious – communities or categories of vulnerable people (for instance, the homeless) have also developed basic wage principles. An example is the Center for

---

9. See Worker Rights Consortium website: http://www.workersrights.org/.
10. Worker Rights Consortium: Model Code of Conduct. Available at : http://www.workersrights. org/coc.asp.

Reflection, Education and Action (CREA) which promotes the 'Purchasing Power Index' and the 'Sustainable Living Wage', insisting on the need to have living wages not only for the well-being of workers but also entire communities and society as a whole. On the basis of the key figure that 42 per cent of homeless people in the United States are working, the US National Coalition for the Homeless – as in other countries – also insists on implementation of the Living Wage Act and highlights the need to apply fair wages to reduce the number of homeless people.

A Too Fragmented and Too Narrow Approach

It is evident that there is still room for action with regard to workers' remuneration at the global level. There is neither an agreed definition nor a common instrument for the calculation of threshold wage levels. There is also no agreement on the manner of implementing a particular wage standard. There are a number of wage concerns that are addressed in a rather diffuse way, lacking the clarity needed for conversion into effective action in the field. Some organizations have insisted on strict compliance with existing national or local regulations, such as on the minimum wage, the payment of wages or all working hours, and social security provisions. Organizations such as Worldwide Responsible Apparel Production (WRAP), the Fair Labor Association (FLA) and the Ethical Trading Initiative (ETI) have included the minimum wage in their codes of conduct, while they also mention the maximum number of working hours and the need to pay social security provisions, as generally required by law. Others have extended their interest to more relative indicators, such as the prevalent wage in a particular industry, although most insist on the living wage concept. This lack of common terminology poses substantial challenges to monitors and social auditors when verifying compliance with codes of conduct and, more generally, the wage-fixing practices of companies along the supply chain.

Moreover, the wage dimensions proposed as the main indicators for wage fixing have been conceived in rather narrow terms so far. It is limiting for codes of conduct to rely only on the legal minimum wage, the prevailing wage in the industry or even the living wage as applicable in the varied national and regional contexts in which companies operate. Table 2.1 clearly shows not only that the number of wage dimensions is limited, but that, in reality, only a few major wage indicators are proposed. Some very different indicators are often grouped together, such as the minimum wage and the prevailing 'industry wage'. Some NGOs– such as the FLA, the Worker Rights Consortium and the ETI – recognize the need to cover a larger set of wage issues, but focus only on the living wage, the minimum wage and the prevailing wage (although the last is not subject to sufficient monitoring in their field work). The ETI, for

Table 2.1 Wage items in NGO codes of conduct, benchmarks or initiatives

Organizations	General wage concept	Wage focus
Ethical Trade Initiative (ETI)	The ETI monitors wage rates paid along supply chains. Recognizing the significance of wage levels with regard to sourcing decisions and the importance, from an ethical point of view, of addressing unacceptably low rates of pay, the members of the ETI have looked at how the living wage provision can be applied in practice, that is, how the living wage provision can be made into an auditable standard	*Living wage* (main wage focus): wages should always be enough to meet basic needs and to provide some discretionary income *Wage legal standards and prevailing wage*: wages and benefits should meet, at a minimum, national legal standards or industry benchmark standards, whichever are the higher *Wage discrimination/wage disparity*: there should be equal pay for equal work, regardless of age, gender, ethnicity or number of dependents *Working time*: legal wage standards to be met, observing the limits on ordinary and overtime work, the appropriate premium rate for overtime and the provision of the correct number of days off and paid holidays *Pay systems*: deductions from wages as a disciplinary measure shall not be permitted *Communication on wages*: all workers shall be provided with written and understandable information about their employment conditions with regard to wages before they enter employment and about the particulars of their wages for the pay period concerned each time they are paid *Real wages*: real wages should be expected to rise over time *Wage share*: need to consider the ability of an economy to deliver a particular distribution of income (proposal to calculate wages expressed as a percentage of per capita GDP)
Fair Labor Association (FLA)	Wages are essential to meet employees' basic needs. Employers shall pay employees, as a floor, at least the minimum wage required by local law or the prevailing industry wage, whichever is higher, and shall provide legally mandated benefits	*Living wage*: employers' recognition that wages are essential for meeting employees' basic needs *Minimum wage/prevailing wage* (main wage focuses): minimum wage as defined by national law or industry wage, whichever is higher

Organizations	General wage concept	Wage focus
Fair Labor Association (FLA) (*cont.*)		*Working hours*: 48 hours plus 12 hours overtime *Provision of benefits*: must provide legally mandated benefits
Fair Wear Foundation (FWF)	Wage and benefits paid for a standard working week shall meet at least legal or industry minimum standards and always be sufficient to meet basic needs of workers and their families and to provide some discretionary income	*Living wage* (main focus): Should meet basic needs of workers and their families and provide discretionary income *Wage standards*: wages should meet at least legal or industry standards
International Labor Rights Fund (ILRF)	All workers are entitled to earn a living wage and a living wage strategy should be put in place, with universally acceptable living wage guidelines promoted in international labour standards and integrated in the social clauses of trade agreements	*Living wage* (main wage focus): workers must be able to meet their basic needs but also to steadily improve their living conditions *Social dialogue*: the employers and the workers concerned shall cooperate in the operation of the (living wage) machinery. Living wage approach advocacy should explicitly support the goal of increased collective bargaining and ILRF must help workers to bargain collectively
Joint Initiative on Corporate Accountability and Workers' Rights (Jo-In Code) (*applied by many organizations, such as the FLA, ETI, FWF, SAI and WRC*)	Wages are one important part of the code developed jointly by multiple stakeholders to promote best practices for cooperation and coordination in order to improve workplace conditions across the world	*Living wage* (main focus): workers have the right to a living wage; wages and benefits shall be sufficient to meet basic needs of workers and their families and provide some discretionary income for a sustainable implementation of the 'living wage' *Minimum wage*: until the living wage is feasible, suppliers should pay at least the legal minimum wage or the prevailing wage, whichever is the higher *Negotiated wage*: right of all workers to form a trade union and to bargain collectively; freedom of collective bargaining will be respected *Communication on wages*: detailed information on wages shall be provided to the workers for the whole working period each time they are paid *Payment of wages*: wages shall be paid on a regular and timely basis

Table 2.1 (cont.)

Organizations	General wage concept	Wage focus
Joint Initiative on Corporate Accountability and Workers' Rights (Jo-In Code) (*cont.*)		*Disciplinary deductions*: deductions from wages shall not be made for disciplinary reasons *Social security*: obligations to workers under labour or social security laws shall not be avoided *Non-discrimination*: do not engage in or support discrimination in hiring, remuneration, and so on. Women and men shall receive equal remuneration of equal value *Payment of overtime*: all overtime work shall be voluntary, not demanded on a regular basis, reimbursed at the premium rate required by the law and shall not exceed 12 hours per employee per week
Labour behind the Label (Clean Clothes Campaign)	Wage should be enough to provide for the basic needs of workers and their families, to participate fully in society and live with dignity	*Living wage* (main focus): Should cover basic needs, include an additional discretionary income and cater for dependents; and take into account the cost of living, social security benefits and the standards of living of others nearby; should be based on a standard working week, before overtime, and apply after any deductions
Social Accountability International (SAI)	Wages paid for a standard working week must meet the legal and industry standards and be sufficient to meet the basic needs of workers and their families	*Living wage* (main focus): wage should provide a worker with basic needs, complemented by some discretionary income *Wage standards*: wages should meet the legal and industry standards *Working hours*: 'standard working week' mentioned *Wage deductions*: There should be no disciplinary deductions
Worker Rights Consortium (WRC)	Licensees recognize that wages are essential for meeting employees' basic needs. Licensees shall pay employees, as a floor, wages and benefits which comply with all applicable laws and regulations, and which provide for essential needs and establish a dignified living wage for workers and their families	*Living wage* (main wage focus): licensees recognize that wages are essential to meet employees' basic needs (the living wage being the 'take home' or 'net' wage, earned during a country's legal maximum working week but not exceeding 48 hours). It must provide for the basic needs of an average family unit of employees in the garment manufacturing sector

Organizations	General wage concept	Wage focus
Worker Rights Consortium (*cont.*)		Must provide a dignified living wage for workers and family *Wage regulations*: wages and benefits – compliance with all applicable laws and regulations *Minimum wage/prevailing wage*: minimum wage as defined by national law or industry wage, whichever is the higher *Working hours*: no more than 48 hours *Provision of benefits*: to provide essential needs
'World of Good' Development Organization Influence on fair trade organizations such as IFAT (International Fair Trade Association), FTF (Fair Trade Federation), and FLO (Fair Label Organization)	Important to enable users to verify that the wages paid to their artisans are 'fair wages' in the sense that they meet international wage standards and also reflect local prices and costs; wages are an important element within fair trade and the aim is 'to ensure minimum fair wages are being met in the global fair trade community'	*Minimum wage*: the proposed tool helps to calculate a floor price for the wages of artisans that would reflect the minimum wage regulations *Communication and social dialogue*: essential to have information on wages available to artisans and buyers that will help inform decisions about fair wages, prices and costs; increased access to information will improve the livelihoods of artisans by increasing their negotiating power and informing the wage design process *Other wage issues*: while the tool is aimed at reinforcing quantitative information and measures on wages, it recognizes that qualitative measures remain central. The organization also recognizes the need to ensure an ethical approach to setting prices and margins
Worldwide Responsible Apparel Production (WRAP)	Workers should be paid at least the minimum total compensations required by local law, including all mandated wages, allowances and benefits	*Legal local standards* (main focus): mandated wages such as minimum wage but also allowances and benefits should be paid

Table 2.1 (cont.)

Other organizations	General wage concept	Wage focus
Center for Reflection, Education and Action (CREA)	Analysis of economic globalization and work on corporate responsibility should also be carried out on wage issues that cut across industries; promotion of the 'Purchasing Power Index' and the 'Sustainable Living Wage'	*Sustainable living wage* (main focus)/ *real wages*: proposal of a 'Purchasing Power Index' based on a standard market basket survey of the evolving prices of extensive lists of commodities; on the basis of the belief that all workers, along with their families and dependents, are entitled to a living standard that reflects the basic dignity accorded to all human beings *Minimum wage*: the calculation of the PPI starts with the legal minimum wage (pro-rated hourly wages) *Other wage issues*: insistence that wages reflect workers' contributions to company growth (wage share) and do not lead to excessive wage disparity within the company, for example, between the CEO and workers at the bottom. Pay systems and working time should also take into consideration the time needed for family, relationships and social life outside work, enabling 'the sustainable growth of human communities'
National Coalition for the Homeless (United States)	Low wages are among the causes of poverty and force many individuals and families to make impossible choices between housing, food, clothing, medical care and transportation. They should thus be raised to allow a living wage that would reduce the likelihood that workers and their families will experience homelessness	*Minimum wage*: should ensure that a full-time worker can afford basic food, clothing and shelter *Universal living wage*: if a person works 40 hours a week he/she should be able to afford basic housing and meet other basic needs *Other wage issues (equal pay for equal work; social dialogue)*: essential for fighting homelessness are the basic rights to free choice of employment, favourable working conditions, unemployment protection, equal pay for equal work, sufficient income, and formation of and participation in trade unions *CSR*: calls to promote living wage policies among homeless, providers to ensure that HCH clinics ensure that their own employees are paid wages sufficient to prevent homelessness

instance, mentions in its documents the need to take into account issues such as income distribution or wage disparity, as well as communication and social dialogue on wages, but in very general terms, while clearly focusing on the living wage. Others have tried to take a pragmatic approach by developing a standard methodology, such as the World of Good Development Organization, with its fair wage guide, although it covers only a limited number of indicators, which may not be sufficient to fully reflect specific local or company conditions and has a rather narrow scope (artisans and crafts).

Thus, NGOs and other civil society initiatives should recognize the need for the application of a more comprehensive and dynamic approach to wages in social auditing.

Too Much Focus on the 'Living Wage'?

In order to better illustrate the diversity of standards set in the codes of conduct, it is important to take a closer look at the better recognized initiatives. Table 2.1. highlights the fact that, so far, NGOs have focused on only a narrow set of wage dimensions. First, NGOs have focused on legal provisions on wages, such as minimum wages, payment of working hours and social security provisions. Second, NGOs have so far also emphasized the living wage. At least six multi-stakeholder initiatives focus on the living wage in their monitoring activities: the Ethical Trading Initiative (ETI), Social Accountability International (SAI), the Worker Rights Consortium (WRC), the International Labor Rights Fund (ILRF), the Fair Wear Foundation (FWF) and Labor behind the Label (Clean Clothes Campaign).

Initiatives by CSR actors have, therefore, so far focused mainly on the living wage, on which there is a growing international debate. Many analysts and NGOs have even advised basing wage requirements along the supply chain exclusively – or almost exclusively – on this dimension, by, for instance, persuading the brands to ensure that their suppliers provide at least a living wage. As an example, 'the ETI board has identified work on the living wage as a top priority for the coming years' (ETI 2007).

The most visible initiatives on wages have concentrated on living wage campaigns. Campaigns have also been launched in a number of developing countries to raise the minimum wage as a way of attaining a living wage. Such campaigns have developed in countries such as Mexico and Indonesia in recent years.

Undoubtedly, the concept is crucial since it is aimed at ensuring basic living standards for all workers. We shall thus merely confirm the need to continue work on such an important and basic principle to better anchor it in the operations of all companies along the supply chain and, furthermore, to make this principle fully operational in companies' everyday practices.

At the same time, there is a need to extend the approach to other wage dimensions, first, because the living wage alone may not be enough to ensure the payment of fair wages along the supply chain – we shall see that the payment of a wage that would ensure basic standards to the workers may be facilitated by the integration of new wage dimensions, such as real wages, the wage share and a number of others (see in Chapter 3) – and second, because of the difficulties (recognized also by the most active proponents of this approach) involved in making the principle of the living wage fully operational and thus fully recognized by all CSR actors. This is why a number of debates have been organized to try to overcome the difficulties or limitations of the living wage approach, which may be gathered into four groups.[11]

First, it often requires detailed studies and a fairly complex methodology to calculate what the living wage should be. It will depend on local cultural habits and conditions, such as the basic food items normally consumed, as well as their prices. There are also many discussions about what type of goods this definition may include, from basic food, accommodation and clothing needs to health care, education and, for example, leisure.

Questions such as what ought to be regarded as 'adequate', in relation to food, housing, clothing and discretionary spending have also been considered. Some organizations – for instance, the ETI – have insisted on including in the list of basic needs 'discretionary spending' for savings and other items.

There have also been some differentiated approaches related to the measurement of average family size or the number of presumed wage-earners per family.

There is also a debate over what the best way would be to measure the existence of the above elements in the various enterprises. Obviously, what workers consider 'basic needs' and how a 'family' is defined vary significantly from country to country.

Second, debates have taken place, not only on the methodology, but also on the type of process on the basis of which the calculation of the living wage should take place. While some have given preference to a sort of 'universal' approach that could be workable and adaptable to the local context, others have argued that such a universal formula for living wages would be too centralized and thus not fully adapted to local needs. They have rather proposed a more

---

11. A number of debates have been organized, for instance by website: (http://www.ethicaltrade. org/ and in particular see Steele, 2000 and Rees, 2007), and by the institutes EPI and PERI in the early 2000s (see http://www.peri.umass.edu/fileadmin/pdf/gls_conf/glw_brenner.pdf and http://www.epionline.org/studies/epi_livingwage_08-2000.pdf); similarly, in 2003, the FLA also hosted a forum on the concept of living wages that proposed a close study of living wages, how it has been measured so far, how it could be installed at the enterprise level and at what cost (Fair Labor Association, 2003).

locally developed method that would put greater emphasis on social dialogue and on consulting the workers to better understand what they interpret as a living wage and how they define their exact needs to ensure living standards in their respective country and social context.[12]

Third, precisely because of the important logistical (and thus time-consuming) framework that it requires, the living wage may be difficult to adjust in accordance with changing conditions, for instance in consumption patterns and price increases. As an example, we might wonder about the possibility of a living wage definition that adjusts quickly to rapid price changes within the current international food crisis, in which the price of basic food items, such as rice, often doubles in the course of a single month (ILO, 2008a).

Finally, the other critique to the living wage comes from the companies themselves, which consider the 'living wage' as a social approach that does not have serious economic foundations and would thus be difficult to accept. While the living wage approach might thus be accepted by companies sensitive to social issues or that could afford it because of their good economic results, it may be systematically rejected by other companies because of what they see as its excessively social and insufficiently economic focus. The integration of wage dimensions and indicators that would be more directly related to economic variables – such as price increases, productivity and technological progress – may thus be more easily accepted by companies and, in the end, help to achieve the primary aims of the living wage method. In the same vein, critics have highlighted that once a pre-determined specific living wage formula was accepted by employers, they would be reluctant to adapt or revise it in accordance with changing circumstances unless social dialogue was established with regard to regular adjustment of the living wage.

The living wage is an essential dimension of the fair wage concept, but it should probably be rendered more flexible to make it fully operational and be combined with other fair wage dimensions.

But NGO Initiatives Provide a Good Basis for an Extensive and Cooperative Approach

At the same time, most NGOs recognize the need to cover a larger set of wage issues. In fact, there seems to be a sort of paradox between the great number of wage dimensions recognized as important by most actors in this field and the rather limited focus of their concrete initiatives on wages.

---

12. For a discussion of the pros and cons of the Universal or Formula Living Wage approach versus the Negotiated Living Wage approach, see Steele (2000).

Having said that, there seem to be many common objectives and similar wage dimensions put forward by the NGOs working in this field which could represent a good basis for more cooperation. The increasing concern and willingness to change wage practices along the supply chain is evident and could be mobilized into a more general movement on 'fair wages'.

2.2 INCREASING CONCERNS AMONG WORKERS AND EMPLOYERS

Trade Unions Sound the Alarm

For the trade unions, it is clear that workers should have the opportunity to play their part in determining what an acceptable wage level is in their own local contexts and this is why they try to play a key role in promoting such a bottom-up approach.

At the global level, trade unions, such as the International Textile, Garment and Leather Workers Federation (ITGLWF), have promoted and supported this view through the inclusion of living wage provisions in codes of conduct. They recognize that they are 'a handle that workers and their representatives can use to help enforce their rights, as part of the mechanisms of normal industrial relations'.[13] On the other hand, they have been less keen on developing a universal formula to measure it, insisting that the right to bargain collectively constitutes the most legitimate method of determining a living wage by local standards.[14] The Federation stresses the important role that workers play in determining what is a living wage.

Current trade union efforts are mainly focused on fighting for workers' rights and they have developed initiatives to ensure decent work for all. Five organizations, led by the International Confederation of Trade Unions (ICTU), recently launched the campaign 'Decent Work, Decent Life',[15] which aims to promote at the global level a notion of decent work which involves not only adequate working conditions, but also social protection for workers and adequate payment. This last factor, for the campaign, is expounded as 'sufficient income for their basic economic, social and family needs, a right that should be enforced by providing adequate living wages'.[16]

---

13. Social Accountability International and ITGLWF (2002).
14. Ibid., p. 49.
15. See website: 'Decent work, decent life': http://www.decentwork.org/.
16. Conny Reuter, Secretary-General, Solidar, ITUC Online, media release, 21 January 2007, cited in 'Decent work, decent life' campaign. Available at: http://www.streetnet.org.za/DWDL. htm.

The Asia Floor Wage alliance is also an initiative aimed at developing an international framework – based in Asia – on wages for the global garment industry. The aim is to calculate a wage floor in purchasing power parity (PPP) terms and taking into account food and non-food costs. The approach should directly help to make progress on the living wage front, while also contributing to progress on minimum wages and collective bargaining on wages.[17]

Similarly, at the European level, the trade unions have launched a major campaign titled 'On the offensive for fair wages' in which they call for pay rises and make clear demands on European decision-makers and the European Central Bank to end their repeated calls for wage moderation and to stop thinking of 'wage moderation as the only adjustment variable' (ETUC, 2008). The ETUC has provided statistics to support their wage claims, for example, on real wages, minimum wages, wage share and wage inequalities. Introduced at the ETUC Congress in Seville in early 2008, this movement led to a Euro-demonstration to demand higher wages in Ljubljana, Slovenia, on 5 April 2008.

Initiatives have also been taken at national level. As an example, the British public sector trade union UNISON launched a fair wage campaign and also developed a fair wages toolkit (UNISON, 2004; 2007) in order to protect the wage conditions of all staff providing public services but transferred to private employers (also with a view to maintaining service quality). The aim was to promote a new Fair Wage Clause or Fair Wages Regulation in public contracting. A concerted campaign in the Scottish health service led to the signing of a Low Pay Agreement.

UNISON has also lobbied for fair wage policies to be incorporated in UK but also European legislation.

Trade union views have also changed on CSR issues (Table 2.2). They are increasingly trying to take advantage of CSR tools, such as codes of conduct, to strengthen social partnerships at regional and global levels. The European Trade Union Confederation (ETUC), at its 2004 Executive Committee Meeting, developed a series of actions to approach CSR from a trade union perspective. These include the recognition that CSR should not be merely a public relations exercise, but requires a sustained effort. It also affirms that the primary concern of CSR must be the quality of industrial relations within a company (ETUC, 2004).

---

17. 'Worker rights groups launch Asia Floor Wage Campaign', 7 October 2009, Maquila Solidarity Network. Available at http://en.maquilasolidarity.org/node/901. See also Position statement of Asia Floor Wage Alliance, June 2009. Available at: asiafloorwage.org.

Table 2.2 Examples of wage items in workers' representatives' programmes

Organizations	General wage concept	Wage focus
Five organizations led by the International Confederation of Trade Unions (ICTU)	Promote at the global level a notion of decent work that involves not only adequate working conditions, but also social protection for workers and adequate payment	*Living wage*: ensure sufficient income for workers' basic economic, social and family needs, a right that should be enforced by providing adequate living wages
International Textile, Garment and Leather Workers Federation (ITGLWF)	Living wage	*Living wage*: inclusion of living wage provisions in codes of conduct
Asia Floor Wage Alliance	Develop an international framework – based in Asia – for a wage floor in global garment industry	*Wage floor*: calculation of a wage floor in PPP terms and taking into account food and non-food costs
European Trade Union Confederation (ETUC)	Pay campaign 'On the offensive for fair wages' Calls on European governments and the European Central Bank to end repeated calls for wage moderation as a response to the crisis	*Wage moderation/real wages*: wages and purchasing power in a downward spiral; rise in real wages needed to boost purchasing power *Minimum wage*: decent minimum wages to combat poverty *Wage share*: wage share in GDP is falling steadily and not following profit growth *Wage disparity*: fall in wage share accompanied by growing inequalities (with drop in purchasing power). Need for genuine equal pay between men and women, fair wages for public sector workers and limits on top incomes *Social dialogue*: need for stronger collective bargaining, including at European level
TUC (UK)		*Wage disparity*: in its submissions to the Low Pay Commission, it argued that the minimum wage should be set at half male median earnings
UNISON (public sector, UK)	Fair Wage Campaign in public sector within the framework of a larger campaign against privatization and the two-tier workforce to ensure that employment, pension and wage conditions remain the same, regardless of who employs workers	*Against competition on low pay*: demanded a new fair wages regulation in public contracting that will protect wage and employment conditions of all staff providing public services, regardless of who employs them, and will also avoid a situation in which contractors compete on the basis of low wages and working conditions Developed a step by step toolkit to help local branches to organize their own fair wage campaign

First Attempts among Enterprises and Brands

Although there are fewer initiatives on 'fair wages' among employers than among trade unions, concern seems to be increasing among employers as well (Table 2.3). This might be due to the global wage trends described in Chapter 1, which may begin to hurt employers. For example, the enormous increase in managerial wages and, correspondingly, the increasing gap between the highest and lowest wages within companies has brought this issue on to the agenda of the boards of most companies and concrete initiatives have been taken to limit increasing wage disparity. In France, as in many other countries, the national employers' organization MEDEF has expressly asked its members to introduce more transparent and more decent systems for remunerating their top managers.

Managers are also increasingly being made responsible for ensuring fair wages along the supply chain. Many brands have committed themselves to codes of conduct which include some benchmarking on wage issues mainly with regard to the payment of wages, the minimum wage and proper payment of overtime. Companies such as Adidas, Nike and H&M have carried out their own auditing to make sure that their suppliers are complying with wage regulations, such as on the minimum wage and payment of overtime.

Others have tried to go beyond purely legal considerations and have started to put pressure on their suppliers or sub-contractors on additional wage issues to ensure fairer wages. For example, some banks in the UK (Barclays, HSBC) have agreed to extend their wage conditions to the employees of their contractors, including benefits and paid holidays. Similar agreements have been reported in the public sector, for instance in East London. Other brands have decided to intervene more directly with regard to wage levels among their suppliers, as in the case of the company School House, which decided in 2008 to impose a doubling of wages on its suppliers in Sri Lanka to ensure a living wage for the workers, and then integrated this increase in their purchasing prices and, therefore, sales costs. With its various human rights guidelines, the organization En Vogue International has also developed a few basic principles on fair wages, notably the payment of the minimum wage and the need for companies to provide a pay slip and to follow written policies and procedures in their wage-fixing processes.[18]

Nevertheless, such initiatives remain rare and isolated and do not form part – at least not yet – of a larger and consistent movement on wages within CSR.

---

18. See website: http://www.en-vogueinternational.com/fairwages.html.

Table 2.3 Examples of employers' initiatives on wage issues

Companies	Initiatives
Public services (UK)	Fair pay claim (2002) in four East London Hospital Trusts employed by the contractors ISS Mediclean and Medirest
Barclays Bank (in agreement with the East London Communities Organisation – TELCO) *Similar agreement at HSBC*	Accepted responsibility for minimum pay conditions for contractors' staff (for example, cleaners) at its new tower HQ at Canary Wharf; staff will receive wage conditions that meet 'socially responsible minimum standards', including employer's pension contribution, 15 days paid sick leave and eight paid bank holidays, bonuses and training
En Vogue International	Developed 'Factory Human Rights Guidelines' with a number of wage guidelines for all its factories and suppliers, stipulating that 'every worker must be paid the legal minimum wage or the local industry wage, whichever is the higher, and must also receive an individual pay slip which clearly identifies regular and overtime wages, other allowances and deductions'
School House, operating in Sri Lanka	Following a report showing that the wages paid by the supplier were below the living wage, the brand asked the supplier to double its wages and committed itself to accepting a corresponding increase in the sales prices of the supplier

2.3 'FAIR WAGE' ENDEAVOURS BY NATIONAL AND LOCAL AUTHORITIES

While the fair wage concept has not yet been incorporated into the CSR process to a significant extent, some examples of 'fair wage' legislation or experience can be found at national and regional level (Table 2.4).

National Level

In Scotland, a first Fair Wage Resolution was adopted in February 1891, which included conditions against subcontracting for contracts of the Fishery Board and Prison Commissioners.

The fair wage was also used traditionally in the British labour movement to define the principle that a worker should be paid the going rate for the work put in, regardless of gender or race. Great Britain had a Fair Wages Resolution (1891, 1909 and 1946) until it was abolished in 1983. It required companies to

Table 2.4 'Fair wage' initiatives by national and local authorities

National level		
Australia	Australian Fair Pay and Conditions Standard	Defines the conditions for fixing minimum wages and fair pay standards
	Fair Pay Commission	Independent body responsible for adjusting federal minimum wage level and classification wages; also produces monitoring reports on economic and social indicators
Scotland	Fair Wage Resolution (1891)	Included conditions against subcontracting for contracts of the Fishery Board and Prison Commissioners
Great Britain	Fair Wages Resolution (1891, 1909 and 1946) The 1946 Resolution was abolished in 1983	Required companies contracting with public authorities to pay the going rate for the trade or industry, based on terms agreed in national collective agreements
Canada	Fair Wages and Hours of Labour Act (1985) Fair Wages and Hours of Labour Regulations	Specifies that persons contracted by the federal government for work involving construction, redevelopment or demolition in any given district must follow certain rules and, in particular, pay a fair wage, not less than the minimum wage, without discrimination and withholding payments or subcontracting, and other labour provisions, such as work classification
United States	Fair Labor Standards Act (1938) Fair Wage Act (1999) Fair Minimum Wage Act (2007) Equal Pay Act (1963)	Established the federal minimum wage Dealt mainly with the minimum wage following the living wage campaign New minimum wage law allowing minimum wage increase Ensures equal pay for equal work and forbids wage discrimination
Chile	Debate on 'ethical wages' (2007)	Public debate on wages and the fair distribution of growth, especially with regard to the combination of very low wages and huge profits in some sectors, such as supermarkets

Table 2.4 (cont.)

Local level		
Yukon (Canada) *Fair Wage schedule also in other districts of Canada, following national Fair Wages and Hours of Labour Act*	Fair Wage Schedule of the Government of Yukon (2005)	Covers several wage issues for employees working in public works projects in Yukon: provisions on the payment of wages, minimum wage, equal pay, wage rates by category, class and job title, Fair Wage schedule to be posted, paid holidays, etc.
Municipality of Toronto (Canada)	Fair Wage Schedule of the City of Toronto (1893; extended recently) Originally confined to construction workers and then extended to non-construction classifications, such as clerical workers.	Contractors and sub-contractors for the city must pay their workers the union rates for different classifications or, for non-union workers, the prevailing wages and benefits in their branch. Stipulates also vacation pay and applicable amount for fringe benefits. Requires compliance also on working hours and conditions of work
Massachusetts (United States)	Minimum Fair Wages Law – Chapter 151	The different chapters of this Law require the payment of reasonable wages, minimum wage rates by occupations in different areas (agriculture, hospitals, restaurants, schools, domestic service, etc.), overtime pay, bonuses, penalties in case of failure to pay, compulsory health insurance, proper pay recording, review by court decision
North Carolina (United States)	Fair Wages (NCFW) (2007)	Focused on increasing minimum wages in keeping with the notion of a living wage
Ohio (United States)	Minimum Fair Wage Standards	Every employer shall pay employees at a wage rate not less than the wage rate specified in the Ohio Constitution and should adjust their wage rate accordingly; it stipulates also the payment of overtime,

Local level		
Ohio (United States) (*cont.*)		(*cont. from previous page*) bonuses, permitted deductions, prohibition of wage discrimination (including 'casual workers'), method of wage computation; penalties/sanctions for non-compliance
120 city/state governments (United States) including Baltimore, New-York, Chicago, San Jose CA, and Los Angeles County	Living wage ordinances	Provide a definition of and ensure compliance with a living wage; tendency to extend the concept to other wage issues
Newcastle City Council, UK	Protocol on Fair Wages	Ensured that new and transferred staff would receive the same pay and working conditions as staff directly employed by the local authority
Greater London Authority (GLA)*	Fair Employment Clause (2002)	Introduced a fair employment clause into its contracting procedures, including the payment of a fair wage (at least equivalent to public sector wages); policy applied in cleaning and catering services for City Hall and new services in Trafalgar Square
City of London (UK)	London Living Wage for contractors (2008)	Agreement concluded by the Olympic Delivery Authority (ODA) to ensure, among contractors working for the 2012 Games venues and infrastructure, the payment of a living wage in London (£7.20 per hour), but also eligibility for 10 days full sick pay, 28 days paid holidays and access to a recognized trade union

Note: * A similar best value code has been signed in Wales covering local authorities and national park authorities (2003); and also within the Scottish health service, with the signing of a Low Pay Agreement.

pay the going rate for the trade or industry, based on terms agreed in national collective agreements.

In the United States, there is a Fair Wage Act (1999), although it deals mainly with the minimum wage, following the living wage campaign. More recently, a new minimum wage law – which allowed a significant minimum wage increase – was entitled the Fair Minimum Wage Act (2007). With regard to other wage issues, other legislative initiatives were developed, such as the Equal Pay Act, which President Kennedy signed in 1963 to prohibit paying women less than men for the same job. Similarly in Canada, the Fair Wages and Hours of Labour Act ensures that companies/persons who enter into a construction contract with the federal government pay a fair wage, at least at the level of the minimum wage and complying with labour regulations (Government of Canada, 2008).

In Australia, the Fair Pay Commission has the task of fixing and adapting the national minimum wage according to the economic, financial and social context and needs, and generally following the preparation of an annual minimum wage review, in which it makes some recommendations after consultations and research, and taking into account necessary indicators – inflation, employment, low pay and so on. It then announces its wage-setting decisions in July each year (Government of Australia, 2009).[19]

A national debate also took place in Chile in summer 2007 – following increased social tensions – around the notion of 'ethical wages' and the fair distribution of growth. While the government set up a working group to study the issue and make recommendations, the item continued to make headlines in the media.[20] Difficult negotiations at the forestry company Celco and the state-owned Codelco mining company could be concluded only after the management agreed to negotiate the wages of subcontracted workers with the relevant trade union, which also shows the need to take into account wages associated with different work contracts. In the case of supermarkets, the critics claimed that supermarket chains were contributing to social inequality in Chile, mainly through 'anti-union' practices and extreme wage disparities. While the ratio between executives and employees is usually around 8 to 1 in Europe, in the Censosud chain the wage disparity between executive salaries and the minimum wage paid by the company was found to be 200 to 1. At the same time, Cencosud recorded USD 319 million profits for 2006. The use of

---

19. For the Australian Fair Pay Commission website, see fairpay.gov.au.
20. See 'Chile debates "Ethical wage"', 14 August 2007, *Valparaiso Times* (http://www.valparaisotimes.cl/content/view/152/25/); 'Chile braces for largest labor demonstration in twenty years', 28 August 2007, *Santiago Times* (http://www.tcgnews.com/santiagotimes/index.php?nav=story&story_id=14540&topic).

multiple trade names in the same chain was also criticized as a tool against unionization.[21]

Regional/Local Level

At regional level, it is also worth reporting, for instance, the 2005 Fair Wage Schedule of the Government of Yukon (Canada) because it covers several relevant wage issues. For instance, it sets the wage rates (by category, class and job title) that can be paid to persons working on a public work contract in the Yukon; these wage rates are annually adjusted to the previous year's consumer price index (CPI). They must also be applied to employees working for sub-contractors. This fair wage schedule also includes provisions on 'the payment of wages' (how often wages must be paid; what wage components are included; how wages should be paid; and the possibility of a wage claim procedure if wages are not paid, with fines against employers); the 'minimum wage' (level; coverage; method of calculation for atypical employees); 'equal pay' (against discrimination between employees on the basis of sex; action to be taken should a breach occur; enforcement procedures); and the rights of employees to bargain collectively on wages. It also requires that the Fair Wage Schedule be posted at the work site so that employees are aware of it. It also requires proper wage recording 'for a period of less than three years with the name, address and occupation of each of the employees, together with his/her rate of pay, the hours worked and the amount for each period worked'. Records are also required to be open to inspection.

Similarly, the municipal city of Toronto implemented a Fair Wage Schedule as early as 1893 –and which is still in operation today – to fight discrimination against workers by subcontractors and suppliers engaged in work for the city.[22] The schedule ensured that contractors for the city paid their workers the union rates or, for non-union workers, the prevailing wages and benefits in their industry. Originally confined to construction workers, the fair wage policy was then extended to non-construction classifications, such as clerical workers. It also required compliance with an acceptable number of working hours and conditions of work. In view of our proposal, it is interesting to note that the Toronto Fair Wage Schedule also mentioned the need to establish stable labour relations and to minimize potential conflicts (that is, social dialogue – in fact,

---

21. 'Chile's top supermarkets panned for poor wages and working conditions', 23 August 2007, *Santiago Times*. Available at: (http://www.tcgnews.com/santiagotimes/index.php?nav=story&story_id=14506&topic).
22. See *Fair Wage Policy*, by the Toronto Fair Wage Office; available at: http://www.toronto.ca/fairwage/index.htm.

wage rates were negotiated between employers' and workers' groups), but also to limit wage differentials between organized and unorganized labor, as well as discrimination (on the basis of race, creed, sex, sexual orientation, age, marital status, family relationship or disability) and to ensure payment at the prevailing rate, not only of the activity but by geographical area. Training obligations and upgrading opportunities were also mentioned as part of the Fair Wage Schedule. Penalties are applied in case of non-compliance; if the contractor or sub-contractor continues not to comply with the Fair Wage schedule it can be disqualified from conducting business with the city, first for a period of two years, and then for an indefinite period of time, if other violations occur.

Other regional initiatives, such as the North Carolinians for Fair Wages (NCFW) in 2007, have also focused on increasing minimum wages in keeping with the living wage concept. Massachusetts General Laws include a law on Minimum Fair Wages that stipulates all minimum wage rates by sectors and occupations, with all requisite details, from the basic wage during normal working hours to overtime rates, bonuses, Compulsory Health Insurance, Inspection and Review process and penalties in case of non-compliance.[23] The Ohio Minimum Fair Wage Standards also require all employers working for the State of Ohio to pay the wage rates laid down in the Ohio Constitution and in accordance with the national Fair Labor Standards Act.[24] Coherence on Fair Wages thus prevails between federal level and the individual states, with a similar situation with regard to the living wage.

In the United States, more than 120 city/state governments have passed living wage ordinances, with a tendency to extend the concept to other wage issues. These living wages are voted on by local electorates or city councils and apply to the employees of companies which do business with the city or county. They have come about as a result of campaigning by community–labour coalitions. It is also worth noting that such living wage ordinances generally achieve a wage rate which is much higher than the US minimum wage, generally following their conclusion that the prevailing statutory federal minimum wage level is not enough to ensure decent living standards for workers and their families, the typical basis used in living wage ordinances being four family members (for instance for Minneapolis, St Paul, Boston and many others).

More recently, in London the Olympic Delivery Authority (ODA) concluded an agreement to promote the London Living Wage for Contractors working on

23. *Massachusetts General Laws* – Minimum Fair Wages – Chapter 151. Available at: http://law. onecle.com/massachusetts/151/index.html.
24. Chapter 4111: Minimum Fair Wage Standards, Code of the Ohio Constitution. Available at: http://codes.ohio.gov/orc/4111.

2012 Games venues and infrastructure. Not only is the payment of a living wage in London demanded (£7.20 per hour), but also eligibility to 10 days full sick pay, 28 days paid holidays and access to a recognized trade union.

CONCLUSIONS

Undoubtedly, there are increasing concerns about wage issues along the supply chain, from all the actors concerned: NGOs, which are increasingly involved in the monitoring of sub-contracting and outsourcing and also increasingly determined to ensure better wage practices among suppliers; trade unions, which have launched campaigns sounding the alarm on wage developments; employers' representatives and individual managers, who have begun to impose some wage standards on their suppliers; and finally, some national and local authorities which have shown that they can provide a useful framework for promoting fair wage practices. This may indicate that a good momentum is building for the launching of a large-scale movement or initiative on fair wages.

Despite these increasing concerns, a coherent approach on wage issues is still lacking. While highlighting a number of key wage indicators in their codes of conduct – such as prevailing wages, wages and productivity, and social dialogue – NGOs' initiatives on wages remain much too fragmented and too focused, first, on a small number of legal provisions and second, and even more strongly, on the living wage concept, which, unfortunately, is constrained by methodological and practical limitations. As a result, NGOs have not yet managed to impose a clear monitoring process on wages along the supply chain. Similarly, trade unions have not been able to have an impact in the field, since they are rarely present at suppliers. Certainly, the fact that employers' organizations have requested fairer wage practices – for instance, in the remuneration of top executives or in response to increases in wage inequality – may help to change things in the wage area. Individual initiatives on the part of brands to better monitor and influence wage practices among their suppliers are also encouraging. However, these initiatives are rare and isolated, and a broader movement of employers in favour of incorporating wages into CSR has yet to emerge. The fair wage initiatives of national and local authorities already referred to include fair wage schedules imposed by a few municipalities to induce employers to behave better if they want to be involved in public works projects. National legislation on wages – for example, on the minimum wage, living wages or fair wages – may also induce employers to avoid getting caught up in a race to the bottom in terms of wages and wage costs.

We thus seem to have arrived at a crossroads. While globalization seems to have led to adverse wage developments – as shown in Chapter 1 – the impetus might be there for mobilizing all the actors concerned to incorporate wages into CSR, although to date this movement does not seem to have found its operational path. It might be that this relative CSR deficit on wages is due to the lack of a coherent approach on wage issues, something that we propose to address in the next chapter.

3. Fair Wages: A More Comprehensive and Multidimensional Approach

INTRODUCTION

In the previous chapter, we saw that there is increasing concern about wage issues, not only from national and local authorities and workers' representatives, but also from NGOs working in CSR and a number of enterprises. At the same time, the approach to wages along the supply chain has remained rather narrow in scope and fragmented in approach.

In this chapter, we propose to integrate all the wage issues looked at so far within the framework of a comprehensive and integrated approach, as necessary and complementary 'fair wage' elements. The process proposed is also intended to extend the notion of 'fair wages' to other, no less important wage issues which also have to be taken into account (such as the non-payment of wages, the wage share in growth, wage bargaining and so on).

The following 'fair wage' approach defines the methodology and tools needed to start organizing the collection of data and programming future evaluation and monitoring activities in this field.

3.1 THE FAIR WAGE CONCEPT: AIMS AND METHODOLOGY

The aim of this approach is progressively to develop an economically rigorous concept of 'fair wages' along a number of key wage dimensions and then to develop robust wage indicators. These different indicators could then help to constitute a matrix, enabling a comprehensive and overall assessment of an enterprise's performance in the wage area.

There are a number of what we might call 'fair wage' developments or dimensions: the payment of wages, the living wage, real wages, the wage share and so on. Each of these 'fair wage' developments or dimensions can be captured by a number of indicators.

These indicators help us to assess the performance of each enterprise with regard to (a) each of the 'fair wage' dimensions; and (b) wage issues and wage policy in general, leading to a total 'fair wage' score.

The performance of each enterprise with regard to the selected indicators will be assessed by a series of open-ended questions on wage issues, by means of one questionnaire for the employers and one for the employees. These are complemented by a series of statistical data on wages requested from the management or the accounting/financial department (see the two questionnaires for the management and the workers in Annex 1; the statistical table is at the end of the management questionnaire). These three sources of information and cumulative answers to the questions will help us – by means of a Fair Wage Matrix – to compile the progressive 'fair wage' score of each enterprise.

3.2 'FAIR WAGE INDICATORS' TO REFLECT 'FAIR WAGE DIMENSIONS'

The first step was to define the various types of wage developments ('fair wage dimensions') which would help to define what a fair wage should be. Once these were identified, it was important to establish the different indicators that would help to evaluate company performance on each of these fair wage dimensions.

We propose a general definition, complemented by an extensive definition of fair wages (Box 3.1).

Box 3.1 Definition of fair wages

General definition
Fair wages refer to 'Company practices that lead to sustainable wage developments.'

Extended definition
Fair wages refer to 'Wage levels and wage-fixing mechanisms that provide a living wage floor for workers, while complying with national wage regulations (such as the minimum wage, payment of wages, overtime payments, provision of paid holidays and social insurance payments), ensure proper wage adjustments and lead to balanced wage developments in the company (with regard to wage disparity, skills, individual and collective performance and adequate internal communication and collective bargaining on wage issues).'

The concept of fair wages should also be based on the optimal identification and definition of fair wage developments. With this in mind, we identified 12 fair wage dimensions (Table 3.1).

Table 3.1 The 12 fair wage dimensions

A fair wage could be defined as:	
1. Payment of wages	A wage which is regularly and formally paid in full to the workers.
2. Living wage	A wage that ensures minimum acceptable living standards.
3. Minimum wage	A wage which respects the minimum wage regulations.
4. Prevailing wage	A wage which is comparable to wages in similar enterprises in the same sector.
5. Payment of working time	A wage that does not generate excessive working hours and properly rewards normal working hours and overtime.
6. Pay systems	A wage that leads to a balanced wage structure/composition between the basic wage and additional bonuses and benefits. A wage that reflects different levels of education, skills and professional experience, as well as rewarding individual and collective performance. A wage that complies with regulations on social insurance payments and paid holidays and is not dominated by disciplinary wage sanctions.
7. Communication and social dialogue	A wage on which workers receive sufficient information in advance (through an individual work contract), in the course of the production process (through regular communication channels) and at the time of the wage payment (with a detailed pay slip). A wage that is negotiated individually (with individual employers) and/or collectively – notably through collective bargaining – between the employer and the workers' representatives who are freely accepted in the company.
8. Wage discrimination/ wage disparity	A system of equal wages for equal work that does not lead to wage discrimination and does not generate unjustified, too high and too rapidly growing wage differentials within the company.
9. Real wages	A wage that progresses at least in proportion to price increases.
10. Wage share	A wage that progresses proportionally along with enterprise sales and profit growth and which does not lead to a fall in the wage share in enterprise performance growth.
11. Wage costs	A wage whose progression does not lead to a dramatic reduction in wage costs within total production costs and as a percentage of employment.
12. Work intensity, technology and upskilling	A wage that progresses along with changes in intensity at work, technological contents and the evolving skills and tasks of the labour force.

1. Payment of wages

The payment of wages should be among the first criteria since most important for the workers is the guarantee that they will be paid in exchange for their work. Non-payment of wages can take three possible forms: (a) simple non-payment of wages, representing part of or a full wage that is expected but never paid; (b) delays in the payment of wages, representing a wage payment that will eventually be paid but with a considerable delay of a few weeks or months; (c) underpayment of wages, representing a payment that is made, but well below the legal or expected rate.

In order to identify forms of non-payment we should first capture whether wages are paid and, if so, regularly; if this is not the case we should try to find out what the average amount of delayed payment is and also identify the average length of delays. It is also essential to identify whether there are any difficulties in paying wages in full, and whether there is any source of underpayment in the company, which might consist of a bonus which is not paid when it should be, or overtime hours that are not remunerated as regulated by law or as stipulated in the work contract.

The payment of wages is enshrined in the International Labour Standards, with Convention No. 95 clearly stipulating that wages should be paid: 'employers shall be prohibited from limiting in any manner the freedom of the worker to dispose of his wages' (Art. 6); 'wages shall be paid regularly' (Art. 12) (ILO, 1992). This is the convention that the ILO used most often when intervening in CIS countries in the 1990s, when these countries confronted massive wage arrears and a general process of barter and non-payment of wages. In some countries, legislation has been adopted on the protection of wages and many have also ratified ILO Convention No. 95.

It is interesting to observe that the number of governments which have ratified the convention on the protection of wages is much higher than the number of those which have ratified the convention on minimum wages. This indicates that the protection of wages represents the basis of any wage payment and explains why we rank it as the first fair wage dimension.

To be able to monitor the proper payment of wages, there should be proper recording of wages in the first place and such records should be open for inspection. Cases of double recording, attempts to falsify wage recording and a refusal to make them accessible generally reflect non-payment of wages or wage underpayment (for overtime, for instance).

2. Living wage

To be fair, wage levels should also allow workers to have decent living standards.

No doubt the living wage is an essential dimension of wage fixing since it measures the ability of wages to provide basic needs to workers and their families and thus to provide for decent living standards.

The Universal Declaration of Human Rights states that 'Everyone who works has the right to just and favourable remuneration ensuring for himself and his family an existence worthy of human dignity, and supplemented, if necessary, by other means of social protection'.

However, there is no international labour convention on the living wage, although the ILO has made clear references to the concept from the start. As far back as 1919, the constitution of the International Labour Organization (ILO) in its charter's preamble refers to 'the provision of an adequate living wage'. This principle was also included in the Declaration of Philadelphia, adopted by the International Labour Conference in 1944, in Article III (d), highlighting the need to promote 'a minimum living wage to all employed and in need of such protection'.

Convention No. 131 on minimum wages, although it does not establish criteria with regard to a living wage, provides a basic framework by stating that the elements to be taken into consideration in determining the level of minimum wages shall, so far as possible and appropriate in relation to national practice and conditions, include the needs of workers and their families, taking into account the general level of wages in the country, the cost of living, social security benefits and the relative living standards of other social groups.

The 2008 ILO Declaration on Social Justice for a Fair Globalization recognizes that 'the ILO has the solemn obligation to further among the nations of the world programmes which will achieve the objectives of full employment and the raising of standards of living, a minimum living wage and the extension of social security measures to provide a basic income to all in need, along with all the other objectives set out in the Declaration of Philadelphia' (ILO, 2008c).

At the same time, it underlines that member states have a key responsibility to establish in this field appropriate indicators or statistics, if necessary with the assistance of the ILO, to monitor and evaluate the progress made.

Nevertheless, despite its emphasis on the concept, the ILO has not yet provided a clear methodology or indicator for calculating a living wage or for implementing this concept in practice, mainly because of methodological difficulties and the extreme diversity of situations at national and local level.

However, there have been attempts to establish a living wage (for developing countries, see Anker, 2006) and highlight statistical and conceptual difficulties. Interesting work has been done on the living wage in the United States where the concept of living wages is popular in relation to minimum wages.[1]

There have also been serious attempts by individual enterprises (for example, in China and Vietnam, and 'fair-trade'-related activities) or by NGOs to establish living wages, but so far there is no universally accepted formula.

---

1. See the book by Pollin et al., 2008, and the interesting work done by two research institutes, EPI and PERI: http://www.peri.umass.edu/fileadmin/pdf/gls_conf/glw_brenner.pdf and http://www.epionline.org/studies/epi_livingwage_08-2000.pdf.

What we propose with the fair wage approach is to integrate the living wage as one, but not the only possible criterion for fair wages at company level. This dimension is essential in order to respond to a paradox: while paying a living wage is seen as a determining criterion in wage fixing at national level – notably through the minimum wage – the living wage has so far not been established as an essential indicator in fixing wage levels at company level.

The identification of the living wage dimension requires a comparison between wages paid by companies and the subsistence or poverty line officially calculated in the country, whenever it exists. It could also be progressively based on the different criteria of a living wage already defined by existing research work on living wages. This fair wage dimension could thus progressively benefit from the significant research currently being done on the living wage at both local and international level. At the same time, we recommend that monitoring on wages not be based exclusively on the living wage dimension.

3. Minimum wages

The third criterion should be compliance with minimum wage legislation, if a minimum wage has been fixed, either by law or collective agreement. This is also an essential dimension since the minimum wage is precisely aimed at ensuring a decent starting wage in all companies and for all workers. This is what is stipulated in ILO Convention No. 131: 'minimum wages shall have the force of law' (Art. 2); 'the elements to be taken into consideration in determining the level of minimum wages shall include the needs of workers and their families, taking into account the general level of wages in the country, the cost of living, social security benefits, and the relative living standards of other social groups' (Art. 3) (ILO, 1992).

Most codes of conduct – either of companies or of NGOs – already take into account this basic requirement. When the brands audit their suppliers they check whether the companies are complying with the local minimum wage in order to avoid any obvious breach of local minimum wage provisions.

This minimum wage dimension is related to many other fair wage dimensions, such as the living wage function, since the minimum wage is aimed at providing basic living standards, or the payment of overtime, since national legislation on minimum wages generally requires that the minimum wage be paid to workers for normal working hours and not for extra hours.

4. Prevailing wages

At the same time, it is important to compare wages in the company with wage levels outside. Wages should, of course, be competitive since they are the main component of labour costs; however, if they remain artificially low compared to competitors in the same sector, at other brand subcontractors or in the economy as a whole, this could reflect too great a downward pressure on wage costs in the company, which could only lead to the payment of unfair wages and may lead to workers' demotivation or high turnover.

Wage levels should thus also be analysed in comparison with other wage practices of similar companies and/or main competitors, something which we shall try to capture in terms of the concept of 'prevailing wages', which is already present in the FLA workplace code of conduct on the 'prevailing industry wage', as well as in several other codes of conduct (see Chapter 2).

5. Payment of working hours
A fair wage should, first, not lead to an excessive number of working hours, above the legal limit. Second, fair wage practices should also include the proper payment of working time. It is not all the same if workers work for 48 or 60 hours a week for the same money or whether or not their overtime hours are remunerated, either in accordance with the legal rates or not at all.

In this area, Convention No. 1 (on initial working hours standards), but also No. 30 (on a maximum 48 hours pre-overtime working week) and No. 47 (on a 40 hours working week) provide a useful framework. In this respect, it is essential to check, first, whether the wage system in itself does not push the workers towards excessive working hours beyond the legal limit and, second, whether working hours are properly remunerated, including overtime.

6. Pay systems
In order to better capture the performance of individual enterprises with regard to the fair wage principle, pay systems should also be scrutinized to see whether they are balanced in terms of their structure and pay components. If pay systems are to be effective, they must normally be expected to reflect different levels of skills, position in the hierarchy, individual performance and the financial state and performance of the company. Different pay schemes and their respective outcomes with regard to workers' well-being must, therefore, be analysed, including the piece rate system, collective schemes – such as performance-related pay or profit-sharing – bonuses for seniority, skills or other things, pay and classification grids, fringe benefits, paid holidays and social insurance payments. This identification would also help us to better understand how wages may be linked to individual or collective performance or to different skills and education levels. Certain bonuses strengthen the link to tenure (seniority bonuses), others the link to attendance (attendance bonuses) or to skills (skills bonuses). Others strengthen the link to collective performance (profit-sharing or profit-related pay schemes) or to individual performance (such as piece rate systems). It may happen, however, that certain bonuses – such as the piece rate system – crowd out the basic wage or other wage components.

Certain elements of pay or wage-fixing may have a beneficial effect on workers' well-being and living standards, such as free accommodation or meals.

Other bonuses may have an alienating effect on workers, such as attendance bonuses that depend on a minimum of 28 to 30 days' work per month. Others provide additional income, such as bonuses for poor health and safety conditions, but are not beneficial to the workers in the long run since they have to put up with low health and safety standards and thus do not contribute to improving working conditions in the company. During the EU enlargement process, the European Commission decided to forbid bonuses paid to compensate for bad health and safety standards.

7. Communication and social dialogue

To be fair, wage-fixing systems should be expected to provide workers with adequate information on wages, from when they are hired (through the individual work contract), during the production process (through regular communication channels) and at the point of wage payment (with an informative pay slip).

Finally, wages can be set by means of collective bargaining and lead to collective agreements, or be fixed through negotiation between the employer and individual workers. Alternatively, they can be fixed unilaterally by the employer or even outside any collective and/or individual agreement, something that would obviously lead to rather different outcomes in terms of fair wage developments.

The importance of having workers' and employers' representatives, as well as collective bargaining, is clearly integrated in ILO Conventions Nos 87 on Freedom of Association and 98 on the Right to Collective Bargaining.

Studies throughout the world have shown that collective bargaining can greatly improve wage outcomes and also, to some extent, limit wage differentials (ILO, 2008a).

8. Wage discrimination and wage disparity

Wage fixing should also not lead to any discriminatory practices and the principle of equal pay for work of equal value should be applied. Wage data by gender or ethnic origin should thus be collected within companies to identify any discriminatory wage practices. In some countries, anti-discriminatory provisions have been adopted and ILO Conventions Nos. 100, 111 and 183 are aimed at ensuring respect for the principle of equal pay for equal work. Similarly, Convention No. 94 stipulates that public contracts should include clauses ensuring that the workers concerned enjoy wages and other conditions 'no less favourable than those established for work of the same character'.

Wage developments should also be analysed according to their possible effects on wage disparity within the company, between the top and the lowest grades, between skilled and unskilled and also between male and female workers. This is even more urgent because huge increases in wage differentials have been observed around the world (see Chapter 1). While economists disagree whether wage disparity is a good or a bad thing for companies and workers, they do agree that the growth of disparity in a company can be counterproductive if it is too fast and does not reflect differentiated performance. In recent years, CEO salaries have increased at incredible rates, while workers at the bottom have often been forced to compete in a race to the bottom.

This is why we retained in our definition the terms 'too high, or unjustified, or too quickly increasing wage differentials within the company'. Other fair wage dimensions, such as the minimum wage, contribute to reducing wage differentials, as shown in comparative studies (ILO, 2008a).

Some studies – for instance, for the Council of Europe (Daloz and Barruel, 1993) – have proposed the development at national level of an indicator comparing the minimum wage to the average wage in order to identify dispersion around the average and the degree of skewness in the income distribution. The ILO has also tried to report on the ratio of the minimum wage to the median wage in a systematic way. While such an indicator (minimum wage to average or median wage) would not be appropriate for monitoring at company level, but rather at national level, these proposals confirm the existence of concerns with regard to wage disparity and the need for monitoring.

9. Real wages

If they are to be fair, wages should also be allowed to evolve according to price changes, so that workers do not suffer from an erosion of their wages in real terms. This requires some monitoring of nominal wages compared to inflation in order to better capture the evolution of real wages. In our field work, we tried to complement the national inflation rate with other data on local inflation rates since the latter will most influence workers' purchasing power. Real wages are important with regard to the aim of sustainable development, since workers employed in supply chains in developing countries will be able to improve their relative position in the global income distribution only if wages progressively rise in real terms.

10. Wage share

Fair wages would also be expected to reflect better company performance in terms of profits, profitability and sales growth. Workers' wages should reflect the contribution they make to the company. Given the declining wage share at the macroeconomic level, we need to raise the question of the distribution of benefits resulting from the production and sales of products and services in individual enterprises. If there is to be sustainable development, the ongoing concentration of wealth in the hands of a few within companies and countries must be challenged, as well as the concentration of wealth in some countries rather than in others. Closer monitoring would also be required at micro level, along the supply chain, in order to ensure, on the one hand, that increased growth in a company is fairly redistributed to the workers through either higher wages or profit-sharing bonuses and, on the other hand, that brands with high profits also grant some flexibility to their suppliers to improve their fair wage performance. This would ensure that wages were finally incorporated into Corporate Social Responsibility.

This would require collecting data on company wages and company performance (profits, sales).

11. Wage costs

The payment of fair wages could also be scrutinized according to the company's wage costs, notably to identify sudden falls in wage costs in proportion to other production costs (raw materials, fixed costs, investments and so on).

Of course, wage costs are seen as a competitive element which, according to economic theory, should not be allowed to increase dramatically, thereby increasing overall production costs, which would be reflected in higher prices for the company's products. On the other hand, if wage costs also decrease significantly in a short period of time it may mean that the company is trying to build its competitive advantage on low wage costs alone, which could turn out to be detrimental to the workers but also counterproductive for productivity and performance. In order to monitor wage costs we should not only monitor their evolution in proportion of total wage costs, but also the evolution of wage costs per employee (that is, unit wage costs) to take into account possible employment changes. A rapid reduction in wage costs may be due to a reduction in employment, but it could also be due to lower wage costs alongside constant or even increasing employment. The wage costs variable is thus a complementary fair wage element which should be analysed in relation to both total production costs and employment levels.

12. Wages and work intensity, technology and upskilling

Wages should also be related to changing employment composition. If a company reduces its labour force, while maintaining the same production volume, this automatically increases work intensity. Adjustment of the production process in accordance with the 'just in time' model or increasing the number and range of goods produced may also lead to greater work intensity. This additional burden and stress should somehow be reflected in wage levels.

Similarly, the introduction of new technology requires some adaptation on the part of the workers and may generate additional stress and more intense working rhythms. Together with training received by the workers this leads to the upgrading of workers' skills, which is particularly precious to the company in terms of productivity and competitiveness. To promote such an increase in the company's human capital, workers should progressively receive higher wages. For instance, training is often aimed at creating a multi-skilled labour force to ensure that workers can fill in for each other, something that improves efficiency and productivity.

A higher ratio of skilled to unskilled workers also leads to increased productivity and production quality and should normally also lead to a higher average wage in the company.

The importance of this fair wage dimension seems to be growing among suppliers, which increasingly need skilled workers, a phenomenon clearly identified in our company case studies. We shall see that, despite this demand for higher skilled labour, managers often do not understand why their average wage is not attractive enough. The relevant gap is due to an average wage – used by the managers as a reference wage – that is not increased alongside progressive upskilling of the labour force. If it were developed, this fair wage dimension may progressively help companies to accompany changes in technology, composition and workforce skills by appropriate revision of wage levels, but also pay systems – for instance, a pay system better related to skills and education, notably through a grading pay scale, is more appropriate to skilled workers than the piece rate system (see case studies in Chapter 6).

Selecting Fair Wage Indicators

Enterprise performance with regard to each of the fair wage dimensions discussed so far will be identified through information on various indicators collected by means of two questionnaires: one for the management and the other for the workers. The indicators will thus be used as reference points or benchmarks for assessing the fairness of wages with regard to distinct wage issues.

We have identified these indicators in order to facilitate their collection at company level or, if information is not available, to employ closely equivalent indicators as viable alternatives.

We have regrouped the indicators within the framework of the 12 fair wage dimensions:

1. Payment of wages
Indicator 1: Unpaid wage amounts and/or unpaid wages as a percentage of total wage fund.
Indicator 2: If not paid regularly, average payment delay (one, three, six months and so on).
Indicator 3: Underpayment of wages (basic wage, bonuses, overtime, and so on).
Indicator 4: Presence of informal or undeclared payments ('under the table' or 'envelope wages') and the proportion of the total wage they account for; presence of fake or double recording.

Source(s) of information:
Company surveys (management; workers; statistical table obtained from accounting or financial department).

2. Minimum living standards (living wage)
Indicator 5: Starting wage in the company compared to the national/local subsistence minimum (poverty line) or any other measure of the living wage.
Indicator 6: Average wage in the company compared to the national/local subsistence minimum (poverty line) or any other measure of the living wage.

Source(s) of information:
On wages – company surveys (management; workers; statistical table); on poverty line or living wage – official local or national source or international data (NGOs and so on).

3. Legal minimum wage (minimum wage)
Indicator 7: Starting wage in the company compared to the national/local statutory minimum wage.
Indicator 8: Difficulty in paying the minimum wage.
Indicator 9: Workers informed or not about the level of the statutory minimum wage.

Source(s) of information:
On starting wages – company surveys (management; workers; statistical table); on the national minimum wage – national data and national legislation; on the provincial or city minimum wage – provincial/city data.

4. Prevailing wage

Indicator 10: Average wage in the company compared to the average wage in the sector (if sectoral data are not available, the average wage in the manufacturing sector could be used).

Indicator 11: Average wage in the company compared to the average wage among competitors.

Indicator 12: Average wage in the company compared to the average wage in the region/district.

Source(s) of information:
On average wage – company surveys (management; workers; statistical table); other information on the economy/sector/region – national data.

5. Payment of working hours

Indicator 13: Compliance with legal working hours and overtime.

Indicator 14: Regular payment of normal working hours.

Indicator 15: Payment of overtime hours and at legal/official/expected rates.

Source(s) of information:
On average wage and working hours – statistical table of the company survey; on legal working hours and overtime pay rates – national authorities.

6. Pay systems (wage composition)

Indicator 16: Basic fixed wage as a proportion of total wage.

Indicator 17: Proportion of total wages paid under piece rate system.

Indicator 18: Existence and use of a salary grid (according to occupation/skills/education/experience).

Indicator 19: Existence of bonuses (linked to seniority, attendance, skills, and so on) and their proportion of the total wage.

Indicator 20: Existence of schemes relating wages to collective or company performance (profits, sales and so on) and their proportion of the total wage.

Indicator 21: Existence, types and roles of non-monetary benefits provided by the company (for accommodation, meals, transportation, health, education, vacations and so on).

Indicator 22: Existence of disciplinary sanctions on wages (for instance, related to attendance – if so, number of attendance days required in the month).

Indicator 23: Payment of all legal social insurance to the whole labour force (if not, percentage of workers not covered).

Indicator 24: Provision of paid holidays as required by law.

Source(s) of information:
Pay systems information – management and worker questionnaires.

7. Communication and social dialogue (negotiated wages)

Indicator 25: Existence of individual work contract stipulating wage conditions.
Indicator 26: Existence of regular communication channels on wages (notice boards and/or letters to workers, for instance, on different piece rates).
Indicator 27: Existence of a pay slip and detailed information provided (total number of hours worked; distinction between normal and overtime hours; pieces produced at different piece rates).
Indicator 28: Existence of workers' representatives (trade unions or works councils) involved in discussions or negotiations on wage issues.
Indicator 29: Existence of an enterprise (and eventually sectoral/national) collective agreement.

Source(s) of information:
Information from management and worker questionnaires and, possibly, national data (on sectoral or national collective agreements).

8. Wage discrimination and wage disparity (differentiated wages)

Indicator 30: Sources of wage discrimination identified from wage statistics by worker categories (men/women; by age; migrant/non-migrant and so on).
Indicator 31: Ratio of lowest wage to highest wage and evolution over time.
Indicator 32: Ratio of unskilled to high skilled workers' wages and evolution over time.

Source(s) of information:
Wage levels by worker categories – the statistical table of the company survey; complemented by management and worker perceptions of wage disparity within the company.

9. Evolution of wages with regard to price increases (real wages)

Indicator 33: Real wages: variation of nominal wages/inflation.

Source(s) of information:
Average nominal wage – statistical table of company survey, complemented by worker and employer perceptions of real wages; inflation – national (and possibly regional) data.

10. Evolution of wages with regard to company performance (wage share)

Indicator 34: Evolution of real wages with regard to the company's profits (if profits not available, with regard to evolution of sales).
Indicator 35 (possibly to be developed at a second stage): Evolution of real wages (at the supplier) with regard to the evolution of the brands' profits.

Source(s) of information:
Data on average wage and profits/sales collected at company level (from statistical table), complemented by management and worker perceptions of wages in light of company performance over last two years; statistics from the brands' profits to be obtained from the respective brand(s) or available secondary information.

11. Wage costs
Indicator 36: Variations in wage costs/total production costs.
Indicator 37: Variations in wage costs per employee (unit wage costs).

Source(s) of information:
On wages and other costs (raw materials etc.) and on the number of employees – company surveys (statistical table); complemented by management reporting on the evolution of wage costs.

12. Wages and work intensity, technology and upskilling
Indicator 38: Evolution of real wages compared to capital/labour ratio.
Indicator 39: Evolution of real wages in relation to introduction of/change in technology.
Indicator 40: Evolution of wages in relation to training expenditure per employee and also the ratio of skilled to unskilled employees.

Source(s) of information:
Data on capital, employment and thus on the ratio of capital to labour; on unskilled and skilled labour force and on training expenditure per employee from the statistical table provided in the company survey; complemented by management and worker perceptions of wage adaptation to work intensity, technology introduction/change and training/upskilling.

3.3 DEVELOPING THE FAIR WAGE TOOLS

In order to capture wage developments at enterprise level and to assess companies' wage performance we prepared a questionnaire with a series of questions on wages and related areas. We identified a number of questions that would help us to collect the necessary information on each of the fair wage indicators and, therefore, help in evaluating company performance on each fair wage dimension.

In order to make up for the possible shortcomings of the questionnaire filled in by the managers, it was essential to complement it with a second questionnaire, completed by the employees. The aim was to identify wage practices that are not reported accurately – that is, not in their totality or real extent – by the employers. A third source of information was expected to be the companies' books with regard to wage payments and other economic data on company functioning and performance.

From these three sources of information we should be able to reconstruct the wage story at individual companies and give an objective score for each fair wage dimension, as well as a general fair wage score for the company as a whole. It should also help us to identify the major wage problems within the company and to help to avoid tensions and conflicts arising as a result. This work will be fruitful for local sub-contracting companies, as well as the brands. Repeated on a regular basis, this will allow us to assess the evolution of a company's fair wage policy and to progressively strengthen its weakest points with regard to both wage determination and wage development.

All the fair wage dimensions identified above were similarly addressed in the two questionnaires in order to obtain the point of view of both employer and workers on each of them.

In addition, the employers' version contained – at the end – a statistical table to be completed by the company accountant with general economic information concerning the company and statistical data on the company's performance and wage levels over the years.

The workers' questionnaire was a much simplified version of the employers', tailored to meet possible educational limitations of the respondents. Two versions of the workers' questionnaire were prepared, one for skilled and another for unskilled workers.[2] This distinction was made based on the assumption that the responses of the two subcategories of workers would be slightly different, given their work profiles, differing skill sets and, by extension, wage levels and pay systems. As an example, the section on minimum wages was not presented to skilled workers, as it was assumed that their wage levels would be considerably higher than the legal minimum wage in the region under survey.

For the interviews, the questionnaires were translated into the language used to communicate with the respondents. The selected fair wage dimensions, indicators and questions are presented in Table 3.2.

---

2. The questionnaire in Annex 2 is the one that was distributed to unskilled workers.

Table 3.2 Summary of fair wage dimensions, indicators and relevant questions

Fair wage dimensions	Fair wage indicators	Questions
Payment of wages – Wages are paid in full and without delay, and without underpayment or informal payments	– Unpaid wage amounts – Average payment delay – Underpayments – Informal/undeclared payments	– Did you have difficulty paying wages last year? – Were there any delays in paying wages last year? – Did you experience any underpayment of workers last year? – On the above three issues, what percentage of the workforce was affected? – What amounts were involved?
Living wage – Wages ensure minimum living standards	– Starting wage in the company compared to the subsistence minimum (poverty line) or any other measure of living wage – Average wage in the company compared to the subsistence minimum (poverty line) or any other measure of living wage	– Do you think the starting wage in the company allows workers to live decently? – Do you think the average wage in the company allows workers to live decently? – Do the wages in your company allow the workers to satisfy their basic needs with regard to: food, accommodation, health care, education, clothing, vacations and entertainment?
Minimum wage – The company ensures at least the minimum wage to all workers and informs them about the statutory minimum wage	– Starting wage in the company compared to the existing national or local minimum wage – Difficulty in paying the minimum wage – Workers informed or not about the level of the statutory minimum wage	– What is the starting/lowest wage in the firm? – Do you know what the minimum wage is in your city/province/country? – How does the starting wage in your company compare to the national/provincial/city minimum wage? – Did your establishment have difficulty in respecting the minimum wage last year?

Table 3.2 (cont.)

Fair wage dimensions	Fair wage indicators	Questions
Prevailing wage – The company ensures a wage comparable to other enterprises in the same sector or to direct competitors	– Average wage in the company compared to the average wage in the sector – Average wage in the company compared to the average wage among competitors – Average wage in the company compared to the average wage in the region/district	– What is the average wage in the company? – How does the average wage in the company compare with the main competitors? Higher, lower, the same? – How does the average wage in the company compare with the average wage in the region? Higher, lower, the same? – What is the average wage for different types of employees?
Payment of working hours – The company wage system does not generate excessive working hours and normal working hours and overtime are paid properly	– Respect for legal working hours and overtime – Regular payment of normal working hours – Payment of overtime hours and at the legal rates	– How many hours do you work? – How much overtime? – Was overtime always paid last year? – At what rate is overtime paid?
Balanced and sustainable pay systems – There is a balanced wage structure between the basic wage and additional bonuses and benefits in the company; – Wages reflect different levels of education, skills and professional experience, as well as individual and collective performance	– Proportion of basic fixed wage to total wage – Proportion of piece rates to total wage – Existence and use of a salary grid – Existence of bonuses (linked to seniority, attendance, skills and so on) and percentage of total wage – Existence of bonuses related to collective performance (profit-sharing and so on) and percentage of total wage	– How are wages in the company fixed? – What percentage of production workers' wages is paid according to a piece rate system? – Is a portion of wages paid informally in cash? – Do you implement a salary grid according to occupation, qualifications, education or experience? – What percentage of your production workers' wages, if any, is paid according to a system of bonuses related to collective performance? – If so, what performance indicators are used (*cont. on p. 81*)

Fair wage dimensions	Fair wage indicators	Questions
Balanced and sustainable pay systems (*cont.*) – Wages are not dominated by disciplinary wage sanctions – The company complies with regulations on social insurance payments and paid holidays	– Existence, types and roles of non-monetary benefits provided by the company – Existence of disciplinary sanctions on wages – Payment of all legal social insurance to the whole labour force – Provision of paid holidays as required by law	(*cont. from p. 80*) (profits, sales, productivity, team performance, other)? – Do you distribute any other monetary bonuses (for seniority, attendance, other)? – What non-monetary benefits do you provide (accommodation, meals and so on)? – Are there any wage or bonus deductions/cuts for disciplinary or other reasons? – Is the company making required social insurance payments for all workers? – What paid holidays do you provide?
Communication and social dialogue – Workers receive sufficient information in advance (through individual work contract), during the production process (through regular communication channels) and at the point of wage payment (with informative pay slip) – Wages are negotiated individually and/or collectively – notably through collective bargaining – between the employer and the workers' representatives, who are freely accepted in the company	– Existence of individual work contract with information on wages – Communication channels on wages – Existence of a pay slip with detailed information provided (total number of hours worked; distinction between normal and overtime hours; items produced at different piece rates) – Existence of workers' representatives (trade unions or works councils) involved in wage negotiations – Existence of an enterprise (and eventually sectoral/national) collective agreement	– How are wages defined and adjusted? Are wages in your company fixed: • unilaterally by the employer? • by individual contract with the worker? • by collective agreement at company level? • following a collective agreement at sectoral or national level? – Does the company provide any regular information to the workers on how wages are defined and adjusted? If so, how? – Do you receive a pay slip? If so, does it show total number of hours worked; distinguish normal and overtime hours; items produced at different piece rates?

Table 3.2 (cont.)

Fair wage dimensions	Fair wage indicators	Questions
Communication and social dialogue (cont.)		– Are workers informed about the social insurance they are entitled to? – Does the company have a trade union representing the workers? – Does the establishment have a workers' committee? – Are any of these organizations involved in helping workers with wage issues?
Wage discrimination and wage disparity – The company applies the principle of 'Equal wages for equal work' and does not practice any wage discrimination. – The pay system does not generate unjustified, too high or too rapidly growing wage differentials within the company	– Discrimination in wage payments (by gender, age, migrant/non-migrant and so on) – Lowest wage to highest wage and evolution over time – Ratio of unskilled to high skilled workers' wages and evolution over time – Women's to men's wages in same occupations and evolution over time – Other indicators of wage disparity over time	– Is there any wage discrimination (against workers who are non-local, older and so on)? – Are men and women paid equally for the same occupation? – Has wage disparity in the company increased, decreased or remained constant? – Between what categories of worker (top/bottom, men/women, permanent/temporary, migrants and others, between other groups)? – What factors explain wage disparity, if any?
Real wages – Wage progress at least in proportion to price increases	– Variations in nominal wages in relation to inflation	– What was the progressive increase in nominal wages last year? – What was the inflation rate last year? – What were the variations in progression rates of different types of worker? – Do you think the wage increases last year were above/at/below price increases?

Fair wage dimensions	Fair wage indicators	Questions
Wage share – Wages progress proportionally along enterprise performance (profits, sales) – Wages (within the supplier) also progress in relation to the growth of profits from its main brand(s)	– Evolution of real wages with regard to company profits (or sales) – For suppliers, evolution of their real wages with regard to their brands' profits	– Would you say that your profit margins last year, compared to the previous year, increased, decreased, remain unchanged? – Would you say that your sales volume last year, compared to the previous year, increased, decreased, remained unchanged? – Would you say that wages followed profits and sales growth last year? – Would you say sales growth last year, compared to the growth of your main competitors, increased, decreased, remained unchanged? – Would you say that the profit margin of your main brand contractor last year, compared with the previous year, increased, decreased or remained constant?
Wage costs – Wage costs do not dramatically decline in proportion to total production costs or as a percentage of employment	– Variations in wage costs/total production costs – Variations in wage costs/number of employees (Unit wage costs)	– Did wage costs last year, compared with the previous year, increase, decrease or remain unchanged? – What is the percentage of wage costs in total production costs? – Compared to the previous year, did this percentage increase, decrease or remain unchanged? – Did wage costs per number of employees compared to the previous year increase, decrease or remain unchanged?

Table 3.2 (cont.)

Fair wage dimensions	Fair wage indicators	Questions
Wages and changes in work intensity, technology and upskilling – Wages progress along with changes in work intensity, technology and the evolving skills/tasks of the labour force	– Evolution of real wages compared to capital/labour ratio – Evolution of real wages in relation to introduction/change in technology – Evolution of real wages in relation to training expenditure per employee and also in relation to the ratio of skilled to unskilled employees	– Over the last two years, has work intensity increased, decreased or remained constant? – Do you think work has become more complex or difficult? – Has the company introduced new technology (new machinery, line automation, computerization)? – Does the company provide training? Compared with previous years has it increased, decreased or remained constant? – Did all the above changes influence the level of wages, and in what direction?

3.4 A FAIR WAGE MATRIX – BASED ON ENTERPRISES' PERFORMANCE ON FAIR WAGE DIMENSIONS

The relative performance and cumulative scores on the different dimensions will help to build a matrix and provide a synoptic overview and assessment of wage issues for each enterprise. The matrix will help in reporting the wage areas in which the enterprise is performing well or poorly, in four categories: fair wage, relative fair wage, relative unfair wage and unfair wage. At both extremes, it will also highlight areas in which the company's wage practices are exemplary and those in which they are unsustainable – this last situation requires urging the company for immediate action.

The answers in each of the fair wage areas will then provide a general assessment and final score with regard to fair wages. This will then help us to better define those areas in which improvements and policy responses would be needed, while the failure to cooperate on the part of the employer could be considered to represent non-compliance with the fair wage principles.

Table 3.3 Evaluation system: the fair wage matrix

	Unfair wage (* unsustainable) 1 to 5/20	Relatively unfair wage 6 to 10/20	Relatively fair wage 11 to 15/20	Fair wage (+ exemplary) 16 to 20/20
Payment of wage				
Living wage				
Minimum wage				
Prevailing wage				
Payment of working hours				
Pay systems				
Communication and social dialogue				
Wage discrimination/wage disparity				
Real wages				
Wage share				
Wage costs				
Wage and work intensity, technology and upskilling				
TOTAL COMPANY FAIR WAGE SCORE				

Notes: Fair wage (16–20)
Relatively fair wage (11–15)
Relatively unfair wage (6–10/20)
Unfair wage (1 to 5/20)

* Unsustainable conditions: 1–3
+ Exemplary conditions: 18–20

3.5 HOW TO OVERCOME EXPECTED DIFFICULTIES

A first informal meeting with field experts (from South America, China, Asia and Europe) in Geneva, in August 2007, allowed us to have a first discussion about the present fair wage concept and the corresponding proposal. This wage initiative was welcomed by the experts, who confirmed that action in this area was needed urgently. In fact, they confirmed that all other CSR initiatives could ultimately act against workers if wage issues were not incorporated. They emphasized, however, that the first steps would be difficult, mainly because of the traditional reluctance of employers – especially among sub-contractors – to provide information on wages. The experts also agreed, however, that these problems could progressively be solved and initial reluctance dissipated through an interactive process on such issues. A discussion took place on the difficulties that might be expected and on how to overcome them.

Employers Not Reporting Wages

It seems very difficult to obtain accurate information on wages at enterprise level. Wages remain something of a taboo and employers often keep two or even three sets of books, which allows them to hide their real practices.

The proposed parallel questionnaires – one completed by employers and the other by the workers – may represent an appropriate solution. If workers describe practices of wage fixing that are not reported by the employer this could be incorporated into the monitoring process and final assessment.

Moreover, the idea here is progressively to convert employers' initial resistance into interactive cooperation on wage issues, which may progressively bring more transparency and thus fairer wage practices. This is why such a process should be accompanied by a general campaign on fair wages, aimed at changing attitudes and practices in the wage area. The proposal to use the completed fair wage assessment in order to help employers – through advice and technical assistance – to improve their performance on wage issues may also represent a desirable development from the employers' side. As an example, when testing the fair wage approach in one of the companies (Company A in Chapter 4), the manager we interviewed was very keen to obtain feedback on its wage policy from our team and to receive some advice on wage policy. Despite his belief in the piece rate system, he knew, for instance, that many Japanese companies try to motivate their workers through profit-sharing schemes and also employee ownership. Interestingly, the manager had tried to promote employee ownership in the early stages, but without much development afterwards. The manager was also looking for solutions to retain skilled workers in the company and realized that not only wage levels but also the type of wage system may have an influence.

Employers Not Reporting Profits

Since employers are also reluctant to provide information on profits – or, if they do, they often declare no profits – it may be difficult to monitor the evolution of wages compared to that of profits. In a country such as China it is, for instance, difficult to obtain information in private enterprises and sometimes also in public enterprises.

One solution may consist of asking employers to report on alternative measures of company performance, such as sales growth, value added growth or the evolution of exports. Alternative measures of the wage share could thus be developed. For instance, if the company reports no profits but a significant increase in sales or even in exports over the same period this may mean that orders have increased and allow the auditors to ask the workers, for example, or other managers, for complementary information and explanations.

Complex Relationship between the Brands and Subcontractors

The nature and contents of the contracts or deals between the brands and subcontractors are difficult to identify. This renders difficult any report on wage issues, especially with regard to the link between wages and economic growth or profits. A brand can make huge profits, while the subcontractors have difficulties coping and thus also in generating profits and paying wages. In this regard, information at the subcontractors' level alone will not be sufficient to assess wage performance and, even more important, to change it.

One solution lies in collecting information on wages and economic performance at different levels: the brand, subcontractors and also possible intermediaries.

Over time, this process should progressively provide a more accurate picture of wage developments and the various fair wage elements. The aim is also to change employers' – and the brands' – attitudes on wage reporting, bringing them to recognize that this exercise may also be in their long-term interests.

Diversity in Wage Practices

Since wage determination is complex, any assessment in this field would not be complete if it failed to collect differentiated information. As an example, the brands are increasingly fixing prices by time units, thus rendering it difficult to capture their implications for wage levels and wage trends. Moreover, pay systems, such as bonuses, may vary by categories of workers (white-collar workers, skilled production workers and unskilled workers; or by specific categories, such as migrants, women and so on). There can also be significant differences between gross and net wages, or between the basic and the total wage (which may include additional monetary payments and be complemented by non-monetary facilities, such as dormitories, free food and other fringe benefits). Similarly, there can be significant differences between major economic activities or sub-activities, as in textiles.

The solution clearly consisted in a detailed questionnaire that allowed us to differentiate between different elements of pay and between different categories of workers. The identification of diversity in wage practices may also lead to the progressive adaptation of the questionnaires and eventually also of fair wage indicators (according to the local context).

Influence of Other Connected Areas of Work

The picture of wage developments would not be complete without information on other areas, such as employment and working time (including overtime), as well as social dialogue and industrial relations in general.

The solution may be to create some links and cross-analyses between our questionnaires on fair wages and other questionnaires used by the FLA, for instance on working time, but also on work organization and other things. The questionnaires on wages should also include questions about overtime and employment levels and structure.

Risk of Collecting Fragmented Information

Due to the expected difficulties in collecting information on wages, the initial assessment may be rather fragmented and not able to provide a comprehensive picture of wage developments. If only part of the required information is available this may even give rise to miscalculations in the fair wage final score: for instance, if we obtain information on wage levels but without knowing the number of hours worked and whether they are properly remunerated. Similarly, for the workers, not getting a fair share of the profits does not have the same weight if the enterprise's other indicators are strong or poor.

The solution can only be found over time and through repeated surveys, which may help us to better identify wage trends over the years and progressively extend our knowledge of how to better capture all 'fair wage' issues in individual enterprises.

Lack of Social Dialogue and Workers' Representatives

One difficulty in terms of progressively improving wage issues in the company is the absence of trade unions from many companies – especially among subcontractors – and the absence of real wage bargaining between employers and workers' representatives.

Although our approach will certainly be more difficult where there are no workers' representatives it may help to change this situation. A monitoring mechanism could first help to improve wage issues, even in the absence of workers' representatives. The aim, however, is not to substitute social dialogue but progressively to strengthen it. In this regard, the fact that social dialogue is one component of the fair wage approach may help to change attitudes and make workers' representatives progressively better accepted by management. Monitoring mechanisms may also empower workers' representatives on wage issues and provide them with the necessary arguments and data to negotiate fairer wage developments, not only in terms of wage levels but also in terms of wage structure and pay systems.

3.6 THEORETICAL FOUNDATIONS

A number of theories have highlighted the role that good treatment of workers – in terms of payment of wages – could have on productivity but also quality of production, turnover, absenteeism and, therefore, company competitiveness overall.

The Efficiency Wage Theory

The fair wage approach is supported, first, by the efficiency wage theory, which has been formulated in four different ways. According to the first model, wages in enterprises are set in order to avoid voluntary departures ('quits') by the employees. If voluntary quits represent an important cost to the enterprise, inversely related to wage levels, it would be rational for the enterprise to fix wages at a level that would minimize such departures and, therefore, its costs (Calvo, 1979; Salop, 1979; Stiglitz, 1974). In a second formulation, higher or 'efficiency' wages are aimed at inducing workers to perform better. Higher wages, in fact, correspond to higher costs of being laid-off for the workers, so that they have an incentive to increase their efforts at work accordingly (Shapiro and Stiglitz, 1984). The third formulation, developed by Akerlof (1982), is close to the second and is based on the notion of gift exchange: the loyalty of the workers to the enterprise – and thus their productivity – increases in parallel with the level of wages. Finally, in the fourth model, enterprises pay wages slightly above the market in order to attract the most skilled and talented employees (Weiss, 1980). These four models, despite their differences, represent different facets of the same reality and are thus very complementary. Empirical work has confirmed not only the payment of 'efficiency wages' by enterprises, but also several aspects of the other proposed theoretical versions (Wadhwani and Wall, 1988). They confirm, in essence, that paying higher wages pays off in human capital terms, as well as in terms of economic efficiency and competitiveness. The fair wage approach which we propose to develop is based on the same roots and is also supported by human capital theory.

The Fair Wage Model

The 'fair wage hypothesis' has also been put forward by a number of scholars. The hypothesis is motivated by equity theory in social psychology and social exchange theory in sociology. According to this hypothesis, employees have a conception of a fair wage; insofar as the actual wage is less than the fair wage, workers put in a corresponding fraction of normal effort, behaviour that can lead to efficiency losses and unemployment, as indicated by different types of evidence provided by Akerlof and Yellen (1990), notably cross-section wage differentials and unemployment patterns (see also Feher, 1991).

An extended version of the fair wage model shows that real wage rigidity – that is, allowing nominal wages to follow price increases – reduces the elasticity of marginal costs with regard to output, with positive effects on unemployment (Danthine and Kurmann, 2003).

Other Theories Supporting Specific Fair Wage Dimensions

A number of theories also provide support for the various fair wage dimensions proposed here. Several studies have shown the positive effects that minimum wages could have, not only on workers' ability to cope, but also on wage differentials and motivation and productivity (ILO, 2008a). An extensive literature has also confirmed the expected positive effects of profit-sharing schemes on productivity and profitability, with an impressive consensus, rare in economics (EC, 1991, 1997, 2006; Vaughan-Whitehead, 1995; Poutsma, 2001).

3.7 ORIGINALITY OF THE APPROACH

Capturing Complementarities between Different Wage Issues

All the fair wage dimensions proposed here are needed in the sense that they help to provide one part of the company's wage story. If one of them was missing, any auditing may risk not capturing one essential dimension of wage practices at the company. While all these indicators are complementary, they may not move in the same direction. Although a significant increase in real wages may normally help to improve the company's performance with regard to other wage indicators, such as the living wage, it does not ensure that there would not be a significant decline in the wage share (if the company registers huge profit growth) or an increase in wage differentials.

Similarly, the minimum wage may not mean much if we do not know what is offered in terms of non-monetary benefits, which may help workers to cope.

The minimum wage is also closely related to the living wage. While the minimum wage is essential for ensuring the living wage dimension, it may not be enough. Statistics show that, in many countries, the minimum wage remains well below the national subsistence minimum or poverty line, as in Russia and the CIS countries in Europe, Peru in Latin America and Bangladesh in Asia (ILO, 2008b). Therefore, even workers who earn the legal minimum wage may find it insufficient to meet basic needs. The living wage condition should thus clearly complement the minimum wage condition.

Moreover, many workers' concerns extend well beyond mere 'bread-and-butter' issues measured by such things as the minimum basket of basic goods and relate more to obtaining recognition from their employers in terms of their work and skills (through better pay systems), or better communication (work contracts, communication on wages) and establishing a permanent relationship with their employers, which would allow them to revisit and renegotiate wages and employment on a regular basis (social dialogue).

The picture of fair wages would also be incomplete without taking working hours into account. When workers are paid very low wages, they have a tendency to work excessive hours in order to make ends meet. Efforts to reduce overtime without tackling poor wages can therefore be problematic. On the other hand, efforts to increase wages are not enough without counting how many working hours are worked and whether overtime payments are properly remunerated. Similarly, the tendency to work excessive working hours is often due to the pay systems themselves, often based on the piece rates that induce workers to accumulate working time and minimize rest time in order to obtain the highest possible wages.

At the same time, it is almost impossible to get companies to reduce overtime and pay better wages without consulting and involving workers' representatives in the whole process. Similarly, no work on the calculation of a living wage could effectively be done in an untransparent process and without involving the workers.

Extending Current CSR Work on Wages

The approach proposed is also original in terms of at least four major aspects:

1. It would make it possible finally to include wage issues in corporate social responsibility and extend the monitoring process to a number of wage elements.

2.   It would propose that wage issues in CSR no longer be confined to the legal dimension, that is, compliance with minimum wage regulations, payment of overtime and payment of wages.

3.   It would also no longer confine the fair wage concept to the living wage concept, but integrate many more elements: basic needs, but also wage evolution, wage share in economic growth and profits, wage structure and wage payment systems, negotiation of wage issues.

4.   In this way, it would also enable us to go beyond a social approach – which mainly underlies the living wage approach, however justifiable it might be – to develop a broader approach which takes into account the long-term effects of wage evolution and wage structure on sustainable growth. Economic sustainability requires that we look at wages as key elements in economic developments, such as productivity, consumption and investment. All stakeholders – not only workers and their' representatives, but also employers – could thus be mobilized around this new process.

CONCLUSIONS

The Fair Wage concept we have presented here is a new approach. It has been proposed as a consequence of our identification of a CSR deficit – notably on the methodological side – with regard to wage issues, despite the fact that wage problems have multiplied along the supply chain and concerns are increasing among all the major actors.

The proposed approach may be rendered operational immediately – as we shall see in the following chapters – and could, therefore, rapidly provide highly informative results in this still poorly documented field.

The approach also has the advantage of tackling wage issues in all their complexity, by monitoring not only wage levels (for instance, in comparison to basic needs, the minimum wage, legal hourly rates or wages prevailing in the industry), but also wage adjustments (together with price increases, company performance and changes in technology and human capital). It also encompasses, for the first time, evaluation of the quality of pay systems, in terms of both fairness and efficiency (of different pay components and pay systems), and also in terms of communication and social dialogue. In this sense, the approach goes further than purely legal standards on wages or the living wage dimension. In fact, we believe strongly that it would not be possible to assess a company's wage practices properly without collecting information on all 12 fair wage dimensions.

The proposed methodology – by virtue of its comprehensive list of fair wage dimensions and indicators, which result in the Fair Wage Matrix –

not only provides a powerful instrument for regular auditing of wages, but also allows us to go much further. It provides companies with the tools and framework they need to better identify the strengths and weaknesses of their wage-fixing system and, therefore, more easily to correct their shortcomings in this complex field.

This process could help in the achievement of definite progress on wage-fixing mechanisms and pay practices along the supply chain, while also potentially influencing the global wage developments reported in our introductory chapter. This would represent a significant contribution to our ultimate goal of sustainable economic development.

4. Pilot Testing in Two Suppliers in China

INTRODUCTION

Our team had the opportunity to test the fair wage methodology in October 2008 when it visited two suppliers in the garment sector.[1] We used the two questionnaires that had been prepared, for both the management and the workers, as well as the statistical table requesting economic information (see Annexes). Responses to the questions led to a full assessment of fair wage practices and to final fair wage scores on each of the fair wage dimensions, as well as on the general wage policy of the companies.

4.1 TWO SUPPLIERS IN THE GARMENT SECTOR: A DIFFERENT PROFILE DESPITE COMMON CONSTRAINTS

The two companies had a number of features in common. They were both in the garment sector, as suppliers of brands for which they export the entirety (100%) of their production volumes. Their management was Chinese.

Beyond these similarities, the two companies were rather different, first in terms of management and second in terms of economic conditions.

Company A was part of a large group headquartered in Pudong, Shanghai, founded in 1967 as a company manufacturing silk products. The company mainly manufactured (sewing) apparel as a subcontractor for Adidas and other brands, such as Calvin Klein, Marks & Spencer, and Phillips-Van Heusen (PVH). As a consequence, Company A was running two parallel assembly lines, the first focusing on sportswear, primarily for Adidas, and the second manufacturing non-sportswear apparel for the other brands. Most of A's shareholders were employees who had been in the company since the beginning and who generally came from the CEO's hometown, Jintan city, only three hours away by road. Between 1,500 and 1,600 people were employed as permanent workers, of whom nearly all were non-local.

---

1. This field work, involving interviews at the two companies, was carried out in April 2008 by the author with the assistance of Lina Arbelaez, Sumathi Chandrashekaran, Lina Marmolejo, Jinghan Zhang from Sciences Po and Eva Chen from the FLA.

The group, which boasts state-of-the-art facilities, undertook major restructuring in 2007, which marked a transition from its traditional silk products-based manufacturing to a more diversified garment production portfolio. At the time of the interviews, the group was undergoing full-scale economic expansion and had six factories in three locations: one each in Kunshan and Suqian, and four in Jintan. Factory A, located in Jiangsu province (one and a half hours from Shanghai) was also responsible for adding the labels to the manufactured goods. Their production was approximately 120–130,000 units per day, most of which was for export to Japan, the United States, the United Kingdom and France.

In comparison, Company B was a relatively new enterprise, having been founded in 1999. It was part of an umbrella garment manufacturing company operating from Hong Kong. This particular factory was located in Tongxiang city, in the province of Zhejiang. Its ownership was entirely private, although the owners themselves were dispersed: 50 per cent of capital ownership was Chinese, and the remainder was split equally between owners located in Hong Kong and the United States. Their production was for different brands, namely Philips-Van Heusen (PVH), Calvin Klein, BCBG, Max Mara and Kohl. Nearly all their goods (approximately 97 per cent) were manufactured for export.

Enterprise B had about 1,200 permanent employees, without temporary or seasonal labor. They did, however, subcontract to other companies in high season. Approximately half the labour force was local, while the remainder came from other rural areas of China.

Company B was clearly in poorer economic shape than company A. The executive director reported facing a marked increase in the costs of production, primarily due to a sharp rise in the price of raw materials, while simultaneously being affected by a decrease in the sales of branded goods outside China, particularly in the US market, which represented 65 per cent of its exports.

Although Company B could count on the reputation of the quality of fabric from Zheitong province – which is known to be far superior to their counterparts in Cambodia or Vietnam – the start of the economic crisis in the United States had a direct impact on the consumption of goods, resulting in lower projected profit margins for the year. Indeed, the manager reported that the factory had not even managed to break even in the financial year so far. At the time of the interview, the manager was seriously considering possible coping strategies and, in particular, becoming less dependent on brands and creating an in-house brand, mainly supplying the Chinese market.

Company A: Good Wage Levels but Intensive Work

Because of its favourable economic circumstances Company A was paying wages above those of its competitors and also offering a good range of monetary bonuses (for seniority, attendance and so on). The company also provided free accommodation, free meals and a number of other non-monetary benefits, such as for transportation, gifts of factory products and so on. At the same time, the number of orders resulted in continuous production, involving excessive overtime and difficult working rhythms. The pay system contributed to this objective of maximizing workers' efforts.

Company B: Low Wage Levels but a Willingness to Improve

By contrast, Company B, as reported by the manager, was facing problems surviving due to difficulties in getting sufficient orders – especially in the wake of the recent collapse of the US market – and competition from other countries. Their difficult relationship with the brands was also pushing them to explore an extension of their production for the local market rather than uniquely for external markets. They thus were having difficulties maintaining wage levels comparable to their competitors, as well as problems offering a wide range of monetary and non-monetary benefits. Despite such difficulties, the management was making every effort to maintain wage levels and also to provide acceptable living standards to its workers. Their wage policy and pay systems reflected this rather complex situation.

4.2 COMPREHENSIVE PICTURE OF THEIR WAGE POLICY

The fair wage approach and the questionnaires for both management and workers allowed us to capture a fairly comprehensive picture of their wage story. It also allowed us to collect enough information on all the different and complementary fair wage dimensions.

The first dimension helps to capture compliance on the payment of wages, while the second and third allow us to check compliance on minimum wage issues and whether the starting wage allows workers to have decent living standards. Then the objective is to check wage levels by comparing the companies' wages to competitors' wages. At the same time, it is important to check how those wage levels are achieved in terms of working time, and whether they take due account of overtime. Pay systems are then analysed to check whether the pay systems are not too problematic or too much dependent on one pay mechanism, such as the piece rate, attendance bonuses or seniority. The more diversified pay systems are, the better they might be expected to be for the workers, who will not have all their income in one basket, but based on a range of performance criteria. Communication channels and social dialogue also are important processes for assessing the fairness of the companies' wage policy. Wage trends are then also analysed to see how wage levels are evolving in accordance with price increases (real wages), company performance (wage share) and changes in working rhythms, technological content and labour skills (wages and technology). Progression of wage disparity and wage costs is also scrutinized to identify whether any wage imbalances could have been generated over time. Table 4.1 summarizes the performance of the two companies on these different fair wage dimensions.

Table 4.1 Performance of Companies A and B on fair wage dimensions

	Company A	Company B
Payment of wages	Paid monthly. No delays reported	Delayed only by a few days from time to time
Living wage	Good, thanks to high wages, additional bonuses and a series of non-monetary benefits	– Poor performance because of low wage levels and too few non-monetary benefits – Good minimum wage policy for those at bottom
Minimum wage	The starting wage corresponds exactly to city minimum wage	Corresponds to the city minimum wage + 20%
Prevailing wage	Well above competitors' wages	– At the same level as competitors' wages, according to management – Below competitors' wages, according to workers, including most skilled employees; confirmed by statistics
Payment of working hours	– Excessive working hours – Overtime exacerbated by the pay system, based on piece rate performance and high attendance bonus – Suspicion that some overtime not paid at the legal rates	– Overtime not excessive – Overtime in general properly paid, except for Saturdays, when it is underpaid
Pay systems	– Piece rate overdominant – No pay scheme related to company performance – Attendance and seniority bonuses – Many non-monetary benefits (accommodation, meals and so on) – Classification grid, but only for skilled workers and dependent on average piece rate performance	– Overdominance of piece rate system – Attempt to relate wages to company performance – Some non-monetary benefits (subsidized meals and so on), but no accommodation – No pay and classification grid

	Company A	Company B
Communication and social dialogue	– Wages fixed by individual work contract – Poor communication on pay system – Information on pay slip confused – Existence of trade unions and of a collective agreement, but social dialogue not really operating	– Wages fixed by individual work contract – Pay slip distributed with full information (total hours worked, distinction between normal working time and overtime, description of piece rate for each type of good) – Nevertheless, poor communication on real economic situation (worsening) of the company – Trade union, but not active on wage issues and no collective agreement
Wage discrimination/wage disparity	– Not much wage disparity – Possible wage discrimination against newly hired workers (those with less than one year's seniority)	– Not much wage disparity – Decreasing wage differentials between those at the bottom (who enjoy higher wage increases) and those at the top, including top managers
Real wages	Nominal wage increase just above inflation rate	– Nominal wage increase above inflation rate, despite economic difficulties – Workers not convinced about the evolution of their purchasing power, probably due to their excessively low wage levels
Wage share	– No wage increases related to company performance – High increases in profits and sales over last two years not accompanied by higher wage increases	– Some attempt to link wages to company performance, but difficult to continue due to poorer performance – The company decided to maintain wage levels despite a clear fall in profits
Wage costs	Wage costs were kept relatively high due to good wage levels and also other benefits. The lack of data offered by the manager led us to believe that wage costs may not have increased as much as claimed by the management. This was confirmed by relatively poor progress in real wages, despite huge sales growth.	Wage costs voluntarily kept at the same level by the manager, despite an increase in other production costs (such as energy)

Regular Payment of Wages

Monthly wages were paid regularly, on the fifteenth of every month, in the two companies. In Company A, the only delay occurred when the fifteenth fell on a Sunday or a public or bank holiday, while in Company B, in months when the fifteenth fell on a holiday, wages were paid a few days earlier or later.

In both companies, there were thus no issues or conflicts with regard to the monthly payment of wages. Subsequent interviews with both unskilled and skilled workers confirmed regularity in the payment of wages. By means of the interviews, notably with the head of the wage department, and by examining their books we were unable to identify fake recording or double recording, although we did suspect that Company A was making employees work many more overtime hours than those recorded in the books.

Living Wage Function and Minimum Wage Compliance

Factory A was found to comply with the minimum wage at the city and provincial level, which was RMB 850. Moreover, all the unskilled workers interviewed were aware that the starting wage in the company corresponded exactly to the minimum wage in the city.

With regard to the 'living wage', the measurement of company performance was difficult since, at the time of the interviews, there was still no official national – or provincial – poverty line. In 2007, the unofficial poverty line in China was accepted as RMB 1,067 per person per year, which was extremely low, much lower than the lowest accepted international level (about $1 per day for one person). This is why revision was under active consideration.[2] Nevertheless, Company A, by implementing good wage levels, was certainly respecting the 'living wage' function, something that was confirmed by unskilled workers, who not only claimed that their wage was sufficient to live decently, but also pointed out that they had even managed to save some money. The skilled workers also believed that their wage was sufficient to live decently because they were provided with free food and accommodation. The provision of fringe benefits – in particular, free accommodation and meals – was thus found to be crucial to help workers to cope with minimum living standards.

Clearly, Company B had more problems keeping wages at an acceptable level. This is reflected in the company's poor performance on the living wage dimension. Both workers and management reported that wages may not be sufficient for the workers to cope. The workers' responses to the question of whether the wage was sufficient to live decently were varied: the local residents

---

2. 'Poverty line may be raised', *Shanghai Daily*, 14 April 2008. Available at: http://www.shanghaidaily.com/sp/article/2008/200804/20080414/article_355794.htm.

said it was enough, whereas the outsiders clearly felt it made life difficult. Clearly, the fact that the enterprise did not provide any accommodation represented a problem in terms of living standards.

However, as reported by the manager, real efforts are being made to protect the most vulnerable workers, for instance, with a systematic policy to establish a starting wage in the company which is approximately 20 per cent higher than the provincial or city official minimum wage, which explains the company's good performance on the minimum wage dimension (Table 4.2).

Table 4.2 Minimum wage compliance in Companies A and B, 2008

	Starting wage in the company	Local minimum wage	Difficulty in paying minimum wage reported	Workers informed about statutory minimum wage
Company A	850	850	No	Yes
Company B	866	750	No	Yes

Prevailing Wage

To measure the prevailing wage, the fair wage approach can rely on three sources of information: questionnaires (i) to the manager and (ii) to the workers to find out whether they believe the average wage in their company is at, above or below the wage paid by their competitors; and (iii) statistical information from the company accountant on average wages by different categories of workers, which we can compare directly to the average wage in the same industry, but at national level.

Both workers and manager in Company A believed that the relative wage was far higher than that of their main competitors in the city/province, but also than the average wage in their home province. This evidence was partly based on personal experience, as some had worked elsewhere, where wages were lower. Data collected on the prevailing wage confirmed that Company A was paying above the market rate, with an average wage of RMB 1,500 in comparison to an average wage among competitors of RMB 1,392. The workers added that they were not envisaging leaving the company because their wage was much more stable and because they received more benefits than elsewhere.

By comparison, Company B was found to perform poorly in terms of prevailing wages. Although the management reported that they paid higher wages than their competitors, workers' interviews and statistics did not confirm this view. When asked to rate wage levels, the workers felt that the wages in this factory were the same as or below those of the main competitors, clearly contradicting the manager's opinion. However, two non-local workers agreed that the wages here were higher than those in their home province.

Statistics confirm that the average wage in the company was below the industry average wage in 2007 (see Table 4.3).

Table 4.3 Average wage in Companies A and B and industry prevailing wage, 2007

	Average wage in the company (RMB)	Average wage at industry level (RMB)
Company A	1,500	1,392
Company B	1,200	1,392

Payment of Working Hours

Working hours was undoubtedly the major wage issue in Company A, as acknowledged by the manager himself at the beginning of the interview. He recognized that, because of the multiplication of orders, the legal limits were difficult to comply with, especially in the busiest months (July–August, according to the workers). The CEO emphasized that the company never subcontracted – to either workers or other companies – to help during peak production periods. On the contrary, small companies contracted them to help with their production when many had been forced to close due to heavy snow. This contributed to an increase in orders and also working time, which plainly appeared to be a general problem, not only during peak periods but throughout the year. The workers had to work six days a week on a regular basis, with Saturdays counting as overtime on double pay. The workers claimed that, on Saturdays, they were not allowed to work extra hours. However, instead of having one day off (Sunday) every week, the workers agreed to work 12 days at a stretch in order then to be able to return to their home province for a full weekend. Some workers reported that sometimes they worked for three weeks (17 days) in a row before getting a break because of the priority given to production orders received from the brands. Given the large number of working hours accumulated by the workers there were good grounds for believing that some of those additional working hours – for instance, on Saturdays, Sundays and holidays – were not always remunerated at the legal rates, thus implying some underpayment problems.

Interestingly, the overtime situation differed between the two assembly lines. Less frequent overtime on the first assembly line was justified on the grounds that they produced goods only for one brand – Adidas – that gave constant and continuous orders, making it possible to better plan the use of overtime. The situation was different in the other production line, which produced for a wider range of brands.

In Company B, the unskilled workers said they worked six days a week, for about eight to nine hours a day (the regulation being eight hours per day, five days a week). Some workers, however, reported working between ten and twelve hours per day. Nevertheless, the number of working hours was much lower than in Company A and workers never had to work for three weeks in a row before having a break.

However, the workers also reported that Saturdays were not paid as extra hours but at the same rate as the other days of the week, thus entailing some underpayment of overtime.

Pay Systems

We tried to identify what the wage-fixing mechanisms and pay systems were in practice and to assess whether they were balanced in terms of composition (between basic fixed wage and flexible pay; between basic wage and bonuses; between monetary wage and non-monetary benefits) and whether they properly reflected different educational attainment, skills and individual and collective performance.

The major finding was the overdominance of the piece rate system in both companies.

This system was found to totally dominate the wage-fixing process in *Company A*, which did not rely on many other wage sources. Not only did the piece rate system apply to all workers on the assembly lines, but, interestingly, it also directly influenced the wages of skilled workers and supervisors, whose wage was based on a multiple of the average wages of unskilled workers. One skilled worker reported that his contract mentioned that he would be paid 1.6 times the average wage of workers on the production line, another worker 2.1 times the same average wage. Only the wages of managers and temporary workers (such as cleaners and gardeners) were not based on the piece rate system.

As a result, pay systems were found to be rather poor and, notably, not to reflect the workers' various levels of education, skills and professional experience, since all of them were paid according to the number of pieces produced. Finally, the overreliance on the piece rate system in relation to production workers also meant that their wage was wholly flexible, since only the payment of the minimum wage was guaranteed, which obviously put the wage at risk of significant variations.

The efficiency of the system can also be questioned. While the piece rate is set in advance only for standardized products, it must frequently be changed for products in relation to which trends change more quickly. For example, for

Adidas, the piece rate is reassessed less often than for others, namely every one or two months. For smaller orders the piece rate is calculated on a per order basis, which imposes a heavy burden on the sample department. According to the manager, this can lead to possible inaccuracies in calculating the time taken to produce one unit.

The wage-fixing system in A is very simple. The manager and head of the wage department explained that to fix wages, they look at average wages among competitors (RMB 1,000 in 2007). They then add 20 per cent more to achieve a target average wage of RMB 1,200, which they then complement with bonuses. This target or reference average wage is divided by 21.75 (number of working days per month) and by 8 hours (hours regularly worked per day) to yield the hourly wage. On this basis, the technical department calculates the number of units of production that workers would have to produce in one hour in order to achieve this target average wage. This leads to the piece rates that represent the main source of payment. It is important to mention that, when the production time per product is calculated, the technical department adds an additional 20 per cent in order to provide the workers with breaks. It emerged in discussion, however, that this 20 per cent extra time had been discussed among the workers, particularly as some of them were unwilling to accept it, as it represented time for extra production and therefore extra payment. One direct implication of the piece rate system is thus to lead workers to minimize their rest periods (even for going to the toilet), as well as holiday breaks, in order to maximize their income. This is a concern in terms of fair wage practices.

The workers' reluctance to accept extra breaks points to their excessive reliance on even that fraction of the wage affected by the extra time calculation. Furthermore, the fact that the workers would be paid only the minimum wage if they were sick or if they were taking a holiday clearly seems to induce the workers to work as much as possible, even beyond their normal mental and physical capacities. This is confirmed by long working hours in Company A.

Overreliance on piece rates also meant that wages were found not to be linked to the company's economic performance, expressed in terms of sales or profits. A series of fixed bonuses were granted, however, such as a seniority bonus of RMB 10 per month for every additional year worked and after a worker has been at the factory for a year, complemented by a series of attendance bonuses: a monthly bonus if a worker had attended a total 21.75 days per month and, in addition, RMB 100 per month at the end of the year for every month in which the target of 21.75 days was met. The skilled workers specified that they received an annual attendance bonus of RMB 1,200 if the leave they took in the course of the year was less than one month, excluding Sundays and public holidays. These attendance bonuses represent an important source of income – approximately 10 per cent of the total wage – and were found to reinforce workers' propensity to work almost all the time.

The non-monetary benefits offered by the factory were particularly high. The workers were given free food and free accommodation, which proved to be essential to maintain workers' living standards. The company also reimbursed their transportation costs for their annual vacation home.

The workers were also covered by insurance, for health, occupational injuries, pensions, unemployment and maternal care. Towards this, the employees paid 20 per cent and the company the remaining 80 per cent. They also pointed out that the factory had encouraged them to contribute to a pension, but had given them the freedom to decide whether or not they wished to do so, given the problems with implementing the system across provinces.

Wage fixing in *Company B* also mainly relied on the piece rate system, combined with the minimum wage. The factory first estimated an internal minimum wage target, based on the minimum wage of the city. For unskilled workers, for instance, the minimum wage target corresponded to the minimum wage in Tongxiang city of RMB 750, to which the enterprise added 20 per cent to achieve a factory minimum of RMB 866. This was then divided by 21.67 days (the number of working days in a month), to reach a daily minimum wage of RMB 40. The figure of RMB 40 was thus the daily target minimum for the unskilled wage, which could potentially be higher, according to the individual piece rate performance of workers.

For skilled workers, the factory increased the RMB 40 (as calculated for unskilled workers) by 20 per cent to arrive at approximately RMB 50 as the daily target minimum wage.

The piece rate was calculated by the technical department by estimating the amount of time taken to manufacture a piece, then adding 30 per cent as extra time for breaks during production. This was tested over a three-day period, with the result that at least the minimum of RMB 40 per day was achieved. This was then used to finalize the piece rate.

In the interviews, some skilled workers thought that this did not satisfactorily match their experience in the industry. They also reported that they would be more interested in receiving a fixed wage according to their education and skill levels. However, no wage grid system was implemented by the company.

Compared to Company A, fewer bonuses were distributed by Company B. There was no seniority bonus. Although it had implemented an attendance bonus system, this was discontinued, based on the argument that this would lead to more democracy and freedom for the workers. Only the management's pay, however, was related to annual profits. To extend this system to all workers, the company undertook a two-year project with a researcher from Zhejiang University in order to improve the bonus system for workers. Details of this system were not available, and only passing reference was made to this project. This reference was perhaps intended primarily to highlight the factory's efforts to introduce or experiment with changes in the pay system.

The performance of Company B in delivering non-monetary benefits was also fairly poor: it did not provide accommodation or transport services.

The enterprise had earlier tried to buy land and to build dormitories, but negotiations with the city government had broken down.

The unskilled workers corroborated that they did not receive any non-monetary incentives or bonuses for transport or accommodation (all of these expenses had to come out of their salary – they received subsidized food but estimated that one subsidized meal at the factory canteen cost between RMB 2 and RMB 5, amounting to RMB 60–150 a month).

Non-local workers reported paying high rents for housing, implying that wages in Company B were clearly too low to allow for decent living standards.

Vacations included 10 days for the Spring Festival, seven days in both May and October, as well as days for the new year holiday, totalling 27 days, besides the weekly Sunday off. However, holidays were paid at a lower rate – in fact, at the minimum wage rate – so that the workers were penalized by being paid below what they would normally get at work. As a result, they had problems coping when they took holidays.

Finally, workers were aware of the mandatory social insurance they were entitled to, and acknowledged that they received it. They said they contributed 20 per cent of the cost, while the company covered the rest.

Communication and Social Dialogue

We tried to assess the information given to workers on wage issues at the beginning of the process (individual work contract), in the course of the production process (on piece rates for instance) and at the end of the process (wage payment and receipt of pay slip). The various communication channels were not developed to the same extent.

In both companies, information was well provided at the beginning of the process through individual work contracts which generally stated the minimum wage, the way their wage would be calculated and the fact that they would be paid on the fifteenth of every month.

In Company A, workers were informed about piece rates in advance by the technical department. Crucially, all the interviewees knew what the rate was for each order, as it was also written on the notice board in advance. However, communication was less good at the end of the process. In particular, the pay slip was found to be hard to read – it was difficult to differentiate between the various wage components (wage, bonuses and so on). In fact, workers reported often not understanding how their wage had been calculated. We were not provided with copies of pay slips, despite our specific requests.

Communication channels were much better in Company B. The number of pieces produced by a production unit was listed on the notice board on a monthly basis. Moreover, the pay slip that was given to us was very precise and clearly distinguished between total hours worked, normal working time and overtime, as well as stating the piece rate.

Nevertheless, there were also communication problems in Company B. For instance, the workers did not know that their company's performance had declined and were convinced that it was doing very well.

Moreover, social dialogue was not developed at all. There were trade unions in the company, but, although they sometimes intervened on wage issues, they were not really involved in wage bargaining. The workers reported that they did not believe that the union had any influence in wage negotiations. There was no collective agreement. The manager repeatedly highlighted that relations with the workers were 'familial', close-knit and based on trust, so that there was no reason to pursue a collective agreement with the trade unions.

Social dialogue was also poorly developed in Company A, which functioned mainly on the basis of paternalistic labour relations. There was a trade union that represented 100 per cent of the workers and even a collective agreement. However, wages did not seem to be much influenced by such mechanisms, but rather were decided unilaterally by the management. Interviews among the workers revealed that they were not aware of the existence of such a collective agreement. Not only did they not know that one had been signed, but none of them even knew what a collective agreement was.

None of the workers knew of any wage problems solved by the trade union, but were aware that they could approach it if they had any concerns in this regard. They reported that the previous year there had been a few cases of pay slips that did not match the personnel record, but they declared categorically that the union would be a last resort, after the accountant and the manager.

Interestingly, despite much higher wages in Company A, workers were much more afraid to respond to the questions and were very worried about not giving the right answer – that is, answers that would put the management under pressure – while the workers spoke much more freely in Company B.

Wage Discrimination and Wage Disparity

Finally, questions on wage disparity were put to the interviewees, first, to check whether there was any wage discrimination against certain groups of workers and, second, to check whether there had been a rapid increase in wage disparity over the years between different groups of workers, and especially between those at the bottom and those at the top.

In both companies, men and women were paid the same wage, according to the interviewees, demonstrating that the piece rate system did not cause discrimination. There were also no disparities between migrant and local workers. Most of the unskilled workers received approximately the same wage, confirming the absence of discrimination. Seniority was treated differently by means of the seniority bonus. However, the perception was that older workers did not receive special treatment in any other way. One skilled worker mentioned that there was no woman at his level, but as far as he knew, women and men were paid the same.

In Company A, however, our interviewing team suspected that new hired workers may be discriminated against in terms of wage payment, although it was difficult to confirm this, since the management refused to allow interviews with workers who had less than one year's seniority.

There was no perceived change in the disparity between top and low levels of wages in the enterprise (A), which was confirmed by our statistical table on wage levels by categories of workers over 2005–2007. The salary of the managers was fixed, so that they could sometimes receive less income than many production workers. The only difference was that the managers received more bonuses. In Company B, the manager even pointed out that the disparity between top and low-level workers had decreased, giving his own salary as an example of one that had remained the same for two years.

The skilled workers, interestingly, felt that the disparity between the top- and lowest-level employees had decreased.

Real Wage Progression

Three sources of information were also used to test real wage progression: the perceptions of the managers and the workers, as well as the statistics provided by the enterprise on nominal wage growth, which we could then compare to the consumer price index, at both national and provincial level.

In Company A, the data show that nominal wages in 2007 had increased by 6.8 per cent (7.3 per cent in 2006), higher than the inflation rate for China in 2007 (4.8 per cent – the inflation rate in Jiangsu province was only 4.3 per cent). It was lower, however, than the figure (+10 per cent for nominal wages) estimated by the manager during the interview. Furthermore, according to some interviewed workers, this wage increase was not enough to cover price increases, while for others it was sufficient. However, one determining factor for them was the fact that Company A provided housing.

In Company B, nominal wages seem also to have caught up with price increases, despite the difficult conditions it was facing. The workers acknowledged that nominal wages had increased, but all felt that the increase did fully not take into account price increases and the cost of living. They confirmed, however, the scale of nominal wage increases stated by the manager. This perception might be due to the fact that wages were low in Company B and not complemented by significant non-monetary benefits, which led workers into difficulties maintaining decent living standards. The data provided by the accountant confirmed that nominal wages continued to increase, in fact by 12 per cent in 2007 (after 4.4 per cent in 2006), well above the national inflation rate of 4.8 per cent and the inflation rate in Zhejiang province of 4.2 per cent. This manager's efforts to pay workers above price increases, despite a decline in profits, should be recognized.

Wages in Relation to Company Growth (Wage Share)

A number of questions allowed us to test the progression of the two companies' wages in relation to economic performance. Apart from the workers' and the managers' opinions, our statistical table – completed by the company from its accounts – helped us to collect direct data on profits and sales growth.

In Company A, sales volumes and exports had both gone up and the management pointed out that, despite increased raw material costs, the company was still at the top within the garment sector.

Both unskilled and skilled workers believed that there had been an increase in the profits of the enterprise, especially in comparison to its main competitors. At the same time, they claimed not to know – and not to be informed – about the company's performance. They also confirmed that there was no connection between wages and enterprise performance. The enterprise statistics confirmed that, in both 2006 and 2007, sales in A had increased continuously, while wage growth had not followed proportionately. Nominal wage growth was above inflation but not by much, and the increase in real wages was low compared to national real average wage increases in China, described in Chapter 1, while real wages did not follow any increase in sales performance.

Table 4.4 Companies A and B wages and performance, 2005–2007

	Sales growth 2005/ 2006	Sales growth 2006/ 2007	Sales growth 2005/ 2007	Nominal/ real wage growth 2005/ 2006	Nominal/ real wage growth 2006/ 2007	Nominal/ real wage growth 2005/ 2007
Company A	Sales: +4.3% Profits: NA	Sales: +8.3% Profits: NA	Sales: +13% Profits: NA	NW: +7.3% RW: +2.5%	NW: +6.8% RW: +2.0%	NW: +14.6% RW: +4.6%
Company B	Sales: +0.1% Profits: –4%	Sales: +1.7% Profits: –5.5%	Sales: +1.8% Profits: –9.5%	NW: +4.4% RW: –0.4%	NW: +12.0% RW: +7.2%	NW: +16.9% RW: +6.8%

In contrast, the manager of Company B emphasized that the company's profits were decreasing, adding that this was due directly to the contractual agreements with the brands, which had not changed since 2005, despite the increasing prices of raw materials and higher labour costs.

Nevertheless the company's performance remained better than that of its competitors, according to the manager, thanks to a slight increase in sales in 2007 (1.7 per cent after virtually no growth – 0.1 per cent – in 2006).

Nevertheless, despite a constant (or only a slight) increase in sales, but a fall in profit margins, the management in Company B decided to keep wages going up, with an increase in real wages which was more significant than in Company A. Real wage increases of 6.8 per cent in 2005–2007 were even higher than sales growth over the same period (1.8 per cent) and higher than the real wage increase in Company A (4.6 per cent). Certainly, this reflected a serious commitment on the part of the manager not to decrease workers' living standards. In fact, he clearly stated that he would prefer to shut down the company rather than reduce wages or fire workers.

Interestingly, despite reported declining profits, the workers believed that the enterprise's profits had increased since more orders were being placed by contracting brands, such as BCBG, Calvin Klein and Kohl. This misunderstanding concerning the real performance of the company was undoubtedly due to the lack of communication on the part of the management, although the latter might benefit from telling the workers the truth about the current difficulties encountered by the company.

These two examples show that wage levels are not enough to assess a company's wage policy, which should also be seen in progression and in comparison to other variables, such as price increases and company economic performance in terms of annual changes in profits and sales.

Wage Costs

The wage costs dimension, within the fair wage approach, is aimed at checking whether there has been a sudden increase or decrease in wage costs. In particular, some erosion of wage costs was expected in relation to the increase in the prices of energy and raw materials experienced in 2007–2008. This would have meant that workers would be worse off since the proportion paid in wages out of total company expenditure would be less and also that the workers would themselves be confronted by an increase in domestic energy prices.

This scenario seems not to have transpired in the two companies we visited.

According to the management of Company A, wage costs had increased in relative terms, compared to previous years, and also in comparison to other production costs. However, no data were provided on either wage costs or total labour costs.

Despite the fact that sales volumes and exports had both gone up, the manager reported that profits were affected because of increased raw material costs, while the terms of reference (prices of goods produced for the brands) with brands such as Adidas remained the same. No data were provided on profits.

The lack of information led us to believe that there was something that the manager did not want to share with us with regard to the wage share in company growth and profits, and also in terms of the evolution of wage costs.

In Company B, the percentage of wage costs in total production costs, including raw materials, was about 28 per cent in 2007, according to the manager (Table 4.5). This was confirmed by the statistics we collected. Despite the increase in the price of raw materials the manager reported that wage costs had gone up, compared to other production costs. This was unavoidable, he added, to ensure that workers would continue to enjoy decent living standards in tandem with price increases, which were particularly high for certain products (energy, food and so on).

The workers in both enterprises had no idea about wage costs and so no significant information could be collected from the workers on this dimension, which motivated us to remove questions on wage costs from the workers' questionnaire in subsequent interviews.

Table 4.5 Wage costs progression, Companies A and B, China, 2005–2007

	Wage costs as a percentage of total production costs in 2007	Progression of wage costs as a percentage of total production costs 2005–2007	Progression of wage costs per employee 2005–2007 (%)
Company A	NC	NC	NC
Company B	28.2	+1.4 percentage points	+21.5

Note: NC = Not communicated.

Wages in Relation to Changes in Production and Technology

A number of questions allowed us to check what changes were occurring in the two companies with regard to work organization, work intensity, work complexity, training and the introduction of new technology, and also to identify whether changes of the kind that require some adaptation and skills on the part of the employees had been reflected in their wages. These matters are important, given the continuous pressure on the workers due to changes in fashion and their need to acquire new technical and adaptational skills, together with their expected effects on compensation.

In both companies, intensity at work has increased over the past few years. In fact, working rhythms were reported by the workers as being very fast and as having increased over the last two years along with increases in the number of orders and a wider range of goods.

There have also been some attempts to introduce new technology, with an overall increase in the level of computerization and automation – for instance, totally new machinery had been introduced in Company A – and an increase in training, particularly in Company B, in which all the workers reported that training had increased in comparison to the previous year.

In both companies, managers and workers reported that this had directly influenced the range of tasks, as well as work intensity. Overall, they felt that work intensity had increased in the last few months. According to the workers, they were having to adapt more quickly to new models and changing fashions. They also felt that their work was becoming more complex, particularly due to changing styles. They added that changes in designs were more frequent and more types of goods had to be produced in the same period of time because of the introduction of new technology.

Nevertheless, all these changes in work intensity and the new technological and adaptation skills required of the workers had not been accompanied by higher wages. Neither additional bonuses nor wage increases were provided for having to deal with such new technology. Moreover, wages were found not to reflect different levels of education or skills, with – notably – little use or even the complete absence of a pay classification grid. It was expected that the piece rate would be sufficient to reward the most skilled employees. Training also did not lead to wage increases or specific bonuses. Nevertheless, the manager of Company B believed that experience and training had made the workers a more valuable asset.

The manager of Company B pointed to a specific concern with regard to the acquisition of new technology: occasionally, new machinery was purchased in order to meet the demands of a certain brand and to ensure that the order was awarded to the company. It happened, however, that, although the factory had clearly complied with these demands, the brands had in the end not placed the expected orders, as a result of which several new machines (specifically adapted for that purpose) were wasted (dead investment).

To sum up our results on wage evolution, Company A was found not to perform well in terms of wage trends. While wage levels were high and were found to adapt to price increases as much as they could, they seemed to have been totally disconnected from the company's performance, despite impressive profits and sales growth. Undoubtedly, the company could have afforded to share more of its profits with the workers and make wages more responsive to economic success. In Company B, the management was able to keep nominal wage growth well above price increases, despite economic difficulties. Notwithstanding a decline in profits in 2005–2007, the management did not want to preside over a fall in wages. The responses to our different questions allowed us to prepare a comparative table on the performance of Company A and Company B on all fair wage dimensions (see Table 4.6).

4.3 CONFIRMING THE NEED FOR A COMPREHENSIVE APPROACH

These – sometimes subtle – differences between the two companies also provide us with interesting insights with regard to our methodology.

From this first analysis we can see that many of the fair wage dimensions are fully complementary, so that it would not have been possible to get the full picture without considering them all.

As a first example, it is not enough to monitor good compliance with minimum wage regulations without taking into account the number of hours worked. It is not all the same whether the workers can achieve the minimum wage within the legal normal working time – as indicated in Chinese regulations, the workers should achieve the minimum wage within 48 hours of normal working hours – or by accumulating overtime hours.

Secondly, it is not enough to look at wage levels without looking at their evolution, year on year. In Company A, wage levels were high, but not adapting much to changing economic conditions, which may cause the employees progressively to lose their 'comparative advantage' with regard to wages.

Thirdly, monetary income is not everything for the workers, who can have better living standards if a number of non-monetary benefits are provided by the company. This provision of fringe benefits can make a considerable difference to a company's performance on the living wage dimension. We could see that this aspect was an important part of the better wage performance of Company A compared to Company B.

Beyond Mere Compliance on Legal Issues

Our testing of the fair wage approach confirmed the need to integrate new dimensions for evaluating companies' wage practices and wage policies. While, so far, wage assessment was based on compliance with wage regulations – mainly on the payment of wages and the minimum wage – it is essential to go well beyond this limited approach and also to analyse less conventional wage dimensions, such as pay systems.

Scrutinizing Not Only Wage Levels But Also Wage-fixing Mechanisms

We could see, for instance, that it is not enough to look at wage levels, but also to study how wages are calculated and distributed. For a similar wage level, whether workers are paid according to a fixed basic rate determined according to a pay and classification grid will not be the same as whether they are paid solely according to their piece rate performance. While the first system might ensure that the workers will be paid whatever their performance or orders received, the second system will vary according to orders and individual performance and so will influence workers' behaviour. While piece rate performance, according to its defenders, may induce workers to work harder, it is also plausible that they may overstress workers, who will try to minimize rest periods and maximize their efforts, with possible risks to their health and also possible mistakes, adversely affecting quality. The ultimate effects on workers' productivity remain to be proven. What is certain, however, is that the pay system and the way in which wages are calculated will not be neutral in terms of worker protection and a company's fair wage performance.

Looking Not Only at Wage Levels But Also at Wage Progression

While wage performance has always been assessed in terms of wage levels, rapidly changing economic conditions require wages to be more responsive to new environments. Very high profits in some activities may require that wages follow economic performance more closely. We have seen, through our two pilot studies, that the wage share is not a dimension that is currently taken into account by either the suppliers or the brands in adjusting and defining wage policies. Such a wage share deficit at micro level may help to explain the wage share deficit identified in Chapter 1 at macroeconomic/global level. The total absence of company interest and policies with regard to such aspects confirmed the need to take them into account.

Relevance of the New Fair Wage Dimensions

Interestingly, there were new dimensions that appeared to be relevant for both companies, such as pay systems, social dialogue and wage share. We shall see in the next section that the analysis of these new dimensions to some extent changed our assessment of wage practices at company level. The elasticity of wages in relation to price increases and profits, for instance, was quite different in the two companies.

Similarly, in our testing of the fair wage approach the contrast was rather striking between increased intensity and complexity at work – due to a series of factors, such as more frequent changes in the type of goods produced and more sophisticated goods, as well as higher technology, with new automated machines to which the workers must adapt, sometimes through specific on-the-job training – and the total lack of consideration for the fact that such trends may increase the workers' skills and so their wage levels.

This also contributes to the declining wage share reported in Chapter 1, which is probably due to the fact that wages do not respond either to better economic performance or increased technological demands.

Despite this lack of consideration, the managers reported to us their worries about losing their labour force and in particular their skilled labour force. For this purpose they were implementing more training, but without adapting wages upward. Modifying their wage policy in order to retain a trained and skilled workforce is the next step, and more systematic efforts should be made to make them aware of it.

4.4 BEYOND AUDITING: A GRADING SYSTEM FOR POLICY ASSESSMENT

The fair wage approach makes it possible, first, to award each company a general fair wage score, according to its cumulative marks on each of the fair wage dimensions (Table 4.6). The approach also helped us to award a score on each of the fair wage dimensions, thereby enabling us – based on the assessment table overleaf – to see at a glance the wage areas in which the companies were performing fairly well (with, in some cases, significant achievements), but also those in which they should be making most progress (where the most serious wage problems were identified).

While the final results may be expected, for instance, to award a better fair wage score to Company A, the comprehensive nature of the approach allows us to highlight interesting and unexpected findings. While better than that of Company B, Company A's score is far from satisfactory, being only slightly above the 50 per cent average. Moreover, it highlights a number of problematic wage areas. Conversely, the generally worse score of Company B also encompasses areas in which the company has shown some encouraging signs.

Company A's strengths are clearly its good wage levels and good provision of monetary bonuses, as well as non-monetary benefits which help the workers to cope. At the same time, this is provided in exchange for a considerable workload and excessive working hours, with some suspicion that they may not all be remunerated at a fair rate. This pressure to 'work hard' is reflected in the pay system, which is based mainly on the piece rate, complemented by a strong attendance bonus which both pushed workers to accumulate the maximum possible working hours and minimize their rest and holiday time. Moreover, the fair wage approach allows us to identify areas in which the

Table 4.6 Evaluation of the fair wage performance of Companies A and B*

Fair wage (16–20), Relatively fair wage (11–15), Relatively unfair wage (6–10), Unfair wage (1 to 5)

	Unfair wage (unsustainable: 1–3) 1 to 5/20	Relatively unfair wage 6 to 10/20	Relatively fair wage 11 to 15/20	Fair wage (exemplary: 18–20) 16 to 20/20
Payment of wage (indicators 1–4)			*12/20*	18/20
Living wage (and so on)	*05/20*			18/20
Minimum wage			12/20	*16/20*
Prevailing wage		*08/20*		18/20
Payment of working time	05/20	*07/20*		
Pay systems	05/20	*07/20*		
Communication and social dialogue		09/20 *08/20*		
Wage discrimination/ wage disparity			13/20	*16/20*
Real wages			12/20 *13/20*	
Wage share		06/20	*14/20*	
Wage costs			12/20	*16/20*
Work intensity, technology and upskilling	05/20 *05/20*			

TOTAL COMPANY
FAIR WAGE SCORE

Company A: 133 on max. 240
Company B: *128 on max. 240*

TOTAL COMPANY
AVERAGE FAIR
WAGE SCORE

Company A: 11.08
Company B: *10.66*

Notes: * Scores for company B in italics.

performance of Company A was fairly poor. This was the case with regard to its communication policy, notably the total absence of details on the pay slip and the lack of social dialogue. There was also no attempt to allow the workers to share in the company's good performance in terms of profits and sales.

Company B seems to exhibit the opposite dynamics, with poor wage levels compared to competitors but a clear willingness to maintain workers' purchasing power – notably through good starting wages – despite poor company performance, with declining profits. The company thus achieves a good score on a number of fair wage dimensions, such as the minimum wage, the wage share and communication, reflecting the detailed pay slip provided to the workers. At the same time, Company B receives a poor score on prevailing wages, real wages and social dialogue.

We can thus see that the two companies in the end have a similar – albeit fairly low – score, while having different problems in terms of wage policy, which leads to different policy recommendations.

CONCLUSIONS

In conclusion, we can confirm that the fair wage approach and grading system proposed earlier worked rather well. It was possible, using the proposed indicators, to award the companies a score on each of the 12 fair wage dimensions. On that basis, we were also able to provide a general fair wage assessment to the two firms.

This methodology, by means of a comprehensive and multi-dimensional assessment, helped us to capture the wage story in each of the two companies.

The method makes it possible to clearly identify areas to be improved and could thus represent an invaluable tool, not only for monitoring/auditing but also for assessment and for providing policy advice with the aim of helping companies to make progress on wage issues.

We could also see that this assessment and the final scores would have been quite different if only a few fair wage dimensions had been taken into account. Company A was found to perform fairly well on the indicators that are normally used for auditing exercises, such as the payment of wages, the minimum wage, the prevailing wage and the living wage. In contrast, Company B was found to perform rather badly on the same indicators – except on the minimum wage. Taking on board a larger number of fair wage dimensions helped us to capture more elements of the wage-fixing system. We were able to see, first, that Company A was clearly deficient in terms of the payment of overtime, and even had problems with compliance. The pay system in Company A was also found to be fairly poor because it relied only on the piece rate system. In fact, Company A received a score at the limit of unsustainability on these two fair wage dimensions (payment of working time and pay systems). Company A was also found not to share improved results with the workers, while Company B, despite its economic difficulties, was making a real attempt to improve real wages, to share the fruits of improved performance with the workers and to increase wage costs (performing better than Company A on these three fair wage dimensions). Both companies, however, did little to adapt wages to changes in work intensity, technology and labour force skills, a dimension that will certainly require more attention. The integration of other new dimensions, such as pay systems, communication and social dialogue or wage elasticity to price increases or to company performance could also help progressively to change the managers' attitudes to the different components of wage policy and also their wage practices. This first run-through allows us in the next chapters to go much further and to apply our fair wage method much more extensively.

Part II

The Fair Wage Approach in Practice

5. First Comprehensive Auditing on Wages

INTRODUCTION

After building up the fair wage approach – its various complementary dimensions, indicators, questions and final assessment matrix – and successfully carrying out some pilot testing, we were able to implement this approach in practice and use it to make concrete progress in our assessment and policy advice on wage issues in the field. This led to the opportunity, with the assistance of the FLA, for the first time to carry out a comprehensive auditing on wages, which we report in this chapter. This exercise allowed us to collect the first – unique and complementary – information on all the different wage dimensions and their interaction with other areas of the world of work, such as working time, production performance and labour force composition.

In Chapter 6, by means of qualitative case studies, we apply the fair wage approach to assess the impact of the current economic crisis on wage issues.

5.1 MONITORING FAIR WAGES ON A LARGER SCALE

The Sample: Focus on China, but with Some Coverage in Other Asian Countries

While the FLA has been carrying out auditing among suppliers for years – with a team of auditors posing a series of questions in a number of areas, on recording, working time, employment and health and safety – this was the first time a comprehensive and full list of questions on wage issues was incorporated in the auditing exercise. This provided an opportunity, first, to check whether the fair wage approach could be integrated as a useful component of the auditing and, second, to collect – for the first time – essential data and information on wage compliance and wage practices. The auditing was carried out in autumn 2008 among 31 companies in China and a few other Asian countries, namely Bangladesh, India, Indonesia, Sri Lanka and Vietnam. Since most suppliers of brands (estimated at 80 per cent) are located in China, the largest number of companies were audited in various Chinese provinces (23

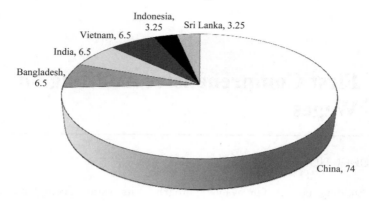

Source: Fair Wage Auditing 2008.

Figure 5.1 Geographical distribution of audited companies, 2008 (%)

companies), while interviewing companies in other Asian countries helped us to identify whether similar wage trends and wage practices could be observed outside China. Figure 5.1 presents the exact composition of the sample. The auditing team used the Fair Wage methodology to collect evidence on all the different dimensions of wage fixing. The methodology worked well since it was possible to collect evidence on almost all fair wage dimensions, with the exception of data on wage costs and also the link between wages and work intensity and technology. Since the audited companies were rather reluctant to provide information on the latter, the team opted to focus on the other ten fair wage dimensions. The qualitative case studies presented in Chapter 6 will complement the auditing notably by collecting information on these two dimensions.

A Tendency to Operate Using Dual Records

Before going into the different wage dimensions, the auditing team checked, by various means, whether the company was producing fake records, involving dual or even triple record keeping (Figure 5.2). This first exercise was telling: 42 per cent of companies were found to be operating in this manner, with official records being prepared for the authorities and labour inspection (generally in compliance with all the relevant labour regulations), but with other sets of records for the brands and, sometimes, for other kinds of external auditing (such as FLA). Clearly, the companies resorting to dual recording had, by definition, compliance problems and had something to hide in terms of wages, working time and other working conditions. In these companies,

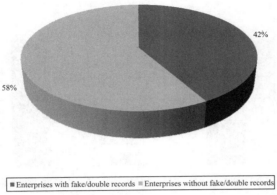

42%

58%

■ Enterprises with fake/double records ■ Enterprises without fake/double records

Source: Fair Wage Auditing 2008.

Figure 5.2 Companies using fake/dual records (%)

the auditing team was particularly careful to reconstitute the 'true' wage story through management and workers' interviews, as well as a meticulous analysis of all the books. This analysis often led to contradictory statements on the part of the management, but the questions on complementary aspects of wage fixing helped, in the end, to obtain a more precise idea of what was going on in terms of wages and working conditions.

Fair Wage Dimension No. 1: Payment of Wages

The first wage dimension was the payment of wages. It was addressed in terms of three questions: the non-payment of wages, delays in paying wages and cases of underpayment. In total, 19 per cent reported having had problems paying wages at all (one in five companies), and 6 per cent reported having been obliged to postpone wage payments: 25 per cent of companies – or one in four – thus reported a problem with wage payment. A total of 58 per cent also reported the underpayment of wages, that is, wages below the level at which they should normally be paid. We shall see that a majority of these cases concern the underpayment of overtime.

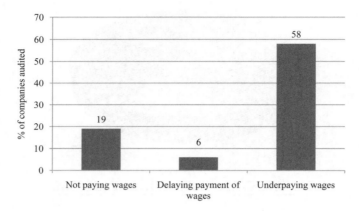

Source: Fair Wage Auditing 2008.

Figure 5.3 Payment of wages (%)

Fair Wage Dimension No. 2: Living Wage

Questions relating to the second fair wage dimension – living wages – resulted in many uncertain answers to the question 'Is the starting wage provided by your company sufficient to ensure workers a minimum living standard?', with a majority of enterprises (75 per cent) reporting that they did not know or not answering at all. This confirms the difficulties involved in enterprises assessing

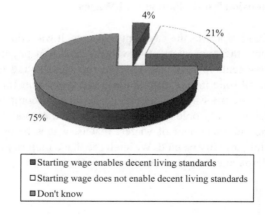

Source: Fair Wage Auditing 2008.

Figure 5.4 Starting wage and living wage (%)

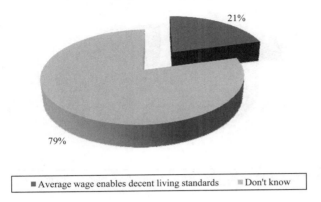

Source: Fair Wage Auditing 2008.

Figure 5.5 Average wage and living wage (%)

and monitoring this wage function, as well as the need to develop a methodology – as already proposed in some quarters, as mentioned in Chapter 2 – to help management and workers to systematically monitor living wages. Our findings did confirm problems in ensuring this basic wage function: 21 per cent clearly stated that they believed the starting wage they were paying their workers was not sufficient to allow decent living standards, while only a very small proportion of companies – 4 per cent – reported that the starting wage they provided (generally corresponding to the official minimum wage) was adequate in this respect. This clearly shows that the minimum wage requirement of ensuring basic needs, as stipulated in ILO Convention No. 131, was not met by most of the audited suppliers. A similar picture emerged when companies were questioned about the living wage function of the company's average wage (instead of the starting wage): the percentage of managers who did not know was even higher (79 per cent), with – as expected – a higher percentage of companies (21 per cent) believing the average wage was sufficient to ensure decent living standards. Nevertheless, the high percentage of companies not answering or which did not know seems to confirm that, according to management, even the average wage level may not be sufficient to enable the workers to cope.

Fair Wage Dimension No. 3: Minimum Wages

The third dimension of fair wages concerns compliance with minimum wage regulations. A total of 23 per cent reported a starting wage that was below the official province or city minimum wage, while a majority (77 per cent) reported paying at least the minimum wage to all their workers. These results mean,

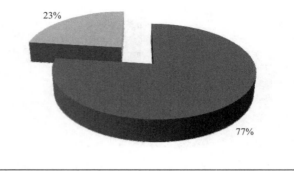

23%

77%

| ■ Starting wage above minimum wage ■ Starting wage below minimum wage |

Source: Fair Wage Auditing 2008.

Figure 5.6 Starting wage compared to legal minimum wage (%)

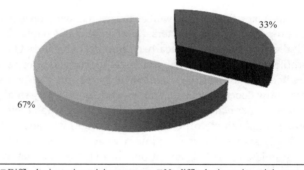

33%

67%

| ■ Difficulty in paying minimum wage ■ No difficulty in paying minimum wage |

Source: Fair Wage Auditing 2008.

Figure 5.7 Difficulties paying the legal minimum wage (%)

however, that 23 per cent – that is, nearly one enterprise in four – were not complying with minimum wage regulations. It is important to note that the auditing was able to obtain such a result only because compliance was measured by checking the company's starting wage compared to the official minimum: if the question had been posed directly to managers the percentage of non-compliants would have been much lower. Nevertheless, many employers – in order to hide their failure to comply with the minimum wage regulations – may have given fake statistics on starting wages, so that we may conclude that the percentage of companies not complying must be much higher.

This was confirmed by the answers to the question 'Did you have difficulty paying the minimum wage in the last two years?', with 33 per cent of managers reporting that they indeed had difficulty respecting the official minimum wage.

Fair Wage Dimension No. 4: Prevailing Wages

The next dimension concerns the prevailing wage. The FLA had already integrated this dimension into their work on wages (see Chapter 2), but without conducting a comprehensive survey of its application in the field. To the question, 'Do you provide a wage that is higher, the same as or lower than the wage provided by your main competitors?', a total of 49 per cent of enterprises reported they did not know, which is already a significant indication that the companies do not use such a comparative approach to define their wage levels. A majority (32 per cent) of the managers who answered the question reported that they were paying at or above the wage paid by their competitors, while 19 per cent admitted paying below what was paid by other suppliers in the same activity and producing similar products.

Interestingly, a majority of managers (61 per cent) replied that they had the feeling that they were paying wages below the provincial or city average wage. This may be due to the fact that the suppliers we interviewed were from the manufacturing sector, which traditionally pays less than companies in other sectors, such as services, banking and others. On the other hand, these companies pay rather higher wages than other manufacturing companies because of their orders from the brands, as confirmed by our qualitative case studies, presented in Chapter 6.

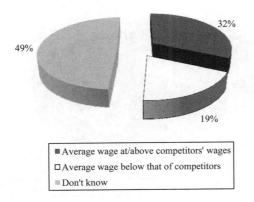

Source: Fair Wage Auditing 2008.

Figure 5.8 Enterprise average wage compared to competitors (%)

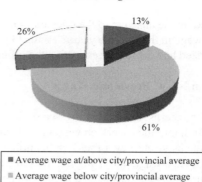

Source: Fair Wage Auditing 2008.

Figure 5.9 Enterprise average wage compared to provincial/city wage (%)

Fair Wage Dimension No. 5: Payment of Working Time

On the payment of working hours, the result was also fairly clear: 68 per cent of companies reported facing difficulties in paying overtime, that is, nearly seven companies out of ten (Figure 5.10). This was a striking finding and confirmed the payment of working hours – and, in particular, overtime – as the main area of non-compliance with regard to wages. Only 32 per cent reported not having such problems, so we can assume that they regularly paid overtime, although

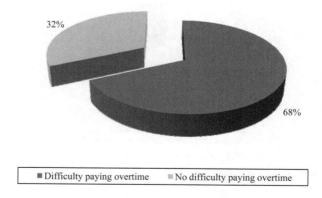

Source: Fair Wage Auditing 2008.

Figure 5.10 Payment of working hours (%)

both the auditing and the qualitative case studies (in Chapter 6) confirmed that the payment of overtime represents the area in which companies are hiding the most and which, in fact, induce them to introduce dual book-keeping. We may, therefore, expect reality to be even worse than the results reported here.

Fair Wage Dimension No. 6: Pay Systems

For the pay systems dimension, we managed to obtain information on the different wage systems used by the companies. The first – rather striking –

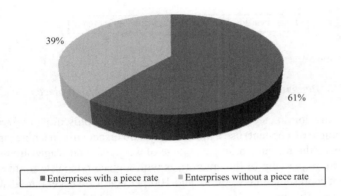

39%

61%

■ Enterprises with a piece rate   ▦ Enterprises without a piece rate

Source: Fair Wage Auditing 2008.

Figure 5.11 Proportion of companies with piece rate system, whole sample (%)

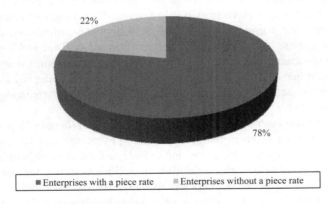

22%

78%

■ Enterprises with a piece rate   ▦ Enterprises without a piece rate

Source: Fair Wage Auditing 2008.

Figure 5.12 Proportion of companies with piece rate, sub-sample on China (%)

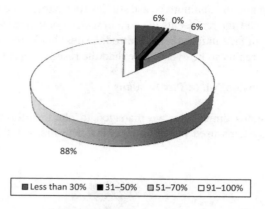

Source: Fair Wage Auditing 2008.

Figure 5.13 Percentage of total wage paid on the basis of a piece rate (%)

result was the dominance of the piece rate system. Not only did a majority of the companies (61 per cent) use a piece rate system (especially in China, among 78 per cent of them), but a high percentage of workers' total wages are paid in this way: in 88 per cent of the enterprises with a piece rate system, this form of payment represented between 91 and 100 per cent of workers' total wages (Figure 5.13). This first result on pay systems means that there is no basic wage that could, for instance, be calculated in accordance with some sort of pay grid, with wage levels reflecting different skills, education and experience.

This was confirmed by answers to the questions on the existence and operation of a pay and classification grid system: 39 per cent of companies reported not using a grid system (Figure 5.14 opposite). Moreover, among those which did use such a system (61 per cent), as we shall see in Chapter 6, our qualitative studies revealed that such use remains rather rudimentary.

The predominance of the piece rate system also means that the pay systems are rather unbalanced since they do not leave any room for introducing other pay systems.

Figure 5.15 shows, for instance, how poorly developed (in only 29 per cent) pay systems related to enterprise performance (profits, sales and so on) are in comparison with those based on individual performance, although such systems are used in some Asian countries, as well as Western ones, and have been shown to motivate the workers and so also to boost productivity.

There were also very few enterprises distributing bonuses related to seniority (22 per cent), or even bonuses related to attendance (35 per cent) (Figure 5.16 overleaf). The percentage of enterprises with both seniority bonuses and

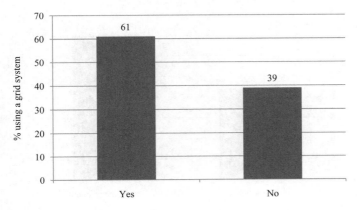

Source: Fair Wage Auditing 2008.

Figure 5.14 Enterprises using wage grids (%)

attendance bonuses was found to be much higher among Chinese suppliers (46 and 56 per cent, respectively – Figure 5.17 overleaf). We shall also see, in the next section, the specific and very strict conditions on which the payment of such attendance bonuses seem to depend among Chinese suppliers.

At the same time, a majority of enterprises (74 per cent) were found to pay at least one form of non-monetary bonus, which can be an important source of non-monetary income and significantly increase workers' living standards.

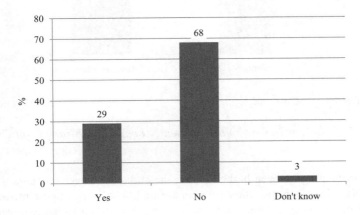

Source: Fair Wage Auditing 2008.

Figure 5.15 Enterprises with wages related to collective performance (%)

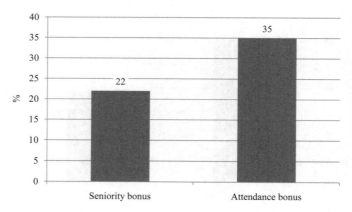

Source: Fair Wage Auditing 2008.

Figure 5.16 Enterprises with other monetary bonuses, whole sample (%)

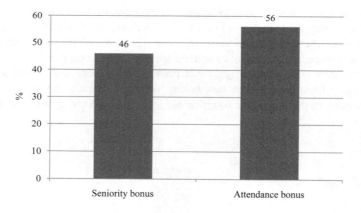

Source: Fair Wage Auditing 2008.

Figure 5.17 Enterprises with other monetary bonuses, sub-sample on China (%)

This percentage was even higher among the audited Chinese companies (83 per cent), where non-monetary benefits are traditionally an important source of well-being, compensating the monetary wage and thus alleviating poverty.

We also asked what types of non-monetary bonus the companies provided. The largest number of companies (61 per cent) provided free meals. Fewer than expected provided accommodation (42 per cent) and even fewer transportation (10 per cent) and medical services (6 per cent).

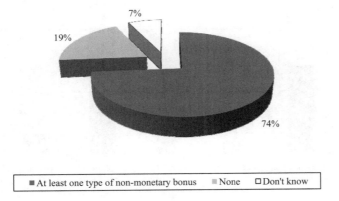

Source: Fair Wage Auditing 2008.

Figure 5.18 Proportion of enterprises providing non-monetary bonuses, whole sample (%)

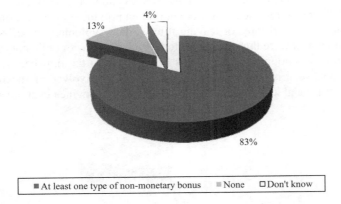

Source: Fair Wage Auditing 2008.

Figure 5.19 Proportion of enterprises providing non-monetary bonuses, sub-sample on China (%)

The percentage of enterprises providing accommodation was much higher in the sub-sample on China (among 57 per cent of audited companies there), which might be explained by the high worker mobility and the importance of migrant labour moving from one province to another. We shall see in our case studies in China that migrant workers generally represent between 70 and 100 per cent of the total labour force of suppliers in the garment sector.

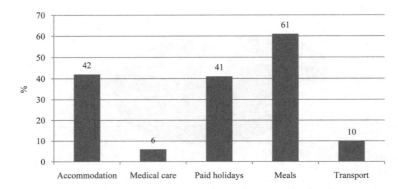

Source: Fair Wage Auditing 2008.

Figure 5.20 Types of non-monetary benefit provided (%)

Under the fair wage dimension on pay systems we also asked whether enterprises were providing (legal) social insurance to all workers (Figure 5.21). A
total of 77 per cent reported they were not, often providing insurance only for
a fraction of the workforce or leaving it to workers' voluntary contributions.
Many companies were thus found not to be complying with obligatory social
insurance contributions. In China, this may be due to the drawbacks of the
current social security system, notably the difficulties involved in transferring
accumulated social insurance contributions from one province to another.

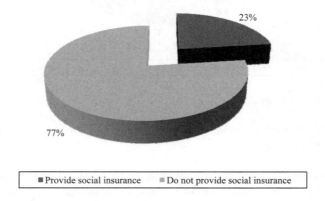

Source: Fair Wage Auditing 2008.

Figure 5.21 Proportion of companies providing social insurance (%)

Unfortunately, during the auditing, we could not investigate whether paid holidays were being granted in accordance with the law, but we asked whether the company was providing paid holidays at all (Figure 5.20). The fact that only 41 per cent replied positively is a first indication that there must be serious non-compliance with regard to the provision of paid holidays, something that we managed to cover more extensively in our case studies (Chapter 6).

Fair Wage Dimension No. 7: Communication and Social Dialogue

Concerning communication and social dialogue in wage fixing, it is significant that only 45 per cent of enterprises reported having individual labour contracts, while only 16 per cent (generally the same ones) also had a collective agreement. Interestingly, 52 per cent of companies reported that wages in their company were fixed unilaterally by the employer, meaning that neither individual nor collective negotiations took place with the workers (Figure 5.22).

A relatively high proportion of enterprises reported having a trade union (55 per cent) and far fewer a workers' collective (16 per cent). Our qualitative surveys in Chapter 6, however, highlight the fact that these trade unions are rarely involved in wage issues, not to mention other working conditions. Moreover, few collective agreements have the aim of establishing clear conditions in wage fixing and other working conditions –although this should be the primary aim of collective agreements.

In terms of communication, the majority of companies (87 per cent) were found to provide a pay slip to individual workers (Figure 5.24). A lower

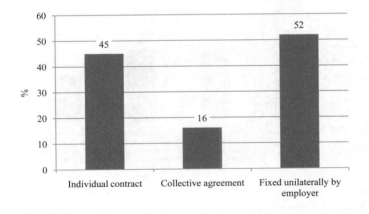

Source: Fair Wage Auditing 2008.

Figure 5.22 Individual and collective negotiations on wages

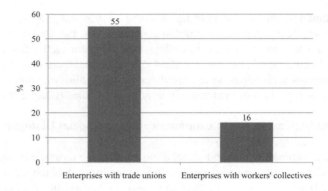

Source: Fair Wage Auditing 2008.

Figure 5.23 Forms of worker representation in the companies

percentage indicated the total number of hours worked on the pay slip, however (48 per cent); or distinguished between regular working time and overtime (48 per cent). Even fewer (32 per cent) were found to detail individual performance according to different piece rates. To summarise, even when pay slips are distributed, they do not always – in at least 50 per cent of audited enterprises – provide the necessary information.

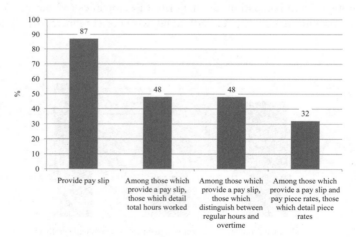

Source: Fair Wage Auditing 2008.

Figure 5.24 Proportion of enterprises which provide pay slips (%)

Fair Wage Dimension No. 8: Wage Discrimination/Wage Disparity

We also asked questions about wage disparity within the enterprise to identify, first, the gap between employees at the top (managers) and those at the bottom (unskilled production workers). Enterprises in the Asian countries in the survey – and even more so in Chinese companies – were found to have a very low disparity between the highest and the lowest wages, generally of less than three times, much less than in Western companies, where the wage gap can reach 30 times. This was confirmed by our case studies. Moreover, no discrimination was found between men's and women's average wages in the audited companies, while both management and workers reported not having observed any wage discrimination against migrant workers. Nevertheless, the wage data collected over three years – from 2006 to 2008 – show that wage disparities were significantly and rapidly increasing.

In fact, a majority of the audited companies (64 per cent) replied that wage disparity had increased within the company, especially between the top and the bottom. This confirms the need to continue monitoring this fair wage dimension in the future.

After questions about wage levels, we asked about wage adjustments in order to better identify what criteria were taken into account when adjusting wages from one year to the next: prices, profits/sales, and labour and capital changes.

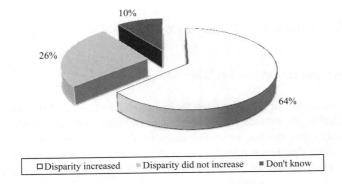

Source: Fair Wage Auditing 2008.

Figure 5.25 Wage disparity, 2006–2008

Fair Wage Dimension No. 9: Real Wages

On the real wage dimension, a significant percentage of companies were found to have increased nominal wages (91 per cent), but below the rate of inflation (in 39 per cent of them, as shown in Figure 5.26). This is despite the fact that the period under investigation (2006–2008) is known to have been relatively stable in terms of inflation, with a national annual inflation rate in China, for instance, well below 10 per cent (6 per cent in 2008).

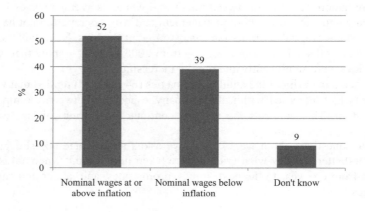

Source: Fair Wage Auditing 2008.

Figure 5.26 Change in real wages, 2006–2008

Fair Wage Dimension No. 10: Wage Share

The responses to our questions on the wage share showed that wages were not adjusted in accordance with enterprise performance. A total of 45 per cent indicated that they had not increased wages in step with the enterprise's growth in profits and sales. In a sense, this result should have been expected, given our previous result indicating the very low percentage of companies operating pay systems related to enterprise performance. Our results, therefore, confirm a disconnection between company performance and wages.

With regard to the wage share, the new crisis conditions are, obviously, changing the situation. While wage growth was found not to have increased in step with profit growth, the current crisis may induce suppliers to cut wages in order to maintain their profit margins or to limit their fall. In some cases, it may be that in 2009 as a whole there will no longer be positive wage growth,

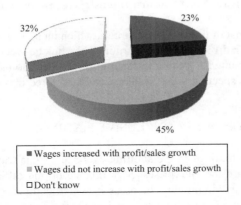

- Wages increased with profit/sales growth
- Wages did not increase with profit/sales growth
- Don't know

Source: Fair Wage Auditing 2008.

Figure 5.27 Wage share, 2006–08

albeit below profit growth, but rather a fall in real wages in parallel with falling profits. This should be monitored to check whether such a decline in wages is not excessive compared to the reduction in profit margins.

It is significant to report that already at the end of 2008 – that is, at the start of the crisis – the only wage adjustments in accordance with company performance were found in those companies that reduced wages following a reduction in profits (this phenomenon was found in 40 per cent of companies experiencing a decline in profits from 2007 to 2008). A downward correlation was therefore observed between wages and profits among the audited companies and, in general, wages were found to have been reduced by even more than the company's reported decline in sales and profits. In contrast, no upward correlation was found in those companies that continued to report increased profits in 2008 (in fewer than 3 per cent of them).

Fair Wage Dimension No. 11: Wage Costs

A few questions were asked and data requested from managers concerning wage costs and their evolution over time – especially in comparison with other production costs and the number of employees in the company – but relatively few companies responded (less than 5 per cent). This made it impossible to produce reliable results on this fair wage dimension and we investigated this issue in the course of our qualitative case studies (Chapter 6).

Fair Wage Dimension No. 12: Work Intensity/Technology and Wages

Similarly, the format of the auditing exercise, which includes many other areas than wages, made it difficult for us to scrutinise the link between wages and the evolution of work intensity, the introduction of new technology, training and upskilling. These aspects are also systematically explored in our case studies.

5.2 SUMMARY OF MOST CONCLUSIVE FINDINGS

To summarize the findings of the auditing exercise on fair wages, Tables 5.1 to 5.4 try to capture the enterprises' performance on the different fair wage dimensions. It clearly highlights the areas in which companies should make most progress, compared to those in which companies were found to require only some changes or even no change at all.

Areas of Non-compliance a Top Priority

First, it is important to highlight those areas in which enterprises do not comply with existing national legislation. This applies in the case of the payment of wages, minimum wages, the payment of overtime and of social insurance contributions. The number of companies that indicated non-compliance in these areas is sufficiently large to make them a priority focus: 58 per cent of

Table 5.1 Compliance on legal wage issues

Enterprises:	
With fake records	58%
Not paying wages or delaying payment	25%
Underpaying wages	58%
With starting wage below minimum wage	23%
With difficulty in paying minimum wage	33%
With difficulty in paying overtime	68%
Not providing social insurance to all workers	77%
Not providing individual labour contracts	55%

Source: Auditing on wage issues, FLA 2008.

enterprises were found to use fake records. Moreover, nearly one-quarter of companies were not complying with the minimum wage legislation, and one-quarter were having difficulty paying wages at all, so that they had to delay their payment. Many were found to be underpaying (58 per cent), confirmed by the high percentage reporting difficulties in paying overtime (68 per cent). Finally, 77 per cent were also found to be failing to ensure that their workers had social insurance.

We should add the lack of individual contracts (absent in 55 per cent of audited companies), although the signing of an individual work contract is obligatory between the company and individual workers before they start work.

Clearly, priority should be given to these areas of non-compliance.

Widespread Low Pay Problem: Need to Increase Wage Levels

In many companies, wages were found to be fairly low. Those enterprises that replied to the questions on living wages reported that their starting wage was clearly not enough to enable the workers to live decently: only 4 per cent of companies reported starting or lowest wages in the company to be sufficient in this regard. This was confirmed by starting wages which were never much higher (and sometimes lower, in one company in four) than the official minimum wage, which is expected to cover only the workers' basic needs.

The wage data collected over three years – from 2006 to 2008 – show that wage disparities were significantly and rapidly increasing.

Table 5.2 Low wage problems

Enterprises where:	
Starting wage does not enable decent living standards	21%
Disparity increased between workers at the top and those at the bottom	64%

Source: Auditing on wage issues, FLA 2008.

In fact, a majority of the audited companies (64 per cent) replied that wage disparity had increased within the company, especially between the top and the bottom, where workers see their situation deteriorating. This confirms the need to continue monitoring this dimension in the future.

Poor Wage-fixing Requiring Systemic Changes

Enterprises were also found to have rather unbalanced pay systems, mainly due to the dominance of the piece rate system, which does not allow any other pay system in companies. This was confirmed by the absence of pay and classification grids or by the low number of enterprises with different kinds of collective performance-related pay systems or other monetary incentives. By contrast, the distribution of non-monetary benefits appeared to be a useful mechanism in most enterprises, helping workers to cope in terms of basic needs, mainly with regard to accommodation, food and health care.

Wages, although already fixed at a very low level, were also not found to follow price increases, so that workers' purchasing power deteriorated in the majority of companies. Clearly, wages should be fixed in such a way that they more closely follow the evolution of price increases. This is even more necessary in the current international food crisis, which is characterised by price volatility with regard to basic food items. We saw in particular that the price of rice more than doubled in only one or two months in 2008. This automatic adjustment to price increases should thus, to some extent, be 'institutionalised' in the wage-fixing mechanisms at company level.

The responses to our questions on the wage share showed that wages were not adjusted in accordance with enterprise performance. A total of 45 per cent indicated that they did not know, while 32 per cent reported that they had not increased wages in step with the enterprise's growth in profits and sales. Our results, therefore, confirm a disconnection between company performance and wages, a result which is not surprising since 71 per cent reported not using pay systems relating wages to collective performance.

Table 5.3 Pay systems and wage adjustments

Enterprises:	
With a piece rate system	61%
Among them, enterprises paying more than 90% of total wages in this way	88%
Not using wage grids	39%
Without a pay system that relates wages to collective performance	71%
Where nominal wage increase remained below inflation	39%
Where wages did not increase with profit/sales growth	32%

Source: Auditing on wage issues, FLA 2008.

Other Areas in Which Progress Needs to Be Made

We were also able to identify other areas in which the companies must improve. This is the case with social dialogue and communication. Not only are wages in too many companies still fixed unilaterally by management, with inadequate individual and/or collective wage negotiations, but the information provided to the workers concerning how wages are fixed and adjusted is very poor. Although the majority of companies were found to distribute pay slips to their workers, these pay slips rarely make a clear distinction between normal working hours and overtime, or between the different piece rates applied by the company.

Even when there is social dialogue, employee representatives such as trade unions or workers' collectives are too rarely involved in negotiations on wages and other working conditions.

Table 5.4 Communication and social dialogue on wages

Enterprises:	Yes
Not providing a complete pay slip	48%
Without a collective agreement	84%
Without trade unions	45%
Without a workers' collective	84%

Source: Auditing on wage issues, FLA 2008.

CONCLUSIONS

This first auditing on wage issues shows that it is possible to collect sufficient evidence in this field, despite expected difficulties and resistance from managers. Through this exercise, we managed to collect evidence on most of the fair wage dimensions identified in Chapter 3. It made it possible for the first time to carry out a global assessment of wage practices among suppliers, with differentiated results, for instance, between China and other Asian countries. If repeated on a frequent basis – for instance, every year – such auditing could help to identify the evolution of wage practices among suppliers, and also to monitor the progress made by individual companies. This could serve as a sound basis for helping individual enterprises to progress in wage-fixing, not only on wage levels but also on pay systems and wage-fixing mechanisms.

These results also confirm the need to adopt a comprehensive and multi-dimensional approach on wage issues: it would be difficult for a company to make progress in one dimension, while not taking care of the others. An integrated approach of this kind must be adopted and used in regular auditing in the field.

6.   Fair Wages within the Crisis

INTRODUCTION

After the auditing exercise, which covered a significant number of enterprises but was constrained in terms of the number of questions we were able to ask, we decided to complement it with more qualitative case studies, looking at three enterprises in different regions of China.[1] This allowed us to look more deeply in our investigation of practices in each of the fair wage dimensions, while giving us a unique opportunity to use our methodology to evaluate the first effects of the economic crisis on wages along the supply chain. The field work was carried out at the end of May 2009.

6.1 ENTERPRISES INTERVIEWED AND METHODOLOGY

In order to improve our understanding of the situation among suppliers we carried out case studies in enterprises in the garment industry in three different provinces of China: Jiangsu, Shandong and Beijing (see Map 6.1).

Map 6.1

---

1. Field work was carried out by Lihui Jin, Caroline Lavoie, Lolita Sagitari and Natalie Unwin-Kuruneri under the coordination of the author and local support from the FLA (specific thanks to Xiaolei Qian for her kind assistance during the interviews).

Table 6.1 Main features of Companies 1, 2 and 3

	Company 1	Company 2	Company 3
City	Nanjing	Qingdao	Beijing
Province	Jiangsu	Shandong	Beijing
Products	Sports goods	Caps and hats (sewing, cutting, packing)	Clothes
Sector	Industry, garment	Industry, garment	Industry, garment
Years of activity	3 (since 2006)	5 (since 2004)	4 (since 2005)
Status	100% foreign investment as affiliate of Taiwanese company	100% foreign investment as affiliate of a large Korean company (Sun Jing International)	100% state-owned company as independent local supplier
Brands	Columbia Umbro Lonsdale Gear for Sports	Califame GPA Zephyr Graph-x	H&M Columbia
Employment	390	280	1,349
% of migrants	50	90	95
City	Nanjing	Qingdao	Beijing
Province	Jiangsu	Shandong	Beijing
Main features	– enjoys support from parent company – fairly confident in the face of the crisis – no compliance with working time regulations – greatest willingness to reform pay systems	– low wages and poor working conditions – long working hours – waves of voluntary labour departures (–40% in 2006–2007)	– very rapid growth and high performance (sales, profits) – systematic strategy to limit wage growth – problems paying overtime

As during our pilot testing (Chapter 4), the interviews were conducted in several steps. First, the general manager was interviewed in order to obtain a general view of the company and the employers' fair wage questionnaire was filled in. Then, workers were interviewed after having been selected by the team in the different assembly lines. Generally speaking, two rounds of interviews were conducted, first among a number of unskilled production workers, and then among skilled production workers, generally working as specialists in the sample department. The financial or accounting department was also asked to fill in a statistical table containing all wage and other economic data (see Annex 1), which could – by providing more objective data – usefully complement the management and workers' questionnaires.

General Situation

Company 1: Confident in the crisis despite strict contracts with brands

Company 1 is located in Nanjing in the province of Jiangsu. It is a sports company affiliate of a large Taiwanese group established 30 years ago and with headquarters in Taiwan, which also operates factories in Vietnam and Laos. The factory visited was in very good condition and produced mainly woven sportswear for American and European brands, including Columbia, Umbro, Lonsdale and Gear for Sports.

This subsidiary was created in 2006 and employed 390 workers at the time of the interview, 50 per cent of whom were migrant workers. Company 1 has the advantage of receiving significant capital support from its parent company, which made it possible for the subsidiary to survive its failure to make a profit in the first two years and, now, to cope with the crisis without serious implications, so far. The first year of profits was expected in 2009, although this was revised in light of the current financial and economic crisis. The company in 2009 remained fairly confident in the crisis, although it was clearly facing decreasing orders. In the current context, the manager clearly stated her dissatisfaction with regard to relations with the brands. She repeatedly said that the conditions of the contract with the brands were much too tight and that the company was being squeezed. In general, the brands impose both very tight deadlines and poor rates for each item produced. This policy has been exacerbated by the crisis. This puts the suppliers in a situation in which they are able to cope only by getting the workforce to do overtime above what is allowed by law, but not paying for such overtime at the expected rate, many overtime hours being remunerated only at the normal rate (as regular working hours during normal working time).

The manager also said that the brands merely closed their eyes to their overtime practices as long as they produced a clean set of records. This situation led to double recording in the company, with one set of books produced for the brand that did not indicate any non-compliance issues, especially in terms of overtime, and another one with the true figures, showing a number of overtime hours well above the legal limit and also a number of overtime hours remunerated below the statutory rates.

Nevertheless, among the three companies, Company 1 displayed the strongest willingness to reform its wage systems. Not only were the workers found to have signed a labour contract stipulating wage conditions, but the company was also trying to reform its wage system by linking workers' wages to the factory's performance and by introducing a pay and grading system. However, this willingness did not always seem to translate into implementation due to a number of weaknesses, notably in internal communication channels or the complexity of its pay systems. Interestingly, the underpayment of overtime on Saturdays, which remained one major drawback, was stipulated in individual labour contracts, although it ran counter to the law.

Another key feature of Company 1 was its confidence with regard to its financial position, despite being a fairly new factory. Not only did the parent group provide it with capital through three years of losses, but it was also considering opening new factories in other provinces, according to the manager.

Company 2: Entered the crisis after waves of voluntary quits

The second company was located in the suburbs of Qingdao city in Shandong province. The factory was four and a half years old, 100 per cent Korean-owned – by Sun Jing International – and produced mainly caps and hats. Although the visit to the factory was facilitated by Zephyr Graph-x, the brand's name hardly ever came up. The main brands the factory produced for were Califame and GPA. The factory employed 280 workers at the time of the interview, 90 per cent of whom were migrant workers. Most were also relatively young and relatively skilled. The main finding was two significant reductions in employment: by 120 employees between 2006 and 2007 (25 per cent of total labour force) and by 70 employees between 2007 and 2008 (20 per cent), a phenomenon explained by the management as waves of voluntary departures. This was confirmed by interviewed workers who explained that many of them were leaving the company to move to better paying provinces (Shandong being among the provinces with the lowest wage levels). This case study thus offered a perfect illustration of the impact of wage levels on labour turnover, especially among a very mobile labour force: migrant, young (thus more mobile) and skilled. This labour force had not been replaced, resulting in a much greater intensity of work and harder working conditions for the remaining workers.

We shall further investigate how the company was performing in terms of fair wages and how it was trying to cope with the high labour turnover, especially in the current economic crisis. The fact that the company was an affiliate of a Korean company may also explain some peculiarities in comparison with the other two companies (such as the absence of the piece rate system, the total lack of social dialogue and use of a suggestion box instead).

Company 3: Outspoken manager revealing anti-crisis strategy

Company 3 was significantly larger than Companies 1 and 2. Located on the outskirts of Beijing, this five and-a-half-year-old facility, created in 2004, employed 1,349 employees, 95 per cent of whom were production workers from all over China, but mainly from Sichuan and Inner Mongolia, while the management (5 per cent) were mostly locals. The company was 100 per cent state-owned under a large group holding that had another five factories with similar activities in garment manufacturing and produced clothing products mainly for H&M and Columbia. Visiting the factory, it was obvious that a wide variety of styles were being produced at the same time, with two large buildings that each housed 12 assembly lines, making a total of 24. A code-of-conduct inspector from H&M accompanied the team to the first meeting, but did not stay for the interviews. The manager was very candid in his answers. Since it was a research project associated with the FLA, he stated that he wanted to 'get the story out' about suppliers in the garment industry. He said that he would try to be much more honest than he was with the usual auditors and that he would frankly reveal the factory's main challenges with regard to wages. In fact, his manner seemed quite open throughout the interviews and often went much further than the workers themselves, who were unaware that their manager had been so frank (Jin et al., 2009).

The manager started by admitting that he had organised specific coaching for the workers with regard to external audits. This was confirmed during our interviews with the workers, who rarely departed from the answers they had been trained to give to the auditors and thus systematically contradicted the manager's more open answers. In fact, from the workers' point of view – at least from that of the unskilled workers: the skilled workers appeared to be more critical – Company 3 appeared to be the perfect company in terms of working hours, pay systems and workers' satisfaction.

The manager clearly stated that his main strategy was to weather the crisis and to emerge as a strong player after other factories have fallen by the wayside. For this purpose he had drafted a three-year wage plan, which was based mainly on constant nominal wage levels, encouraged by the current government's policy of freezing the minimum wage. Nevertheless, he reported that, owing to the crisis, the company's relations with the brands had become even more tense than before, because they were imposing even more difficult terms in the contract negotiations. His exact words were that he was being 'beaten down' by the brands in terms of contracts. His only solution was, first, to stop increasing wages and, second, to reduce his raw materials budget by 'beating down' his suppliers at the other end of the chain.

6.2 THE WAGE STORY IN THE THREE COMPANIES

The interviews carried out in tandem with the fair wage questionnaires (see annexes) allowed us to collect systematic information on the various and complementary fair wage dimensions and to reconstitute the wage story in the three companies.

We systematically analysed what the prevailing pay systems were; whether they were balanced in terms of composition and evolution; and also whether the workers were well informed about how they worked. Within each dimension, compliance with local labour law was also evaluated.

No Delays in Paying Wages but Flagrant Cases of Underpayment

In general, no cases of non-payment of wages or delays in paying wages were reported in the three companies. Wages were paid on a regular basis, generally once a month. In these companies, both management and workers were not expecting more difficulties in paying wages owing to the crisis.

No cases of informal – or under-the-table – payments in cash were reported in the three companies under study. Cash payments were very infrequent and reported as being used to bridge a gap when new recruits had not yet set up a bank account, which is required for payment by direct and automatic transfer, generally every month.

At the same time, clear cases of underpayment were reported, generally in the areas of working time and the payment of overtime.

Company 1 admitted not honouring the double-time payment expected for overtime on Saturdays, as prescribed by law. The manager clearly indicated that such a payment would impose too heavy a burden on the company, thereby making it less competitive in relation to the group's other factories in Vietnam and Laos, ultimately threatening its survival. Surprisingly, the employees did not realise this and believed they were being paid double-time for Saturday work, thereby indicating the importance of communication – or, as here, the lack of it – in employees' perception of the wage-fixing process.

In Company 3, the manager openly admitted not voluntarily paying overtime at all, thereby breaking the law. Indeed, the intention was to push this strategy harder in response to the crisis in order to further reduce labour costs, as a coping strategy. The workers also indicated that wage deductions were applied if they were unable to meet the daily production targets. In order to avoid this, workers had to work longer hours and accumulate additional overtime, which was not paid by the management.

In fact, two aspects of underpayment of wages in Company 3 should be noted. On the one hand, overtime on Saturday was not counted as overtime, so that there was underpayment of work on Saturdays, as well as of overtime in general. On the other hand, it seemed that when the target number of pieces was not achieved, workers had to stay late, with a number of additional working hours not being paid at all. This amounts more to the non-payment of wages rather than to underpayment.

Minimum Wage: Fragile Compliance

We tried to assess the minimum wage from a number of different perspectives:

1. Was the starting wage in the company at least at the level of the statutory regional/city minimum wage?
2. Could the minimum wage be achieved within the basic working hours and without accumulating overtime?
3. Had the company experienced difficulties paying the minimum wage in the past?
4. Were the workers informed about the statutory minimum wage, as required by law?

No cases of non-compliance with the official minimum wage were reported by the management. At Company 1, however, some workers reported that they had experienced difficulties in being paid the minimum wage in the past.

At Company 2, the company's starting wage was exactly the provincial minimum wage of RMB 760, topped up with a bonus of RMB 100 for food, making a total of RMB 860 per month. Given that deductions were reportedly taken from the food allowance for disciplinary reasons, however, we cannot conclude that the RMB 100 was included in wages every month. At the same time, the fact that 40 per cent of the workers had left the company in 2006–08 may be explained by such wage deductions and also the very low wages in the company. Furthermore, only one in four of the employees interviewed knew the correct statutory minimum wage, which is a matter of concern since, by law, employers must notify workers of a change in the minimum wage within 10 days of the effective date and this information must be published in at least one official local publication.

Nevertheless, there were no difficulties in ensuring the basic legal minimum wage, as reported by both management and workers.

At Company 3, the situation was even more confusing. The manager did not know the starting wage in the company and had to ask one of his assistants to provide this information. Although he did not get a precise answer, he replied that the provincial minimum wage was RMB 800 and that the starting wage in his company was above that level, at least by a little. On the workers' side, a few employees reported that the starting wage in the company was RMB 800, while others reported that it was 830. Among the skilled workers, one man initially said that the starting wage was RMB 800, but was prompted by a young woman that the legal minimum wage was 830, so he changed his answer to say that the starting wage was, indeed, RMB 830 and above the provincial minimum wage. The interview dynamics were interesting, given that the manager had said that the workers had received coaching for the audit (Jin et al., 2009).

Our question about compliance with the official minimum wage obviously made both management and workers particularly anxious. The fact that the manager did not know what the official minimum wage was, was also an indication of his lack of awareness of minimum wage compliance at his company. This means that there might well have been cases of non-compliance, even if not directly reported during the interviews.

In any case, considering that overtime was not paid – especially in Companies 1 and 3 – there is good reason to believe that this starting wage was the final wage received by the workers for their normal work plus overtime, making it a flagrant example of non-compliance both with overtime and minimum wage regulations (which stipulate that the minimum wage should be paid for basic working hours only).

Table 6.2 clearly shows that the management reported that their starting wage was at least the official provincial minimum wage. In fact, we can see in all three cases that the starting wage corresponded exactly to the statutory minimum and no more, thus showing the impact of minimum wage regulations

Table 6.2 Minimum wage payment in the three companies, 2008

	Company 1	Company 2	Company 3
Starting wage in the company (a)	850	760 (+ 100 for food)	800
Local minimum wage (b)	850 (city of Nanjing)	760 (city of Qingdao)	800 (city of Beijing)
a/b (in %)	100%	100%	100%
Doubts concerning whether the minimum wage was also paid for overtime work	Yes	Yes	Yes
Reported difficulty in paying the minimum wage	Yes (workers)	No (management) No (workers)	No (from both manager and workers)
Workers informed about the minimum wage level	All workers informed	No (1 in 4)	Various answers from the workers

among suppliers. However, where workers did not know what the statutory minimum wage was, as in Company 2, it was difficult to know for certain from the workers whether it was applied or not.

Living Wage: A Function Difficult to Ensure

When asked about their living-wage function, the management of Company 1 responded that wages in the company allowed workers to ensure their basic needs, a statement only partly confirmed by the workers, some of whom reported that their wage did not allow them to live decently. They did report, however, that the non-monetary benefits provided by the company played an important role, such as accommodation (free of charge to all migrant workers), food, health care and education. Workers complained about the fact that wages were too low to permit holidays or entertainment, which should be considered in light of the company's non-compliance with its obligation to provide paid holidays.

Company 2 – characterized by the lowest wage among the three companies – gave rise to the worst report with regard to living wages, with workers (mainly very young) reporting that they were not satisfied with their living standards. In particular, they reported that their wage did not enable them to afford better clothing, not to mention holidays or entertainment. They also added that their capacity to afford education was very limited. This confirms the need to approach the living wage dimension through different categories of basic expenditure. The company tried to compensate for living wage deficiencies by providing food, accommodation and health care via an on-site doctor and provision of free medication.

Table 6.3 Living wage in the three companies

	Company 1	Company 2	Company 3
Wages allow decent living standards	Yes (management) No (for workers)	Yes (management) No (for workers)	Yes (management) No (workers)
Areas of complaint	Holidays, entertainment	Clothing, education, holidays, entertainment	Education, holidays
Important role of non-monetary benefits (accommodation, meals, and so on)	Yes	Yes	Yes

In Company 3, the workers were even more assertive, reporting – and contradicting the manager at least on this point – that the wage they received was not sufficient to enable them to live decently. Some of the workers expected that, owing to the crisis, their wage may not be sufficient even to cover basic needs. They also confirmed the usefulness of the non-monetary benefits that they were getting from the company, such as dormitory accommodation and subsidized meals.

However, we also discovered from the interviews that a number of non-monetary benefits or bonuses – for food, for instance, as in Company 2 – could be withdrawn in case of absenteeism or for some other disciplinary purpose. Such benefits should not be made dependent on work discipline since they would thus represent an unstable source of income for the workers and so undermine their living wage function.

With regard to the living wage, the decision of the local authorities to freeze the minimum wage could have clear implications in terms of wages at the lowest level and thus generate an increasing number of low paid workers and working poor.

Wages below Market Rates or Prevailing Wages

The highest average wage was found in Company 3, at RMB 1,467 a month in 2008, which confirmed national statistics suggesting higher wages in state-owned enterprises compared to private enterprises. Company 1 was somewhere in the middle, with an average wage of RMB 1,310, while the lowest wages were found in Company 2, with RMB 1,200. Indeed, Company 2 scored lowest in terms of the living wage function of pay and also in terms of the prevailing wage. This had direct implications on labour force turnover, with 40 per cent of workers quitting the company in 2006–2008.

In general, both management and workers indicated that the average wage in their company was probably higher than – in Companies 1 and 2 – or at least the same as (in Company 3) those of their competitors. However, the interviews showed that neither workers nor managers knew much about wages in competing companies. Most of them (for instance, in Company 2) even admitted not knowing about the industry average wage in their province.

The data collected at the companies which we compared to national and provincial data did not confirm the optimism shown by management. In the three companies, the average wage was clearly below the national average wage for this industry (clothing), of RMB 1,547 (see also a/b ratio in Table 6.4). It was also well below the provincial average wage even for Company 2, located in the low-pay province of Shandong (see a/c ratio in Table 6.4). This provincial average, however, includes non-manufacturing companies in sectors traditionally paying much higher wages, such as banking and services.

In Company 2, workers admitted that they were not even sure whether their wage was higher than the average wage in their province of origin – although seeking a higher wage is the primary objective of migration within China. This is an additional indication of very low wages in this company, which partly explains why such a large proportion of employees decided to leave.

Another interesting result was the management's conviction – in all three companies – that they would do better than their competitors in the face of the crisis and that the wage gap with competing companies would increase further. This answer was given even in Company 3, where the manager planned to freeze nominal wages to cope with the crisis. This self-assurance in relation to competitors may mean that the situation in the industry as a whole is expected to be particularly bad, so that even the companies with a moderate wage policy may do better than other companies. On the other hand, it may also be due to a management strategy of minimising the expected effects of the crisis in order to avoid panic among the workers.

Moreover, it is important also to take into account the final wage rather than the average wage. For instance, in Company 3 – which showed the highest wages of the three – the fact that workers were not paid for overtime clearly meant that more working hours did not lead to higher wages. Similarly, in Company 1, the fact that more non-monetary benefits were provided played a major role. This confirms the need to use a number of criteria when assessing fair wages within companies.

Table 6.4 Prevailing monthly wage (in RMB) in the three companies, 2008

	Company 1	Company 2	Company 3
Average wage in the company (a)	1,310	1,200	1,467
Prevailing (average) wage in textiles, clothing, shoes and caps manufacturing at national level (b)	1,547	1,547	1,547
Prevailing (average) wage at province level (c)	2,281* Jiangsu province	1,941 Qingdao city, Shandong province	3,726 Beijing city
a/b	84.6	77.5	94.8
a/c	57.4	63.1	37.7

Notes: * For 2007 (data for 2008 not yet available in June 2009).

Source: National Statistical Bureau.

Unbalanced Pay Systems

The three case studies again confirmed the predominance of the piece rate system, which was applied in two out of the three companies and represented a high percentage of their total wage: 80 per cent in Company 1 and 90 per cent in Company 3. However, in Company 1, an attempt had been made to start paying skilled workers a fixed wage, while most unskilled production workers continued to be paid under the piece rate system.

Table 6.5 Structure of wages in the three companies, 2008

	Company 1	Company 2	Company 3
Pay system	– Unbalanced in favour of piece rates, but some other incentives (based on attendance, seniority) and a collective bonus	– Pay system without piece rates and relying on a basic wage (hourly wage) according to a pay grid + bonuses – Not much diversification of bonuses and too much reliance on full attendance	– Uniquely relying on piece rates and an attendance bonus
Piece rate	80% of total wage	No piece rate system	90% of total wage
Attendance bonus	– 20% of annual bonus – Paid for a presence of 26 days/month and time off of no more than 48 days/ year – Absenteeism penalised by wage cuts	– Full attendance during the year rewarded by a few days off – But need to accumulate 30 days presence each month for a whole year	– For 26 days presence per month, Monday to Saturday – Severe penalties for every day not worked
Seniority bonus	– 30% of annual bonus, with RMB 50 for each year of service	– Seniority bonus – Technical bonus for skilled workers (also dependent on full attendance)	– Included in the basic wage and representing 1% of total wage per month
Collective bonus	– Paid on an annual basis according to sales growth	– No collective bonus	– No collective bonus related to company performance

At the same time, we were able to identify an unreasonable insistence on full attendance, which demanded that workers work at least 26 days a month in Companies 1 and 3, and even more in Company 2, where not only wages, but also bonuses and non-monetary benefits – such as meals – were dependent on attendance. This obliged workers to accumulate working days without any rest or sick leave.

A series of monetary bonuses were also distributed in the three companies, but were found to be a source of confusion: the composition or structure of wages was not very transparent and workers were generally unaware of the system in place. This clearly undermined the effectiveness of such bonuses: if workers do not know how their bonus is calculated, it cannot have a positive effect on their motivation and productivity.

Very Strict Attendance Bonus

The case studies confirmed the observations obtained through the auditing exercise related to the widespread use of very strict attendance systems (or bonuses), which oblige workers to keep their days off to a minimum.

In Company 1, the attendance bonus was paid only if the worker was not absent more than four days a month, corresponding to the four Sundays in a month, and no more than 48 days a year (that is, four days per month $\times$ 12 months), with the attendance bonus being reduced in proportion to the number of days missed. This system obliged the workers to work every Saturday throughout the year if they did not want to lose their attendance bonus and, moreover, at an illegal rate: instead of the 200 per cent which they should have been paid for overtime on Saturdays they received only the weekday overtime rate of 150 per cent. According to the workers, such basic conditions for working on Saturdays had been incorporated into their labour contract, although this clearly contravened national labour law, which requires at least two rest days per week. The same provision (26 days per month attendance) was found in Company 3, which was also applying penalties to sanction absenteeism: a 50 yuan deduction for every day of absence and dismissal for three consecutive days of absence. Full attendance was even stricter in Company 2. Unauthorised days off taken by the employee, even for sickness, resulted in the loss of the attendance and technical bonus and an immediate cut in the monthly food allowance and monthly wage. This is very strict because workers will inevitably become sick at some time during a full year.

These strict conditions to reduce absenteeism (such as direct sanctions or an excessively high number of working days) explain why this type of bonus was found not to be very effective in motivating the workers.

Tensions between the Minimum Wage and the Piece Rate

In the companies in which the piece rate represented most of the workers' wages, piece rate pay was at odds with the minimum wage in the sense that, while many workers' piece rate pay was often found to be below the official minimum wage, the company ended up paying the official minimum wage anyway. This was found to be demotivating for those workers who managed to earn at least or slightly above the minimum wage and who could see that the poorest performers were getting the minimum wage, come what may. To strengthen workers' motivation it would be necessary to set piece rates much higher, so that good performers were able to earn much more than the minimum wage. Conversion to a basic wage that reflected workers' skills, not in terms of their piece rate attainment but their levels of education, skills and performance, would also improve efficiency since it would ensure a basic wage higher than the minimum wage for higher-skilled workers.

In addition, overreliance on the piece rate system leaves no flexibility for increasing wages in accordance with inflation. Furthermore, it also makes it impossible to take into account other fair wage dimensions, such as the wage share, social dialogue, skills and so on.

Skilled and Unskilled Workers' Pay Systems at Odds

In Company 1, two systems coexisted: while most production workers were paid according to the piece rate, most skilled workers were generally paid a monthly basic wage, especially those in the special orders department, who produced items from the beginning to the end of the process, something that required a broader set of skills and typically took more time than items produced on the assembly line. Skilled workers involved in the sample department were also paid a basic monthly wage. The problem is that the statistics provided by the manager clearly showed that the average wages of unskilled workers – especially those performing well in terms of pieces produced – were much higher (RMB 1,742) than the average wages of skilled workers (RMB 1,294), which was clearly demotivating for skilled workers paid only a fixed basic wage.

Obviously, in Company 1, there was a high level of dissatisfaction among skilled workers, first because they were paid less than unskilled workers and, second, because there were two parallel systems, one for those skilled workers paid on a monthly basis and the other for skilled workers paid according to the piece rate, who generally ended up with a better wage that those on a basic monthly wage. This highlighted the need for a coherent and transparent pay system in the company.

It was also because of the coexistence of such different pay systems that the wages of supervisors and foremen – which depended on the piece rate performance of the team of workers they supervised – were reported to be much higher than the wages of managerial and executive employees, who were considered to be 'clerks' and were thus paid on a monthly basis.

But problems can emerge even when all the workers are paid under the same system. This was the case in Company 3, which used piece rate payments for both skilled and unskilled production workers, and to some extent also in Company 1 on those assembly lines on which both unskilled and skilled workers were paid according to a piece rate system. Although piece rates were much higher for skilled workers because a piece produced by them represented higher quality and more complex work, they could accumulate fewer pieces, so that in the end they often attained a lower wage than unskilled workers. As an example, in Company 1, skilled and unskilled workers were involved at different stages of the production process. Unskilled workers had the task of producing the front of a shirt, with long straight lines, which was easier to cut and sew than a collar or sleeve, with several seams, which is what the skilled workers did. As a result, unskilled workers ended up well ahead of many skilled workers.

It might be because of these problems inherent in the piece rate system that the wages of skilled workers were found to be below those of unskilled workers. Many companies, as a consequence, complemented piece rate payments with a skill or production bonus, which increased in accordance with workers' skills and position. However, such bonuses were found to be fairly marginal with regard to total pay and thus did not make up for the drawbacks and inconsistencies of the piece rate system.

In the companies interviewed (especially Company 3), skilled workers complained openly about the piece rate system, reporting that this pay system did not properly reward differences in skills and education. They also complained that they were not involved at all in determining the different piece rates, for which the technical department (also called the 'sample department' in some companies) was exclusively responsible.

This finding confirms the total inadequacy of the piece rate system in rewarding different skill levels, contradicting the opinion of many managers at suppliers, who stated that the piece rate system was the best system for rewarding skills, since higher skills naturally lead to the production of a higher number of pieces and, therefore, higher pay. The problem is, as already mentioned, that the pieces produced by skilled and by unskilled workers are often not the same. This also confirms the need to have a more structured system relating the wage – or at least a substantial part of it – to skills and education to make sure that wages better reflect internal grading. This underlines our categorization of skills and technology as a fair wage dimension, on the understanding that wage levels should normally evolve alongside individual workers' characteristics in terms of training, acquisition of new skills and know-how.

In some ways, Company 1 has been much more innovative in its pay systems. Not only has it tried to put some workers on a basic monthly wage, but it has also sought to develop an annual bonus related to company performance. Interestingly, the skilled workers there clearly stated their preference for extending the annual bonus instead of relying too much on piece rates. These are certainly the first steps in the right direction for the purpose of progressively ending the dominance of the piece rate system. On the other hand, it shows that, whatever new system is applied, it should first be explained to the workers. There should be regular communication concerning calculation methods and its application to the whole labour force. Company 1 had gone some way by converting half of its skilled workers to a fixed basic system. Progressively, however, this should be applied to all skilled workers and then also to unskilled workers within the framework of a coherent grading system in order to avoid any discrepancies in wage levels.

Table 6.6 Average wages (in RMB) by categories of workers, 2008

	Company 1	Company 2	Company 3
Unskilled workers	1,742	1,000	1,100
Skilled workers	1,294	1,400	1,557
Average wage	1,310	1,200	1,467

Sources: Interviews in the three companies.

Misuse of the Salary Grid

Although a salary grid was reported to be in use in all three companies, it is doubtful that it was being used effectively. In fact, if 80 to 100 per cent of wages were paid on a piece-rate basis, there was clearly little flexibility left for paying the employees according to a classification/pay scale. Indeed, the managers were unable to provide any details on the number of grades and categories, and on the exact contents of each category. Typically, the skilled workers in Company 1 were not aware that any grid system was being applied. The fact that the wages of unskilled workers were above those of skilled workers provides a clear example of how poorly the wage reflected different skill levels. In Company 3, there was a total absence of grading since the manager was convinced that the current piece rate system fully rewarded skills, education and experience.

Even in Company 2, which used a fixed basic wage rather than a piece rate system, the grid system seemed to be used more for calculating the 'technical skill bonus' than for defining the different levels of basic wages.

Table 6.7 Use of a pay grid

	Company 1	Company 2	Company 3
Pay grid	Yes, but not used for wage fixing	Yes – used for pay system of all workers but with a focus on determining 'technical skill bonuses'	No – the piece rate system is believed to reward the most skilled

Some Isolated Attempts at Pay Based on Company Performance

At all three companies, both management and workers reported the absence of a link between company performance and wages, although Company 1 had implemented a pay system related to sales volume, which was expected to account for 20 per cent of annual wages. Initially related to sales because of the absence of profits in the first two years of operation, the management intended to convert this annual bonus into a profit-sharing scheme, once profits were actually made. This annual bonus could represent up to one monthly wage, as reported by one skilled worker who had received an annual bonus of RMB 900 in 2008 (making a monthly average wage of RMB 1,294). This attempt contrasted strikingly with the fairly unique pay system implemented in Company 3, in which piece rate payments represented more than 80 per cent of the total wage, as also observed in other companies during the auditing exercise. Unfortunately, although Company 1's scheme was an interesting attempt to make the pay system less dependent on piece rate performance, the management had not complemented this new system with sufficient communication and information. As a result, some workers reported that they did not know that this system was in place, while others were receiving some sort of annual bonus, but did not know it was related to the company's sales performance. But if workers do not know what their bonus depends on, what kind of incentive is that? Any positive impact such a scheme might have had on workers' motivation to work harder was therefore seriously limited.

In contrast with performance-related pay, the three companies reported that they were applying seniority bonuses. These could be fairly substantial, as in Company 1, which disbursed an additional RMB 50 per month for each year of service, representing an important source of income for workers with 3–4 years of service (4 years × RMB 50 = RMB 200 per month, making an annual RMB 2,400, nearly two average monthly wages). While this could be considered rigid because it is not a flexible pay component, this type of bonus can help to motivate workers to remain at the company and so serve as a useful tool for reducing high staff turnover, especially among skilled employees.

164 *Fair Wages*

Importance of Non-monetary Benefits

In addition to monetary bonuses, a significant number of non-monetary services were provided by the three companies. In Company 1, free accommodation was provided for migrant workers. Meals, health care, transportation and scholarships for children were also subsidized by the company. Provision of free accommodation for migrant workers should be accompanied by benefits for local workers, but this did not seem to be the case in the company.

Significant benefits were also provided in the other two companies (see Table 6.8): accommodation, meals, basic medical care and transportation during Chinese New Year.

Company 2 tried to compensate low wages by providing food, accommodation and health care, including an onsite doctor and provision of free medication. This was reported to constitute an important source of income by the workers. On the other hand, it was not sufficient to prevent massive labour turnover, mainly motivated by a desire for better wages at other companies and possibly in better paying provinces.

Table 6.8 Non-monetary benefits and paid holidays

	Company 1	Company 2	Company 3
Non-monetary benefits	Free accommodation for migrant workers, health care, free meals and transportation, scholarships for children	Free accommodation and meals, medical care, and transportation for Chinese New Year (but not for all workers)	Accommodation, subsidised meals, free medication, transportation Since 2009, workers required to pay for electricity and water
Paid holidays	Not provided (confirmed by manager and workers)	Not provided	Not provided, except for five days during Chinese New Year

At the same time, the three companies were found not to comply with the 11 legally mandated paid holidays (see Table 6.9). In lieu of paid public holidays, workers at Company 1 were offered vouchers to be used in grocery shops, while workers in Company 3 were offered a few paid holidays during Chinese New Year, although this was not confirmed by the workers. In Company 2, the workers did not report being paid for the legally mandated public holidays.

Table 6.9 Paid public holidays under the law, China, 2009

Public holiday	Number of days
New Year, (January 1)	1
Spring Festival	3
Ching Ming Festival	1
Labour Day (May 1)	1
Dragon Boat Festival	1
Mid-Autumn Festival (Lunar New Mid-day)	1
National Day (October 1, 2, 3)	3
TOTAL	11

Source: Chinese Labour Contract Law (2008).

Confirmation of Widespread Non-compliance with Social Insurance Regulations

The management of Company 1 candidly admitted that the company was not providing all the statutory social insurance schemes. Not all workers were included – rather than implementing such payments on a mandatory basis the company had decided to make them voluntary. The same situation was reported by some workers in Company 2, who added that they had not enrolled in the scheme owing to the cost. In Company 1, workers did not even receive the necessary information: interviewed workers were not able to name the exact type of insurance and the amounts involved.

The situation was even worse in Company 3, at which social insurance was not paid by the management at all, except for work-related injuries. The management drew our attention to the fact that migrant workers from another province would never get back any money they might pay for insurance when moving on to another province or returning to their original province. The system was not computerized and there was no trace of individual social insurance contributions. Workers in Company 3 also reported that the enterprise had a policy of hiring only agricultural workers, who hold an 'agricultural household card' which requires lower social insurance payments from the company. Rather than trying progressively to cover the maximum number of employees the company recruitment policy was aimed at minimizing social insurance payments, leading to discriminatory employment practices.

Improper Payment of Working Time Confirmed

As already described, overtime payment represented the main source of underpayment, especially in Companies 1 and 3. In Company 1, Saturdays were treated as normal working days. Curiously, the workers were convinced that they were being paid legal overtime rates, even though the manager clearly stated that overtime was not paid any extra on Saturdays. Some workers even reported not working at all on Saturdays, indicating the pressure put on workers giving interviews of this kind to conceal the truth in fear of management retaliation.

In Company 3, the management admitted not paying overtime at all, while workers reported that overtime was paid, again illustrating the effectiveness of the coaching sessions which the manager admitted having organized. In Company 3, which, as we have seen, had increased sales and seemed to be popular among the brands, one cause of the underpayment problem was difficulties in completing orders. The workers confirmed that they were not given sufficient time to meet orders, so that they had to work additional hours to produce the necessary number of pieces, as the company raced to meet its quota.

Table 6.10 Payment of overtime

	Company 1	Company 2	Company 3
Total working hours	According to the Manager: 8 hours a day + 2–3 hours a day OT According to the workers: six-day working week	8 hours per day for five working days + OT	Above legal regulations: 8 hours per day for six working days
Overtime	Non-compliance with legal five-day working, with Saturdays treated as normal working days	Within the legal limits of 36 monthly OT hours per month; always paid but workers unaware of legal OT rates	Underpaid on Saturdays OT often not paid at all

In Company 2, both managers and workers reported that overtime payments were made in accordance with the law, but most workers were unaware of the prevailing legal rates for overtime. Obviously, there was some flexibility for management with regard to overtime. Full transparency with regard to overtime payments should include the provision of proper information on legal regulations, especially on the payment of overtime.

Box 6.1 Legal regulations on working hours, China, 2009		
A. Working time	Source: Decision of the State Council on Revising the Provisions of Working Hours of Workers	Workers and staff shall work 8 hours a day and 40 hours a week.
B. Overtime	Source: Labour Law of the People's Republic of China	Extended working hours for a day shall generally not exceed 1 hour; if extension is called for due to special reasons, the extended hours shall not exceed 3 hours a day on condition that workers' health is guaranteed. The total extension in a month shall not exceed 36 hours.
C. Overtime payment	Source: Labour Law of the People's Republic of China	1. 150 per cent of the normal wages if the extension of working hours is arranged; 2. 200 per cent of the normal wages if the extended hours are arranged on days of rest and no deferred rest can be taken; 3. 300 per cent of the normal wages if the extended hours are arranged on statutory holidays.

Source: Jin et al., 2009

Real Wages: Not a Management Priority

Perceptions of nominal wage rises in response to price increases often differed between management and workers. In Company 1, the management clearly said that nominal wages had increased by more than 20 per cent, on average – that is, above the inflation rate of 5.9 per cent in 2008 – thus resulting in significant real wage increases. In contrast, the workers reported having been paid RMB 50 more as a seniority bonus, but also that they had not received any other increase, so that their basic wage had gone down in comparison to prices. In Company 2, the manager said that wages had increased by 35 per cent in 2008, which was much higher than the rate of price increases. However, strangely enough, the workers did not know whether their wage had increased. It is difficult to believe that they could have overlooked a 35 per cent increase. Only a few skilled workers mentioned that their nominal wages had increased, but at a much lower rate than price increases and they complained about their declining purchasing power. In fact, this seems to be the main reason why 40 per cent of the labour force (70 per cent of whom were – relatively young – skilled operatives) had left the company since 2006.

In Company 3, real wages seem to have increased in tandem with the sharp increase in the legal minimum wage in 2008. However, workers reported that they did not feel that their wage had been adjusted to price increases. Moreover, the new strategy of the manager – to keep nominal wages constant during the crisis – should translate, in practice, into a fall in real wages and workers' purchasing power.

In the three companies, this uncertain situation with regard to real wages – with the statements of management and workers at odds with one another – tended to contradict the managers' assertions that, in order to overcome the crisis, it was important, while keeping wage costs low, to avoid decreasing wages in order not to demotivate the labour force and to attract and retain skilled workers. The managers interviewed did not really consider the effects of such a policy (of constant nominal wages) on real wages. In fact, the manager of Company 3 reported that he did not know what the inflation rate was in 2008, a lack of knowledge and reflection on the issue that was confirmed by the other managers, and which directly confirms the need – and legitimises our objective – to develop greater understanding of this fair wage dimension – real wages – and to have it progressively integrated in suppliers' wage policy and overall strategy.

The notion of real wages should also be better explained to the workers. In Company 3, the workers seemed satisfied with the manager's statement that wages would not be cut despite the crisis, without realizing that in fact they will lose purchasing power, especially if prices continue to increase rapidly, as was the case in China in early 2009. This is even more surprising since they clearly said that their wages would certainly not be sufficient to cover their basic needs during the crisis. When specifically asked whether 'their wages managed to keep up with price increases last year?' and whether 'they were expecting their wages to keep up with price increases this year?' they clearly answered both questions negatively, showing that they could understand the issue if it was presented in a straightforward and transparent way.

Wages Totally Disconnected from Company Performance

In general, the workers in the three companies did not even know how their company was performing. Even in Company 1, where sales-related pay was introduced, the workers – who continued to have the same volume of work, including overtime, even during the crisis – were convinced that the company was doing well, while the management was reporting decreasing profits or even an absence of profits.

This was the result of a policy of lack of transparency concerning profits when growth in most Chinese suppliers was skyrocketing. On the other hand – and more positively – this illustrates that the management is not using the crisis as an excuse or an opportunity for adjusting wages and working conditions downward.

However, this also leads to a number of discrepancies. This absence of transparency concerning the real situation of the company may be counterproductive for the management, too, because it cannot refer to the effects of the crisis as justification for seeking to reduce labour costs. The management of Company 1 clearly expressed its willingness to make workers' wages more sensitive to economic performance and company profits. In Company 3, the management stated firmly that performance improvements were never translated into higher wages.

The data provided by the accounting departments of the three companies confirmed the disconnection. Both profit margins and productivity were found to have improved in Company 2 without being reflected in wage increases. Company 3's significant sales growth in 2007–2008 (more than 20 per cent) was also not reflected in nominal wages, which the manager would like to keep constant as far as possible.

This poor connection between wages and collective performance may also be explained by the weakness of a wage structure that remains dominated by the individual or piece rate system. Since the piece rate system is believed to encourage individual workers to work harder and faster, both the management and the workers do not seem to have the incentive to value collective rather than individual performance. Nevertheless, in all three companies, the managers recognised that pay schemes related to collective performance would need to develop in the future.

Sign of Progress on the Wage Front: Wage Costs Increasing

As in the auditing survey, the managers of the three companies reported that their wage costs had increased by 30 per cent as a proportion of their total production costs (up to 45 per cent in Company 1). This was due – according to the management of Company 1 – to the sharp increase in the local minimum wage, which had increased in Nanjing by 20 per cent. Similarly, wage costs increased by 16 per cent in Company 2, despite a fall in employment. The unit wage costs clearly increased by 50 per cent, something that can be explained only by increased overtime – even if a good part of it remains unpaid – to compensate the voluntary resignations of 40 per cent of the labour force. Despite its clear 3 years' strategy to keep nominal wages constant, Company 3 has succeeded to maintain wage costs in 2007 and 2008 with even a slight increase, of 1 per cent, in comparison to total production costs. This might be partly due to the managers' successful plan to 'beat down' its suppliers' prices for raw materials (energy and so on).

Nevertheless, this increase in wage costs also confirms the impact of recent improvements in national legislation on developments at enterprise level. If minimum wage regulations had been absent in China, wage costs would certainly have deteriorated rapidly alongside the increasing price of energy and other production costs.

Increased Wage Disparity Despite Minimum Wage Increase

For this purpose, we studied wage levels and progression in different classifications: between the top and the lowest workers; men and women; permanent and temporary; migrants and different ethnic groups; and other groups.

The case studies confirmed the findings from the auditing exercise, that is, increasing wage disparity within the companies. First, between the wages at the top – of managers – and wages at the bottom – of unskilled production workers, generally paid the minimum wage rate. This was confirmed by the workers in all three companies. An increasing gap is also emerging between unskilled and skilled production workers, thus confirming the increasing weight of the skills premium – with the exception of Company 1, at which skilled workers were found to be paid less than unskilled workers. Certainly, this wage disparity between the top and bottom grades would have grown even further if the minimum wage had not been increased significantly in 2007–2008.

An increase in the wages of other higher ranking categories, such as supervisors – whose wages are often higher than those of managers – should also be noted. This might be explained by the fact that managers are considered administrative employees paid at a basic fixed wage, while the wages of supervisors are generally related to the piece rate performance of the workers they supervise. This situation might also lead to potential distortions in terms of motivation and decision-making (even corruption among managers).

At the same time, no sources of wage discrimination, especially of migrant workers – but also by gender – have been reported in the three companies, even during the crisis. Only discrimination against non-agricultural employees during the recruitment process was reported in Company 3, because they cost more in terms of social insurance payments.

Poor Communication and Lack of Social Dialogue

Different questions addressed to managers and workers allowed us to collect information on the quality of communication on wages before, in the course of and after the production process.

Wages were fixed in the three companies by an individual contract with each worker, which is an important achievement in compliance with Chinese regulations. It means that workers receive information in advance on what their wage level should be.

At the same time, weaknesses were identified within the company in the communication process accompanying production. We saw earlier, for instance, that workers were not all aware of the provincial or city minimum wage to be applied by the company (as in Company 2).

In Company 1, the workers also reported generally not knowing in advance how much they were going to be paid for each piece they produced.

The case studies confirmed the findings from the auditing that pay slips were distributed in most enterprises. After some investigation, however, we realised that this pay slip generally did not provide basic information, such as the total number of hours actually worked, and also did not clearly distinguish between the payment of regular working time and overtime. This was the case in Company 1, at which one rather rudimentary way in which the workers could calculate overtime payments was to subtract the minimum wage from their total basic wage. Undoubtedly, in these circumstances – no proper recording of working time – the workers could not easily recognise cases of underpayment. Similarly, in Company 3, the workers could see their individual piece rate performance in an attachment to their pay slip, but without any distinction between normal working hours and overtime, something that is to be expected in a company that often does not remunerate workers for overtime.

Box 6.2 Legal regulations on social dialogue, China

'Labour unions should establish a collective bargaining mechanism with the employer in order to safeguard the lawful rights and interests of workers and monitor the implementation of employment contracts and collective contracts by employers'.
Article 6 of the Law of the People's Republic of China on Employment Contracts

---

A series of questions also made it possible to assess social dialogue in the three companies. Contrary to the Chinese Labour Contract Law, which stipulates that trade unions or a workers' committee must be involved in collective bargaining, no social dialogue seemed to exist in the three companies. On the contrary, the absence of collective agreements helped to keep the workers in the dark concerning their wage conditions. In Company 1, there was no trade union which the workers might have asked for more information on wage levels and wage determination. Workers reported the existence of a workers' committee, but it was involved, not in wage issues but in the organisation of trips and the distribution of gifts to the workers on national holidays. The only way of discussing wage concerns was to go to see the head of the Human Resources department, which indicated a rather paternalistic and individual approach to wage issues. The same deficiency was found in Companies 2 and 3, in which there was a trade union, but it was involved not in bargaining, rather in 'welfare organization'. We might wonder whether the existence of social dialogue may have helped Company 2 to retain some of the workers who voluntarily left the company. In Company 3, the management even reported being very sceptical about the role of trade unions and instead developed communications via cell phones and a letter box. In Company 2, skilled workers did not know about the existence of a trade union. In conclusion, either social dialogue simply did not exist or it had taken a very paternalistic form, as in the (Korean) Company 2.

Higher Intensity at Work without Wage Increases

As part of our investigation of the payment of a 'fair wage' we tried to discover whether wages were linked to changes in work organisation, training and structural changes in the factory. The purpose was to find out, first, whether work intensity, technology or job complexity had changed and, second, whether these changes had had any effect on wages.

In general, increased work intensity and complexity was reported by both workers and management in the three companies. This was to be explained by more frequent changes in clothing styles, but also the demand that more goods be produced in the same period – as reported by one manager with regard to increasing pressure from the brands – and changes in the operation of the assembly lines. In some enterprises – such as Companies 1 and 3 – this increased complexity was also accompanied by the introduction of new technology and more training. The situation was particularly tight in Company 2, in which the voluntary departure of 40 per cent of the labour force in the last two years had obviously been accompanied by more overtime, but also greater work intensity and more stressful rhythms of work. This situation – more stressful work not accompanied by wage compensation – led to a vicious circle, compelling even more workers to leave the company.

In the three companies under study, the assessment is that wages did not keep up with increased work intensity or complexity. This was confirmed by the workers and also, to some extent, by the management. This can only be counter-productive with regard to efforts to reach the companies' targets and/ or strategy to retain highly skilled workers, however. Highly skilled workers must be properly remunerated in order to discourage them from offering their skills to another company for higher wages.

What is more, during the interviews neither management nor workers could understand why such organisational changes – even when accompanied by significant training and skills upgrading – should lead to wage increases. These perceptions may be influenced by the dominance of the piece rate system: both the workers and the management believed that improved skills will be directly reflected in increases in the number of pieces produced and so in higher wages. If a fixed basic wage system dominated, based on a proper grading system, workers' attitudes may also change with regard to the link between work organisation, skills and wages.

The companies' different answers on each of the fair wage dimensions helped us to compile Table 6.11 on their fair wage performance.

Table 6.11 Fair wage performance of the three companies

	Company 1	Company 2	Company 3
Payment of wages	– No problems reported	– No problems reported	– Non-payment of overtime reported
Living wage	– Wages allow employees to meet their basic needs	– Basic needs in terms of food, accommodation and health care satisfied – But complaints with regard to education, clothing, vacations and entertainment	– Disagreement between workers and management – Doubtful whether the starting wage in the company is above or below the official minimum wage
Legal minimum wage	– Starting wage above local minimum wage – But difficulties paying the minimum wage reported by workers	– Starting wage exactly at the provincial minimum wage (RMB 760) + a bonus of RMB 100 for food – No difficulty in paying legal minimum wage	– Evidence pointing to a starting wage exactly at the official minimum wage, but including OT (unpaid), meaning non-compliance with minimum wage provisions
Prevailing wage	– Wages slightly higher than competitors' wages according to the manager – Higher or the same according to the workers – Lower according to statistics	– Average wage lower than competitors according to statistics – Managers unaware of provincial average wage in the industry	– The same as competitors for both the manager and the workers – Not sure in terms of total wage because of unpaid OT – Lower according to statistics
Payment of working hours	– Non-compliance: overtime not properly paid on Saturdays because treated as normal working day	– Have always managed to pay overtime – However, workers were not informed about legal overtime rates	– Non-compliance: OT often not paid at all as part of coping strategy, or under-paid (i.e. on Saturdays) – If production targets not reached, additional (unpaid) OT

Table 6.11 (cont.)

	Company 1	Company 2	Company 3
Pay systems (see Table 6.5 for more details)	– Unbalanced in favour of piece rate (80% of total wage) – Distribution of various bonuses, but not easy to identify – Significant non-monetary benefits (meals, accommodation, and so on)	– Pay system without piece rates and relying on a basic wage according to a pay grid – Not much diversification of bonuses and too much reliance on full attendance	– Unbalanced in favour of piece rate (90% of total wage) – Attendance bonus – Significant non-monetary benefits
Social insurance payments	– Not paid to all workers	– Not paid to all workers	– Often not paid at all – System not computerised – Recruitment of agricultural workers in order to minimise social insurance payments
Communication and social dialogue	– Wage conditions fixed in individual labour contracts – Workers confused and unaware of their bonuses and wage structure – Only semi-informative pay slip – No negotiations on wages and workers' committee not active in them	– Wage conditions fixed in individual labour contracts – Pay slip received with information on total hours worked; distinction between pay for normal working hours and overtime – Suggestion box – Trade union, but not involved in pay issues	– Wage conditions fixed in individual labour contracts – Pay slip with piece rate performance, but no distinction between normal hours and overtime – Trade union in the company but not involved in bargaining – No social dialogue but suggestions box and communication via cell phone – External communication: workers trained to answer audit questions

	Company 1	Company 2	Company 3
Wage discrimination /wage disparity	– No wage discrimination – Increasing disparity between top and bottom – Increasing disparity between skilled and unskilled	– No wage discrimination – Low wage disparity – But increasing between lowest paid workers and the management and between skilled and unskilled; between production and administrative workers	– No wage discrimination but employment discrimination in favour of agricultural workers – Low wage disparity but slightly increasing between skilled and unskilled, especially during the crisis
Real wages	– For the workers, wage did not follow price increases	– Have increased according to the manager but no confirmation from the workers	– Workers clearly stated that nominal wage did not keep up with price increases (especially among the unskilled) – Manager confirmed constant nominal wages strategy
Wage share	– Wages did not keep up with company performance, despite a bonus related to sales growth	– Total disconnection between company performance and wages	– Lack of correlation between profits and wages confirmed by both management and workers
Wage costs	– Wage costs have increased along with the minimum wage increase	– Wage costs have increased more than other production costs	– Wage costs have been maintained due to a parallel reduction in real wages and raw material prices
Work intensity and technology	– Wages did not keep up with more complex and intense work production process – New technology but no impact on wages	– Higher intensity at work mainly due to sharp fall in employment despite same volume of orders, but no effect on wages, leading to more quits – Higher complexity of work but no impact on wages – Training but no effect on wages	– Wages did not keep up with higher intensity at work, increased training and new technology

6.3 MANAGERS' AND WORKERS' FAIR WAGE ASSESSMENT

At the end of the interviews, both managers and workers were asked to assess their company's wage policy. In particular, they were asked to say whether they considered wages paid in the factory fair, unfair or neither fair nor unfair. They were then requested to identify those fair wage areas in which they considered that the company should try to make most progress, some progress or did not need to change. The answers are summarised in Table 6.12.

Table 6.12 Workers' and managers' fair wage assessment

'Globally, would you say that the wages paid in the company are:'

	Company 1	Company 2	Company 3
Fair		Manager Workers	Manager Unskilled workers
Unfair			
Neither fair nor unfair	Manager Workers		Skilled workers

The managers generally believed that wages in their company were fair, as in Companies 2 and 3, while the manager's opinion in Company 1 was more attenuated. Workers in Company 2 also evaluated their wage as being fair, which is fairly surprising considering the very low wages in this company (the lowest among the three companies at which interviews were conducted) and the fact that a significant proportion of the workforce had left because of wages and working conditions. The workers justified their answer by saying that they had an individual labour contract, as well as regular payment of wages. This testifies eloquently to the low standards workers have to endure at suppliers in the garment industry in China. It also confirms the importance of having work contracts within the framework of a fair wage policy, something which the auditing exercise revealed was generally missing among suppliers in China. Nevertheless, the same workers were much more critical in their assessment with regard to individual areas (see Table 6.13).

Interestingly, there were differences between skilled and unskilled workers in Company 3. Despite the fact that skilled workers managed to maintain purchasing power better than unskilled workers, who experienced a decrease in real wages, they reported being much less convinced of the fairness of the wage system in their enterprise. This is to be explained in terms of their low assessment of the piece rate system, which does not appropriately reward differences in skills, education and professional experience.

Table 6.13 Workers' and managers' assessments of various fair wage dimensions

'Among the following wage areas, could you specify those in which you believe your enterprise needs to make most progress, some progress or does not need to change':

	Managers			Workers		
	Most progress	Some progress	No need to change	Most progress	Some progress	No need to change
More regular payment of wages			1, 2, 3			1, 2, 3
Wages that better enable decent living standards	3	1,2		2	3	1
More compliance with minimum wage			1,2,3			1,2,3
Wages more comparable to wages in other, similar enterprises		3	1,2	2,3		1
Wages that better reward overtime	1,3		2	1	2,3	
Better balanced and motivating pay systems		1,2,3		2	1,3	
Better communication and more negotiations on wages, both individually (with individual workers) and collectively (with workers' representatives or trade unions)	3	2	1	1,2	3	
Less wage disparity		1	2,3	1	2	3
Wages that better keep up with price increases		1,3	2	1,2	3	
Wages more closely related to enterprise performance	3	1,2		1,2,3		
Better progression of wage costs		2,3	1		1	2,3
Wages that better reflect changes in work intensity, technology and upskilling		3	1,2	2	1,3	

Notes: 1 = Company 1; 2 = Company 2; 3 = Company 3.

Surprisingly, in none of the three companies did workers expressly state that they found their wage unfair, which may be due to fears of retaliation from the management – as we have seen, internal coaching for external audits was sometimes organised by the management to influence workers' answers. However, differences with regard to assessment became much more frequent when we asked both management and workers to name the wage areas in which they believed the most improvement was necessary.

We can see from Table 6.13 that there were important differences between the assessments provided by managers, on the one hand, and workers, on the other. In general, managers were obviously more satisfied – or did not dare to be more critical of their own policy – and thus tended to place their answers in the right-hand column. Workers wanted more areas to change and thus tended to place their answers in the left or middle columns.

The labour–management relationship is also important. For instance, workers in Company 1 were much more open in their answers (identifying five areas as requiring most progress), while workers in Company 3 were clearly much more afraid of the implications their answers might have (identifying only two areas as requiring most progress). Workers in Company 2 were also rather open and critical, identifying seven areas (out of the 12 fair wage dimensions) in the left column, as requiring most progress. While this might be partly due to the fact that workers were less afraid to speak the truth, it obviously also reflects particularly a bad fair wage performance on the part of this company, which helps to explain why it experienced significant labour turnover in 2006–2008.

The case of Company 3 is particularly interesting. A very open management combined with very reserved workers – partly because of the coaching they received in advance of the auditing – led to the contrary situation, in which the manager was much more critical of wage practices, identifying four areas as requiring most progress: payment of overtime, social dialogue, wages that better enable decent living standards and wages better related to economic performance. By contrast, the management in Company 1 identified only one area – better payment of overtime – as requiring most progress, while the manager of Company 2 did not single out even one area in which most progress would be needed.

This comparative table is revealing and exhibits significant results concerning the various fair wage dimensions. In certain areas, manager and workers agreed that there was no need to change, as in the case of the regular payment of wages in all three companies. There also seems to be a consensus between the manager and the workers of the three companies in terms of compliance with the minimum wage. This was confirmed by our objective assessment, performed on the basis of all interviews and statistical information from the companies.

There were also areas which were identified by both management and workers as needing most progress, such as better rewarding of overtime, in Companies 1 and 3, an area that our general auditing exercise also identified as one of the weakest wage areas. Workers and management also identified a need for improvement with regard to better balanced and motivating pay systems, wages more closely related to enterprise performance and pay systems leading to less wage disparity (although this was more often raised by the workers).

There were also areas in which the two sides did not reach the same conclusion: as an example, the management in Companies 1 and 2 did not believe there was a need to strengthen communication and social dialogue, while workers put it among the priority items. The same applied to the issue of wages that better reflect price increases (especially in Companies 1 and 2), an area identified as among those most in need of progress by workers, but as less in need by the manager. In Company 2, there was also clear disagreement between management and workers with regard to prevailing wages, with workers putting this issue among its top priorities and the management considering it a non-issue.

Interestingly, in Companies 1 and 3, the manager seemed to be more concerned than workers about the issue of wages better ensuring decent living standards (while the opposite was true in Company 2). The manager in Company 1 clearly stated that there was a need to improve wage levels to improve workers' living standards, but that this was not feasible at present (2009) because labour costs were already too high compared to the other group affiliates in Vietnam and Laos.

In contrast, the workers seemed more keen than the manager on having wages better reflect organizational and technological changes (especially in Companies 1 and 2).

These differences may also sometimes be due to asymmetric information. As a typical example, workers in Company 1 were not really aware of the fact that their overtime on Saturdays was not remunerated as it should be. As a result, they indicated that the company should be making only 'some' progress in this area, while the management – clearly better informed about its own policy – knew perfectly well that they were not respecting the law and that they should be making 'most' progress in rewarding overtime. There was also a gap in Company 1 between workers' and management perceptions of the company's wage practices in relation to price increases, with workers indicating that real wages had gone down, while the management said the opposite. The same applied to social dialogue: the management did not believe that more negotiations, either individual or collective, were needed, especially during the current crisis, while the workers wanted to see a more negotiated wage policy.

In general, in the two companies in which the piece rate system dominated, workers expressed their dissatisfaction with wages that did not reflect skills and education, and reported that this dimension would need most progress (Company 1) or at least some progress (Company 3). Interestingly, it was Company 2 – which did not rely on piece rates, but on a basic wage and grid system – at which workers reported that no change was needed in this area, reflecting their satisfaction with the extent to which wages reflected skills, education and professional experience.

There were also differences between the opinions of skilled and unskilled workers, as in Company 1, where skilled workers – who were found to be paid less than unskilled – wanted the company to make some progress to improve the link between wages and organisational and technological changes, while unskilled workers did not see any need for change in this respect. In Company 3, skilled workers were more concerned about whether wages were comparable to those of competing companies.

6.4 REACTIONS TO THE FINANCIAL AND ECONOMIC CRISIS

The interviews enabled us to observe the reactions to the economic crisis in the three companies and to identify the effects it was having on wage practices.

At the same time, state intervention to overcome the crisis has created a new operational framework for Chinese companies. In this section, we first provide an overview of government measures within the economic crisis and then identify the effects of the crisis in the three individual enterprises and their fair wage performance in this new context.

National Response to the Crisis

The Chinese government, like other industrialised countries, has reacted swiftly to the crisis. Its measures, aimed initially at providing assistance to the banking sector, have been extended to other areas, including employment and working conditions. In this last area, the objective has clearly been to preserve as many jobs as possible, thereby avoiding massive layoffs. A number of measures have thus been proposed to help enterprises cope with the crisis and to induce them to retain their labour force.

The factories' strategies for facing the crisis, therefore, have to be implemented in such a new policy context. On 17 November 2008, the Chinese government delayed the annual minimum wage increase. Delaying the minimum wage increase was intended to stabilise wage costs in order not to increase the burden on factories experiencing difficulties as a result of the crisis. The minimum wage freeze allowed the government to kill two birds with one stone: (i) it helps factories to manage wage cost growth by allowing them to stay in business without resorting to layoffs; and (ii) it helps workers to keep their jobs and incomes.

Table 6.14 Anti-crisis measures taken by national authorities, China, 2009–2010

Direct assistance to avoid job losses	– Local government unemployment benefit surplus to subsidise struggling enterprises
	– Government subsidies for peasants/migrant workers
Onsite vocational training	– Training: national and local authorities encourage enterprises to provide onsite vocational training for employees who would otherwise be laid off and offer financing for such programmes
	– Possibility of delaying tax payments
	– Enhanced role of state-owned enterprises in maintaining employment
	– Close monitoring of foreign companies operating at low capacity or closing down
Measures to ease the unemployment burden	– Spread out layoff compensation payments: allow companies which have difficulty paying compensation for layoffs in a lump sum to pay in instalments (with approval of workers and/or trade unions)
	– Guidance from government (layoff plans)
	– Inclusion of migrant workers in formal channels (job information)
	– Increase unemployment benefits and medical benefits
Wages	– Freeze minimum wage at 2008 level
Working time/wages	– Flexible working hours and pay
Social insurance	– Temporary delay (six months) of social insurance contribution payments for enterprises in difficulty – Temporary reduction of social insurance contribution rate for enterprises in difficulty for a period that should not exceed 12 months – If local bureaus have a surplus after paying unemployment benefits, the surplus can be used to pay a social insurance contribution subsidy to enterprises which are experiencing difficulty, but have already taken active measures, such as onsite training, rotation resting, post shifting and other measures to avoid laying off workers
Social dialogue	– Enhance role of trade unions – Trade unions must be informed about payment delays – Settle labour disputes promptly – Pilot negotiations and collective agreements (for instance, at provincial level)

Source: Circular on *Easing the burdens on enterprises and stabilising labour relations*, 2008.

Later, in December 2008, the central government released a circular describing several policy changes designed to ease the burden on enterprises and stabilise labour relations. The circular, released jointly by the Ministry of Human Resources and Social Security and the Ministry of Finance, allowed enterprises in difficulty to delay the payment of social insurance contributions for six months, reduced contribution rates and introduced the possibility of a subsidy for paying social insurance and/or workers' wages, financed from the surplus unemployment benefits of local governments. The central government also made it possible for enterprises to access financing for onsite vocational training as a means of avoiding layoffs.

With regard to employment, several subsidies have been proposed to help companies to keep their labour force and avoid layoffs. Keeping certain categories of workers in employment, such as migrant workers and peasants – through subsidies or training programmes – has also been a specific target. The government has also started closely monitoring the operation of multinational companies to ensure that they will not implement significant layoffs.

One obvious way of protecting employment consisted in providing enterprises with opportunities to reduce costs. Employers' social insurance contribution rates have been lowered and the possibility of delaying tax or even social contribution payments has also been introduced. It is for the same reason that the decision to freeze the minimum wage in 2009 was also taken at national level, before being implemented in every province in China. More flexibility in the use of working time and wages has also been introduced. The measures taken at national level are summarized in Table 6.14.

Measures have also been taken with regard to unavoidable layoffs. Enterprises that had difficulty paying severance payments to laid-off workers in a lump sum were allowed to pay in instalments, after negotiating with the enterprise's trade union.

What Implications at Company Level?

Our interviews enabled us to collect information on the companies' reactions to the economic crisis.

Towards a collapse of production?

The global recession that is affecting all industrialised countries, which represent the main export markets of Chinese garment suppliers, has obviously had an impact on their operations. In this context, we can only expect real wages to go down and thus also the wage share.

Not surprisingly, the three visited companies reported a decline in profits in 2009 and acknowledged having more difficulties than before in getting new orders. Large orders from brands, in particular, were more difficult to obtain.

Nevertheless, the three companies remained fairly confident that they would manage to overcome the crisis. In Company 1 – and also Company 2 – this was certainly due to the support of the parent company that helped them to survive despite the current lack of profits. This may also be the reason why both the managers and the workers reported that they expected their company to do better than its competitors in the crisis. In Company 3, the manager was confident about his three-year plan to improve its competitiveness.

This self-confidence on the part of the three companies could be explained in a number of other ways. First, it might reflect the more comfortable financial position of companies that have an established relationship with the brands, especially if they are supported by a parent company. Obviously, these companies have more capacity and margins to survive the crisis than small companies, many of which are already closing down. The manager of Company 3 reported that he expected many small companies to close down and that only the largest would survive, competing fiercely for contracts.

At the same time, we believe that this does not fully reflect reality. After all, even parent companies have run into trouble during the crisis, which may also impact directly on their affiliates. Parent companies also have a tendency to compare the respective labour costs of their affiliates, so that the management of affiliates in China may quickly become vulnerable. We believe that the management was expressly optimistic about the crisis because it was afraid of giving the workers the impression that they may have difficulties in the future and eventually have to implement some layoffs or reduce wages. The management knew that the immediate reaction from the workers would be to leave the company for a better paying competitor in the same province or in a better paying province. Interviews with both the management and the workers confirmed that, even during the crisis, the management was afraid that workers would leave the company. At the same time, it is surprising that, despite management fears, workers so far had been unable to establish a better bargaining position and obtain better wages. This may be explained by the absence of organised labour and workers' representatives within the companies. The labour force remained fragmented, was poorly informed about wages and working conditions and its relations with the manager tended to be on an individual basis, represented by individual labour contracts and the absence of collective bargaining and collective agreements. It is possible, moreover, that, as the crisis continues and employment prospects deteriorate, workers may find it increasingly difficult to move from one company to another or from one province to another.

Employment: limited adjustments

Interestingly, in the three visited companies, employment had so far not been the adjustment variable for coping with the crisis. Company 1 did not foresee any employment cuts, although it intended to temporarily freeze new hiring in the expectation of decreasing orders. Company 2 will also not engage in employment cuts, especially since in 2006–2008 it already lost a significant number of employees (40 per cent), who moved to better paying provinces. Company 3 also decided to retain all its labour force during the crisis, also in the belief that this would leave it in a better competitive position after the crisis is over. This decision not to cut employment is due to a combination of phenomena. First, those companies that produce for external markets to survive will need to continue working for brands. Since they are already working at their maximum capacity, reducing the labour force but making the remaining employees work more intensively with more overtime does not seem very realistic – although this is what Company 2 seems to have tried to do so far. They need, therefore, to retain their labour force to keep going with the same production volume, and even if they face decreasing orders they still have the flexibility to reduce overtime payments to bring down their labour costs – although we saw that companies already do not pay overtime according to the law. The second explanation may have to do with the national regulations on employment, which are rather strict compared to other countries. It is interesting to note that the companies complained about too rigid employment regulations in China, which do not allow companies to get rid of their employees without significant costs.

Overtime as a possible adjustment variable
These factors led the three interviewed suppliers to find other strategies to cope with the crisis. Some opted for simple non-payment of overtime, as in Company 1, where overtime on Saturdays will continue not to be remunerated in accordance with legal rates. When asked about the crisis, the management replied that overtime will certainly be at the core of the adjustment process, in the first instance, with overtime being reduced in order to cope with decreasing orders, but then with continuing underpayment of overtime in order to reduce labour costs, while still meeting tight deadlines which would not be possible without overtime.

Company 3 also clearly stipulated that, during the crisis, the non-payment of overtime would be part of the coping strategy. They would thus rely even more than before on unpaid overtime, as reported by the – particularly open – management. Interestingly, the workers, who had been well coached in preparation for the auditing, reported either – in the case of the unskilled – that they had never worked overtime, or that – in the case of the skilled workers – that they had worked overtime which had always been paid, although they were unable to explain how the system worked, thereby confirming that no overtime payment system existed in the company.

In contrast, Company 2 – which was expecting more problems paying overtime during the crisis – was exploring possible ways of reducing overtime.

Whether this was a realistic strategy in a company which had already lost 40 per cent of its employees, and thus can have only limited flexibility to implement work sharing, is another question.

Other areas seem to be directly affected by the crisis. Training was among the first budget headings to be cut by management, as in Company 3. This may well have adverse effects on the quality of the labour force, although the latter was identified by all three companies as a core factor in their future competitiveness. The initiatives taken by the national authorities to encourage training may, to some extent, limit this adverse effect on human resources.

Wages again the residual at the end of the chain
The decision by local authorities to freeze the minimum wage may have direct implications. While the increase in the official minimum wage in 2007–2008 played a role in maintaining wage costs in proportion to total production costs, and limiting wage disparity, the crisis, together with the decision by local authorities – on instructions from central government – to freeze the minimum wage may reverse wage trends.

When asked about it, the management at all three companies claimed that they did not anticipate any additional difficulties in the payment of wages in the context of the crisis. No change in their wage practices was planned. However, the elements they provided led us to think exactly the opposite.

First, it is interesting that all three companies that experienced an increase in their wage costs in 2007–2008 were not expecting any further increase in these wage costs during the crisis. The manager of Company 1 justified its announced wage freeze on the basis of the local government decision to freeze the minimum wage after its historic increase in 2008 (from RMB 750 to 850). We can thus predict that wage costs will fall in 2009 in many Chinese suppliers, especially in comparison with other production costs, thereby again showing that wages are the adjustment variable. This confirms the need to continue monitoring wage costs as a fair wage dimension.

Second, the minimum wage freeze may also lead to the stagnation of the lowest wages in comparison to the wages of other categories of employee, such as managers, but also skilled workers and supervisors. This might also lead wages to lose some of their living-wage function in the crisis, while also potentially increasing wage disparities, as we shall see below. Workers in Companies 1 and 2 were not sure what would happen to the minimum wage in light of the crisis, indicating that they were not entirely confident.

Third, real wage decline was to be expected. While keeping the nominal wage constant – that is, reducing real wages – was clearly a coping strategy in Company 3, a decline in real wages was also expected in the other two companies. In Company 2, the manager clearly stated that wages would not be adjusted to price increases and the workers were not sure whether they would soon experience even some nominal wage cuts. In Company 1, which so far had maintained relatively high wages, notably by complementing basic wages with an annual bonus related to enterprise performance, the management did not anticipate any increase in nominal wages in 2009, which would mean that wages would lose some ground compared to price increases.

These expected downward wage trends rather contradict the statements made by the managements of the three companies concerning the importance of avoiding falling wages during the crisis: in Company 2 in order not to lose any more workers, in Company 3 to motivate skilled employees and in Company 1 to avoid labour shortages in the province of Jiangsu in the face of expected labour migration to higher wage areas, such as Shanghai and Guangdong.

This trend may reduce workers' living standards even further, as reported in the visited companies. It may also further motivate workers to leave the company to find better pay elsewhere, something that may be catastrophic for Company 2 at a time when they need their workforce to be able to respond to the orders of their contractors, thereby ensuring that they will be able to overcome the crisis. Unless the crisis – with fewer employment opportunities – reduces labour mobility between provinces.

Paradoxically, the managers may really have believed that by keeping nominal wages constant they were doing the right thing in order to preserve workers' purchasing power, without realizing that constant nominal wages mean declining real wages and lower worker purchasing power. It could also be that they know but do not want to frighten the workers. As openly stated by the manager in Company 3, 'wages constitute an important signal to workers concerning the company's health and stability. If they are reduced, the company gives a signal that it is not doing well. The workers become nervous and leave for a more stable environment.'

Many managers put the responsibility on the contractors. The managers said that under the conditions imposed by the brands, combined with the crisis, they did not know how long they could keep the business running. This is why, in Company 1, some diversification has taken place: the management has invested outside Nanjing, which is very likely to expand in the coming years, so that the value of their land can only increase, thereby enabling the company to recoup its investment at any time by selling its facilities and the land purchased at a reduced price.

Decline in some bonuses and even non-monetary incentives
Owing to the crisis, the three companies' non-monetary benefits seem to have become less generous, although the opposite policy might have been expected by the workers. It was significant that, in 2009, the workers in Company 3 were asked by the management to start paying for their electricity and water consumption, previously paid by the company. This clearly reduced the

workers' living standards. At the same time, the companies continued not to provide paid holidays, as requested by the law. There were no signs of any willingness in the three companies to comply with this legal obligation in 2009–2010. This might also be due to poor labour inspection to ensure legal compliance on work issues, a fact that could only be worsened by the urge towards greater flexibility in the world of work – for instance, in terms of flexible working hours and pay – introduced by the government in the face of the economic crisis.

Minimum wage policy effects on wage disparity and working poor

Due to the crisis, a further increase in wage disparity was foreseen by both the management and the workers in Companies 1 and 2. In Company 3, the signs were perceived to point in the same direction, with skilled workers reporting that their nominal wages had increased, while unskilled workers reported that they had not. Skilled workers also appeared to be more confident that they would weather the crisis without serious problems, while unskilled workers reported that they were worried.

This increased wage disparity could be the first direct consequence of the minimum wage freeze at local level. There was also a more pronounced difference between those at the bottom and those at the top or in the middle.

Second, this might also be due to the expectation that skilled workers will be able to cope with the crisis, since they continue to be in demand, especially because of their ability to leave in order to find better wages and working conditions elsewhere. We might expect, however, that, if the crisis prevails for many months and even years, the ability of workers to move from one company to another might be significantly reduced.

Tensions with regard to pay systems

Within the crisis, tensions also seem to have arisen within internal pay systems, dominated by piece rates. In Company 1, the use of this system in the crisis had become more and more problematic. In fact, in tandem with decreasing orders, most workers were not achieving piece rate payments above the mandatory minimum wage. This was found to be very poorly motivating, especially for those who worked hardest and in the end did not receive much more than those who did less and were paid the minimum wage anyway. The piece rate was, therefore – and even more than before – clearly at odds with the minimum wage. If the crisis persists, this might lead to wage levels below the legal minimum wage, even if the minimum wage rate does not increase.

The crisis could offer a good opportunity among some suppliers to shift from the piece rate system to another, more motivating and better adapted pay system. This was echoed by skilled workers, who reported that their wages did not sufficiently reflect their skills and educational background, a link that they would like to see systematically introduced by their company. This claim should not be neglected by the management, which stated that one of its objectives in the crisis was to better motivate the workers – especially the most skilled ones – and to retain their services.

Managers' new interest in linking wages to company performance

We have seen that, in recent years, the managers have not been very keen on sharing increased sales and profit growth with the workers – there was no link between company performance and wages. In the interviews, we noticed that the reduced number of orders and general economic recession had led the managers to reconsider the link – non-existent so far – between wages and company performance, with a hidden agenda of allowing wages to fall when there was a dip in performance.

In general, the managers stated the need to link wages to individual performance even more than previously, while also improving the part of wages related to collective (enterprise) performance, so that they would go down in the case of a profit reduction and rise in a period of increased profits. This also corresponds to a fundamental wish on the part of the workers to see their wages linked to company performance. At the same time, experience in other countries shows that, while the promotion of profit-sharing schemes can be effective in periods of expansion, the same cannot be said for periods of economic slowdown, when their introduction could be interpreted by the workers as an attempt by the management to reduce workers' wages in response to the crisis.

Nevertheless, the period of crisis could be useful in changing attitudes and preparing for the development of profit-sharing or performance-related pay schemes, if managers were ready to develop such schemes as soon as economic growth reappears.

Uncertain effect on work intensity

The crisis may affect intensity at work in a number of possible directions. On the one hand, decreasing orders may lead to less intensive working conditions, as expected by workers in Company 2. With wages remaining constant, workers may thus enjoy less stressful working rhythms.

On the other hand, in Company 1, the manager said that the decreasing number of large orders was leading to more frequent changes on the company's assembly lines in order to cope with multiple, diverse small orders, so that, ultimately, the impact on work intensity may not be positive. It may also result in more, not less overtime, especially because brands still impose the same timeframes for the delivery of orders, even though there may be fewer of them due to the crisis. Thus, overtime and even work intensity may increase, which is what seems to have happened in Company 2.

Table 6.15 Reactions to the crisis in the three companies

	Company 1	Company 2	Company 3
Employment	– No cuts expected – But new recruitments frozen due to expected decrease in orders – Labour migration observed to better paying provinces (Shanghai, Guangdong)	– In 2007 a considerable number of employees lost who moved to better paying provinces – Would like to retain its labour force	– No cuts expected
Production	Decreasing orders		Imposing tighter contracts on suppliers
Profits	Plans to make 2009 the first profit-making year called into question by the crisis; support from parent company to maintain employment and wages	Reduced profits expected	Further profit reduction expected by management; but not confirmed by statistics showing continued profits
Business strategy	Not defined	Not defined	Continuing to get contracts with brands but cutting wages and increasing overtime
Normal working time	–	–	–
Overtime	– Payment of OT expected to be more difficult – Non-paid OT on Saturdays will continue	– Payment of OT expected to be more difficult – One solution, according to the manager, is to limit OT, if possible – Remains to be seen whether this is realistic after 40% decline in employment level in 2006–2008	Will be increased without being remunerated

Table 6.15 (cont.)

	Company 1	Company 2	Company 3
Wages	– Despite relatively high wages, no further wage increases anticipated (meaning a real wage decline) – Tensions between minimum wage and use of piece rates	Real wage decrease expected (possibly also nominal wage cuts, according to workers)	Deliberate policy not to increase nominal wages anymore (so real wages will fall)
Bonuses and non-monetary benefits	– Decreasing	– Decreasing	– Workers are now asked to pay for their electricity and water
Other working conditions	–	Intensity at work increased, along with 40% voluntary quits, but it may now decline with decreasing orders	Training reduced
Social dialogue	– Necessary to manage the crisis, according to the management – Workers declared that social dialogue could help them keep up with crisis developments and effects on company	Social dialogue seen as important within the crisis, by both the manager and the workers, but the trade union must redefine its role (get involved in bargaining)	Not seen as a priority during the crisis, although the workers have expectations in this field

Moreover, the crisis may also lead to a reduction in employment and thus, in the end, to a higher work volume for the remaining workers. This might lead to more, not less intensive working conditions. This is why it is important to check how the employment level of the company has been evolving: if orders remain the same, or even decrease, but employment is significantly reduced, we might expect a more intensive production process. Although this should normally lead to higher wages, increasing unemployment and the general climate of economic crisis may weaken the workers' bargaining position even further, with corresponding adverse effects on wages. In fact, as we have seen, real wage declines have already been observed in the interviewed companies.

Good intentions on social dialogue not put into practice

Two of the three managers interviewed (at Companies 1 and 2) reported that they believed it was necessary to strengthen social dialogue with the workers in response to the crisis. However, this willingness does not seem to have been followed by much action to promote collective bargaining and social dialogue – even communication channels – with the workers. In Company 2, the lack of social dialogue was said by the manager to be the direct outcome of a poor trade union strategy and efforts to promote collective bargaining. While this may be partly true, no doubt the management could also play a significant role in developing social dialogue, notably by allowing workers' representatives to be more closely involved in such issues as working conditions, wages and even the company's strategy to cope with the crisis. In Company 3, there was an overt antipathy towards trade unions and a clear determination to undermine their potential role in the management of the company: 'the trade unions are not useful and do not work in China because if you give people rights they do not know how to use them'. It seemed to be deliberate management policy not to involve the trade unions in collective bargaining.

6.5 'FAIR WAGE' LESSONS

The case studies were useful because they complemented the auditing exercise well, first, by providing more information on the different practices and policies implemented by suppliers on wage issues and, then, by helping to identify their coping strategies for overcoming the current crisis, as well as their direct effects on wages.

Confirmed Need for a Comprehensive Approach

These case studies on wage reactions during the crisis confirmed the need to analyse wage trends in their different dimensions in order to get the full story. In Company 3, for instance, the decision of the manager to keep nominal wages constant – thus decreasing real wages – should be seen in light of his strategy to further increase non-paid overtime. In combination, this is likely to mean not only more intensive and longer working hours, but also decreasing purchasing power. The workers will work even more but will lose out in terms of wages, a situation that could lead, at the very least, to general demotivation, but which also threatens more serious social tensions on the workers' side. This would be detrimental both to workers and management, as well as the company as a whole.

Absence of a Clear Coping Strategy during the Crisis

More generally, Companies 1 and 2 lacked a clear strategy to overcome the crisis. They tried to cope by means of adjustments, such as non-payment of overtime, but no deep restructuring or reorientation of production was planned. For instance, no thought had been given to possible redirection of trade flows.

This absence of a clear strategy is obviously reflected in working conditions among suppliers, with wages appearing again, in most cases, as the ultimate adjustment variable. While this became a de facto effect in Companies 1 and 2, it was clearly formulated by the manager in Company 3 as part of a strategic plan based on a restrictive policy, in terms of both wages and raw materials, aimed at coping with onerous contract terms imposed by the brands.

Direct Effects on Wages and Working Conditions Legitimize 'Fair Wage' Monitoring

Interviews in the visited enterprises showed that real wages were expected to suffer in the crisis, together with non-monetary benefits, which the companies had provided fairly generously so far. A deterioration in working conditions was also to be expected, with a greater risk of unpaid overtime and increased work intensity without wage compensation. In Company 2, the manager clearly stated that they will face more difficulties honouring the payment of overtime and that one solution might be to reduce overtime. However, the brands do not permit much flexibility with regard to schedules, so that the ultimate solution for suppliers consists in retaining overtime, but reducing payment for both overtime and regular working time. This explains the discrepancy between the workers and the managers with regard to company performance during the crisis: while the managers report declining profits, the workers have the feeling that the company is doing fairly well, if not even better than before, based on the amount of overtime they are being asked to do and their assessment of orders received.

As more factories close and others stop hiring new employees, this should result in lower mobility between provinces, which will increase downward pressure on wages. While worker mobility was previously an incentive for suppliers to offer decent wages to retain skilled labour, the reduced prospects for migration may induce factories to lower wages, especially if they are themselves squeezed by the brands. Since workers will have fewer opportunities to seek work elsewhere, they may be forced to accept lower wages or working conditions. All fair wage dimensions will thus require continuous monitoring.

Table 6.16 Main effects on fair wages expected from the crisis

Payment of wages/underpayment	Expected to increase
'Living wage' function of minimum wages and wages in general	To be reduced together with expected decline in real wages
Starting/minimum wages in the companies	To be frozen in response to national/local policy unless companies decide on another policy route
Prevailing wage	Wages compared to competitors will depend on the capacity of the enterprises to survive the crisis and also to get orders from the brands
Payment of overtime	Further non-compliance reported
Pay systems	No improvement expected
Social dialogue	Expected to develop with new opportunities for discussions within the crisis
Wage disparity	Wage disparity increasing between workers at the bottom and the others, mainly because of the minimum wage freeze
Real wages	Will depend on inflation but should be expected to decrease slightly, with even nominal wage cuts in many companies; minimum wage freeze should further reduce workers' purchasing power
Wage share	To be further reduced, with wages decreasing more than company profits
Wage costs	To be decreased in tandem with the minimum wage freeze and other restrictions on wage increases
Wage intensity	– In many suppliers, lower number of orders may lead to lower work intensity – In others, it may be increased because of more diversified orders and, in some cases, reduced employment but with same or similar sales volume; such changes will not be reflected in wages

Role of the State: Extending the Scope of Non-compliance?

The policy changes proposed by the state in response to the crisis has undoubtedly had a significant impact on wages among Chinese suppliers. This new policy environment may have the direct result of confirming wages more generally as the main adjustment variable. With employment trumping wages, the new crisis policies may reflect a step backwards in relation to the progressive 2008 Labour Law as far as wages are concerned. The shift in minimum wage policy is the most illustrative, if one compares the impressive increase in 2008 to the general freeze in the statutory minimum wage in 2009. Similarly, the new flexibility granted to factories with regard to social insurance greatly lowers the threshold for compliance, even though the state now at least insists on and thus legitimises the companies' payment of social security to the workers. This legitimisation will, however, elude workers in factories that have hitherto evaded social insurance payments: the factories that were not paying their contributions in the past will certainly not put themselves in the spotlight by participating in the payment delay programme.

The new policies have had adverse effects not only on minimum wages, but also on wages in general. Suggesting a nominal wage freeze represents a fairly strong sign to the employers that they should freeze wages in general and reduce their wage costs. Workers will thus immediately feel a decrease in purchasing power, especially if inflation resumes its rise or if the international food crisis continues. This focus on nominal wages rather than real wages is worrying from a fair wage standpoint.

Finally, the crisis may also have a direct effect on enforcement mechanisms. There are indications that the economic crisis may prompt governments to turn a blind eye to factory non-compliance in the name of job protection and social stability. Company 3's manager was confident that the government would rather see factories not pay overtime but keep employees than implement massive layoffs.

The new policy environment may nevertheless have some positive effects on factories and their wage policies. By strengthening the role of trade unions in the discussion of layoffs and/or the implementation of flexibility measures, the government may help to instil a culture of social dialogue in factories. This will ultimately depend on the capacity of the trade unions to transform themselves into real actors in social dialogue and collective bargaining.

Another positive aspect of the Chinese policy response to the crisis is the encouragement of onsite vocational training. Training was, admittedly, not prevalent in the factories we visited and our auditing exercise confirmed that this is a general phenomenon in almost all companies. If training can help to lower costs by increasing productivity, however, some pressure could be taken off wages.

Companies Facing Alternative Wage Strategies

At the moment, the Chinese government has decided to freeze the minimum wage in order to give priority to employment and companies seem to be at a crossroads in terms of wage policy.

On the one hand, the most obvious and tempting route for companies may be to follow the minimum wage freeze, which may help them to reduce labour costs and so maintain employment. At the same time, the facilities proposed by the government – to reduce or postpone employers' social insurance contributions – will also help to reduce labour costs. A restrictive wage policy, however, may turn out to be counterproductive. A minimum wage freeze at company level would certainly have detrimental effects on the most vulnerable workers and their living standards. Such a freeze, if it were reflected throughout the wage scale, would also mean a deteriorating wage situation for all workers, with obvious effects, not only on the workers and their purchasing power, but also on the company, with risks of continued labour turnover, reduced productivity, lower production quality and lower motivation and attendance. This may affect companies' competitive base, which is crucial for emerging from the crisis and developing rapidly thereafter.

On the other hand, companies may decide to follow another route and to define their own wage policy in light of their own circumstances. In Company 1, attempts to improve pay levels and systems may help the management to meet its objective of retaining a highly skilled labour force. Similarly, in Company 2, given its specific employment context, with 40 per cent of employees already having left the company, the management may opt for a strategy aimed at keeping its current labour force, while strengthening its wage policy by both improving its pay system and progressively increasing wage levels. Finally, Company 3 may also use its high performance in terms of sales and profits to invest in both technology and human resources – notably through a good wage policy – so that they would be better positioned to compete. Training current employees to produce better quality products could reduce waste and help to maintain profitability. Currently, the Chinese government is providing subsidies for training employees who would otherwise be let go by companies in distress. Company 3 could take advantage of these subsidies to train its employees and strengthen its competitive position post-crisis.

The management may thus consider going beyond the minimum wage freeze proposed at central level in order to maintain workers' purchasing power and follow a higher value-added route that could pay off in the current crisis. Good quality products and a motivated labour force could only result in increasing orders from the brands and lead the companies into a better competitive position, as long as the immediate external pressures are not too high to reduce their labour costs overall.

Responsibility and Action on the Part of the Brands

The crisis has made the suppliers even more vulnerable with regard to the brands. They are more dependent than before on their contracts and their bargaining position is deteriorating. Competition between suppliers for contracts will be even tougher, especially in a general climate of bankruptcies involving the most vulnerable – generally smaller – companies.

This heightens the urgency of wage initiatives along the supply chain and in particular of making the brands more sensitive and thus more responsive to wage issues among their sub-contractors. In particular, suppliers reported that when the prices of raw materials increased at the end of 2007 and early 2008 the brands did not relax their policy, but imposed even tighter conditions. This obviously led suppliers to offset increasing raw material prices, not by raising prices – because of the inflexibility of the brands – but by reducing wage costs. According to the manager of Company 3, the brands are aware of this situation and of the implications for wages and working conditions, but continue to operate a 'Don't ask, don't tell' policy. The manager added that it is well known that the garment industry depends on overtime, with most of it not being paid, so that the brands have a responsibility. If, alongside the current economic slowdown, the prices of raw materials also increased, the impact on wages would be catastrophic.

CONCLUSIONS

Our case studies and our fair wage approach – and its comprehensive nature – allowed us to provide a first assessment of the effects of the current economic crisis on the wage front. The crisis is, in fact, expected to influence almost all the fair wage dimensions identified in this book. While real wages are expected to go down, together with wage costs, a fall in real wages – and, in many cases, also nominal wages – higher than the decline in profits was reported and should lead to a further deterioration of the wage share. The minimum wage freeze imposed by the government in this area has also directly influenced companies' behaviour in this regard, with worrying effects expected in terms of declining living standards and increased wage disparity. At the same time, the government's priority of maintaining employment was interpreted as carte blanche for non-compliance on such important matters as the payment of wages, underpayment and the non-remuneration of overtime, which was clearly expected in the three interviewed companies. Such adverse trends identified in this exercise provide further justification for continuing the monitoring exercise. This book has proposed a methodology for this purpose that will be pursued further by the FLA. It is also clearly urgent to start addressing these issues along the supply chain, not only with the suppliers, but also with the brands. We could see how much the brands' policies and, sometimes, lack of flexibility (or willingness) to renegotiate the terms of their contracts with their suppliers, together with their lack of involvement on fair wage issues – such as the non-payment of overtime and excessively low wages – was, in the end, influencing wage practices along the supply chain. The crisis clearly shows the responsibility they should assume in such important areas. Incorporating wage issues in the CSR process has become more important than ever, if CSR objectives are to be met.

Policy Conclusions

7. Towards a Fair Wage Campaign

7.1 LESSONS FROM GLOBAL WAGE TRENDS

The wage trends identified in Chapter 1 paint a rather worrying picture. Wage moderation with inadequate adjustment of real wages, a continuous decline in the wage share and increasing wage differentials seem to show that the global economy is beset by problems in the redistribution of economic wealth between capital and labour. Many eminent economists have claimed that this failure to redistribute the fruits of growth, with low wages that are insufficient to sustain consumption and increasing income disparity, is one of the main causes of indebtedness and so of the financial crisis that has now turned into a deep recession. This means that the crisis will not be resolved in its full profundity unless solutions are found to these income problems.

Moreover, our data show that, while wages have struggled to keep up with economic growth for the last 15 years, they tend to be even more vulnerable during and immediately after economic crises – as illustrated by repeated crises in Latin America, Asia and Central and Eastern Europe – in consequence of which we might expect the current economic crisis to lead to even more unbalanced and unsustainable wage developments. Wage data in 2008–2009 already show a decline in real average wages and minimum wages.

7.2 CSR DEFICIT ON WAGES

At the same time, a number of wage problems have been identified along the supply chain, notably, a growing number of working poor, with wages among suppliers which often are not sufficient to provide workers and their families with a living wage. As a result, concerns are growing with regard to wage issues within the framework of corporate social responsibility (CSR). A number of NGO initiatives on living wages or fair wages have been launched, reflecting CSR actors' own concerns. We have seen that the trade unions have rung the alarm bell about wage trends and have launched a major campaign to promote more sustainable wage developments, while enterprises themselves are beginning to be concerned by a number of wage issues, such as wage disparity and the remuneration of top managers, the increase in the number of low-paid workers and its impact on consumption, and difficulties retaining motivated and skilled employees. A number of governments and municipalities have also launched initiatives to maintain wage standards in tandem with processes such as privatization, outsourcing and increased capital and labour mobility. A number of standards also exist at international level, notably based on the ILO conventions. Nevertheless, all these initiatives remain rather limited in scope and in the number of wage dimensions that they take into account.

Both international and national initiatives put the emphasis on the minimum wage, the protection of wages, wage discrimination and the payment of hours worked, while many other dimensions remain uncovered, including real wages, the wage share and living wages – for instance, there are no International Labour Standards in relation to the latter. This might also be the reason why, so far, NGOs – through benchmarking and codes of conduct – have mainly put their efforts into monitoring companies' legal compliance with regard to existing international labour standards on wage issues. At the same time – and, in this case, in response to the absence of standards at national and international level – most NGOs have decided to develop the living wage concept and make it operational on the ground. While this movement has been beneficial and has helped to increase wages in many parts of the world – with very good examples in many US states and Canada – the approach may have become too focused on living wages, behind which many other wage problems remain hidden. Moreover, initiatives on wages within CSR have remained too fragmented, with no coherence in terms of the issues covered and without the development of general principles and overall coherence by CSR actors. This seriously undermines any attempts to move forward in this area, especially since wages continue to represent a major component of labour costs over which employers are keen to maintain full control, despite isolated attempts on the part of the brands to improve the wage-fixing process among their suppliers.

All these elements point to a need to launch a strong movement to incorporate wages into CSR. Table 7.1 confirms that relatively few of the 12 fair wage dimensions presented in this book benefit from ILO Conventions: protection of wages, minimum wages, discrimination and working time. Of course, even in the areas that are covered by International Labour Standards, auditing and enforcement, though easy in principle, are often difficult in practice. Even after an ILO convention has been ratified and transposed into national legislation, implementation is often lacking. It befalls the companies themselves to ensure proper implementation. Furthermore, some International Labour Standards were put in place a long time ago and may not always reflect the new reality and the needs of workers in a globalized context. This requires not only an updating and strengthening of some ILO conventions – such as the one on minimum wages, which is rather general, or those on social dialogue – but also more initiatives and benchmarking along the supply chain.

Table 7.1 Fair wage issues covered or missing at international level

	ILO Conventions	Other
Payment of wages	Convention 95 on protection of wages	
Minimum wage	Convention 26 (1928) on minimum wage Convention 131 (1970) on minimum wage	
Living wage	No specific convention; – but included in the Constitution of the ILO in 1919 (preamble to the Charter) – in Art. III (d) of the Declaration of Philadelphia, adopted by the International Labour Conference in 1944 – included indirectly in Convention 131 on minimum wages as one criterion for minimum wage fixing – included indirectly in Convention 156 and Recommendations 131 and 135 – included in ILO declaration on social justice for a fair globalization in 2008	Universal Declaration of Human Rights (UDHR) (1948), Article 23(3) UN Covenant on Economic, Social and Cultural Rights (ICESCR) (1966), which includes 'the right to a living wage', Art. 7(a)
Prevailing wage	Nothing	
Working time	Convention No. 1 on Hours of work (Industry), complemented by No. 30 on Hours of work (commerce and industry) and No. 47 on Forty-hour week.	
Pay systems	Nothing	
Social dialogue	Conventions No. 87 on Freedom of association, No. 98 on the Right to collective bargaining, Conventions No. 135 and 154	
Wage discrimination/disparity	Conventions No. 100 and 111 on equal employment opportunities and non-discrimination; also Convention No. 183 on Maternity protection	
Real wages	Nothing	
Wage share	Nothing	
Wage costs	Nothing	
Wages, work intensity, technology and upskilling	Nothing	

Even more needs to be done in those wage areas that do not benefit from any international convention, such as living wages, but also pay systems, real wages and the wage share. It is essential that all CSR actors take responsibility in these areas.

7.3 FAIR WAGE APPROACH TO INTEGRATING WAGES IN CSR

In this book, a new approach – the Fair Wage approach – is proposed, precisely to extend the number of wage dimensions taken into account and also to try to promote a methodology which may help to address all the different dimensions in a complementary way in any work involving auditing, assessment or policy advice among companies operating along the supply chain. Based on a number of wage dimensions, themselves captured by a range of fair wage indicators, this tool is proposed with the aim of helping directly to identify the various strengths and weaknesses in a company's wage policy, notably through drawing a Fair Wage matrix. Its purpose is also progressively to change mentalities and the scope of analysis in this field.

The fair wage approach is aimed at promoting responsibility on wage issues among actors in the supply chain, thereby enhancing wage practices among suppliers. It may also help to foster cooperation and responsibility on wages among the brands and encourage governments to establish a level playing field.

7.4 FAIR WAGE APPROACH BACKED UP BY FIELD WORK

The fair wage approach implemented through a first auditing of 31 companies and the qualitative case studies not only was extremely useful, but also yielded unique information. First-hand information was obtained on the different wage practices and policies implemented by suppliers, which also helped to identify the effects of the crisis on wages, as well as the place of wages in company coping strategies. The findings from the field work confirmed the need for the proposed fair wage approach. First, problems were identified in each of the 12 fair wage dimensions, confirming the need to retain all of them and to address them in mutual interaction.

At the same time, the field work confirmed that the problems of wage fixing along the supply chain will continue to prevail during the crisis and will even grow worse, since wages were again found to be used as the ultimate adjustment variable at all stages of the supply chain, with clear implications for all fair wage dimensions: enterprises were expected to have more problems in paying wages overall, but especially overtime and, in some cases, even the minimum wage. The companies investigated also did not intend to adjust wages to price increases or any measure of company performance or changes in work intensity, which may mean that wages perform their basic living wage function even less than before.

This field work on wage reactions within the crisis confirmed the usefulness of analysing wage trends in their various dimensions in order to get the full wage story. In Company 3, for instance, the decision of the manager not to decrease nominal wages must also be seen in terms of its potential effects on real wages – which will, therefore, decrease – and his strategy to further increase unpaid overtime, which in combination are likely to lead, not only to more intensive and longer working hours, but also to decreasing purchasing power for the workers. This is despite continuous improvements in sales and profits which in no way appear to be reflected in wages. This situation could lead, at the very least, to general demotivation, but also to social tensions on the workers' side. This would be detrimental to the workers, the management and the company as a whole.

The need to address wages along the supply chain is thus even stronger within the current crisis.

7.5 CONDITION NO. 1: SEEKING A NEW COMMITMENT ON WAGES FROM THE BRANDS

Our field work has helped to show that, as a result of the crisis, the suppliers are more vulnerable than ever in relation to the brands, having become more dependent on their contracts. In parallel with their weaker bargaining position, competition between suppliers to win contracts from the brands has become even tougher, in a general climate of bankruptcy among the most vulnerable – generally smaller – companies.

This makes it more urgent to launch wage initiatives along the supply chain and in particular to make the brands more sensitive and responsive to wage issues among their sub-contractors. In particular, suppliers reported that, when the prices of raw materials increased at the end of 2007 and early 2008, the brands did not relax their policy, but imposed even stricter conditions on their suppliers. Unable to respond to increasing raw material prices by raising their prices – because of the inflexibility of the brands – they sought to reduce wage costs. According to the managers of the interviewed companies, the brands are aware of this situation and its implications for wages and working conditions, but continue to operate a 'Don't ask, don't tell' policy. One manager added that it is well known that the garment industry depends on overtime, most of it unpaid, and so the brands have a certain responsibility.

There is thus a clear need for urgent action to ratchet up wages, especially in the global garment industry. Retailers have a critical role to play, since their buying power and influence over suppliers is often great. They clearly must do more to encourage their suppliers to be good employers and to integrate ethical trading principles into their core business decisions. Furthermore, the prices they pay their suppliers must allow the latter to pay their workers enough to live on without having to accumulate excessive hours. Any attempt to promote fair wage practices will be unsuccessful if the brands are not involved and participate in defining – and implementing – the different fair wage indicators and dimensions proposed. If a number of fair wage practices were simply imposed on the brands' operations in one country, it would be easy for them to relocate in search of more relaxed wage conditions elsewhere. In contrast, a brand's commitment to a number of fair wage practices could ensure that these are applied in all its operations, hopefully spilling over to other brands and suppliers.

7.6 CONDITION NO. 2: SETTING UP A GENERAL COOPERATIVE PLATFORM

It is also clear that brands alone cannot improve the wages of workers in their supply chains in far-off countries. Collaboration between brands and retailers, governments, suppliers, trade unions and other local organisations in sourcing countries is essential to achieving widespread, lasting change.

First, a new type of relationship is needed between the brands and their suppliers. Ensuring that wages provide a living wage, but also that they will be periodically adjusted to price increases, company performance and relevant changes in work intensity and technology certainly are not policies that the suppliers will be able to implement on their own without cooperation and support from the brands. Brands can also look for ways of rewarding suppliers for increasing wages – for example, by advising them on how to increase productivity. They can also signal to governments in sourcing countries that they prefer to buy from countries where conditions for workers are improving.

The action of NGOs is also essential to ensure that suppliers and brands work effectively in the right direction, as well as to ensure that fair wage practices are progressively introduced along the supply chain. We have seen that there is an increasing determination among NGOs to encourage better wage standards among suppliers, but they have suffered from a lack of coherence. We should thus channel their mobilization capacities towards a more coherent and more comprehensive framework, as proposed in the fair wage approach.

Cooperation between employers and workers is also essential. For example, calculating and agreeing on what a living wage should be in each country and region requires negotiations between workers' representatives, trade unions – where they exist – and employers' associations. Similarly, the elaboration of more balanced and more efficient pay systems should be done in collaboration between managers and workers' representatives. Trade unions could also help NGOs and company representatives to identify – and implement – the necessary wage indicators that may help to improve the situation.

Finally, there is also a clear need for self-sustaining efforts on the part of governments and brands, since one influences the other in both good and bad practices. We have seen that, in the past, there have been a number of national and local initiatives on wages, which emerged together with increased mobility of capital and labour and outsourcing. This has led, for instance, to the conclusion of fair wage or living wage agreements at local level, imposed by local authorities, such as the London Living Wage or the Fair Wage Schedules in several regions of Canada. Similarly, the increasingly global nature of trade and of labour markets calls for new initiatives on fair wages, both at national and local level.

Many elements of the multidimensional approach to fair wages might be envisaged as part of government wage policies. Governments could develop similar indicators and even add new ones which would be more appropriate to national than company level, such as the percentage of low-paid workers in the country (measured by the percentage of wages below two-thirds of the median wage) or wage disparity measured by the ratio of the minimum wage to the median or average wage.

Similarly, it may be necessary to instigate cooperation or common policies on wage issues between countries or regions. It is in this spirit that a number of common European minimum wage policy guidelines recently emerged at EU level: increased labour mobility in the EU after its enlargement to 27 countries has led, not only to public debates (on the possible implementation of a statutory minimum wage in Germany and Sweden) and action (national collective agreement in Austria) on minimum wages at national level, but also to proposals to establish common minimum wage-fixing principles at EU level, precisely to avoid social dumping with regard to minimum wages (Schulten, 2008; Vaughan-Whitehead, 2010).

A common approach at international level to develop a number of commonly agreed fair wage indicators may also be effective in ensuring real and general changes in wage practices along the supply chain, especially since the new global environment, with greater and easier movement of labour and capital, highlights the inadequacy of unilateral approaches. If a company is forced to pay a determinate living wage or higher wage in one country, it may simply relocate in search of cheaper labour, engaging in the kind of 'race to the bottom' already described in Chapter 1, with countries competing to provide the lowest possible wages in order to attract investment.

Enforcement mechanisms or internationally recognized fair wage benchmarking would be particularly useful.

7.7 CONDITION NO. 3: INSTITUTIONALIZING FAIR WAGE ASSESSMENT

We saw in Chapter 5 that the first step consists of collecting information on wages by inserting new questions on wages in the auditing exercise, but also by means of a number of case studies and interviews with both the managers and the employees. This led to a first general assessment of the situation in terms of fair wages and the identification of the most acute wage problems encountered at company level.

There is a need to continue the exploration of wage issues started in this book. Only more detailed and comprehensive assessment will help to make the public aware of what the wage problems are along the supply chain, while also helping CSR actors to better understand the value added that their mobilization on such fair wage issues might immediately provide.

The monitoring process on fair wages could be implemented more systematically in order to collect regular information on wage issues at enterprise level. Obtaining answers to the fair wage questionnaires on a regular basis – for example, annually – would help to follow the progression of individual enterprises and also help them progressively to face and solve fair wage problems. This regular process would also help to change employers' mentalities on wage issues and to bring these issues into the public domain. The FLA has adopted the Fair Wage approach and has built a self-assessment questionnaire on fair wages which the suppliers can fill in online. Obviously, such assessments and reviews will have to be carried out with the agreement of the brands, which, ideally, would participate in this approach. Open access to facilities and operations would also be needed.

7.8 PROPOSAL NO. 1: AN INTERNATIONAL FAIR WAGE NETWORK

The wage assessment introduced in the previous section can be used to develop a number of policy conclusions and identify areas in which improvements are needed and concrete action is urgent.

A multi-stakeholder strategic group, comprising employers – including suppliers and brands – workers' representatives, NGOs, independent researchers and academics, could be set up and asked to launch initiatives in this area. It would be ineffective if the fair wage approach was implemented by only one NGO or just a few brands. There should be a general movement towards better wage practices.

We propose, therefore, the creation of an International Fair Wage Network which could regroup all the actors involved along the supply chain and present in the CSR arena, who would be ready to commit themselves to work to promote better wage practices.

The idea is thus to take advantage of an interactive process, involving NGOs, managers, workers' representatives and researchers in order progressively to improve wages. The aim is gradually to move individual factories 'up the ladder', not only in terms of paying 'living wages' – which obviously remains a key element in assessing the fair wage scores of individual companies – but also on other elements we believe should be part of the 'fair wage' approach. In order to succeed, this process would require a step-by-step approach to overcome the possible difficulties involved in collecting information and avoiding possible initial reluctance from the different stakeholders.

The decision to launch such a network was decided among CSR actors at a first fair wage conference convened by the FLA in October 2009 in Washington. It led to the creation of a Fair Wage website (Fair-wage.org). This network represents a necessary tool for launching the cooperative platform already mentioned. It would also ensure the coherence needed in the wage area and help to liaise the proposed fair wage approach in relation to all wage initiatives at international and national level, for instance on living wages. It represents a key step in incorporating wage issues within the CSR process and could be followed by a fair wage campaign.

7.9 PROPOSAL NO. 2: A FAIR WAGE CAMPAIGN

There is a clear need to launch a campaign for better wage practices along supply chains and to engage the responsibility of the different actors, including the brands, on wage issues.

All relevant actors should be invited to do more to remind retailers of their responsibilities, including on wage issues. NGOs trying to better monitor the supply chain should be invited to present their views on wages and on fair wage indicators. Consumers could signal that they take fair wage practices into account when making their consumption decisions and that they prefer to buy from companies which have shown the most serious commitment to fair wage practices. Trade union representatives should continue to put pressure on companies to develop better wage practices. This campaign could also be an excellent opportunity for the brands to show their commitment to fair wages and to start to incorporate wages among their CSR standards.

One of the first initiatives could be the organization of a major international conference in which all stakeholders would participate and a comprehensive 'fair wage assessment' could be presented and debated, and policy issues discussed.

Some initial steps to raise public awareness on wage issues have already been taken at international level. For example, in September 2006, following the failure of the Bangladesh tripartite wage board to propose an acceptable minimum wage for the garment industry, the Clean Clothes Campaign (CCC) decided to intervene in the debate. After developing their key arguments for a minimum wage increase, they called on the different members of the MFA Forum Bangladesh buyer group to ensure that their factories would pay at least TK 3,000 (USD 35.53) as the entry-level wage. It is interesting to note that, among the key arguments to justify such an increase, the CCC mentioned issues such as price increases, but also the four-and-a-half-fold economic growth in the garment sector since 1994, increasing exports, increasing wages in other industrial sectors, the increased cost of basic food items and the new official (and independent) calculation of the living wage, as well as compliance with national law and international labour standards. The year 2009 was also characterized by the Asian Floor Wage Campaign, aimed at inducing brands and their suppliers to pay at least a minimum living wage, calculated in terms of purchasing power parity and on the basis of a minimum basket of goods intended to provide the minimum calories needed by workers and their families. This campaign managed to attract the attention of the public and the media in many Asian countries.

We should also mention the fair wage guide proposed in 2005 in the informal artisan economy by the fair trade crafts community. It was aimed at creating global standards for the payment of fair wages (in terms of which piece rate payments to artisans are converted into a daily-wage equivalent according to prices, materials and time) and creating a fair trade craft product label.

It is this type of approach that the current proposal seeks to implement in a more systematic and comprehensive way – notably by extending it beyond the garment industry and also taking into account more wage dimensions – and which could be promoted and legitimized by launching a large-scale campaign and a general mobilization of multiple stakeholders.

7.10 PROPOSAL NO. 3: A NEW WAGE BENCHMARKING APPROACH

While, as we have seen, many NGOs are already working on wage issues – mainly living wages – there is a need not only to widen the approach to more fair wage dimensions and indicators, but also to start to combine such efforts in order to develop a coherent and robust approach to wage issues along the supply chain.

A first step could consist in the reassessment and redefinition of wage indicators and also wage benchmarks by CSR actors. Their respective weights in the fair wage matrix may also be defined.

Wage standards need to be changed. For example, it is common to see the same standards proposed by different NGOs, such as the provision that 'wages should be fixed at the national minimum wage or the prevailing industry wage'. Nevertheless, we saw in our field work in China that this provision does not make much sense as, in a way, it puts the minimum wage and the industry average wage on the same level, while the majority of suppliers may adhere to the minimum wage but hardly pay the – difficult to achieve – average industry wage. Since most companies may have difficulties in respecting such a provision on the prevailing industry wage a more attainable standard may have to be set and, in any case, it must not be confused with the minimum wage. This led the FLA recently to change this provision.

Second, rather than concentrating only on legal wage issues (such as the minimum wage and overtime payments) – which should obviously remain basic requirements – or on living wages, codes of conduct (and thus companies' commitment to fair wages) should integrate many more wage items. Wages should not only provide a living wage, but also be complemented with non-monetary benefits; furthermore, pay systems (such as the piece rate) or bonuses (as for attendance) should be used in a balanced way which does not impose too much stress on the workers – for instance, inducing them to accumulate working hours and minimize rest time. Employers should, instead, promote balanced and diversified pay systems that reward individual and collective performance, while also reflecting workers' education, skills and professional experience. Workers should also receive all necessary information on their

Table 7.2 New proposed benchmarks on fair wages

General commitment to fair wages

Companies recognize that their practices should lead to sustainable wage developments. With this purpose in mind, individual employers commit themselves to paying fair wages, that is, wages that adhere to wage regulations and are determined through balanced wage fixing and wage adjustment mechanisms, as defined below.

Fair wages – specific benchmarks

Local/national law

Individual employers commit themselves to respecting wage regulations, such as on the payment of wages, the payment of the minimum wage and the payment of overtime; they should also respect the payment of social insurance and the provision of paid holidays and apply anti-discriminatory regulations and principles on equal pay for equal work.

Living wage

The manager should ensure that all wages paid in the factory are sufficient to ensure minimum living standards.

Prevailing wage

The enterprise should, as far as possible, try to pay the average wage prevailing at industry level.

Table 7.2 (cont.)

Pay systems

Employers shall not impose a pay system (such as a piece rate) or bonuses (for example, for attendance) which could be stressful for the workers and adversely affect their health, for instance by inducing them to accumulate working hours and limit (or minimize) rest time. The employer should thus make every effort to use a balanced pay system that does not rely on a single wage source, but rather diversify wage components to ensure a healthy and motivating work environment. The pay system should also ensure that wage levels appropriately reflect the different levels of education and skills of the labour force.

Individual labour contract and information on wages

Employers should sign a labour contract with each individual worker which stipulates the wage the worker can expect to receive (for normal working hours, as well as overtime; and for the basic wage, as well as other wage components, such as bonuses for seniority, attendance or individual and/or collective performance, including any deductions), and the wage-fixing mechanisms, so that the worker can see how his or her wage will be calculated and regularly adjusted. Regular information on wages – especially when pay rates are changed – should also be ensured.

Pay slip

A pay slip should be distributed to each worker at the time of the wage payment and no less than once a month. This pay slip should specify the total number of hours worked and distinguish between the payment of normal working hours and the payment of overtime.

Collective bargaining on wages

Employers shall make every reasonable effort to develop a collective process of negotiations on wages, through collective bargaining on wages with workers' representatives, trade unions being welcome in the enterprise.

Real wages or wage progression in tandem with price increases

Whatever pay system they use, employers shall ensure that nominal wages are increased annually and adjusted at least up to the annual inflation rate (or annual price increase) to avoid a decline in real wages and workers' purchasing power.

Share in company growth or wages tracking company performance

Employers shall make every reasonable effort to ensure that workers' wages are somehow related to company performance (such as annual profits or sales) and thus increase in tandem with better company results. In case of a downturn in company performance (lower profits or sales from one year to the next), the employer shall also make sure that any possible slowdown in wage progression is not greater than the slowdown in the company's results.

Wages in tandem with changes in work intensity, technology and human capital

Employers shall ensure that higher intensity at work, more adaptability on the part of the labour force with regard to technological changes or the acquisition of new skills – notably through training – will be accompanied by proportionate wage increases.

wages and how their wages are calculated – notably through the conclusion of individual labour contracts and the regular distribution of detailed pay slips – and should also be allowed to negotiate their wages collectively through their representatives. Employers should, in addition, ensure that wages are adjusted on a regular basis to the cost of living and that they track company performance.

In summary, we should ensure as far as possible that individual employers are committed and ensure the practical implementation of the various fair wage dimensions, as well as the fair wage benchmarks, both general and specific, proposed in Table 7.2.

It is important to maintain a fairly flexible approach while trying to make progress on the different fair wage dimensions.

While all the fair wage benchmarks should be considered together in order to ensure that no important dimensions are overlooked, it may not be possible for companies to implement all of them at once. They should therefore be considered as objectives that companies may decide to aim for in accordance with a certain time schedule. While adherence to certain fair wage dimensions is more imperative and should be more immediate, especially where there are legal regulations – such as the payment of wages, minimum wages, payment of overtime, payment of social insurance and paid holidays – progress will not be possible on wages in general if other fair wage dimensions are not improved, such as pay systems or social dialogue. It is thus in the interest of all actors, employers included, to ensure the progressive improvement of their fair wage performance in those areas as well.

To help companies in their efforts to implement better wage practices, fair wage training schedules could be proposed to NGO field officers, as well as to individual company managers and even workers' representatives.

7.11 PROPOSAL NO. 4: FAIR WAGE CERTIFICATION

One of the objectives of the fair wage campaign should be to get the brands to agree to implement a basic code, which includes fair wage dimensions, in all their factories and also to put adequate and effective efforts into ensuring that the code is followed by their contractors, subcontractors, suppliers and licensees. In exchange, these brands could receive some sort of fair wage certification for their products, which would confirm that these goods have been produced on the basis of fair wage practices. This fair wage certification would ensure that workers in those brands' factories enjoy relatively good wage conditions, while also providing these brands with a competitive value added in the form of a quality label for their products. Setting up such a fair wage certification scheme could give rise to a spillover effect among suppliers and brands.

7.12 PROPOSAL NO. 5: INTEGRATING FAIR WAGES INTO FAIR TRADE

There is now a groundswell of opinion in favour of including fair wages as a core part of fair trade initiatives. Since trade is the engine of the global economy, and also for economic growth, and since labour costs are an important part of trade competitiveness, it could represent an important vehicle for changing wage standards.

Not only is this an important social objective, but there is also an economic justification, which is that it would enable workers in the South steadily to improve their standards of living and thus fuel the demand on which global trade is based.

One possibility would be to include a social clause on fair wages in regional or multilateral trade agreements. These would ensure, for instance, that the goods bought under such an agreement have not been produced by workers being paid below the living wage, comply with basic wage regulations or respect basic fair wage dimensions.

Others have proposed, as a complementary tool, an international convention on certain wage issues, such as living wages.

However realistic this last objective may appear, the fair wage approach, as proposed in this book, is aimed at changing the daily wage practices of brands and suppliers and, through this, at improving the role of wages in international competitiveness and global trade. No doubt this objective could progressively be achieved through international cooperation and the commitment of all CSR actors to the fair wage concept.

CONCLUSIONS

Adverse global wage trends, the limitations of traditional social standards in this area and the increasing public awareness of wage problems are major factors which clearly point to a need for new approaches to influence wage practices worldwide. Undoubtedly, in a world dominated by global trade and accelerating mobility of capital and labour – and in which individual brands have become the leading actors – incorporating wages into the area of corporate social responsibility represents the best way of changing wage practices in depth and extensively along the supply chain. The current CSR deficit on wages – identified in this book – should therefore be addressed. This first requires the development of a coherent and multidimensional approach that would lead enterprises to look at wage costs in a fundamentally different way, while continuing to improve their competitiveness. This is why a new approach – the fair wage approach – has been proposed in this book, underpinned by significant field work.

To work effectively, a number of conditions must be put in place. First, the brands should be committed to this new approach. In other words, the commitment to incorporate wages into CSR should be real and not merely opportunistic. Brands will have to show, by concrete initiatives in the field, that their behaviour is changing with regard to wages. Second, we should ensure that the brands' efforts are not isolated but, on the contrary, amplified by establishing a general cooperative platform, on which all those concerned – NGOs, employers' and workers' representatives, academics, local and national governments – will cooperate and exchange views in order to ensure that their actions in this field will, as far as possible, converge and be self-sustaining (rather than neutralizing each other). We have seen, for instance, how essential it was to have a coherent vision encompassing brands, suppliers and national governments on wage developments. Third, the best way to ensure long-term results and avoid backward steps would be to institutionalize the fair wage approach, not only for auditing purposes but also to increase our knowledge of the issues and our ability to provide concrete policy advice. CSR on wages will be successful only if it goes beyond a purely monitoring or auditing role – for which convergence between the actors would, for obvious reasons, be more difficult – to encompass a more cooperative approach between CSR actors, who would work together to identify ways of progressively improving wage practices along the supply chain.

The proposed approach is new and requires concerted action, for which we have listed a number of concrete proposals: setting up an international fair wage network, launching a global fair wage campaign and modifying benchmarking on wage issues to include all wage indicators and dimensions presented in this book, which could lead to a sort of international 'fair wage' certification – a 'fair wage label' – to be gradually integrated into the package developed to ensure fair trade.

The claims made in this book are far from trivial, being directed towards responding to one of the most significant drawbacks of the market economy. Since income distribution between labour and capital has been identified as a major root cause of the current financial and economic crisis, concrete improvements are called for on the wage front, and not only enterprises – especially the brands – but all CSR actors have to make it happen. Such concerted action on wages is essential to strengthen the sustainability of our economic system in a more global environment.

Bibliography

Akerlof, G. (1982), 'Labor contracts as partial gift exchange', *Quarterly Journal of Economics*, 97, 543–69.

Akerlof, G. and J. Yellen (1990), 'The fair wage effort hypothesis and unemployment', *Quarterly Journal of Economics*, 105 (2) (May), 255–84.

Anker, R. (2006). 'Poverty lines around the world: A new methodology and internationally comparable estimates', *International Labour Review*, 145 (4).

Arbelaez, L., S. Chandrashekaran, L. Marmolejo and J. Zhang (2008), 'Corporate social responsibility and fair wages', prepared for the FLA under the supervision of D. Vaughan-Whitehead, Sciences-Po, Paris.

Asian Development Bank (ADB) (2007), *Key Indicators 2007: Inequality in Asia*, Manila: ADB.

Bosch, G. and C. Weinkopf (eds) (2008), *Low Wage Work in Germany*, New York: Russell Sage Foundation.

Calvo, G. (1979), 'Quasi-Walrasian theories of unemployment', *American Economic Review*, 69 (2) (May).

Caroli, E. and J. Gautié (eds) (2008), *Low Wage Work in France*, New York: Russell Sage Foundation.

Council of Europe (1998), Document concerning Article 4, Paragraph 1 of the Charter, Cycle XIV-2, Strasbourg, 10 June.

Daloz, J.-P. and M. Barruel (1993), 'Research into a method of defining "decent" and "fair" wages within the meaning of Article 4, Paragraph 1 of the Social Charter', mimeo (March).

Danthine, J.-P. and A. Kurmann (2003), 'Fair Wages in a New Keynesian Model of the Business Cycle', Cahiers de recherche 0320, CIRPEE. Available at SSRN: http://ssrn.com/abstract=396080.

EPSU (2006), 'Tackling low pay', EPSU Policy document, Brussels.

ETI (Ethical Trading Initiative) (2000), 'The "living wage" clause in the ETI base code – how to implement it?', D. Steele, Information Officer (June). Available at: www.ethicaltrade.org/Z/lib/2000/06/livwage/content2.shtml.

ETI (Ethical Trading Initiative) (2003), 'Linking wages, overtime and productivity', Chapter 5 of Key Challenges in Ethical Trade: Report on the ETI Biennial Conference 2003. Available at: www.ethicaltrade.org/Z/lib/2003/12/eticonf/page05.shtml.

ETI (Ethical Trading Initiative) (2007), 'A "living wage" for workers in global supply chains – a comment', by Dan Rees, Director of the Ethical Trading Initiative (24 September). Available at: www.ethicaltrade.org/Z/lib/2007/09/living-wage-eti/index.shtml.

European Commission (1991), *PEPPER I Report – Promotion of employee participation in profits and enterprise results in the member states of the European Community*, ed. M. Uvalic, *Social Europe* Supplement No. 3/91, Luxembourg.

European Commission (1997), *PEPPER II Report – Promotion of employee participation in profits and enterprise results in the member states of the European Community*, COM (96) 697 Final, Brussels, 8 January.

European Commission (funded by) (2006), *PEPPER III Report – Promotion of employee participation in profits and enterprise results in the new member and candidate countries of the European Union*, ed. J. Lowitzsch, Inter-University Centre Split/ Berlin, Institute for Eastern European Studies, Free University of Berlin.

European Commission (2007), 'The labour income share in the European Union', in *Employment in Europe*, Brussels: EC.

European Trade Union Confederation (ETUC) (2004), *European Trade Unions and CSR – Report* (May). Available at: http://www.etuc.org/IMG/doc/CSRCESfinal3_EN1.doc.

European Trade Union Confederation (ETUC) (2008), 'On the offensive for fair wages' (19 November). Available at: http://www.etuc.org/a/4561.

Fair Labor Association (2003), *Beyond Questions and Principle: Exploring the Implementation of Living Wages in Today's Global Economy*. A Report by FLA's Living Wage Forum (20 October), Columbia University. Available at: http://www.fairlabor.org/all/resources/livingwage/FLA_livingwage_forum_report.pdf.

Feher, E. (1991), 'Fair wages and unemployment', Department of Economics, University of Technology, Vienna.

Ferreira, F. and M. Ravallion (2008), 'Global poverty and inequality: a review of the evidence', World Bank Policy Research Working Paper No. 4623, Washington DC: World Bank.

Government of Australia (2009), *Submission to the Australian Fair Pay Commission – Minimum Wage Review 2009* (20 March). Available at: http://www.workplace.gov.au/workplace/Publications/News/Minimumwagereview20.

Government of Canada (2008), 'Construction contracting with the Canadian Government', Human Resources and Skills Development Canada (HRSDC) (15 January). Available at: http://www.canadabusiness.ca/servlet/ContentsServer?cid=10819452 03446&lang=en.

Hopkins, M. (2007), *Corporate Social Responsibility and International Development, Business and Economics*, London: Earthscan.

ILRF (International Labor Rights Fund) (1999), 'Empowering workers towards a living wage – a position paper' (fall), Washington DC. See also: www.laborrights.org.

IMF (2007a), 'The globalization of labor', in *World Economic Outlook: Spillovers and Cycles in the Global Economy* (April), Washington DC: IMF.

IMF (2007b), 'Globalization and inequality', in *World Economic Outlook: Globalization and Inequality* (October), Washington DC: IMF.

International Labour Office (ILO) (1992), *International Labour Conventions and Recommendations 1919–1991*, 2 volumes, Geneva: ILO.

International Labour Office (2005), *Key Indicators of the Labour Market* (KILM), 4th edition, Geneva: ILO.

International Labour Office (ILO) (2008a), *Global Wage Report 2008/09 – Minimum Wages and Collective Bargaining towards Policy Coherence*, Geneva: ILO.

International Labour Office (ILO) (2008b), *World of Work Report 2008 – Income Inequalities in the Age of Financial Globalization*, ILO–International Institute for Labour Studies, Geneva: ILO.

International Labour Office (2008c), 'ILO Declaration on Social Justice for a Fair Globalization', adopted by the International Labour Conference at its 97th Session, Geneva, 10 June 2008.

International Labour Office (2009), *Global Wage Report – Update 2009*, Geneva: ILO.

International Trade Union Confederation (ITUC) (2008), *The Global Pay Gap*, Brussels: ITUC.

ITGLWF (2002), *How to Use Codes of Conduct to Help Secure Fundamental Worker Rights*. Available at: http://www.itglwf.org/pdf/HowtoUseCodes-pp43-56.pdf.

Jin, L., C. Lavoie, L. Sagittari and N. Unwin-Kuruneri (2009), 'Fair wage: bolstering corporate social responsibility in times of crisis', prepared for the FLA under the supervision of D. Vaughan-Whitehead, Sciences-Po, Paris.

Jo-In (Joint Initiative on Corporate Accountability and Workers Rights) (2007), Report on End Conference, Bogazici University, December.

Krueger, A. (1999), 'Measuring labor's share', *American Economic Review*, 89, 45–51.

Kuznets, A. (1955), 'Economic growth and income inequality', *American Economic Review*, 45, 1–28.

Labour behind the Label (1999), *Threadbare – A Report on Wages in the Fashion Industry* (22 October).

Layard, R. (2006), 'Happiness and public policy: a challenge to the profession', *The Economic Journal*, 116 (March), C24–C33.

Li, M. and P. Edwards (2008), 'Work and pay in small Chinese clothing firms: a constrained negotiated order', *Industrial Relations Journal*, 39 (4), 296–313.

Lloyd, C., G. Mason and K. Mayhew (eds) (2008), *Low Wage Work in the United Kingdom*, New York: Russell Sage Foundation.

Luebker, M. (2007), 'Labour shares', ILO Technical Brief No. 1, Geneva: ILO.

Lustig, N.C. and D. McLeod (1998), 'Minimum wages and poverty in developing countries: some empirical evidence', conference report, British Library Shelfmark 98/01176, 62–93.

Maquila Solidarity Network (2002), 'Are apparel manufacturers getting a bad WRAP?', Memo No. 12 (November). Available at: http://en.maquilasolidarity.org/sites/maquilasolidarity.org/files/codesmemo12_0.pdf.

Organisation for Economic Co-operation and Development (OECD) (2007), *Employment Outlook*, Paris: OECD.

Poutsma, E. (2001), *Recent Trends in Employee Financial Participation in the European Union*, Luxembourg. Available at: http://www.eurofound.europa.eu/pubdocs/2001/12/en/1/ef0112en.pdf.

Rechnungshof (2007), *Bericht gem. Art 1–8, Bezügebegrenzungsgesetz BGBl.* I No. 64/1997.

Salop, S.C. (1979), 'A model of the natural rate of unemployment', *American Economic Review*, 69 (1), 117–25, March.

Schulten, T. (2008), 'Towards a European minimum wage – fair wages and Social Europe', *European Journal of Industrial Relations*, 14 (4), 421–39.

Shapiro, C. and J.E. Stiglitz (1984), 'Equilibrium unemployment as a worker discipline device', *American Economic Review*, 74 (June).

Steele, D. (2000), 'The "living wage" clause in the ETI Base Code – how to implement it', Ethical Trade Initiative (June). Available at: http://www.ethicaltrade.org/Z/lib/2000/06/livwage/index.shtml.

Stiglitz, J.E. (1974), 'Wage determination and unemployment in LDC', *Quarterly Journal of Economics*, 88, 194–227.

Stiglitz, J.E. (1986), 'Theories of wage rigidities', in J. Butkiewicz et al., *Keynes's Economic Legacy: Contemporary Economic Theories*, New York: Praeger Publishers, 153–206.

Stiglitz, J.E. (2009), Address to ILO special sitting, 304th Session of the Governing Body and its committees, trilingual transcript, pp. 6–25.

Stockhammer, E. (2008), 'Wage flexibility or wage coordination? Economic policy implications of the wage-led demand regime in the Euro area', Political Economic Research Institute Working Paper No. 160, Amherst, MA, University of Massachusetts.

Trades Union Congress (1997), *The National Minimum Wage, TUC Evidence to the Low Pay Commission* (26 September).

UNISON (2004), *Fair Wages – How to End the Two-Tier Workforce in Public Services and Achieve Fair Wages* (June). Available at: http://www.unison.org.uk.

UNISON (2007), *Fair Wages Toolkit*. Available at: http://www.unison.org.uk.

United Nations Development Programme (UNDP) (2007), *Poverty in Focus: The Challenge of Inequality*, Brasilia: International Poverty Centre.

Vaughan-Whitehead D. (1995), *Workers' Financial Participation – East–West Experiences*, Labour–Management Relations Series, Geneva: ILO.

Vaughan-Whitehead, D. (2003), *EU Enlargement versus Social Europe? The Uncertain Future of the European Social Model*, Cheltenham, UK and Northampton, MA, USA: Edward Elgar.

Vaughan-Whitehead, D. (2010), *The Minimum Wage Revisited in the Enlarged EU*, Cheltenham, UK and Northampton, MA, USA: Edward Elgar.

Wadhwani, S. and M. Wall (1988), 'A direct test of the efficiency wage using UK micro data', Discussion Paper No. 313, CLE, London School of Economics.

Weiss, A. (1980), 'Job queues and layoffs in labour markets with flexible wages', *Journal of Political Economy*, 88, 526–38.

World Bank (2007), *Global Economic Outlook*, Washington DC: World Bank.

Annexes

Annex 1 Fair Wage Questionnaire (employers)*

CONTACTS:

Establishment name: _____

Province: _____City:_____

Telephone number: _____ Email:_____

Person interviewed:

Name:_____

Position:_____

Date of interview:_____ Time of interview:_____

Name of field officer:_____

Comments:_____

_____

_____

_____

GENERAL ECONOMIC INFORMATION

1. What are the main products/services provided by this establishment?

_____

2. What is the exact ownership of this establishment on January 2009:

State-owned:	___%
Municipally-owned:	___%
Private local:	___%
Private foreign:	___%
Total	100%

---

* This questionnaire is addressed to managers; a second questionnaire is addressed to the workers. The information collected through this questionnaire will be kept *strictly confidential* and the name of the company will not be identified, if this is the wish of the company management.

3. Is this establishment a subsidiary/affiliate of an enterprise/parent company?

Yes	No

If so, what is the main country of origin of the parent company?

_____

Name of the parent company: _____

4. Is this establishment a sub-contractor of another enterprise?

Yes	No

If so, what is the main country of origin of the brand/contractor?_____

Name of the brands: _____

_____

5. How many years has this establishment been in operation? _____ years

6a. How many persons, including management, did this establishment employ on 1st January 2009 including full-time, part-time, regular workers, temporary, casual, contract, unpaid family workers and apprentices, and those on temporary absence and leave:

_____ persons

6b. What is the percentage of workers used on a temporary/seasonal* basis? _____% (*with less than one year seniority in the company)

6c. What is the percentage of employees who are not locals?   _____%

7a. In 2008 did you have to get rid of part of your labour force?

Yes	No

7b. If so, by what percentage did you have to reduce your labour force?
_____%

7c. If so, what employees were made redundant:

Mainly temporary/seasonal workers	
Mainly non local workers	
All types of workers	

8. Do you think that you may envisage employment cuts in 2009?

Yes	*No*

I. Payment of wages

9a. Did you have any difficulty in paying wages last year?

Always	
Often	
Sometimes	
Rarely	
Never	

9b. If so, what was the percentage of the workforce affected? _____%

10a. Did you experience any delay in paying wages last year?

Yes, with more than 2 months delay	
Yes, with a 1-2 months delay	
Yes with a 1 to 4 weeks delay	
Yes, with less than one week delay	
No, I always could pay wages in time	

10b. If so, what was the percentage of the workforce affected? _____%

11a. Did you experience any under-payment* of workers last year?
(* Under-payment refers to the payment of pay rates below the legal or standard requirements, either for normal working hours, overtime, payment of bonuses and so on)

Often	
Sometimes	
Rarely	
Never	

11b. If so, what type of under-payment (for working hours, overtime, bonuses and so on)?
(please specify: _____)

12. Do you expect the current economic crisis to generate:

Difficulties in paying wages	
Delays in paying wages	
Under-payment of wages	

II. Living wage

13a. Do you think the *average wage* distributed in your company allow workers to live decently*?
(* refers to a wage level that allows the workers to respond to their basic food, accommodation and other basic living standards needs)

Yes	No

13b. Do you think the *starting wage* distributed in your company allows workers to live decently?

Yes	No

14. Do wages distributed in your company allow workers to satisfy their basic needs in regard to:

	Yes	*No*
Food		
Accommodation		
Health care		
Education		
Clothing		
Vacation and Entertainment		

15. In front of the current economic crisis do you expect wages:

To better cover minimum living standards	
To cover less minimum living standards	
No change	

III. Legal minimum wage

16. What is the starting wage in your company? _____
(The starting wage corresponds to the lowest (first) wage scale in the company)

17. What is the national/provincial statutory minimum wage: _____
Don't know: _____

18. How is the starting wage in your company compared to the national/provincial minimum wage:

Higher	*Lower*	*Same*

19. Did your establishment last year have difficulty in respecting the minimum wage level:

Always	
Often	
Sometimes	
Rarely	
Never	

20. Within the current economic crisis do you expect difficulties in paying the minimum wage?

Yes	*No*

IV. Prevailing wage

21. What was the company's average monthly wage in 2008? _____

22. How was this average wage compared to the:

	Higher	*Lower*	*Same*
Average wage in main competitors			
Average wage in your province			

23. Within the current crisis do you believe that paying wages above those of competitors will become:

More important than before	
Less important than before	
The same as before	

V. Social dialogue and communication

24. Are wages in your company fixed:

Unilaterally by the employer	
By individual contract with the worker	
By collective agreement in your company	
Following a collective agreement fixed at sectoral or national level	
Other (specify: _____)	

25. Does your establishment have:

	Yes	*No*
A trade union		
A workers' committee		

26a. Do the workers receive a pay slip?

Yes, all workers	*Yes, only production workers*	*Yes, only white-collar workers*	*No*

26b. If so, does this pay slip provide:

	Yes	*No*
An assessment of total hours worked		
A distinction between regular hours pay and overtime pay		
A description of individual piece rate performance		

27. Are workers informed about the social insurance they are entitled to?

Yes	*No*

28. In the current crisis do you believe that you should reinforce the dialogue with the employees?

Yes	No

VI. Pay systems and wage structure

29. What percentage of your production workers' wage is paid according to a *piece rate* system ? (from 0% if there is no piece rate in the enterprise to 100% if the totality of workers' wage is paid from a piece rate system):

0% to 30%	
31% up to 50%	
51% to 70%	
71% to 90%	
91% up to 100%	

30a. Is there a part of wages you give in cash in an informal way to the workers?

Yes	No

30b. If so, what is the percentage of their total wage paid under this form?
___ %

31. To determine wages do you use a *salary grid* according to workers' occupation/qualifications/education/experience?

No	
Yes, for skilled employees	
Yes, for all employees	

32a. What percentage of your production workers' wage is paid according to a system of bonuses related to *collective performance*?

0%	
1 to 5%	
5 to 10%	
10 to 25%	
25 to 50%	
More than 50%	

32b. To what indicators of enterprise performance are these bonuses related?

Enterprise's profits		
Enterprise's sales' growth		
Enterprise's productivity		
Team's performance		
Other performance target (specify:_____ _____)		

33. Are there *other monetary bonuses* you distribute?

	No	*Yes*	*If yes, % of total wage*
Related to seniority (and if so, % of total wage)			
Related to attendance (if so, % of total wage)			
Other bonus (specify:_____ _____)			

How many days a month should the employee work to get such attendance bonus? _____ days

Other bonus
(specify:_____)

34. Do you provide the following *non-monetary benefits*?

Free/subsidized accommodation	
Free medication/medical care	
Paid holidays	
Free/subsidized meals	
Free/subsidized transportation	
Yes, other (specify: _____)	
None	

35. Is the company making all required social insurance/security payments to the government?

Yes, for all workers	
Yes, for some workers (_____% of labour force)	
No (please explain: _____)	

36a. In the current crisis do you believe you should implement a change in the way wages are fixed?

Yes	*No*	*Don't know*

36b. If so, which change do you believe would be desirable? _____

_____

VII. Payment of working hours

37. Did you always manage to pay overtime last year?

Always	
Often	
Sometimes	
Rarely	
Never	

38. How much is overtime paid (as a multiplier of pay rate for normal working hours: x1.0; x1.5 and so on)?

During the normal working week (Monday to Friday)	X__
On Saturday	X__
On Sunday	X__
On holiday period	X__

39. Do you expect the current crisis to lead to more difficulty in paying overtime?

Yes	*No*	*Don't know*

VIII. Wage disparity

40. Would you say that *in general* wage disparity in your enterprise in the last 2 years would have:

Increased significantly	
Increased slightly	
Remained unchanged	
Decreased slightly	
Decreased significantly	

41a. *In particular* would you say that wage disparity in your enterprise in the last 2 years would have increased, decreased, or remained unchanged:

Between:	*Increased*	*Decreased*	*Remained unchanged*
Top and lowest level workers			
Men and women			
Permanent and temporary workers			
Migrants and others			
Different ethnic groups			
Between other groups of workers (please specify: _____)			

41b. Are migrant workers coming from rural areas (or neighbouring countries) hired on different conditions?

Yes	No

If so, please explain: _____

42a. Do you expect wage disparity to increase if the crisis continues?

Yes	No	Don't know

42b. If so, why? And between what categories?_____

IX. Real wage

43. What has been the increase in nominal wages last year (2008)? ___ %

44. What was the inflation rate last year? ___%   Don't know: __

45. Do you think the wage increases in your enterprise last year:

Were above annual price increases	
Approximately the same as price increases	
Were below annual price increases	

46. With the current crisis and compared to the past do you expect that wages:

Will adjust better than before to price increases	
Will adjust less than before to price increases	
No change	
Don't know	

47. Do you expect cuts in nominal wages this year?

Yes	No

X. Company economic performance and the wage share

48. Would you say that your profit margin last year (2008) compared to previous year (2007):

Increased		
Decreased		
Remained constant		

49. Would you say that your sales volume (or activities) last year (2008) compared to previous year (2007):

Increased	
Decreased	
Remained constant	

50. Would you say that wages have been following profits and sales' growth last year (2008)?

Yes, fully		
Yes, to a great extent		
Yes, but to a limited extent		
No, there was no correlation		

51. In 2009 do you expect your profit margin:

To increase	
To decrease	
Not to change	

52. What will be the impact on wages?

Will be increased	
Will be reduced	
Will not change	

XI. Wage costs

53. Did your wage costs last year compared to other production costs (raw materials, energy, transportation and so on):

Increased	
Decreased	
Remained constant	

54. What was the percentage of your wage costs compared to total production costs in 2008?
        ___%

55. How do you think wage costs will behave within the current crisis?

They will be reduced compared to other production costs	
They will increase compared to other production costs	
No change	
Don't know	

XII. Wages, training and technology

56. Over the last two years do you think that the work in the company has become more complex (more difficult), less complex or remained unchanged?

More complex	
Remained unchanged	
Less complex	

57. Would you say that the intensity at work:

Increased	
Remained unchanged	
Decreased	

58. Among the factors that might explain more complex/intensive work, did you experience over last two years:

More frequent changes in style	
More goods to produce in the same period	
Changes in the operation of assembly lines or in the way work is organized	
Other (mention: _____)	

59. Was new technology introduced in the last two years?

Yes	*No*

60. Did your training expenditure last year (2008) compared to previous year (2007):

Increase	
Decrease	
Remain constant	

61. Did all these changes lead to some wage increases?

Yes, to a great extent	
Yes, to some extent	
No, left wages unchanged	
In fact decreased wages	
Don't know	

62. Do you expect the crisis to generate higher work intensity in your enterprise?

Yes, to a great extent	
Yes, but to a limited extent	
No	

General assessment of wage policy

63. Globally, would you say that the wages you pay to your employees are:

Fair	
Unfair	
Neither fair nor unfair	

64. Among the following wage areas could you specify those in which you believe your enterprise needs to make most progress, some progress, or no need to change:

	Most progress	*Some progress*	*No need to change*
More regular payment of wages			
Wages reflecting decent living standards			
Wages reflecting price increases			
Wages rewarding overtime			
Wages being comparable to wages in similar enterprises			
Wages being closely related to enterprise performance			
Wages reflecting employees education, skills and experience			
Wages reflecting organization and technology changes			
Wages being better communicated and negotiated individually (with individual workers) or collectively (with workers' representatives)			
Wages leading to less wage disparity between workers			
Other (specify: _____)			

65. Among the areas in Question 64, in which ones do you expect more difficulties because of the crisis?

_____

66. Do you think it would be desirable to further increase wage levels in the company?

Yes	No

67. What factors among the following do impede the company to do so?

	Yes, to great extent	Yes, to some extent	No
Wage costs already too high			
Other production costs (raw materials, energy and so on) too high			
Contracts with the brands too tight			
Productivity too low			
Lack of prospects on internal market			
Lack of prospects on external market			

Statistical Table

	2006	2007	2008
EMPLOYMENT			
Total number of employees			
Number of unskilled operatives			
Number of skilled operatives			
Number of supervisors, foremen			
Number of sales, service employees			
Number of clerical employees			
Number of managerial, and executives			
Number of men			
Number of women			
Number of migrant workers			
WORK CONTRACTS			
Number of permanent employees			
Number of fixed-term employees			
Number of interim agency workers			
Number of full-time employees			
Number of part-time employees			
Number of self-employed			
Number of sub-contracted employees (through outsourcing to another firm)			
WAGES			
Average wage for all employees			
Wage for unskilled operatives			
Wage for skilled operatives			
Wage of supervisors, foremen			
Wage of sales, service employees			
Wage of clerical employees			

	2006	*2007*	*2008*
WAGES (*cont.*)			
Wage of managerial, and executives			
Lowest wage in the company			
Highest wage in the company			
Total wage costs			
Total production costs			
% of wage costs / total production costs			
% of training expenditure (% of total expenditure)			
ENTERPRISE RESULTS			
Profitability = (cash flow) / (fixing + circulating capital)			
Profit margin = turnover – total expenditure			
Annual sales (in local currency)			
% of production exported			
WORKING HOURS			
Average weekly hours (Total including overtime)			
Weekly normal hours			
Weekly overtime hours			

Annex 2 Fair Wage Questionnaire (workers)*

GENERAL INFORMATION

1. How long have you been in the factory? _____months

2. What are you doing (type of work)?_____

3. In what assembly line are you working?_____

4. For what main brands? _____

5a. What city do you come from ?_____

5b. How far is it from here? _____hours by road

5c. How often do you go back home? every _____weeks

I. Payment of wages

6a. Is your wage regularly paid?

Yes	No

---

* This questionnaire is addressed to the workers; a second questionnaire is addressed to the managers. The information collected through this questionnaire will be kept *strictly confidential* and the name of the company will not be identified, if this is the wish of the company management.

6b. If so, how often?

Daily	
Weekly	
Monthly	
Other (specify: _____)	

7a. Did you experience any problem in being paid last year?

Yes	*No*

7b. If so could you evaluate what was the amount of non-paid wages in percentage of your monthly wage?

Less than one monthly wage	
Between one and 1.5 monthly wage	
Between 1.5 and 2 monthly wage	
More than 2 monthly wages	

8a. Did you experience any problem of delays in wage payment?

Yes	*No*

8b. If so, what was the average delay before being paid?

More than 2 months delay	
1–2 months delay	
1 to 4 weeks delay	
Less than one week delay	

8c. If so, is the problem mainly concerning some categories of workers?

Yes	*No*

If yes, please specify which category(ies):

_____

8d. If so, what was the reason given by the management for not paying you

_____

9a. Did you experience any under-payment* of workers last year?
(* Under-payment refers to the payment of pay rates below the legal or standard requirements, either for normal working hours, overtime, payment of bonuses and so on)

Yes	No

9b. If so, what type of under-payment* (for working hours, overtime, bonuses and so on)?
(please specify: _____)

10. Do you expect the current economic crisis to generate:

More difficulties in being paid	
More delays in the payment of wages	
More under-payment of wages	

II. Living wage

11. Is the wage you get sufficient to live decently*?
(*refers to a wage level that allows you to respond to your basic food, accommodation and other basic living standards needs)

Yes	No

12. In particular does your wage allow you to satisfy your basic needs in regard to:

	Yes	*No*
Food		
Accommodation		
Health care		
Education		
Clothing		
Vacation and Entertainment		

13. In front of the current economic crisis do you expect that your wage:

Will better cover minimum living standards	
Will cover less minimum living standards	
Will experience no change	

III. Legal Minimum wage

14. What is the starting wage in your company?   _____
(The starting wage corresponds to the lowest (first) wage scale in the company)

15a. Do you know whether there is a statutory minimum wage in your province?

Yes	*No*

15b. If so, what is its level?   _____per month
                                      _____per hour (eventually)
                                              Don't know: ___

16. How is the starting wage in your company compared to this provincial minimum wage:

Higher	*Lower*	*Same*	*Don't know*

17. Did your establishment last year have difficulty in respecting the minimum wage level:

Yes	*No*

18. Within the current economic crisis do you expect your enterprise will have difficulties in paying the minimum wage?

Yes	*No*

IV. Prevailing wage

19. What is your monthly wage? _____

20. How would you say are the wage levels in your company compared to the:

	Higher	*Lower*	*Same*
Average wage in main competitors			
Average wage in this province			
Average wage in your home province			

21. Within the current crisis do you believe that your company will:

Be doing better than other competitors and thus pay higher wages	
Be doing worse compared to other competitors and thus pay lower wages	
Be doing the same than before	

V. Social dialogue and communication

22a. Did you sign an individual work contract with your employer?

Yes	*No*

22b. If so, is this work contract saying something about your wage?

Yes	No

22c. If so, what does it say? _____

23. Does this establishment have a trade union representative?

Yes	No

24. Does this establishment have a workers' committee?

Yes	No

25. Did the trade union (or the workers' committee) help you in the past on wage issues?

Yes	No

26a. Is your establishment covered by a collective agreement?

Yes	No	Don't know

26b. If so, does this collective agreement cover wage issues?

Yes	No	Don't know

27a. Do you know in advance how much you will be paid under the piece rate system?

Yes	No

27b. If so, how (notice board, oral communication and so on): _____

28a. Do you receive a pay slip?

Yes	No

28b. If so, does this pay slip provide:

	Yes	No
An assessment of total hours worked		
A distinction between regular hours pay and overtime pay		
A description of individual piece rate performance		

29. Are you informed about the social insurance you are entitled to?

Yes	No

30. In the current crisis do you believe that the dialogue with the management should be developed?

Yes	No

VI. Pay systems and wage structure

31. Are you mainly paid according to a piece rate system?

Yes	No

32. What percentage of your wage is paid on this piece rate basis? (from 0% if there is no piece rate in the enterprise to 100% if the totality of workers' wage is paid from a piece rate system):

0% to 30%	
31% up to 50%	
51% to 70%	
71% to 90%	
91% up to 100%	

33a. Is there a part of your wage you that is given to you in cash in an informal way?

Yes	No

33b. If so, what is the percentage of your total wage paid under this form? ___ %

34a. Do you consider that the current pay system in the establishment is rewarding sufficiently your skills and experience?

Yes	No

34b. If not, explain: _____

35. Do you benefit from a basic wage which is calculated according to a salary grid that takes into account your individual qualifications/education/experience?

Yes	No	Don't know

36a. Do you receive bonuses related to collective (enterprise) performance?

Yes	No

36b. If so mention which one: _____
(related to profits, sales, team's results and so on)

37. Do you benefit from other monetary bonuses such as:

	No	Yes	If yes, % of total wage
Seniority bonus (and if so, % of your total wage)			
Attendance bonus (and if so, % of total wage) How many days a month should you work to get such an attendance bonus? _____ days			
Other bonuses (specify: _____)			

38a. Are some of these bonuses or any source of your wage cut for any disciplinary reason or other reasons (absenteeism; contribution requested for accommodation and so on)?

Yes	No

38b. If yes, please describe: _____

39. Do you benefit from any of the following non-monetary benefits?

	Yes	No
Free/subsidized accommodation If so, would you consider the conditions for accommodation acceptable? YES _____ NO_____		
Free medication/medical care		
Paid holidays		
Free/subsidized meals		
Free/subsidized transportation		
YES, other (specify:)		
None		

40. Are you covered by any insurance provided by the company?

Yes	No

Please describe: _____

41a. In the current crisis do you believe the company should modify its pay system?

Yes	No	Don't know

41b. If so, which change do you believe would be desirable? _____
_____

VII. Payment of working hours

42a. How many hours do you work:

Per day	
Per week	

42b. Among those how many are normal working hours and overtime?

	Normal working hours	*Overtime*
Per day		
Per week		

43. Did the company manage to pay overtime last year?

Always	
Often	
Sometimes	
Rarely	
Never	

44. How much is overtime paid (as a multiplier of pay rate for normal working hours: x1.0; x1.5 and so on)?

During the normal working week (Monday to Friday)	X__
On Saturday	X__
On Sunday	X__
On holiday period	X__

45. With the current crisis, do you expect to be less remunerated for overtime?

Yes	*No*	*Don't know*

How many days of vacation were you allowed to take last year? _____

Would you like to increase this number if possible?

Yes, but with the same wage	
Yes, even if with some wage loss	
No	

Fair Wages

With the current crisis do you expect to have less holidays?

Yes	No	Don't know

VIII. Wage disparity

46. Would you say that in general wage disparity in your enterprise (between the top and the bottom; or between categories of workers) in the last 2 years would have increased:

Yes	No	Don't know

47a. In particular would you say that wage disparity in your enterprise in the last 2 years would have increased, decreased, or remained unchanged between:

	Increased	Decreased	Remained unchanged
Top and lowest level workers			
Men and women			
Permanent and temporary workers			
Migrants and others			
Different ethnic groups			
Between other groups of workers			
(please specify: _____)			

47b. Are migrant workers coming from rural areas (or neighbouring countries) hired on different conditions?

Yes	No

If so, please explain: _____

48a. Do you expect wage disparity in your company to increase if the crisis continues?

Yes	No	Don't know

48b. If so, why? And between what categories?_____

IX. Real wage

49a. Did your nominal wage increase last year compared to previous year?

Yes	No

49b. If so do you think that this wage increase:

Was above annual price increases	
Approximately the same as price increases	
Was below annual price increases	

50. With the current crisis and compared to the past do you expect that your wage:

Will adjust better than before to price increases	
Will adjust less than before to price increases	
No change	
Don't know	

51. Do you expect cuts in nominal wages this year?

Yes	No

X. Company economic performance and the wage share

52. Would you say that your enterprise profit margin last year (2008) compared to previous year (2007):

Increased	
Decreased	
Remained constant	

53. Would you say that your enterprise sales last year (2008) compared to previous year (2007):

Increased	
Decreased	
Remained constant	

54. Would you say that your wage has been following your enterprise's profits and sales' growth last year (2008)?

Yes, fully	
Yes, to a great extent	
Yes, but to a limited extent	
No, there was no correlation	

55. In 2009 do you expect your enterprise's profit margin:

To increase	
To decrease	
Not to change	

56. What do you expect will be the impact on your wage?

My wage will be increased	
My wage will be reduced	
My wage will not change	

XI. Wage costs

57. Do you think that your enterprise's wage costs last year compared to other production costs (raw materials, energy, transportation and so on):

Increased	
Decreased	
Remained constant	

58. How do you think wage costs will behave within the current crisis?

They will be reduced compared to other production costs	
They will increase compared to other production costs	
No change	
Don't know	

XII. Wages, training and technology

59. Over the last two years do you think that the work in the company has become more complex (more difficult), less complex or remained unchanged?

More complex	
Less complex	
Remained unchanged	

60. Would you say that the intensity at work:

Increased	
Decreased	
Remained unchanged	

61. Among the factors that might explain more complex/intensive work, did you experience over last two years:

More frequent changes in style	
More goods to produce in the same period	
Changes in the operation of assembly lines or in the way work is organized	
Other (mention: _____)	

62. Was new technology introduced in the last two years?

Yes	No

63. Did you follow more, less or unchanged training last year (2008) compared to previous year (2007):

More training	
Less training	
Unchanged	

64. Did all these changes (intensity/complexity/technology/training) lead to some wage increases?

Yes, to a great extent	
Yes, to some extent	
No, left wages unchanged	
In fact they decreased wages	
Don't know	

65. Do you expect the crisis to generate higher work intensity in your enterprise?

Yes, to a great extent	
Yes, to a limited extent	
No	

General assessment of wage policy

66. Globally, would you say that the wages paid in the company are:

Fair	
Unfair	
Neither fair nor unfair	

67. Among the following wage areas could you specify those in which you believe your enterprise needs to make most progress, some progress, or no need to change:

	Most progress	*Some progress*	*No need to change*
More regular payment of wages			
Wages reflecting decent living standards			
Wages reflecting price increases			
Wages rewarding overtime			
Wages being comparable to wages in similar enterprises			
Wages being closely related to enterprise performance			
Wages reflecting employees' education, skills and experience			
Wages reflecting organization and technology changes			
Wages being negotiated individually (with the individual workers) or collectively (with workers' representatives)			
Wages leading to less wage disparity between workers			
Other (specify. _____)			

68. In the near future do you expect the wage policy to get better or to get worse?

To get better	
To get worse	
Not to change	

Index

Organizations and Activism series

Series Editors: **Daniel King**, Nottingham Trent University and **Martin Parker**, University of Bristol

---

Organizations and Activism publishes books that explore how politics happens within and because of organizations, how activism is organized, and how activists change organizations.

Forthcoming in the series:

Sociocracy at Work:
Possibilities and Limitations of an Alternative Democratic Model of Organization
Martyn Griffin, Daniel King,
Ted Jennifer Rau and **Jerry Koch Gonzalez**

Organizing Food, Faith and Freedom:
Imagining Alternatives
Ozan Alakavuklar

Out now in the series:

Anarchist Cybernetics:
Control and Communication in Radical Politics
Thomas Swann

Guerrilla Democracy:
Mobile Power and Revolution in the 21st Century
Peter Bloom, Owain Smolović Jones and **Jamie Woodcock**

Find out more at

bristoluniversitypress.co.uk/organizations–and–activism

Organizations and Activism series

Series Editors: **Daniel King**, Nottingham Trent University and **Martin Parker**, University of Bristol

---

Find out more at

bristoluniversitypress.co.uk/organizations–and–activism

REIMAGINING ACADEMIC ACTIVISM

Learning from Feminist Anti-Violence Activists

Ruth Weatherall

BRISTOL
UNIVERSITY
PRESS

First published in Great Britain in 2022 by

Bristol University Press
University of Bristol
1–9 Old Park Hill
Bristol
BS2 8BB
UK
t: +44 (0)117 954 5940
e: bup-info@bristol.ac.uk

Details of international sales and distribution partners are available at bristoluniversitypress.co.uk

Cover design by blu inc, Bristol
Front cover image: Unsplash/Alexander Ant
Bristol University Press uses environmentally responsible print partners
Printed and bound in Great Britain by TJ Books Limited, Padstow

Contents

Series Editors' Preface

Organizations and Activism

Daniel King and Martin Parker

Organizing is politics made durable. From co-operatives to corporations, Occupy to Facebook, states and NGOs, organizations shape our lives. They shape the possible futures of governance, policymaking and social change, and hence are central to understanding how human beings can deal with the challenges that face us, whether that be pandemics, populism, or climate change. This book series publishes work that explore how politics happens within and because of organizations and organizing. We want to explore how activism is organized and how activists change organizations. We are also interested in the forms of resistance to activism, in the ways that powerful interests contest and reframe demands for change. These are questions of huge relevance to scholars in sociology, politics, geography, management, and beyond, and are becoming ever more important as demands for impact and engagement change the way that academics imagine their work. They are also important to anyone who wants to understand more about the theory and practice of organizing, not just the abstracted ideologies of capitalism taught in business schools.

Our books will offer critical examinations of organizations as sites of or targets for activism, and we will also assume that our authors, and hopefully our readers, are themselves agents of change. Titles may focus on specific industries or fields, or they may be arranged around particular themes or challenges. Our topics might include the alternative economy; surveillance, whistleblowing, and human rights; digital politics; religious groups; social movements; NGOs; feminism and anarchist organization; action research and co-production; activism and the neoliberal university, and any other subjects that are relevant and topical.

'Organizations and Activism' will also be a multidisciplinary series. Contributions from all and any relevant academic fields will be welcomed.

The series will be international in outlook, and proposals from outside the English-speaking global north are particularly welcome.

This book, the third in our series, confronts the question of academics as activists, as scholars who wish to use their institutional power and position to produce some sort of impact beyond the academy. The desire to make a difference, to change theory and practice, is an ambition if not an imperative for the critical scholar. As the oft-cited statement by Marx from the *Theses on Feuerbach* puts it, 'philosophers have only interpreted the world in various ways. The point, however, is to change it'. Critical studies has recently been going through a turn to 'engagement', 'co-production', and the reinvention of 'action research' – demands to get directly involved with others outside the walls of the university who are also interested in producing change. The call is to work with activists, unions, sympathetic businesses, third sector organizations, citizens and any constituencies interested in bringing about social change. The assumption is that if only academics left the ivory tower behind, got our hands dirty, and worked collectively and constructively with potential allies, then we can bring about constructive social change.

This book provides a story about Ruth Weatherall's grappling with and challenge to these assumptions. She entered the field armed with the tools of academic work, the theories, methods, plans, ethical approvals, and concepts, all with the intention to enact an academic activism that not only brought about change, but doing so in a manner aligned with the goals of the research. She passionately believed she could use her research expertise to benefit an anti-violence feminist collective further both their goals of social justice and her own research. Yet she was undone by these encounters. In this beautifully written account, Weatherall provides us with a narrative of the way in which her assumptions were 'shattered' by the engagement, and forced to rethink what her academic activism could and should mean.

Reimagining Academic Activism directly confronts what it means to be an agent of change, an academic working in, with, and alongside a social justice community organization – feminist anti-violence activists. It is an invitation to rethink the assumptions that shape academic activism. Rather than the neat divisions between academics and activists, theory and practice, reason and emotion, abstracted knowledge and embodied knowledge, these lines become blurred. Seeing how her colleagues embodied the theoretical positions they held, how they learnt *from* their experiences, Weatherall came to an understanding that 'women are experts in their own reality'. She was learning from her colleagues involved in social change, learning from the emotion, the passion, grief and anger used as starting points for their activism.

This is also a book about feminist anti-violence activism. As we write these words in the UK, a vigil in memory of Sarah Everard who had been abducted and killed was violently broken up by the police. Protests in Australia, India, Hong Kong, Mexico and many other countries continue to highlight the everyday violence against women throughout the world. This book provides us with a nuanced and timely insight into the work of this collective as they work with women experiencing domestic violence. In particular it explores the role of the body in anti-violence activism, the unsettling of identities and the importance of vulnerable bodies. Set in Aotearoa New Zealand, Weatherall, as a Pākehā (White New Zealander) describes the way in which her continued engagement in anti-violence activism began to unsettle her understanding of what it meant to be a women, and how recognizing this precarity to violence can help dismantle the normative distinction between victim and non-victim. This is a powerful and powerfully written document, one that takes the reader on a journey of tensions, complexities, and contradictions and concerns a topic than we all have some investment in.

We hope you enjoy this book. If you want to discuss a proposal yourself, then email the series editors. We look forward to hearing from you.

Preface

In a square in central Sydney on a warm evening in late November 2018, one rose is laid for each woman killed by domestic violence this year in Australia. So far, there have been 63. Different country, I think, same rotten feeling. I am practised at citing such numbers: 137 women are killed every day by an intimate partner around the world; one in three women in my home country of Aotearoa New Zealand will be subjected to violence at the hands of their partner; LGBT+ folk are at least twice as likely to be subjected to sexual violence by an intimate partner than their heterosexual counterparts, but are less likely to seek help for fear of discrimination. The numbers are practically etched onto my skin. There is a pressing need to create a more just world for women and gender minorities. The numbers alone support that conclusion. But the numbers, while shocking, can feel impersonal. The jolt from numbers can quickly pass. A moment of disbelief, or pain, or maybe even anger. Then gone. Violence might as well be woven into the very fabric of our societies. It is vital to see that each number is a person, and each person is a history; a community; a society; a story. I carry these stories in my bones.

Yet, I cannot think of the dead without remembering those who work to find them justice. They stand before me laying roses as pedestrians pass by to signify that these deaths are a social shame; they march in the streets with placards stating 'I can't believe I still need to protest this shit'; they sit with victims in the family court; they meet with government representatives; they sit around tables in cold, damp offices making collective decisions; they demand workplaces take responsibility for their employees. Mostly, I think of the buzz of an open-plan office first thing on a Friday morning. I think of my voluntary work alongside one collective of feminist anti-violence activists. I think of women shouting to one another. Laughing with one another. Having serious whispered conversations. Closing doors. Opening others. I think of the faces of my colleagues. White women. Brown women. Old women and young women. They all look tired. Overworked. Active. Angry. I think of their work to change the history; the community; the society; the story.

This earth will turn over.

I am a researcher who spent months working with feminist anti-violence activists. I joined their collective as a researcher intent on understanding how social justice organizations create social change. For nine months (and many return visits thereafter), I listened to them debate ideas as a collective; I talked with them individually about activism; I observed them at their work; I engaged in work with the collective as a volunteer. As such, I was both working with and working for the collective. I saw the members of collective as colleagues as well as participants. In the early days of my research, I wanted to be an academic activist. I understood that position to involve doing research to further the political goals of a social movement, in which the academic activist is directly involved. I assumed that meant my purpose was to (co)create theory about how social justice could be achieved and thereby improve the practice of activism for my colleagues and, possibly, other similar organizations or groups in the movement.

This book, simply put, is a story about how my assumptions were wrong. This book is a story of how listening to and learning from women[1] working in a feminist anti-violence collective impelled me to reimagine academic activism. The core lessons I learnt from the collective involved shifting how we think about who holds knowledge, expertise, and theory; recasting emotion and embodied experience as fundamental to knowledge; and working *with* difference, rather than in spite of difference, to develop solidarity in our fight for social justice. In relation to these tools, I follow the lines of connection and divergence between academia and activism throughout this book. This journey takes us away from the initial lines I drew between academia and activism, and spills into new intellectual terrain.

On the day I joined the collective, I came equipped with many 'academic' tools at my disposal. I had a stack of ethics forms to safeguard participants' confidentiality, several scholarly books containing theoretical frameworks relating to social change, a head full of various methodology handbooks on how to do a good ethnography, a potent (if not also naïve) desire to contribute to social justice, and several neat notebooks of varying sizes for recording my observations. I also took with me a vast array of assumptions about what it meant to do 'engaged' or 'activist' scholarship. At that time, my initial assumptions of what was academic were clear: I had theory, I had a research plan and research questions, and I had ideas about how to cocreate knowledge with my participants. My role in the collective, then, would be to observe and analyse the actions and political know-how of my colleagues, which would be supported and expanded by (scholarly) theories of social change. In my mind, I had already drawn lines between what was academic (theory, knowledge, research) and what was activist (practice, political know-how, action).

My experiences as an ethnographer with the collective, however, catalysed a permanent change in how I understood the relationship between academia, activism, and social justice. The change was spurred by my colleagues' feminist approach to anti-violence activism. The feminist anti-violence movement has, since its inception, developed a sophisticated and insightful body of work about violence, gender, and social norms. Of particular relevance here is the movement's collective knowledge of the connection between the social, physical, and economic violent subordination of women and gender minorities in their household and the (hetero)sexist social norms and institutions which reify that violence. Although I had encountered these arguments in my academic reading and completely endorsed the position, it was the way my colleagues *embodied* that theoretical position that pushed me out of my complacency and caused me to examine how my conceptualization of the 'academic' and 'activist' was shaped by those patterns of inequality.

I remember the moment that catalysed the change acutely. I still can feel myself in that warm room, feet curled underneath me on the sofa, listening to my colleagues discuss how the collective worked alongside victims of violence. One of my colleagues summarized the collective's approach: *women are experts in their own reality*. It was a reversal of hierarchy. Through lived-experience victims understood violence better than anyone (traditional 'experts' included). The collective learnt *from* women and gender minorities, and walked alongside victims to support them in what they needed. For those engaging in social justice work, an empowerment-centred approach is unlikely to seem radical. When looked at from a theoretical standpoint, however, reimagining the roles of the victims and activists draws different lines between knowledge, expertise, and embodied experience.

For my colleagues, the stakes were clear. If the stories of women and gender minorities are not centred in anti-violence activism, patterns of gender inequality are reified. Over many decades feminist anti-violence activists have clearly established that the social devaluation of women and gender minorities, their experiences and their needs, is both a cause and consequence of domestic violence. To disrupt harmful social, political, and institutional norms which reified gendered violence, my colleagues took a position which aimed to ensure that women's stories were heard, believed, and considered authoritative. Unsettled by this approach, I questioned which categories I was reinforcing and what the political and social effects of my current ideas about academic activism were. The lines I had drawn were problematic and operated to maintain a division between thinking and doing. Accordingly, I had reified categories about 'academia' and 'activism' which obscured the interconnection of theory and practice and thereby failed to adequately respect, practice, and reimagine my colleagues as experts in their own reality. After that day, I continued to question the lines between theory and practice, reason and emotion, abstract knowledge and embodied knowledge. And soon, I questioned the ground on which I stood.

In this book, I ask the question 'how can we reimagine "academia" and "activism" in a way that provides novel avenues for social change?'. Part of answering this question involves looking at what is conceptualized as 'academic' and what is 'activist', as well as exploring the possibilities and limitations of these conceptualizations for social change. These are important questions for both academics and activists to ask because fighting for social justice involves examining our position within interlocking systemic inequalities and undertaking interconnected action which disrupts inequality within these systems. For activists and academics to disrupt inequality and recreate a more just world, they must be equipped with ideas about how and why injustice occurs, and how it could be changed for the better. This book presents a systematic exploration of the 'how and why' of academics and activists in the context of the anti-violence movement. I draw on my ethnographic experience with the collective to describe how and why I reimagined academic activism and offer an alternative based on what I learnt from my colleagues in the collective.

This book makes liberal use of a 'before/after' structure to imitate my evolving understanding of social change, academia, and activism. I oscillate between empirical material and conceptual material throughout the book, to the point where the two often become indistinguishable from each other. I embrace this liminal space. I explore tensions between different conceptualizations of academia and activism. I argue against static understandings of those identities and alternatively propose that social change is less about having the 'right' tools and more about what happens when we learn from one another to pick up those tools in our own fight against injustice. I describe this exploration as rhizomatic, and I follow lines in all directions. I also write to give a sense of everyday life in the collective. My colleagues are given pseudonyms to maintain a sense of them as whole, complex people. These writing strategies are intended to emulate the core messages from this book and to embody the approach which I learnt from my colleagues.

This book is organized into four parts and a conclusion. Part I explores how academia and activism are conceptualized in a way which creates and maintains a separation between theory and action. The conceptualization of academic/activist is the focus for Chapter 1. Calls for academics to become more involved in communities and social movements usually operate on the assumption that academics are too involved in *thinking* and not enough in *doing*. Similarly, calls for activists to partner with researchers are often made on the basis that rigorous research, *theory*, and data are much needed in social movements to increase legitimacy and theoretical grounding for their *actions*. From the basis of that unsettling moment within the collective (which I come back to in more depth in Chapter 1), I go on to explore how these separations can be limiting and harmful.

In Chapter 2, I set the stage for my own holistic reimagining of academic activism. I discuss how I took a rhizomatic approach to rethinking the interconnections of theory and practice. To do so, I return in more depth to the specific historical, geographical, and socio-political moment of my colleagues and our feminist anti-violence work. I outline in greater detail the context of the community sector in Aotearoa New Zealand and the anti-violence movement. This detail offers a sturdier foundation for understanding the knowledge of the movement and academics, the action undertaken, and the way that theory and practice are intimately intertwined. One of the most important aspects of Part I is the deconstruction of the categories of academic and activist. While I continue to refer to these identities in the remainder of the book, the reader will carry a sense of the nebulous interconnection between the two.

Part II focuses on reimagining the role of emotion within social justice work. I begin with a discussion of the (disputed) decline of activism within the community sector in favour of more 'gloves on' approaches which work with institutions, such as the government. These stories of decline often hinge on neoliberalism, told either a tale of submission or resistance to neoliberal ideology. To interrupt the inequalities perpetuated by neoliberalism, I draw out the emotional aspects of feminist anti-violence work. As I note in the chapter, it is hardly contentious to claim that activism and emotion are connected. My focus in Chapter 3, however, is on the way that emotion is a *consciously considered* part of activism and is part of 'world making' (in terms of how we relate to each other). It is important for all involved in social justice work to consider how their theories and actions are informed by emotion to form connections with others.

To illustrate, I focus in Chapter 4 on the strong emotions of passion, grief, and anger, which were intertwined with my colleagues' work. The strong emotions I encountered in my volunteer work with the collective were part of forming connections to victims of violence and identifying which organizational practices were helpful or harmful to victims. Emotions like these cause us to be 'beside ourselves', making and remaking our ties to each other. I look at how the consciously considered emotions were part of debating the kind of world in which we wish to live. I then turn the emotional lens to looking at commonly implicated emotions for academics when engaged in social justice scholarship. Although academics are expected to passionately connect to their cause, there is an assumption that they should still continue to engage objectively (that is, with a lack of emotional orientation). As I learnt from my colleagues, however, emotional orientations related to objectivity limit the connection to those impacted by inequality. I suggest how emotional relations in academic/activism could be reimagined to deepen connection, theorization, and action.

Part III is made up of three chapters that explore the body in academic/activist work. Feminist anti-violence activism has paid particular attention to the body as a site targeted with physical and institutional violence. The anti-violence movement, as a whole, has developed sophisticated and powerful ideas that demonstrate that domestic violence is underpinned by sexism and heterosexism. Accordingly, an individual's experience of violence is shaped by their gender identity, race, ability, sexuality, migrant status, and so on. Domestic violence is, then, a social, political, and cultural problem that requires social, political, and cultural solutions. My colleagues consistently debated these ideas, refining and expanding them in relation to their lived experience along multiple lines of identity. Anti-violence work brought to the surface their own vulnerability as cis-women, women of colour, indigenous women, and LGBT+ folk.

In the three chapters of Part III, I explore how the body was positioned by my colleagues as a site of political action. In Chapter 5, I first unpack how they celebrated their gendered identities as well as understanding their own bodily experiences (in addition to the bodies of other victims) as political. I then move to looking at which bodies were excluded from my colleagues' common conceptualization of gender identities in Chapter 6. I look at how the conceptual exclusion of LGBT+ folk was interconnected with their exclusion within my colleagues' actions. In Chapter 7, I discuss a more radical conceptual approach to victims of violence offered by my colleagues. Their approach was grounded in a body's vulnerability to political, social, or cultural inequalities. In the context of anti-violence activism, this was a powerful way of thinking about and engaging in the protection of bodies from violence. In relation to Chapter 7, I then move to considering how these lessons are relevant for the intersection of academia and activism in terms of the interconnection of thinking/doing and recognizing and responding to vulnerability.

Part IV focuses on stories and social change. Stories are often an important part of social justice work. They give a human face to abstract issues (such as gendered violence). They offer insight into pathways to change. They help form connections between us. Stories can be an inroad to empathizing with others, even when those struggles are not our own. At a personal level, the stories we tell about ourselves give insight (to ourselves as well as to others) into the complexity of our lives and the nuances of our sense of self. In Chapter 8, I (re)tell the stories of six of my colleagues with an emphasis on how they understood themselves as feminists (or not), as activists (or not), and women (or not). Together, these stories create a rich tapestry of experience of anti-violence work and the threads of power which shape our sense of self and our conceptualization of activism.

In Chapter 9 I unpack the complexities of my colleagues' stories. I give particular attention to how the multiple accountabilities they carry (such as an accountability to their government funders as well as an accountability to victims of violence) shape their sense of 'activist' self and the way they undertake social justice work. I use a theoretical frame of the 'micro-politics' of identity to explore how the changes and differences in their identities illuminate a multiplicity of approaches to social justice. Often, these positions would conflict with their differing accountabilities or with the position of other members of the collective. My colleagues utilized their accounts (both in my formal research and informally every day), to support or resist the collective's practices and debate the role of the collective. Rather than looking to erase the differences between them, a micro-political account offers a way thinking about how we can organize *through difference*. Conflicting accountabilities, the ebbs and flows of power, and complex accounts of oneself, are important for how we conceptualize our sense of self. I conclude the chapter by arguing that difference is fundamental in creating solidarity towards large-scale emancipatory projects.

Finally, the Conclusion brings together the lessons learnt from my colleagues. Drawing on the famous sentiment from Audre Lorde – 'the Master's tools will never dismantle the Master's house' – I outline how the reimagining of academic/activism can offer new tools for dismantling inequality. The intimate connection between theory and practice becomes, once again, central to the final chapter as I summarize how academic/activism was intertwined in complex, and sometimes unexpected, ways. The conclusions are not a step-by-step guide for academics to 'engage' with communities or activists (or vice versa). Far from it. The conclusions aim to provoke reflection on our approach(es) to social justice and the unique historical, geographical, and socio-political contexts in which we operate. Such reflection asks us to examine what happens when we focus on what grows from the 'and' of theory *and* practice, mind *and* body, emotion *and* reason, or knowledge *and* action. The tensions, contradictions, and exclusions that emerge from focusing on the interconnection of 'and' are productive. Such tensions are indicative of the ongoing, necessary *work* to confront inequality and learn from those who are experts in their own reality.

PART I

The Academic/Activist

1

Setting Out

If I were to turn left when I exited my apartment in the morning, I would meander my way down the hill, through the central business district, past parliament and the high court, and end up at the business school building of my university where my office was located, the primary site of my academic work. If I were to turn right when I exited my apartment in the morning, I would wander down the other side of the hill, through the main shopping precinct, past the bars and restaurants, and almost leave the central city by the time I reached my other office, the site of my activist work as part of a feminist anti-violence collective. Sometimes I would travel between the two halfway through the day, dragging my tired body from one end of the city to the other. During this period, I was both 'academic' and 'activist'. I was undertaking a research project about social change in anti-violence activism. As part of this research, I was a 'voluntary ethnographer'; a researcher embedded in the community organization I was studying, contributing to the social justice cause alongside my colleagues at the same time as conducting my research. My life was a state of constant transition between these worlds.

I had plenty of time to reflect during my regular transitions. I would think about anti-violence activism and the stories of violence I heard throughout the day. I would think about different theoretical approaches to domestic violence, flicking through pages of books or scrolling through journal articles in my mind. Sometimes these thoughts would bleed into one another. Sometimes they would refuse to blend. I tried (and failed) many times to capture that liminal period in my fieldnotes, or poetry, or journal during my ethnography. I couldn't quite capture that feeling that my ideas and identities were spilling over the lines I tracked through the city. I also couldn't quite capture that eventual sense that my academic self and activist self ceased being separate somewhere on that winding trail during my regular transitions. No matter whether I turned left or right, no matter where I started or ended the day, I carried something with me.

The liminal space between academia and activism, and the associated senses of disorientation and connection, are at the core of this book. Throughout, I grapple with the duality of being both 'academic' and 'activist' by reimagining how we draw lines between these identities. I write for those who, like me, frequently contemplate how academics and activists can work alongside each other in pursuit of social justice. Academics are regularly asked to connect to the 'real world' and undertake research in a way that will generate 'impact' for communities. Academics who have collaborated with activists, however, often feel similar tensions as I did as I traversed my cityscape. Academic activism is often considered a 'hybrid' identity (Petray, 2012), an identity in the borderlands (Naples, 2010), an identity not easily reconciled (Hale, 2019). Activists too often come away from these encounters with academics feeling undervalued or frustrated (Varkarolis and King, 2017). The liminal space between academia and activism is a space fraught with complexity. But it is also a space of immense potential. I write about the lines of connection between academic activism and anti-violence activism with an intent to explore possible new pathways to a different, more just, world.

I came into my project about social change in community activism through the lens of academic activism. I saw myself as engaging with feminist anti-violence activists and contributing to their on-the-ground political action by providing research expertise as well as producing research that would (broadly) support ending violence against women. My sense liminality, however, marks how the ground moved beneath my feet. Importantly, my transition was not only from one side of the city to another, but from one way of thinking about the connection of academia and activism to another. The more I learnt from the collective about their approach to feminist anti-violence activism, the more unsettled I became with my neatly held divisions between what was considered 'academic' and what was considered 'activist'. I had thought of myself as building bridges between theory and practice, knowledge and action, which were situated on opposite sides of the cityscape. What I learnt from my colleagues in the collective, however, was that knowledge/action, theory/practice, academia/activism and so on, are intimately intertwined.

Thus, while this book is about reimagining the notion of the 'academic activist', it is primarily a book about my colleagues and their work as part of a feminist anti-violence collective. My transitions across the cityscape only became relevant through my engagement with my colleagues. I was inspired by their work as a collective to centre the embodied knowledge of victims of gendered violence as well as their work sharing victims' stories to unpick the social, political, and economic inequalities which reinforce violence. Moreover, my colleagues' anti-violence work was underpinned by a commitment to understanding and practising decolonization, collectivism, feminism, and diversity. All their work with victims, the government, businesses, and other activist groups was guided by these commitments. Accordingly, my colleagues had an intricate and sophisticated understanding of intersecting systems of inequality and were experts at practising their core commitments in a wide variety of situations. The way my colleagues undertook their work was inherited from the early days of the feminist movement in Aotearoa New Zealand. The collective carried on the tradition of creating novel ways of organizing that were anti-hierarchical and non-violent. In short, I quickly found that I had much to learn.

How I came to reimagine academic activism by learning from my colleagues is central to this book. As Sara Ahmed (2012: 2) argues: 'every research project has a story, which is the story of an arrival'. This 'story of an arrival' examines why we come to frame an issue in the way that we do and the political and theoretical implications of this framing. Two stories of arrival are core to this book: my institutional story of arrival and my empirical story of arrival. My institutional story of arrival is related to my engagement with research about academic activism and the plethora of other ways in which academic work is argued to influence the world. My empirical story of arrival is grounded in my time with a grassroots anti-violence feminist collective. This empirical story follows my engagement with my colleagues and how their sophisticated theories and interconnected practices diverted, and deepened, my institutional story of arrival.

Accordingly, the institutional and empirical stories of my arrival are intertwined. As many researchers who have undertaken similar ethnographic style work will tell you, the dual identities of being both researcher (observer) and member of the society or organization (participant) impels a deeper, although more fractured and complex, understanding of both identities (Kondo, 1990; Behar, 1996). Dual identities are more than the sum of their parts; we grow and spill from the 'and'. In the remaining part of this first chapter, I first focus on my institutional starting point and my project on identity and social change. I discuss my initial understanding of academic activism and how academics and activists could collaborate through a focus on academic literature. As I enter into the anti-violence movement, however, I explore how my assumptions were disrupted. These moments spill into the subsequent chapter.

Setting out

The viewpoint I had at the outset of my research project that there is a divide between academia and activism is well entrenched in academic debate. Reiter and Oslender's (2014) edited collection, *Bridging scholarship and activism*, for instance, uses this division as their starting point; quoting Marx's widely cited statement: 'philosophers have hitherto only interpreted the world in various ways; the point is to change it'. The title of the collection puts particular emphasis on separation. The 'bridging' implies that academia and activism are discrete activities on opposite sides of a canyon; or as I felt it, on opposite sides of a cityscape. Reiter and Oslender, and the writers in their collection, call for greater movement between academia and activism: asking for bridges to be built and crossed repeatedly. In their introduction, Reiter and Oslender outline a kind of crisis of legitimacy, in which academics have become increasingly detached from the world outside their 'ivory tower' and too narrowly focused on publishing esoteric (read: confusing and impenetrable to anyone outside – and often inside – academia) articles only a handful of people will read. Activists, on the other hand, are down in the dirt, in touch with grassroots communities, making change happen but lack a certain rigour to their activities and could benefit from institutional research (albeit of the engaged kind). Academia and activism could be a productive couple, if only academics were to rethink their role in society.

The characterization of academia as a place of rigour and knowledge, and activism as a place of emotion and action, is fairly pervasive throughout interdisciplinary academic commentary on academic activism. Many others follow a similar characterization of academia and activism as in Reiter and Oslender's collection (Speed, 2006; Naples, 2010; Khasnabish and Haiven, 2015; Couture, 2017). Flood et al (2013) argue that academic activism is composed of four elements: (1) producing knowledge to inform social change; (2) a methodology of research which realizes social change through the research process; (3) a pedagogical commitment to social change education; and (4) seeking to disrupt inequalities within academia itself. Academic activism, then, is a kind of 'hybrid identity' which (uncomfortably) balances cultural critique and political action (Petray, 2012). As Sudbury and Okazawa-Rey (2009: 3) argue in their edited collection about activist scholarship, academic activism involves 'the production of knowledge and pedagogical practices through engagements with, and in the service of, progressive social movements'.

There is a kind of veneration of social movements which saturates these perspectives. While academia may have more rigour and theory, social movements have true and just causes at their heart. Accordingly, academia should meld to activism and become more 'active' and 'practical' in the process (Speed, 2006; Reiter and Oslender, 2014). Radical interpretation of the world is all well and good, but if it is not matched with political action, then it will never reach its potential. In this vein, academia is argued to have much to add to activism, and there is vast potential in academics resisting institutional demands to narrowly focus on topics of academic interest (Varkarolis and

King, 2017), partnering with communities (Brennan, 2019), and bringing their knowledge to the aid of social justice (Sudbury and Okazawa-Rey, 2009; Yerbury and Burridge, 2013; Khasnabish and Haiven, 2015).

As I started my research project, I found that my own field of critical management studies (CMS) was replete with similar debates. From the very inception of my field, academics had debated among themselves how best to create change 'out there' (Alvesson and Willmott, 1992). This was a particular concern for 'critically' minded scholars, who were intent on questioning and challenging taken-for-granted assumptions about issues as broad as capitalism, neoliberalism, managerialism, neo-colonialism, and the importance of gender, race, (dis)ability, and class to work and organization (Alvesson et al, 2011; Pullen et al, 2017). The 'C' in CMS seemed, therefore, to be more closely connected with activism in its often-damning critique of mainstream managerial and capitalist practices and heartfelt calls for a radically different and more just future. By the time I entered the fray nearly 40 years after the conception of my field, the debates had shifted very little. In fact, there were ongoing calls that came out in academic journals which wanted more 'performative' research (King and Learmonth, 2015) and research that worked with alternative organizations and their social movement kin (Parker et al, 2014b) as a way of bringing a *doing* to critical work. I heartily chuckled at the comment that CMS scholars are too often 'writ[ing] notebooks full of bad poetry that no one else will read' (Parker, 2013: 168) and took the sentiments of bringing the *doing* to my critical work to heart.

It is worth widening our view here, to acknowledge that academic activism is one way, among many ways, of thinking about how change happens through academia. For instance, I had entered the university system at a time when there was an increasing fixation on 'research impact'. Research impact is concerned with a greater connection between academics and the world beyond academia, usually characterized as 'industry' and sometimes 'community'. Edited collections such as *Achieving impact in research* (Denicolo, 2014) or *Bad to good: Achieving high quality impact in your research* (Woodside, 2016) argue that research impact is understood as a 'paradigm shift' from a focus on curiosity driven, academically excellent research, to accountability driven, targeted, outcome-focused research. Meaningful outcomes are considered by proponents of research impact to be a natural flow on from good research (hence the pointed title 'bad to good'). In simple terms: academics develop knowledge with the intent of being useful and then apply it in community or industry settings to improve on what is already present. In a similar way to academic activism, then, knowledge is not considered useful unless it is tied to action.

The quest for research impact, however, is rather a horse of a different colour to academic activism. Research impact is often conceptualized as the white horse with an academic champion proudly astride, having accepted their responsibility to industry and intending to improve their outcomes. Less metaphorically, research impact presents itself as a politically neutral and logical next step for researchers to produce knowledge for the good of all. Research impact is often also framed in relation to a 'crisis of legitimacy' (Denicolo, 2014), but one in which the university is required to produce knowledge for all because universities are (increasingly partially) publicly funded. In this sense, academics are conceptualized as needing to produce 'bang' for the 'public buck' by producing knowledge that is good for all rather than of benefit to an elite group of cloistered scholars. Knowledge for the every(wo)man.

As Rhodri Thomas (2018) explores, in *Questioning the assessment of research impact*, however, the conceptualization of research impact and the role of the academic is problematic. Thomas argues that research impact is underpinned by neoliberal values and assumes that universities should inform industry in a unidirectional 'impact'. In this way, academics are framed as influencing industry or community if they undertake appropriately structured research. Thomas also underscores that the seemingly neutral political framing of research impact overlooks the power dynamics and social inequalities which form the fabric of research and society. Academics are situated in a relationship with communities in which they hold (value free) knowledge and set out to improve industry or community practice. Thomas contests this framing and argues that academics should focus on teaching as their primary method of knowledge distribution, and therefore changing where they can achieve social impact. In spite of such critiques, research impact remains an influential way of thinking about the role of academics in creating social change.

Where research impact is the white horse with the champion academic astride (who has finally sorted out their priorities and realized impact should naturally flow on from good research), academic activism is more of an untamed beast, pretty sure that staying in the comfy stables is a bad idea but also unsure how to run free on the open plains. Again, less metaphorically, academic activism has an explicit political dimension embedded in a distrust of institutions (including the university). In comparison to research impact, academic activism is less concerned with 'tinkering' with the social world and more concerned with radical reimagining of the social landscape in the name of social justice. Moreover, whereas research impact is a unidirectional flow, Hale (2019) underscores that academic engagement with activists is (or at least, should be) mutually constituted. Unlike research impact where research is the 'ideal' fit for solving practice problems, Hale argues that the mutual 'contributions materialize not through some idealized fit between activism and scholarship but rather through engagement with their multiple contradictions' (2019: 22). Academic activism is more struggle than flow. But a productive struggle.

The conceptualization of both research impact and academic activism I have presented here are ways of thinking about the relationship between academics and communities (and sometimes activists) and social impact/change. My point is not to depict research impact as 'bad' and academic activism as 'good'. Alternatively, I use this contrast to highlight the various ways that we can draw lines around what is 'academic' and what is 'activist' and between academic/activist and social change. The lines we draw have varying effects: research impact tends to overlook power dynamics; academic activism comes up against institutional norms. Crucially, the lines I have mapped here can be continuously remapped. There are many ways of conceptualizing the academics, activists, and communities (as I will return to in the next chapter). These are not static identities. What is important, then, is our knowledge of the lines we draw and our capacity to understand the possibilities and limitations of drawing lines in that way. These lines are shaped by institutional and social norms, political commitments, and power dynamics that permeate our relationships with others.

At this stage of my institutional story of arrival, however, my understanding of academic activism was dramatically less nuanced. I was acutely suspicious of research impact and its neoliberal (over)tone and felt that academic activism which situates academics developing theory *with* activists in service of the movement more clearly aligned with my political and ethical commitments. In the company of research about bridging academia and activism, I thought extensively about how my own research could provide that level of academic 'rigour' and community 'engagement' that were necessary for activist research. A feminist ethnography seemed a complementary research methodology that would allow me to work in the field with activists while continuing my academic research about identity and social change. I was prepared for the struggle between values and priorities (Hale, 2019). I wanted to research, as Naples (2010) (drawing on Anzaldúa (2012)), describes, in the borderlines between activism and scholarship, and had dreams of carrying academic/activist knowledge across these borders. I also questioned whether I should remain in academia if I was truly dedicated to creating social change. Surely if I was so dedicated to social justice, I should be out 'in the field' instead of cloistered in my comfortable office with its panoptical view of the city below me?

Settling in

This theoretical background provided me with the starting point to thinking about academic activism. As I have noted, however, my institutional story of arrival is only one of my intertwined stories of arrival at reimagining academic activism. I also have an empirical story of arrival. Armed with my initial view of academic activism, I came out from behind my books and entered into 'the field'. Specifically, I started volunteering with an anti-violence feminist collective in Aotearoa New Zealand as part of my ethnographic research project about identities and social change. I was to volunteer with this collective for nine months as I also observed, interviewed, and analysed my colleagues' actions. At the outset of my volunteer work, I carefully explained to the collective how my research expertise could benefit them and that I would be dually dedicated to their social justice mission as well as my own research. In more poetic terms, I offered to be a bridge between the academic world and the world of activism. I did, of course, see my research on identities and social change as ultimately beneficial to the collective's work, but this was to be a separate contribution to my 'on the ground' contributions to their activist work.

The collective specialized in supporting women and children subjected to domestic violence. My homeland, Aotearoa New Zealand, has some of the highest rates of violence against women in the developed world. One in three women will be subjected to physical or sexual abuse from an intimate partner, and one in two women will be subjected to psychological or emotional abuse (Fanslow and Robinson, 2011). A feminist perspective on gendered violence has helped activists to unpick the ways in which institutional and individual violence against women is intertwined with the systematic devaluation of women (Ali and Naylor, 2013) as well as trans and non-binary folk, their needs, and experiences (Ristock, 2011). The likelihood of violence is also tied to other identities, with Māori women being twice as likely as Pākehā[1] women to be subjected to violence (Te Puni Kōkiri, 2010) and bisexual women being most likely to be subjected to sexual violence from a partner (Dickson, 2016). Feminist activists have, accordingly, identified the multiple, interlocking systems of inequality which compound gendered violence (Wilson et al, 2016).

There has been a prolonged activist-led response to violence against women and gender minorities in Aotearoa New Zealand, with many networks of activists emerging from the women's liberation movement in the 1960s and 1970s (Else, 1993). Various activist groups have achieved huge shifts in public attitudes towards domestic violence as a gendered, social problem. Importantly, these organizations were grounded in feminism. Feminism is a particular way of thinking about social justice, usually related to gender inequality, and often centres on thinking about how our gendered experiences shape how we interact with one another in ways that are just or unjust (Ahmed, 2017). Feminist organizations opposing forms of gendered violence have taken many forms such as collectives, coalitions, and leaderless networks. These alternative ways of organizing have helped anti-violence activists to unpick systems of violence through creating new ways of organizing which attempt to be non-violent and democratic (Ferree and Martin, 1995; McMillan, 2007). Feminist anti-violence activism has, from this basis, successfully repositioned domestic violence as a social issue and impelled governments, businesses, and communities to address gendered violence.

The need for anti-violence activism is ongoing, however. Gendered violence continues to be a pervasive social issue globally, with one in three women subjected to violence at the hands of a partner (UNODC, 2018). Moreover, anti-violence activists have grappled with ensuring their activism is intersectional and combatting issues arising from 'mainstreaming' of anti-violence work (Bordt, 1997); such as a de-radicalization of anti-violence work when it is addressed by businesses as an individual economic issue, rather than collective political issue (Weatherall et al, 2021). To add another layer of complexity, many once informal anti-violence groups have now been formalized as community organizations in the third sector. While this formalization has benefits, such as increased funding and public legitimacy, there are also limitations and complexities of doing political work in a more institutionalized way, such as being less willing to critique funders including the government (Arnold and Ake, 2013).

The collective was integral to the activist response to domestic violence in Aotearoa New Zealand. They continue to work throughout the country with victims of violence to support them in whatever they need, from counselling, to support in court, to emergency housing, to caring for pets, to empowerment programmes. Broadly speaking, the collective considers this individual activism. The collective also engages in systems activism, including conducting feminist-oriented research; meetings with government officials; training judges, lawyers, and health care professionals; protests; petitions; and public education. As a volunteer, I supported the systems activist team of about twenty women (the number fluctuated over the course of my voluntary work). The collective structure meant that power was decentralized, and systems activists worked for the individual activists, who in turn worked for victims of violence. Additionally, the collective was guided by four core principles: decolonization, diversity, collectivism, and LGBT+ Pride. As with other feminist activist groups in Aotearoa New Zealand (Huygens, 2001, 2011), the collective attempted to share power equally between Māori and Tauiwi[2] and to centre lines of identity which shape individual and institutional violence against victims.

The situation of the collective in the broader context of the community sector was significant. The community sector in Aotearoa New Zealand is dominated by cultural, recreation, civic, and advocacy organizations;

with small, grassroots groups making up about 84 per cent of the sector (Sanders et al, 2008). Although the sector has a significant economic impact, contributing 5.3 per cent of gross domestic product and employing 4.4 per cent of the workforce, it is the *social* impact of the community sector that is seen as most significant (McLeod, 2017). Community sector organizations engage in social support and activism; two features considered foundational to the sector itself. As part of my project, I also talked with a variety of community sector experts and activists in addition to my voluntary work with the collective. My conversations with these experts spanned a range of topics, but the core focus was on the role of community organizations in creating change in Aotearoa New Zealand. Without exception, these conversations underscored that community organizations amplified the voice for those impacted by inequality and held government and the private sector to account for those oversights and failings (Neilson et al, 2015).

My position in the collective and the broader community sector as both an 'insider' who was dedicated to the social justice cause of the collective, and an 'outsider' who was bringing an academic perspective to the organization's activities seemed, at first, to neatly coalesce with the research I was reading about academic activism. I was crossing that bridge every day, deepening my knowledge of the collective and their ongoing role in anti-violence activism and analysing that knowledge through theory. My work in the field informed my teaching on a university subject about ethics and organizations. In my ethnographic work I consistently invited feedback on my observations from my colleagues and incorporated the feminist principles of the collective into my research. Inspired by my colleagues' collective organizing, I also began creating a community within my university in which we supported one another to communally flourish in spite of the neoliberal context. This work continued after I left the field and moved institutions. If we return to Flood et al's (2013) definition of academic activism, I was certainly engaging in all four areas of their criteria, from research, to teaching, to engagement with the grassroots community.

And we could continue to understand my ethnographic work in this vein. I used my research skills in the collective to carry out a study of economic abuse in Aotearoa New Zealand which was a contributing factor to the passing of the landmark *Domestic Violence − Victims' Protection Act*. I met with police to argue for better responses from the judicial system. I went to meetings with politicians to advocate for the removal of benefit sanctions for women who refused to name the father of their child. We planned a protest in parliament, sticking black tape across our mouths if the government refused to pass legislation that would benefit victims of violence. I heard stories from victims who were subjected to abuse and shared these in magazines, newspapers, radio, social media, and television. My academic training gave me sharp analytical insights and my dedication to the social justice cause gave me a useful outlet for those skills.

All the while I took copious fieldnotes, undertook interviews with my colleagues, and delved into my (oh so theoretical) Judith Butler to analyse the relationships between identities and social change. I reflected on the role of the community sector, and regularly attended (and presented at) forums between researchers of the community sector and community sector activists. In my teaching, I encouraged my students to consider domestic violence as an industrial issue and committed to pedagogical practices that developed critical thinking and active citizenship. I connected with and supported other women in my department. In short, I was attempting to embody the principles of academic activism that I had carried with me into the field. Had I continued in this vein, from this point I would have gone on to demonstrate how these experiences offered insight into how academics could cross the bridge to activism. But my story of my arrival changed. Not long into my ethnographic work, the bridge collapsed.

2

Unsettling the In/Out

Academics who venture into 'the field' and engage with activists are frequently unsettled by the complexity of negotiating the lines of their academic and activist identities. As Reedy and King (2019) elucidate, those lines cross multiple other lines of identity such as insider and outsider or participant and friend. These lines of identity are further complicated by simultaneous, and sometimes divergent, institutional commitments to research and political commitments to the social justice cause of the movement. Consequently, academic activists often have a tangled sense of self and are unable to neatly distinguish one line from another. Other activist ethnographers have underscored, however, that examining the tangled lines of identity is essential to understanding the messy, multifaceted process of social change (Naples, 2003). As Behar (1996: 6) puts it, 'what happens within the observer must be made known ... if the nature of what has been observed is to be understood'. In other words, we can better understand social change if we come to terms with how we were changed.

It is unsurprising, then, that when I started volunteering with the collective, I quickly became unsettled. I was concurrently a volunteer, a colleague, a researcher, an insider, an outsider, an activist, an academic, and, in the end, a friend. For the first few weeks, I continued to carry my initial assumptions about academics and activists. But these lines became increasingly tangled as I repeatedly crossed the cityscape. My fieldnotes show a marked evolution from my 'academic' stiff and formal observations of my participants, to a vulnerable exploration of how my ideas and identities were unsettled as I learnt more from my colleagues. It was not that I had lost my sense of self as a researcher, academic, or activist. On the contrary, the more tangled I became, the more I was able to understand the margins I had drawn around my identities and the more I was able to understand the value of disrupting those lines. Inspired by my colleagues, I started to draw and redraw those lines. I allowed my sense of self to become undone, so I could see what emerged from the middle.

In the Preface, I have already referred to an experience which sparked my undoing. It is important to note, however, that my undoing was not a straightforward process from one set of ideas about academic/activist to another. Far from it. The reimagining I undertook was a messy endeavour in which I followed those tangled lines of identity. My focus shifted away from bridging fixed lines and towards exploring the value of the numerous ways academia and activism *could* be interconnected. Thus, the change in my understanding of academic activism cannot be reduced to a single moment, or 'root'. It is a non–linear succession of moments that surprise us, inspire us, unsettle us, repel us, and change us. Those moments take us in many directions. Accordingly, the moment which I recapitulate here draws together ideas from the previous chapter, and points to other lines to follow:

I was sitting in a warm, comfortable room with several of my colleagues. On our arrival at our workspace this morning, five of us had filtered into a training room for a day of reflection about working with women and gender minorities who were subjected to intimate partner violence. From an ethnographic perspective, I was particularly interested in this day of reflection as it seemed to align with my interest in the connection between identities and social change perfectly. Notebook in hand, I came prepared to collect my data. At the same time, I was interested beyond my research, as I was keen to learn more about how to effectively provide women and gender minorities with support.

We settled into our chairs as I took in and made notes about the room. There were stacks of boxes along one wall, spilling over with donated bath products, new toys, and clothing for victims of violence. We did not accept second-hand goods. Victims deserved more than someone else's castoffs. The furniture we sat on was mismatched and old. An excellent and interesting contrast, I felt, to the shiny products that surrounded us. A spring was uncomfortably digging into my back; a reminder to stay alert and observant of uncomfortable realities. There was a whiteboard at the front of the room towards which the furniture was orientated.

Two women – Serena and Jules (who we will meet again later in the book) – started by telling us about the feminist approach of the collective to working with women and gender minorities. Serena gently explained how her starting point was that 'women were experts in their own reality'. Victims of violence, she explained, had extremely sophisticated understandings of their experience, what safety meant, how violence alters your sense of self, who can be trusted to help, and skills for surviving their reality. Even if victims sometimes did not have the language to articulate those experiences in words, they carried that knowledge in their bodies. Seeing victims otherwise (that is, in need of specialists or experts to tell them what to do) was part of a patriarchal undermining of women's and gender minorities' embodied knowledge. Jules explained that it was the role of the collective to learn from the skills and knowledge victims already possessed rather than to provide 'expert advice'. Serena and Jules also emphasized that the collective was still a centre of expertise (collated from learning about the experiences of many victims of violence), but that this expertise was directed to other institutions – such as the judicial system – and not to victims of gendered violence.

I was unsettled by this account. That moment stayed in my mind for the rest of the day, even as the conversation moved on. What was it about this account that was so unsettling? I repeatedly asked when I was back in my university office. I kept repeating the phrase to myself: *women are experts in their own reality*. A few days later, as I was still searching from an answer, I stumbled across an academic article that gave me the language to voice my discomfort:

> [the] view [that academia involves the production of knowledge and activism involves political action] is based on a series of taken-for-granted and highly problematic ontological dichotomies, including mind/body, theory/practice, reason/emotion, abstract/concrete and 'ivory tower'/'real world'. Perhaps most fundamentally, these serve to set up thinking and reflecting in opposition to doing or acting. (Eschle and Maiguashca, 2006: 119)

Eschle and Maiguashca (2006) write from an explicitly feminist position, drawing on feminist work to challenge the subordination of the body, practice, and emotion, and to critique the unhelpful dichotomy of academic/activist connected to those divisions. Their article deeply resonated with my experience in the collective. I was surprised, and more than a little ashamed, that I had so readily accepted (gendered) divisions between academia and activism. And the revelation initiated the collapse of my academic/activist bridge.

The conceptualization of knowledge, embodiment, victims, and activists proposed by Serena offered me insight into my problematic construction of academia and activism. Serena underscored that the collective considered that expertise about gendered violence was primarily held by victims, rather than the activists. Activists learnt from women and gender minorities about their simultaneous conceptualization and embodiment of their reality. The collective was providing victims with language to articulate their knowledge *differently*, certainly, but their starting point was that women and gender minorities already had a sophisticated understanding of gendered violence. Importantly, the collective considered certain kinds of knowledge, particularly embodied knowledge, as core to creating change for victims. To put it another way, concepts such as safety or violence were simultaneously understood and embodied by victims in their unique reality. Those supporting victims of violence must learn from that interconnection.

The approach of the collective, as well as my accompanying reading, spurred me to further question my own ideas about academic activism. If I took direct inspiration from my colleagues, should my role be to *learn* from activists? Should I put emphasis on embodied knowledge? Could I reimagine my approach to academic activism by following the collective's tools and ideas? Were any aspects of my initial approach useful? Although my sense of self and my ideas about working with activists were unsettled, I felt that it was a useful movement. I recognized that the lines I had drawn between academia and activism were unhelpful and contrary to my political commitments to social justice for victims of violence. Thankfully, to undo these lines and draw new ones, I had access to the wealth of sophisticated, thought-provoking ideas of the collective as well as the writing of other scholars grappling with similar questions which I could follow.

(Re)settling in and out

I began to seek out diverse ideas about how the relationship between academics and activists could be understood. As Shayne (2014) highlights through their edited collection, *Taking risks: Feminist activism and research in the Americas*, there are many ways to engage in social justice work. These approaches, however, do not necessarily frame their work using the terms 'academic' or 'activist'. Feminist research, queer research, indigenous research, action research, and many others, are all approaches to social justice research which offer a unique conceptualization of the entanglement of researchers and communities. Encouraged by the collection, I started to engage with the writing of researchers and communities working in a variety of traditions. I focused my exploration specifically on work which resonated with the commitments of the collective: decolonization, feminism, collectivism, and LGBT+ pride.

I reflected on my responsibilities as a Pākehā researcher to the Tangata Whenua[1] of Aotearoa New Zealand as I read Linda Smith's (2012) powerful treatise, *Decolonizing methodologies*, which encouraged indigenous researchers to resist the ongoing harms of colonization by reimagining their approach to research. I considered my place and responsibility to the queer community by reading Eve Sedgwick's (1994) complex account of how to craft liveable futures for queer youth in *Tendencies*. The feminist dedication to giving voice to women's stories in *Troubling the angels* showed me how research could represent academic and community interests simultaneously (Smithies and Lather, 1997). The work of feminist anti-racist scholars in *This bridge called my back* compelled me to recognize and value difference through our organizing processes as well as through writing (Moraga and Anzaldúa,

2015). These writers, as well as others, developed my imaginative capacity for how the relationship between researchers and their communities could be understood.

If we circle back to the components of academic activism that Flood et al (2013) outlined, the research I engaged with incorporates these dimensions, albeit to differing degrees. The approaches all articulate their political commitments and understanding of social justice; a methodological approach aligned with those political commitments; and their concrete attempts to create liveable futures for those subjected to inequality. In spite of those foundational similarities, the approaches are still very different. The decolonizing methodologies of Linda Smith as a Māori women reclaiming and mobilizing indigenous knowledge in Aotearoa seems worlds apart from Eve Sedgwick's gathering students in her home to learn about queer history during a liberal arts degree in the United States.

What these diverse approaches offered, then, were geographically, historically, and socially specific (re)imaginings of the relationship between academics, activists, communities, the university, and (ultimately) social justice. These approaches were not 'bridges' between different worlds, but holistic reimaginings of how researchers and the communities within which they were embedded could work together for social justice. The power of each of the approaches grew from an entanglement of the unique moments in which they lived with their pursuit of social justice. These singularities incorporated the attention to 'moments' and the concurrent practices which would help to bring social justice into those settings. Thus, while my reading circled me away from my starting point to other social issues, in other traditions, in other contexts, I appreciated the resonance of those ideas with the work of the collective. My imaginative capacity thus magnified, I continued to (re)draw my lines of academic activism.

At first, I was particularly keen to explore how my collective's emphasis on victim's embodied knowledge of violence could be utilized to help me reimagine academic activism. I embraced my colleagues' 'learning from' approach and thought of my colleagues as experts of their reality which I had a responsibility to understand. Aziz Choudry (2020) advocates for a similar approach, emphasizing that academics need to learn from how activists think, learn, and generate knowledge, and to do so, we must recentre our understanding of activist scholarship as not primarily tied to the university. As I continued to make my transitions across the cityscape, however, I felt that I wanted to further question those lines which draw a fixed difference between academic and activist.

My emerging approach to academic activism was enhanced and shaped by my engagement with Deleuze and Guattari's exploration of the rhizome. In *A thousand plateaus: Capitalism and schizophrenia*, Deleuze and Guattari suggest that knowledge could take inspiration from the rhizome. Instead of having a singular root, a rhizome is a type of plant that consists of multiple, semi-independent nodes that follow lines, but grow and spread in their own way. As they describe: 'any point of the rhizome can be connected to anything other, and must be. This is very different from the tree or root, which plots a point, fixes an order' (1987: 5). Through this conceptualization they suggest that we could take a non-linear or non-hierarchical approach to research, argumentation, and theory. (Un)structuring research in a rhizomatic way means that there is no 'root' from which all branches and leaves bud and develop. Alternatively, there are ceaseless connections formed in semiotic chains, overlapping lines which are followed rather than fixed points, there are multiple entryways, and there are multiple points of breaking and reconnecting. As Deleuze and Guattari argue, we should take inspiration from:

> The wisdom of plants: even when they have roots there is always an outside where they form a rhizome with something else ... Follow the plants: you start by delineating a first line consisting of circles of convergence around successive singularities then you see whether inside that line new circles of convergence establish themselves, with new points located outside the limits in other directions. (1987: 11)

I should follow the wisdom of plants and the wisdom of women. Both are experts in their own reality. The wonderful variety of approaches to social change I continued to encounter in my readings and my work alongside my colleagues were those circles of convergence. The collective's commitments to decolonization, feminism, collectivism, and LGBT+ pride were lines which overlapped with gendered violence and allowed my colleagues multiple ways into tackling that violence. My colleagues were grappling with how to continue these commitments in an ever-changing political, social, and economic context. Their own activist lines crossed other lines of their identity. Significantly, this complexity meant their activism was never singular. Alternatively, their work consisted of successive singularities which grew from the intersection of the social context, anti-violence work, and their own identities. These dimensions were endlessly mutating.

In paying attention to the 'successive singularities' of my colleagues, I could explore the circles of convergence between academia and activism connected to this context. I could follow the interconnections of theory and practice, reason and emotion, body and mind between my work and my colleagues' work. A rhizomatic approach resonated with my desire to 'unfix' the order of academic activism and alternatively understand how academia and activism could grow and spread in the context of my work with the collective. In this way, I could continue to learn from my colleagues while exploring other lines of difference and how the context of feminist anti-violence work could lead academic activism in new directions. With this intent in mind, I turn back to my empirical story of arrival, to explicitly bring my worlds into contact and trace the lines. I return to my unique geographical, historical, and socio-political moment in which I entered into the anti-violence movement and worked alongside activists who fight against gendered violence in Aotearoa New Zealand. This time, however, I focus on the circles of convergence.

Into the field(s)

Effectively, I had been part of the community sector all my life; raising donations for charities as a child, participating in non-profit sporting clubs, volunteering at various organizations during university. But this time felt different. I was entering the sector with the explicit aim of developing academic knowledge about the role of community organizations in creating social change. The community sector goes by many names: the not-for-profit sector, the charity sector, the for-purpose sector, the voluntary sector, civil society (Corry, 2010), to name but a few. Whatever name these organizations go by, they form a vital part of our social landscape. The particular role(s) which community organizations play in society is widely debated by academics, practitioners, and policymakers alike. More economically minded policymakers and academics propose that community organizations fill in the gaps in the provision of goods and services that government and business do not, if those needs are not sufficiently utilitarian or profitable (Ghatak, 2020). More civically minded policymakers and academics consider community organizations a fundamental role in democracy through which citizens can participate in democratic processes and have their voices heard (Fung, 2003). Still other policymakers and academics argue that community organizations play an explicit social justice role, serving communities subjected to various forms of inequality (Dale and Onyx, 2005). The many roles of community organizations exist concurrently and overlap with each other. That plurality of form and function is both enriching and bewildering in equal measure; there are many lines to follow.

In my specific context of Aotearoa New Zealand, the role of community sector was significantly influenced by ideas and forms of civil society transported by British colonists (Tennant et al, 2008). Uniquely, however, community organizations were also strongly shaped by Tangata Whenua and Māori models of organizing (Tennant, 2005). The dual lines of influence in the sector refract the relationship between White British settlers (or Pākehā) and the indigenous Māori which was codified in Te Tiriti o Waitangi/The

Treaty of Waitangi in 1840 (Bell, 2006). The rights of Māori were violated by the Pākehā settlers following the treaty in many ways. Māori land was confiscated, Pākehā attempted to abolish the language, Te Reo, and many Māori experienced displacement of from their *iwi*[2] (Walker, 2004). By Māori, for Māori organizations have therefore played a fundamental role in tackling intersecting political underrepresentation, economic inequality, and institutional racism (Tennant, 1989; Rawiri Waretini, 2012). In addition to the social, political, and economic roles of community organizations delineated by mostly Western scholars (Hull et al, 2011), there is an important cultural role which shapes form and function and leads us, once again, in new directions.

The struggle for social justice is an important dimension of many community organizations, in many different forms. Researchers and practitioners within the community sector understand community organizations as adding immense social value to peoples' lives (Neilson et al, 2015). Community organizations can play an important advocacy or activist role. Organizations embedded in the community can amplify the voice of citizens and influence elites (like governments) to tackle systemic social issues (Shaw and Allen, 2006; Erakovic and McMorland, 2009). Importantly, community organizations also offer a range of vital social services as a material response to pressing social problems such as homelessness, domestic violence, or mental health (McLeod, 2017). These organizations, then, possess a wealth of evolving knowledge about collective efforts to achieve social justice. The close connections between social justice community organizations, the government, businesses, and communities result in a high degree of potential political and social influence.

I entered the community sector, however, at a tumultuous time. In the year I started my research project, Garth Nowland-Foreman wrote a strongly critical essay about the 'crushing' weight of government control over the sector (Nowland-Foreman, 2016a). Additionally, trade union activists and academics Sandra Grey and Charles Sedgwick published a similarly damning report about the degradation of the sector's capacity to engage activism only a few years prior (Grey and Sedgwick, 2013b). Since the 1980s, the sector had been increasingly formalized and professionalized, with many socially or civically minded members of the sector mourning the devastation decades of neoliberal policy had wrought (Laurie and Bondi, 2005). Aotearoa New Zealand was not alone in undergoing these neoliberal shifts. Similar contexts including Australia, the UK, and Canada were likewise affected (Hull et al, 2011), which had ripple effects in non-Western contexts (Bernal and Grewal, 2014). While the influences of neoliberal policies on the community sector have been many (and I return to this in Part II), I want to focus here on the influence these policies have had on the role of community organizations in social change.

When I began my formal interviews with members of the community sector there was a palpable sense that the sector had become less radical and increasingly institutionalized over the past 30 years. The decline of civic participation and collective action in tandem with the rise of institutionalized forms of social service echoed on the international stage. Discussions by academics and community members in the similar contexts of Australia (Onyx et al, 2010) and the UK (King, 2017) also had been severely impacted by government policies and changes in social attitudes. Crucially, these environmental changes also change the lines of power. For instance, whereas community organizations may once have strongly opposed changes to legislation or the distribution of resources which compounded inequality, fear of losing government funding could curtail activism. The worry, then, was clear: activism in the community sector was losing its bite. In spite of the numerous challenges facing community organizations, activists in the sector remained dedicated to their cause. Their activism, however, looked different.

Academic and activist Jenny Onyx charted this transition in the context of Australia. Onyx and colleagues map a noticeable shift from community organizations engaging in direct, targeted, and critical 'outsider' activism to adopting softer, more institutional approaches in the neoliberal political and economic environment (Onyx et al, 2010). Even with the movement towards 'advocacy with gloves on', however, Onyx and colleagues emphasize that a binary between 'radical' and 'institutional' activism is unhelpful. Alternatively, they underscore that community organizations developed complex and strategic approaches for an environment which was not particularly conducive to radical change. In other words, activism is not a 'one-size-fits-all' prescriptive model. Community organizations shift and change their activism as the social, political, or economic conditions change. These changes, of course, are not neutral. Different approaches to social change have different political and social effects.

As I started my work with the collective, I experienced and observed these fault lines. As I noted in Chapter 1, the collective had started as a loose network of volunteers that emerged from the feminist movement of the 1960s and 1970s. Over time, however, they had become increasingly formalized as they received funding from various sources including government. While this allowed them to provide more support for women, children, and gender minorities subjected to violence, it also came hand-in-hand with a suite of monitoring and auditing practices required by funders. The collective's closer relationship with government gave them access to policymaking but at the same time made members less willing to publicly criticize government (in)action. Māori were equal partners and received half of the resources (even when those resources were donated to Pākehā), but the organization still grappled with systemic racism and the intergenerational violence of colonization in the collective as well as outside. Additionally, while the collective remained dedicated to non-violent organizing principles and continued to operate as a collective, external pressures had led them to appointing a CEO. While the CEO reported to the collective, she was the 'face' of the collective in outward-facing media. Most of my colleagues still considered themselves feminist activists and the collective continued to advocate for radical change, but there were numerous tensions as a result of concurrent institutionalization and formalization.

At the same time as I was feeling these various pressures 'in the field', I was reflecting on how these experiences resonated with my role at the university. Supposedly, the community sector was my 'out there', the world beyond my ivory tower and my pile of books. Yet, my reading about the sector, my discussions with community sector members, and my work at the collective felt close to my experience at the university. I was hearing discussions about the degradation of academic freedom, the commercialization of university education (Parker, 2018), the whiteness of the academy (Molisa, 2010), and the perceived decline in radical academic thought (Alvesson and Gabriel, 2013) and action in favour of 'gloves on' approaches like research impact. Those challenges seemed eerily parallel to the degradation of civic action, the professionalism of the community sector, the systemic racism impacting Māori, and the shift towards institutionalized activism. In fact, universities in my context of Aotearoa New Zealand were actually registered as not-for-profit organizations with a public mandate to be the critic and conscience of society (Grace, 2010). Like the community sector more broadly, universities had undergone a similar transition towards business-like behaviour and more institutionalized approaches to social change.

These circles of convergence further solidified for me that there was much to be gained by looking at what grew *between* academia and activism. Treating academia and activism as discrete fields was unhelpful. Activism in the community sector was not a straightforward 'doing' of social change or simplistically 'radical' in its approach. On the contrary, community sector organizations had complex and often contradictory relationships with institutions. Core values such as community, democracy, and social justice were always being (re)negotiated as the social, political, and economic context changed. These struggles played out in a different way in academia, but in ways that resonated. The complex relationship between academics focused on social justice and an increasingly corporatized university, exemplifies that reverberation. Accordingly, academia cannot be reduced to impact-ready theory or institutionalized approaches to change. There are multiple lines of connection we can follow which highlight the overlaps and divergences. The connections offer unique ways of thinking about and undertaking social justice work. We grow from that in between.

Into the feminist anti-violence movement

My engagement with the community sector altered the course of my empirical and institutional story of arrival. I was shifting my institutional story through learning from members of the community sector. I no longer considered academic activism to be a 'bridge' between two different worlds, with reason/emotion and knowledge/practice firmly situated on the opposite sides of a cityscape. The more I learnt from my participants, and the more I read on the variety of approaches to creating social change, the more I struggled with uncertainty about how I wanted to approach academic activism. The bridge collapsed, I wandered away from the remains, and now I was sensing my way through a nebulous landscape. A quote from Clifford beautifully encapsulated my thinking: 'we ground things now, on a moving earth' (Clifford and Marcus, 2011: 22). The earth continued to move, and I with it, into the feminist anti-violence movement. I have already delineated how I set out and was unsettled as a volunteer ethnographer with the collective. I return to those circles of convergence to explore how I found productive lines to follow.

Anti-violence feminist activism has a long history in Aotearoa New Zealand (Else, 1993), as it does in other Western countries. The importance of feminism to anti-violence social movements cannot be overstated (Nichols, 2013). Even before focusing my research on anti-violence feminist activists, I had considered myself a feminist. At the time of entering the field I considered feminism a fairly stable social movement interested in gender equality. Naturally, it seemed to me, it followed that I should engage with *the* women's movement (as I so casually assumed the singular at this point in my history) as part of being a feminist and academic activist. From the moment I engaged with my colleagues in the collective, however, I realized how simplistic my version of feminism was, and how ignorant I had been of the rich and complex history of feminism in Aotearoa New Zealand and beyond.

The 1960s, 1970s, and 1980s are often perceived as a radical and progressive time for the feminist anti-violence movement (Ferree and Martin, 1995). Collectives were born, shelters were created, women came together to fight for justice, and manifold innovations in politics, thought, and practice emerged. More recently, however, the movement globally was perceived to be in decline, de-politicized and overly professionalized (Barrett et al, 2016), and increasingly fractured along different lines of identity (Connell, 2019). The collective, born in this radical period, was grappling with these issues. There were tensions between Māori, who often rejected feminism as a Western concept privileged over indigenous ways of imagining women's equality (Irwin, 1990), and Pākehā, who wanted unity in their search for justice. There were tensions between straight women, who wanted to focus on men's violence against women, and queer women, who felt the erasure of their experiences and voices in that narrative. There were tensions between cis-women, who wanted 'women's' only spaces, and trans and non-binary folk, who were often excluded from these spaces. There were tensions between old women, who firmly rejected government involvement in their activities, and young educated women who wanted to engage with institutions and provide more professional services. There were tensions between migrant women, who experienced additional layers of racism or discrimination, and women with the privilege of citizenship, who were afforded protections by the state. There were tensions between women and gender minorities in all of their complexity and diversity.

In the second week of my volunteer work with the collective, I came face-to-face with these tensions. I was fortunate enough to attend a gathering of the collective during which they discussed many of the issues they were facing in their work with victims of violence along the various lines of identity. As part of these discussions, the members of the collective would literally organize along those lines of identity. During the gathering Māori would meet with Māori while Pākehā met with Pākehā. Lesbian women would meet with lesbian women, while straight women met with straight women. I was impressed and intrigued at the collective's direct confrontation of the issues which permeated the broader feminist anti-violence movement. This was not a happy picture of justice, however, as I quickly learnt from my colleagues:

> In the late afternoon during the gathering, I was sitting with a group of my colleagues in a cold corridor discussing the day's events. In this instance, I was primarily listening, rather than adding my own opinion on the way the collective structured their activism. I was surprised that in discussing the meetings along lines of identity, my colleagues primarily communicated feelings of exclusion. Gracie explained how she had been told as a bisexual woman that she wasn't 'gay enough' to attend the discussion with the lesbian women, but too gay for the meeting of straight women. Kimberley told us that as a light-skinned urban Māori she felt out of place with the Māori women raised on the *marae*. Emily hated that her pursuit of a PhD had compromised her legitimacy with some activists because of her increasing interest in feminist theory. Riley felt that it was absurd that Pacifica women like her had to attend the meeting with Pākehā women because the collective only divided along two lines of racial identity. My colleagues were frustrated that their complex sense of self and experiences were reduced to simple lines of identity. While there was no doubt that difference was important to the collective's activism, the lines of feminism, identity, and activism were significantly fractured.

As with the way my empirical story of arrival compelled me to rethink the community sector, this experience early in the field sparked a reimagination of my theoretical (feminist) approach to social justice. I went back to the academic literature, moved by my colleagues' struggles and concerned by the evidence I felt I had gathered which confirmed the decline of anti-violence feminism. Yet, as I delved into the history of feminist organizing and the feminist anti-violence movement, I found nothing but these tensions and debates. The course of feminism never did run smooth. From the earliest moments of the feminist movement, feminists of colour argued that we must address and grapple with the differences *between* women (Arnold and Ake, 2013; Moraga and Anzaldúa, 2015). Feminists from non-Western contexts (Ferree and Tripp, 2006) and indigenous thinkers (Green, 2007) argued that feminism was only one way of thinking about women's empowerment and emancipation. Queer feminists questioned static notions of gender identity (Butler, 2006a). What I found, then, was many (many) ways of thinking about gendered social justice which refracted the unique contexts and knowledge of activists with a myriad of different, intersecting, gender, sexual, racial, geographic, and other identities. Far from undermining a feminist movement, however, these scholars and activists recast diversity as a point from which to consider our experiences of overlapping injustice rather than something to be 'overcome' or 'erased' (Lorde, 1983).

Arnold and Ake (2013: 558) summarize this need to reframe wonderfully. They suggest an alternative story of the anti-violence feminist movement, which is worth quoting at length, as:

> A movement [which] has consistently reinvented itself and its feminist frameworks, learned from its mistakes, and continues to challenge systems that fail survivors of abuse. The implicit and explicit nostalgia for the grassroots origins of the movement threatens to overshadow the attention to the progress and innovations the movement continues to inspire. At the same time, such nostalgia obscures the fact that internal conflicts and tensions – including the debate over the issue of decline itself – have been ongoing since the movement's beginnings.

Like the broader anti-violence movement, then, the collective had consistently engaged with these tensions throughout their history. The conflicts I encountered in those early days of my ethnography were part of the ongoing reinvention of feminism in relation to a shifting social landscape. This perspective of feminism as a diverse collection of voices which aimed to understand our interconnected experiences of gendered injustice resonated strongly with my experiences with my colleagues. They were fighting for justice through their differences, rather than in spite of their differences, and conflict was a necessary part of the collective struggle for ending gendered violence.

In feminist anti-violence work, then, theory and practice were always intimately intertwined. Since the beginning of the anti-violence movement, feminists, activists, and scholars have collaboratively reimagined domestic violence as a public, gendered issue embedded in broader social systems including colonization, capitalism, and patriarchy (McMillan, 2007). Importantly, this collective theoretical contribution has been developed through innovations in practice, such as experimentations in collective, decolonizing, and leaderless organizing (Ferree and Martin, 1995; McMillan, 2007; Huygens, 2011). My colleagues were continuing that legacy. They explored the margins of feminism and whether the collective's practice accounted for their difference. For my colleagues, theories of feminism and feminist practice were entangled. The conflicts and tensions were part of the necessary and productive work to question the margins of social justice frameworks and spill into new terrain.

I felt the echoes of the struggles of the anti-violence movement to reflect difference, counter institutionalization, and consistently reimagine their feminist frameworks, in my experience at the university. A nostalgia for a bygone university era of untamed radical academic thought free from pressures to publish, resonated with the nostalgia for the 1960s anti-violence movement. Similarly, many identities, such as Māori, are subjected to exclusion in academia through theory (for example, disregarding *mātauranga Māori*) and practice, and there are ongoing tensions and debates about how this can be changed. My struggle to reimagine my role in social justice was undertaken in a context in which academics were increasingly asked to codify their social impact. The integration of theory and practice, however, seemed less present in my university but a convergence which held potential. My colleagues created new ways of thinking about justice in tandem with new organizing practices which exemplified their theories. Perhaps, I considered, I could explore the '*and*' of theory and practice, and even the '*and*' of academia and activism, in my attempt to reimagine academic activism.

My journey of arrival, thus far, has circled away from my initial fixed ideas of academia and activism. At the outset, I considered academic identity bound by knowledge and theory and activist identity by practice and political know-how. My role as an academic activist would be to bridge those worlds. My empirical story of arrival drastically unsettled those concepts, and the bridge between them. As I took steps away, I immersed myself in the rich body of work by other researchers which holistically imagined their approach to social justice by embedding their concepts within unique social, historical, and geographic contexts. This social justice work was as diverse as anti-racist university teaching, social work with victims of sexual violence, organizing debates or discussions to share ideas of justice, providing public commentary on inequality, or volunteering for social movements. This work may not always be presented as 'activist', but it is vital to illustrate the diverse ways we can think about the connections between academics, communities, and social justice. As I engaged in my voluntary work with the collective, I moved in and out of these different ideas, not as binaries of ways of being, but as a complex, interconnected constellation of possibilities. I carried these lessons wherever I wandered in my cityscape.

Seeking new directions

In the two chapters of Part I I have followed my evolving understanding of academic activism. At the outset of my research project, I was passionate about contributing to the anti-violence feminist movement and considered (a particular kind of) academic activism to be core to that aim. Accordingly, before I joined the collective, I already had ideas of what constituted activism, feminism, and academia. I had clear lines around each position and the connection between each position. As I soon realized when I joined the collective, those lines were not fixed. Through my intertwined institutional and empirical stories of arrival, I have traced how my lines were undone. Simultaneously, I have taken inspiration from my colleagues to retrace the rhizomatic possibilities of reimagining academic activism. My aim in Part I has been to evoke the unsettling and thought-provoking process of undoing and to explore the rich variety of possibilities which can grow from that undoing. I have maintained, however, that those possibilities are entangled with the unique social, political, and economic context and consequent interlocking systems of inequality. To tackle social issues, such as gendered violence, we must continue to (re)invent our social justice frameworks in relation to the ever-shifting lines of inequality.

In the subsequent parts of this book, I delve deeply into three frameworks of activism and social change that I learnt from my colleagues. Respectively, I follow the lines of consciously considered *emotion* and ethical responsibility, the lines between vulnerability, the *body*, and violence, and the (micro) politics of *storytelling* about feminist identity and accountability. These three focal frameworks were significant to my colleagues and their anti-violence activism. Importantly, however, the frameworks do not neatly layer or offer a holistic, definitive account of 'feminist anti-violence activism'. Alternatively, each part is a necessarily partial account of activism, social change, and academia which circle us in new, and sometimes unexpected, directions. Through those accounts I continue to redraw the lines of 'activist' and 'academic' and, as in Part I, consider the political and social effects of those arrangements. The rhizomatic approach I adopt continues to invite us to look at the tools of social change that emerge from the interconnection of academia and activism which could be transposed to other places, issues, or movements.

PART II

Ties That Bind; Ties That Break

3

Outside of Ourselves

When I (re)entered the community sector in Aotearoa New Zealand as both academic and activist, I was met with a community sector facing immense contemporary challenges for survival. My initial discussions with community members, as I have mentioned in Part I, highlighted a growing despair at the lack of 'bite' of the sector and concern for the ways it had become subservient to the power of neoliberalism. Nevertheless, there was still a strong sense that activism continued to be a vital dimension of the community sector and without some form of activism or advocacy that the community sector was failing to live up to its social promise. In both my conversations with people in different parts of the sector and in the collective, I observed that being part of the community sector was also a deeply cherished aspect of the self. Activist identity was often intimately interconnected with the community sector, but the influence of neoliberalism on the sector had caused many of my participants and colleagues to question whether this sense of 'activist' was lost. The community sector, including the collective, was grappling with a possible loss of radical social change and outsider activism.

During my conversations with a broad range of community sector activists, before I started volunteering with the collective, I eagerly gathered their perspectives about the community sector and its role in social change. Most of the issues raised by my participants seemed familiar to those I'd already encountered in the academic literature. My participants enthusiastically told me about the immeasurable and positive contributions the community sector made by supporting communities across our country. Kelly described this well when she told me:

'[In the community sector] it is the people who live in those communities that make the decisions ... there is a really personal connection and it is local ... I don't think the government responds with such heart that the people on the ground actually have, because it is the stuff they care about.'

The tales my participants shared with me, however, were always enmeshed in a palpable concern regarding the vast difficulties facing many community organizations in Aotearoa New Zealand. Neoliberalism, my participants argued, was continually posing challenges to the sector, and was perceived as threatening the survival of small or radical groups, the capacity of the community to engage in activism, and the democratic potential of the community sector. In fact, the challenges of neoliberalism often became the focal point of discussion, coming to form a frame for understanding the contemporary state of the sector and its activism.

From these conversations, I felt like I had received an induction to the community sector. As I moved into my volunteer ethnographer role, I expected my time with the collective to be enmeshed in many of the same concerns. But I gradually felt that something from my understanding had been missing. Certainly, the frame of neoliberalism was important and had serious impacts on the form of activism in the sector and I re-encountered many of the tensions surrounding neoliberalism and observed, and participated, in their reconstruction during my anti-violence work. Once I began my voluntary role, however, I experienced a shift and expansion of my theoretical understanding of both the community sector and activism. My colleagues helped me to reimagine the importance of emotional connections in community sector activism. There was something more about actually being immersed in the issues and daily activities of a community sector organization; the embodied emotional dimension that I had mostly overlooked in my initial understanding of the tales of activism in the community sector.

These strong emotions were intertwined with a theoretical debate about activism. My colleagues were particularly thoughtful about the emotions present in their work and were acutely aware that certain strong emotions were damaging for victims of violence. Pity and sympathy, for instance, were seen as condescending and positioned women as 'helpless' victims. Part of their role in the collective was to engage in activism to challenge how we thought and felt about victims of violence. Rather than pity or sympathy, my colleagues were bent on fostering passionate anger that women and gender minorities were disproportionately subjected to intimate partner violence. Inspired by my colleagues, I followed the lines between strong emotions, community sector work, activism, and academia.

I have incorporated this shift in my understanding into the structure of Part II. In Chapter 3, I begin by recapitulating the familiar tale of the community sector, neoliberalism, and activism. I follow a realist storytelling tradition, emphasizing the relatively stable, sweeping portrait of the community sector often painted by community sector workers and academics. Once I have presented this familiar tale of the sector, however,

I offer an alternative understanding by exploring the nuanced and dynamic relationship(s) between emotion, identity, forms of organizing, and activism. In Chapter 4, I specifically focus on the everyday life of my anti-violence colleagues and pay specific attention to consciously considered emotions, unfinished endings, ambiguities, and possibilities for change embedded in their work. In reference to the complexity of my colleagues' work, I look at the lines drawn around what 'counts' as activism in the neoliberal context of the community sector and explore the socio-political effects of those boundaries.

A familiar tale of the community sector

I started my empirical story by asking a range of people from the sector to tell me about the role of the community sector, the contributions they felt it made to the people of Aotearoa New Zealand, and what it meant to them to be involved with the sector. I encouraged them to share how social change in and through the sector had changed over time with me. The tales they told felt familiar. There was the initial establishment of the proud activist history of the community sector, highlighting the benefits for community bonds in Aotearoa New Zealand. This was followed by an invasion of the community sector by neoliberal ideology, usually pushed by the government, which corrupted the community spirit of the sector and impeded their capacity to create change. My participants' accounts of the contemporary state of the sector were ambivalent; many of them seemed unsure how to challenge neoliberalism or which elements to embrace for the benefit of their communities. My ensuing overview of the community sector and its role in creating change for communities follows the flow of this tale. My participants are given pseudonyms to acknowledge their localized understanding of this history, and I've interwoven their accounts with research about the community sector and its impact.

History and contribution: community spirit

At first, the empirical and institutional stories of activism in the community sector seemed neatly aligned. Most of the research I was reading about the community sector echoed what I was hearing from my participants in the field. All of my participants assured me of the importance of the bicultural roots of the community sector; the involvement of the sector in diverse aspects of life in Aotearoa New Zealand; and affirmed that the sector played a primary role in creating positive change for the people through activism, embedded in the felt needs of the community.

Promptly, however, my participants would put aside these more formalized 'definitions' and move to issues that seemed to lie closer to their hearts: communicating the *kaupapa* (values base) of the sector and how it strengthened the social fabric of our country. The sector was more than the outcomes it produced; it was an activist spirit that contributed to social cohesion, empowerment, and promoting positive change for communities (Neilson et al, 2015). Kelly and Himene both described the sector as something personal and local, something embedded in people's needs. Adam understood it to be a place of democratic renewal through which people developed a sense of citizenship. Community organizations were considered by Tamara and Nick to be part of the social fabric of Aotearoa New Zealand. Across my interviews, my participants argued that this was a sector that searched for, and fought for, the common good.

A central emphasis of my participants in communicating the *kaupapa* of the sector was outlining a set of unique values that they believed were fundamental to community organizations. The values were attached to community organizations that had social justice missions which, when followed, were argued to help create change. Calvin and Adam argued that the community sector valued democratic cooperation. Others, such as Elisabeth, were more sceptical of the actuality of democratic cooperation, but did agree that there was a perception that community organizations provided the possibilities of democratic cooperation towards shared goals. Abigail highlighted that community organizations valued mutual aid, expressed through the phrase '*aroha tētahi ki tētahi*' (let us look after one another). This phrase encapsulates the value of reciprocal care and affection between people in the community sector. Adam similarly stated that the community sector valued work that was "of and for" the community; the work of an 'I' embedded in a 'we' of the community. Additionally, Kelly explained that her work across the country with a wide range of community organizations had shown her that they uniquely valued the localized and the personal. Importantly, social justice organizations, Shiner told me, were grounded in personal and social transformation. As she said to me, "it isn't just the 'doing good' factor, it is … [about] what you might become."

The *kaupapa* of the community sector was argued to support what my participants understood as the most significant contribution of the sector: fostering and maintaining the social fabric of Aotearoa New Zealand through social justice and activist or advocacy work. The sector was perceived by my participants as a place of connection; a tie drawing people together. For my participants, the community sector was about creating a better future together rather than acting in isolation, drawing together people from different parts of society. Significantly, the community sector was thought of as a place through which marginalized community voices could be heard by the government and by the public. As Grey and Sedgwick also found of the community sector, they 'perceive themselves as ... speaking up for the most marginalised of our society; ensuring that policy meets the real needs of New Zealanders; and ensuring a better society' (Grey and Sedgwick, 2015: 4). The intimate connections between community organizations and their communities ensured that this 'voice' reflected the interests of community groups (Grey and Sedgwick, 2013a). Activism was therefore perceived by my participants as the act of fostering social bonds within and between communities and using that connection to amplify voices to demand a better future. Importantly, community sector activism was embedded in the *kaupapa* of the sector: democratic cooperation, *aroha tētahi ki tētahi*, empowerment, and transformation.

The engagement of the community sector with issues surrounding the Treaty of Waitangi/Te Tiriti o Waitangi, demonstrated for many of my participants the way in which the sector was embedded in communities. Calvin explained to me that although the community sector had no formalized responsibility to the Treaty/Te Tiriti (unlike the government), community organizations were either *kaupapa Māori*, or were active in their attempts to understand their bicultural role. Tamara similarly noted that community organizations were more interested in considering what biculturalism *felt* like, rather than interpreting policy decisions. Abigail argued that this was because the community sector was open and willing to respond to social issues authentically. Himene highlighted how organizations like hers that were *kaupapa Māori*, and operated by and for Māori, were foundational to the sector; demonstrating how the response to need was by and for the people. Community organizations had deep-rooted ties to their communities to which they attempted to respond to the *felt* needs of the people in a way that fostered positive social change. Their activist work was connected to their community sector values. It was embodied work. Democratic work. Emotional work. Transformative work.

Colliding with the market: the impacts of neoliberalism

Critical research about the community sector in the field of management and organization studies is rife with concern about the collision between neoliberalism and the community sector (Eikenberry et al, 2019). And rightly so. Neoliberal policies in the West have had substantial impacts on community organizations, community activists, and on the marginalized communities whom they support (Hull et al, 2011). International research has argued that neoliberalism has limited democratic localized engagement (Woolford and Curran, 2013); something seen as so central to community sector activism. The community sector in Aotearoa New Zealand has also experienced wide-ranging impacts of neoliberalism that have impacted democracy, shaped the way community organizations engage in activism and advocacy, and impacted the depth and breadth of need in communities (Laurie and Bondi, 2005).

The relationship between the state and the community sector in Aotearoa New Zealand changed during the 1980s after the implementation of neoliberal policies. Funding became based on the purchase of services through competitive short-term contracts argued to increase competition and therefore the efficiency and quality of services (Tennant, 2006). Crucially, this led the government to be seen as pushing neoliberal ideologies on the sector that were contrary to community engagement and activism (Grey and Sedgwick, 2013a; Neilson et al, 2015). Shiner explained that she noticed an immediate shift "almost overnight" from community organizations being groups of common interests and enthusiasm, to competitive organizations that had to jump hurdles of formalities to form and get funding. Generally, community sector organizations were now expected to exhibit, as Adam put it, a "neoliberal spirit" that was enterprising, individualist, and risk-taking (Larner and Butler, 2005).

My participants primarily understood neoliberalism as an ideology; focusing less on policy changes and far more how they perceived the spirit of neoliberalism to "take away the essence of community", as Shiner noted. Neoliberalism was usually conflated with community organizations assimilating business-like behaviours. My participants presented a number of different features of neoliberalism. Kara, Robin, and Shiner felt there were pressures to adhere to bureaucratic and hierarchical organizational structures that promoted tight, centralized control by elite individuals. Jane explained to me that it had become necessary to have "a solid organization in the style that people, as in the establishment, the government funders, the non-government funders, are comfortable with" to obtain funding and therefore survival. Himene and Kelly shared the common concern that community organizations were expected to have a one-size-fits-all approach to service provision that was prescriptive and directive. Adam and Calvin thought that neoliberalism constructed individuals as competitive, rational, and independent from the community, and organizations as needing to be entrepreneurial.

Ultimately, my participants who held a primarily negative view of neoliberalism were concerned that it promoted behaviour that was exploitative, oppressive, and contrary to community spirit. In turn, the neoliberal shift impacted the way groups in the sector understood and undertook activism. Once radical groups had become increasingly institutionalized and worked *with* (and sometimes for) government and business. One-size-fits-all services were professionalized and worked to integrate their clients into society rather than to transform society. Individualistic norms damaged democratic cooperation within and beyond community organizations. Community organizations lost their visions of a different social landscape as they were forced to spend time engaging in endless reporting requirements and funding applications. It's hard to imagine a different future when you are trapped monitoring the present.

However, some of my participants shared an ambivalence about the effects of neoliberalism in the community sector and contemplated if there were different opportunities for activism. Tamara, for example, thought that the community sector needed to "get over being worried about being managers" in order to effectively govern their organizations, and Phillip was certain that "if you want to run a big organization you need an IT shop and you need to have an HR shop. It is almost inevitable if you want to be really impactful". There remained, nevertheless, a perceptible sense that there was the possibility of corruption; that by embracing neoliberal ideology something intangible and precious would be sacrificed. Phillip, for example, was also concerned that by "participating in the machine ... somehow the *kaupapa* seems to get tainted or corporatized". Michael was also concerned about whether it was possible to "marry" the demands of quantifiably measured outcomes (implemented by funders in a neoliberal spirit) and activism for transformative change. Although neoliberalism had diluted some of the sector's power, some of my participants therefore explored the positive benefits for efficient and effective achievement of their organizations' goals.

My participants' concern about neoliberalism was set in contrast to the *kaupapa* of the sector. On the one hand, the community sector perceived values of democratic cooperation, orientating around localized lived experience, empowerment of the marginalized, *aroha tētahi ki tētahi*, and transformation as important. On the other hand, the collision of the community sector with neoliberal ideology had resulted in the promotion of hierarchy, individualism, competition, entrepreneurialism, and generic service provision. Even those who perceived that neoliberalism had benefits for efficient and effective organizational governance – such as Phillip and Tamara – were hesitant to embrace neoliberalism wholeheartedly. The foundational values that my participants considered part of activism were in danger of 'corruption' if neoliberalism continued to be dominant. As Onyx and co-authors highlight, however, a binary of radical activism and institutional compliance is unhelpful (Onyx et al, 2010). My participants offer insight into the complexity and variety of ways of thinking about community sector activism. Some of these approaches are disrupted or corrupted as neoliberal values permeate the sector, but my participants also emphasize that they continue to be committed to the *kaupapa* and will undertake transformative, community sector activism in some form.

Dissolving community spirit and voice?

The impacts of neoliberalism were considered by many members of the sector to be taking society down a very dangerous road which threatened the social fabric of Aotearoa New Zealand. Many of my participants could not emphasize enough how intensely they perceived neoliberalism as a danger to the sector (Larner and Craig, 2005; Nowland-Foreman, 2016a), with Adam stressing: "it makes my skin *crawl*". Critical research about the community sector has provided wide-ranging discussion about whether the relationships between the state, private sector, and community sector have moved beyond neoliberalism (Larner and Butler, 2005; Larner and Craig, 2005; Laurie and Bondi, 2005; Nowland-Foreman, 2016a). Government departments in Aotearoa New Zealand, for instance, have claimed to have moved to a 'partnership model' based on mutual cooperation, but both scholars (Larner and Butler, 2005) and community sector workers (Grey and Sedgwick, 2013b) have found that the partnership model is embedded in the same market-driven ideology that was a feature of neoliberal policies. Similarly, my participants reaffirmed that neoliberalism was a continual challenge and that it made fulfilling the activist role of the sector difficult (Elliott and Haigh, 2013).

One of the most significant outcomes of the neoliberal reforms to funding structures was that community organizations became afraid to speak out for or against policy changes (Grey and Sedgwick, 2015). The perceived need of community organizations to exhibit neoliberal behaviours in order to gain funding, and their dependency on these short-term funding contracts, had made it difficult for community organizations to engage in radical activism against the government or other institutions. Phillip explained that community organizations did not want to be seen "biting the hand that feeds you". However, Robin considered activism to be core to the community sector, so if this ability was constrained, they would lose an important dimension of their work. Without limited capacity to speak out on social issues, my participants felt that community sector organizations were not able to fulfil one of their primary functions: to give voice to the marginalized. Additionally, the rigid focus of neoliberal contracts on individual outputs and quantifiable measures was seen as harmful as it excluded the intangible contributions of the sector to communities in Aotearoa New Zealand (Larner and Butler, 2005; Neilson et al, 2015). The tension between neoliberalism and preserving community sector activism was described as reaching a breaking point; pursuing social justice had become almost unviable.

Overall, the tale emphasized the challenges of neoliberalism. Community activism seemed to be dissolving in an environment of neoliberal ideology. Neoliberalism was gradually more normative and the lines between community organizations, private organizations, and public organizations were increasingly blurred (Douglas, 2015). Nevertheless, the tales told by my participants would ultimately revert to (re)emphasizing the positive contributions of the community sector to Aotearoa New Zealand; coming back to the *kaupapa* and activism of the sector. Nick's response was fairly characteristic:

'The sector shouldn't be overlooked. It is such a powerful force in life. Everyone is part of a community and it is a force. If it is degraded in any way, a lot of life gets lost or isn't going to function as well as it should. You've got to keep that generation of enthusiasm and you can't ever stop.'

The familiar tale: the only frame?

The familiar tale is often treated as foundational knowledge by members of the sector and by critical scholars (Sanders, 2015; Eikenberry et al, 2019). The tale can be understood as characterized by a binary: 'neoliberalism'/ 'community'. Neoliberalism is seen as an invasive force that has irrevocably shaped the community sector and situated them in a market economy. Community, on the other hand, is positioned as the preferred state of the sector that has been corrupted or even possibly lost. Furthermore, neoliberalism was perceived as the dominant system by members of the sector which governed how they operated. Most research about the community sector characterizes it in a similar way; either expressing grave concern about the state of democracy and activism in the sector as a result of neoliberalism (Grey and Sedgwick, 2015), or championing the value market-based principles to enhance the skills and efficacy of the sector (Douglas, 2015). In both cases, neoliberalism is the frame for understanding how community organizations operate and engage in activism.

The familiar tale thereby directs our attention towards how activism can continue in a market economy. Through the familiar tale, scholars and community sector members have indeed gained a deep understanding of the contemporary challenges facing social justice organizations and have begun to unpick how these challenges are, and could be, negotiated to continue towards their social justice goals. New forms of activism, such as insider activism, that echo the *kaupapa* of the sector are emerging and help activists to navigate the neoliberal environment. However, dominant ways of understanding aspects of society, such as the familiar tale I set out here, operate to close down alternative ways of understanding social systems (Foucault, 1977). Treating 'neoliberalism' as foundational knowledge for understanding the sector and its role in activism can close down the possibilities of thinking about the experiences of community sector activism in different ways. As such, the multiplicity of experiences and dimensions of community sector activism can be overlooked or underemphasized, thereby constraining how we think about activism in this sector. Accordingly, considering alternative ways of understanding the community sector and activism, which are overlooked or marginalized in this familiar tale, can help us to think more creatively about how scholars and activists alike can foster social change in and through the community sector.

Alternative understandings; alternative organizations

In order to explore other ways of understanding activism in the community sector, I became interested in thinking about different (read, non-neoliberal) ways of organizing. I was, of course, particularly inspired by my colleagues who continued to function as a collective even with the pressures from government, businesses, and some members of the community to adopt neoliberal values and a business-like structure. The collective had its own unique *kaupapa* which valued feminism, decolonization, collectivism, and LGBT+ pride. The values underpinned how they organized activism. As I outlined in Part I, the collective distributed resources equally along lines of identity, dedicated time and space to speaking out the concerns of a particular group (for example, queer women), and maintained a non-hierarchical structure even though they assigned certain roles, like CEO, to assist in receiving funding or to participate in developing legislation. The neoliberal context did, nevertheless, shape their practices. I found, however, that following lines of emotion and collective organizing I could better understand how my colleagues continued to fight for social change and reimagine their activism.

In my field of organization studies, a group of scholars have focused on 'alternative organizations' or those organizations which actively attempt to organize in ways that are not capitalist, hierarchical, or neoliberal (Parker et al, 2014b). In other words, those organizations which 'encourage forms of organising which respect personal autonomy, but within a framework of cooperation, and which are attentive to the sorts of futures they produce' (Parker et al, 2014a). The definition is deliberately kept broad in recognition of the almost infinite possible ways of organizing. Nevertheless, these scholars argue that there is a pressing need to organize differently (again, read non-neoliberal and non-capitalist) to dismantle social inequalities related to the uneven distribution of wealth, gender and racial discrimination, and an individualism which divides people from their communities (Cheney et al, 2014; Sutherland et al, 2014; Reedy et al, 2016).

The broad definition of alternative organizations is therefore tempered by an explicit agenda to focus on organizations which actively attempt to create social change and a better, more democratic, future for us all. A focus on alternative practices of organizing (without assuming they are *inherently* better) follows the political imperative to engage in affirmative action towards social justice organizing, rather than restricting scholarship to critique of extant practices or resistance to mainstream practice. The alternative organizing manifesto, accordingly, is a way for academics and activists to share their practices and the contexts within which those practices helped us towards social change. The *kaupapa* and practices of the collective echo this literature as well as the *kaupapa* of the community sector described by my participants.

Despite the influence of alternative organizations, such as indigenous organizations (Love, 2019), feminist organizations (Ferree and Martin, 1995), or cooperatives (Ranis, 2016), globally, research on alternative organizations in my field of management and organization studies is relatively recent. Additionally, the primary focus of such research has been on what alternatives there are to capitalist organizations, thus taking a labour and production focus (Cheney et al, 2014), or on alternative internal structures (such as anarchism) with an emphasis on promoting democracy and providing alternatives to neoliberalism (Land and King, 2014). Researchers in this area also argue, however, that alternatives to labour and production organizations, while extremely important, are not the only possibilities that alternative organizations embody.

The emphasis when researching alternative organizations, these scholars have argued, is on imagination; the endless permutations of organizational form that could alter our social landscape. After all, our daily experiences are shaped by any number of different organizations or forms of organization including reading groups, found families, schools, circuses, activist networks, walking groups, and so on. All these forms of organizations are structured differently, often in non-capitalist or non-neoliberal ways (even if sometimes informed by those logics) and alter our social landscapes. There is a lot of opportunity for us to learn from alternative organizations, describe how they function, and thereby imagine and develop novel ways of conceptualizing how organizing might shape our social landscape. Importantly, these forms of alternative organizing integrate their practices with their knowledge of systems of inequality. For instance, the way the collective was organized directly counteracted gender inequality by following lines of gender, race, and sexuality, adopting a non-hierarchical structure, and dedicating organizational time to sharing and learning from women's experiences.

Research which focuses on the community sector has also considered how community organizations might embody alternatives to neoliberal models of organization. Bernal and Grewal, for instance, argue for understanding NGOs as distinctive forms of organizing, which differ from market or state organizing primarily due to the influence of feminist politics (Bernal and Grewal, 2014). Bernal and Grewal maintain that NGOs are shaped, but not governed, by neoliberalism, and that in their pursuit of change, community organizations regularly engage in alternative organizing practices. Neoliberalism, capitalism, and hierarchy remain useful considerations for understanding the day-to-day practices of community organizations, but they are not the only influences. Put alongside work from scholars focusing on how some community organizations can be alternative organizations (Land and King, 2014; Jensen and Meisenbach, 2015; Jensen, 2017), Bernal and Grewal's collection indicates that the community sector is usefully understood as a potential space for alternative organizing, which can help us better understand how community organizations achieve social change.

Additionally, much research about the community sector in relation to democracy and citizenship has been centred on practices which could be understood as 'alternative organizing' (e.g., Eikenberry, 2009; Dodge and Ospina, 2016; Connor and Yerbury, 2017). Alterative organizing practices are seen to benefit marginalized people by engaging in collective education (The Trapese Collective, 2014) and social support (Jensen, 2017) without embodying market values. Accordingly, developing our 'toolkit' of alternative organizing practices is important for understanding how activism gets done in and through community organizations and to provide the foundations to apply these practices to other contexts.

My consideration of how some social justice community organizations can be understood as forms of alternative organization is not to detract from the importance of the impacts of neoliberalism on the community sector, or to offer a discrete alternative to the binary. My aim is to consider how we can draw out an array of activist practices by focusing specifically on the 'community' aspects of the sector and explore how these aspects can be mobilized for social justice. As such, describing alternative ways of organizing in the community can help scholars and activists alike to more effectively imagine how we might tackle social inequalities. The different lines community sector activists or academics draw around what constitutes 'activism' in a neoliberal context need to be questioned. The focus on alternative organizing helps us to break the binary of 'radical activism' and 'institutional compliance' by drawing out the many shades of social change in a complex, evolving community sector context. The creative ideas which emerge from this examination can also be translated into other contexts or to other issues.

The community sector, according to my participants, was made of those shades. Some organizations actively attempted to provide alternatives to neoliberalism by offering a space for democratic cooperation, empowerment of marginalized people, transformation of the social landscape and of people's identities, and to promote *aroha tētahi ki tētahi*. Other organizations adopted some neoliberal values in an uneasy marriage with other values. Some organizations continued to position themselves as outsiders and others marched into institutions to make change on the inside. In order to enact and embody the *kaupapa* of the community sector, still other activists engaged in alternative organizing practices with passion. These (constrained) choices of how to organize to achieve social change were deeply meaningful for my participants. Our discussion of community sector activism and the challenges they faced in supporting their communities, was always articulated in passion, or anger, or worry, or excitement, or grief. These strong emotions seemed irrevocably intertwined with decisions about how to come together and fight inequality.

On emotion and organizing

My institutional story of arrival related to the relationship between organized activism and emotion was inspired by my engagement with Judith Butler's work on the ek–static (Butler, 1997, 2006b). In the early stages of this research project I had been interested in Kate Kenny's use of Butler's work on the *ek-static* to understand the importance of strong emotions like passion in an environmental justice community organization (Kenny, 2010). When I reread Kenny's research late in my time as a volunteer, it resonated with my experience. I felt that likewise in the collective, certain strong emotions were particularly salient and had extensive implications for organizing for social justice. As I began to understand that certain kinds of strong emotions were significant for my participants, I felt that, like Kenny, Butler's conceptualization of the *ek-static* was useful for understanding activist identity in the community sector. In particular, the *ek-static* helps us to think through how emotions can reify or break social norms and potentially remake our relationships with one another.

Judith Butler's conceptualization of the *ek-static* is embedded within her work about identities and change. Through the *ek-static*, Butler offers a way of understanding the emotional dimensions of identities. She argues that there is a 'passion and grief and rage we feel, all of which tear us from ourselves, bind us to others, transport us, undo us, and implicate us in lives that are not our own, sometimes fatally, irreversibly' (Butler, 2006b). In other words, the notion of the *ek-static* refers to the emotional state of being beside oneself with a passion, grief, or rage that moves use to form ties with others. We become beyond ourselves and can recognize our self in someone else.

This connection is not a link between separate individuals, but a binding between and around us, through which a community can emerge (Butler, 2011b). We have passionate attachments to other people that result in our being intertwined with the lives of others (Butler, 2006b). The reverse is also true, we can also become undone. Our passion, rage, or grief can undo our ties and drive us apart from one another. We have a passionate desire to be recognized by others and legitimated as recognizable human subjects. Our identities are limited and governed by powerful social norms and when we fall outside the norms of recognition, we can experience an abjection; a disconnection from others (Butler, 2006a). Identities that fall outside of these norms are often made particularly precarious, and some identities are targeted with material and symbolic violence (Butler, 2006b). Emotions, therefore, can operate to exclude.

Butler's conceptualization of the *ek-static* is useful for exploring how certain emotions move us and operate to 'bind' or 'unbind' subjects and objects. Organizing in ways that involve being 'outside of ourselves' in community sector activism entails fostering the conditions for emotions to move us. Additionally, the *ek-static* can offer us insight into the ways in which organizing around emotion can reify social norms; the moments when certain people are 'othered' in community organizations, as Kenny demonstrates in her study. In short, the framework of the *ek-static* helps to focus on the significance of particular intense emotions for catalysing change that were salient in my experiences of the community sector. Here, in Chapter 3, I frame my use of the *ek-static* within research that has focused on emotion and affect in organization studies. Research on emotion and affect act as a basis for understanding the role of emotion in organizing and for the construction of identity in different organizational contexts. From this basis, I return to Butler's notion of the *ek-static* in order to explore the role of the specific emotions – passion, grief, rage – in the collective and draw from here lessons about how emotion informs activism, academia, and organizing alternatively for social justice in Chapter 4.

Prior to the explosion of academic interest in emotion in organizing in the 1990s, emotion had been treated by researchers as an unsuitable or absent dimension of organizational life (Fineman, 2000). Since the publication of the research of Hochschild about emotion labour (Hochschild, 1979 [1983]; Hochschild, 2012), emotion has become recognized as an important part of organizational life by both mainstream and critical researchers; albeit in differing ways (Fineman, 2000; Ashkanasy and Cooper, 2008). Mainstream (positivist) research typically treats emotion as psychological: an internal state of feeling, naturally occurring, triggered by the external environment; usually opposing rationality. From this perspective, emotion is seen as something experienced by a worker as a consequence of the organization, the work, their personality, and their interactions with colleagues (Ashkanasy and Cooper, 2008). In this vein, emotion in activist work would be considered as a natural response to injustice, relationships with fellow activists, and those outside of a social movement. Importantly, in mainstream research about emotions and organizing, emotions are perceived as something to 'control'; both in terms of regulating certain emotions, such as rage (Troth et al, 2017), and in terms of eliciting certain emotions at given times or spaces, such as kindness. Activists then would control or unleash their emotions in certain circumstances (such as a protest) and aim to elicit certain emotions during their activism (such as empathy for victims of gendered violence).

Although conventional studies have made the importance of emotion in the workplace mainstream, they tend to share a problematic de-politicization of emotion and minimize or ignore the ways that emotion is social. Critical perspectives on emotion have taken up these latter themes and demonstrate how emotions are political, emergent, and contingent on social and cultural norms (Sieben and Wettergren, 2010). Most prominently, research about emotion in critical management and organization studies has drawn from social constructionist and/or psychoanalytic perspectives to critique conventional perspectives on emotion in organization and provide alternative ways of theorizing emotion (Ulus and Gabriel, 2018). Social constructionist perspectives largely draw on insights from sociological and anthropological studies of emotion and explore emotion as constituted in social interaction, describing how social context shapes the experience and expression of emotion. From this basis, critical research about emotion has demonstrated the problematic (political) ways in which emotion is utilized for functionalist ends to regulate emotions in organizing and maintaining social norms.

Within the broader research on emotion I have sketched, I found the work of Sara Ahmed on the cultural politics of emotion to be useful for thinking about the relationship between activism, emotion, academia, and social justice. Ahmed theorizes emotion as a form of 'world making' that involves a process of endowing objects with meaning and value through emotion (Ahmed, 2014). Ahmed's theorization of emotion pays specific attention to how emotions can both reify exclusionary social norms *and* have the potential to open up different futures. Thus, understanding emotions as a form of world making is particularly beneficial for understanding how certain kinds of emotions operate as alternative organizing practices which can remake our social landscapes. Ahmed has also discussed the role of emotion in feminism, which is particularly relevant to my colleagues, in her discussion of the 'feminist killjoy' who raises uncomfortable emotions in unconventional spaces (Ahmed, 2017).

Ahmed (2014) builds from sociological and anthropological traditions of understanding emotions as a form of cultural and social practice. She argues that emotions are produced as effects of the interaction between objects and subjects. Emotions are thus relational, in that they involve a (re)action to objects and an interpretation of whether objects seem to be 'beneficial' or 'harmful' etc. Emotions, therefore, involve an orientation of our relationships towards or away from each other, depending on our perception of the meaning and value of our feeling attached to objects. Objects could be a person (or group of people), an action, text, an image, a practice, or an idea. For example, the image of the hungry child used in an activist campaign for food justice can be the object of emotion. We see the image and our interaction with the image shapes the emotion (for example, compassion) we attach to the image; the object seems as deserving of compassion. Our orientation towards or away from others (for example, hungry children) is shaped by our attachment of certain emotions to the object. The process of interpretation of feelings and the attribution of emotions is embedded in histories of association (such as the perception that children are innocent), and over time certain objects are consolidated as the 'sticking point' of particular emotions.

As well as consolidating or reifying particular orientations to one another, emotions can also involve movement. Emotions, Ahmed argues, are effects of circulation (Ahmed, 2014). It is the objects, she contends, rather than the emotion itself which gets circulated; allowing emotions to 'move' and change the orientation of our relationship with one another (for example, the image of the hungry child is circulated as an object of compassion). A change in the interpretation of our feelings or displacing of the object as the 'cause' of a particular emotion can therefore remake the orientations of relationships to one another. Additionally, a change in our interaction with objects – such as a change in the types of action we engage in – can also shift how we understand objects. For example, our compassion could mean we volunteer for a food bank which changes the interpretation of our feelings about the image of the hungry child from an object of compassion to an object of anger (that in a world where food is readily available some children should go hungry). Our orientation towards the child and therefore how we act towards the issue of food justice then also changes. In other words, emotions are implicated in the creation of objects and involve the repetition of certain actions rather than others, which can change our orientation to the object. Emotions, therefore, can also remake our social landscapes.

Alternative organizing, emotion, and the community sector

Understanding emotions as a form of world making (Ahmed, 2014) underscores that emotions are not erased or caused by certain modes of organizing, but that the making of emotions is implicated within forms of organizing. Hence, we could understand that emotions are shaped by capitalist ways of organizing. For instance, the exploitation of certain kinds of emotional labour (particularly of women) to financial ends evidenced so strongly by Hochschild is a dimension of capitalist organizing (Hochschild, 2012). Neoliberal organizing in the community sector also shapes emotion. Pedwell (2012) highlights that in international aid organizations, neoliberalism promotes the commodification of compassion as a useful 'tool' for workers to enterprisingly employ to achieve their goals. She argues that this has the problematic effect of ultimately 'fixing' the people that the organization seeks to help as the object of compassion and other (usually privileged) people as the subject or the distributors of compassion.

Emotion as world making underscores, however, that if we are made through processes of organizing emotion, we can also be remade. There are alternatives. The possibilities of activists who foster different kinds of emotional relationships are evidenced by feminist or women's organizations that take the localized emotion bonds between women as their core organizing practices (Hanisch, 1970; Burstow, 1992; Ferree and Martin, 1995), thus increasing their sense of responsibility for one another in an attempt to engender change. Emotion is, therefore, an important dimension of organizing that has significant potential to remake our social landscapes.

The significance of emotion in activist organizing is not a new concern and it has long been recognized that in various ways emotion is particularly salient and significant in these contexts (Mason, 1996; Goodwin et al, 2001). Importantly, however, emotion is often seen as fundamentally linked to achieving social justice in community organizations, in that organizations should seek to promote certain kinds of emotional identification (usually empathetic) between workers, donors, community members, and public servants and marginalized people (Wilkinson, 2009; Pedwell, 2012). Emotion is therefore often naturalized in relation to community organizations; we should have natural responses to injustice. My overview of emotion as a form of 'world making', however, underscores that emotions are social, political, and threaded with power. Seemingly, 'natural' responses to injustice are actually part of more complicated processes of endowing objects of inequality with value. It is essential, then, to analyse the types of emotion, the objects of emotion, and the social and political implications of that emotional attachment. As I turn back to the tale told by my participants, then, I look at the ways emotion, values, organizing patterns, and activism are woven into a framework of social justice.

My participants emphasized that they perceived the creation of emotional bonds between members of the community as fundamental for community sector activism. Tamara explained that in the community sector, "people really care about what they are doing, they are enthused, they are energetic and committed. And there is a lot of energy, and, sort of, passion". What differentiated the sector for Kelly was that "uniquely this [is a] sector that people give their time to. Because of their passion they give up their weekends or their nights, they go to meetings and they don't get paid for it. There is something else there that feeds them". The "something else there that feeds them" is similar to what Tamara was trying to communicate; that there were emotional bonds that emerged through the way the community sector was organized. The emotional energy of the sector was founded in a sense of commonality; shared interests; *kaupapa*, philosophy, or passion.

In all my interviews with my participants, emotion was not just a response; it was a movement. Phillip explained: "I think that the most important thing is that we are a sector in that our coming into existence and our passion and energy for our continuing existence comes from a set of values." These values were the community values I identified earlier of democratic cooperation, empowerment, transformation, and *aroha tētahi ki tētahi*. Abigail considered the community organizations they worked with to organize around their passions both "physically and spiritually"; Jane simply called this way of orientating work "the love factor". The emotions seen to be prevalent in community organizations were linked to these values. As Shiner explained: "the impetus is not just the passion ... but the flexibility, the freedom, the enthusiasm". For Shiner, the emotion of passion was fundamentally linked to the ways the community sector organized. Nick emphatically described how the community sector changed the social landscape: "we are talking to each other and getting to know one another, something happens, something dissolves".

Not all emotions were positive or had positive effects in this tale. Just as emotions were the ties between members of the community sector, they could also keep people apart and cause connections to become unbound, or 'stuck' in particular configurations of social relationships. Elisabeth told me a story of two organizations who provided the same work in the community, just down the road from each other, which harboured such an animosity that they would never work together. Emotional connections can result in exclusions; maintaining boundaries between 'us' and 'them' that can have harmful effects (Ahmed, 2014). Additionally, many of my participants were concerned that the "fire has gone out of the belly", as Tamara put it, as a consequence of movement towards neoliberal ways of organizing, which changed the emotional orientations between people and precluded certain kinds of emotions such as passion or enthusiasm. Nonetheless, there was a strong sense that emotional bonds remained important to activist organizing and that through negative emotions an affirmative politics could still be maintained. As Calvin told me: "what brings them together in almost every case is some passion, some interest, some ideal, some goal. And that's outside of ourselves."

Having established my theoretical framework from my conversations with people from the sector and academic literature, I now seek to apply these ideas to the collective to look more closely at how emotions and activism were intertwined in the collective. My focus is on how emotions and activism informed social change. I am cautious to reemphasize, however, that the emotion I discuss is not 'natural'. The interconnection of emotion, activism, and social change does not necessarily foster social justice. As both Pedwell (2012) and Brewis (2017) note, emotion that 'fixes' objects and subjects in social norms, by orientating emotion as a tool or possession of an individual, reinforces harmful neoliberal models of organizing that marginalize non-normative people. For organizing alternatively, the focus must be on how emotion encourages the *moving* of subjects and objects and dismantles normalized boundaries between 'us' and 'them'. I also do not wish to generalize empirically from the example of my collective. Instead, I aim to describe how these practices worked in the collective and thereby offer a way of thinking about community sector activism, academic activism, and alternative organizing.

In order to expand on these ideas and to offer a localized exploration of the role of emotion in achieving social justice in alternative organizing and activism, I will continue to draw on Butler's conceptualization of the *ek-static* (Butler, 2006b) within my broader frame of emotion as a form of world making. I return to Butler as she specifically theorizes the relationships between emotion and identity in the frame of social justice through three emotions − passion, grief, and rage − which were salient in the collective. She also focuses on how emotions can remake social landscapes by pushing subjects 'outside of oneself', thereby attempting to avoid 'fixing' subjects and objects. Her work helps me to give an account of emotion that pays specific attention to how we move and what moves us, in ways that open up different kinds of relationships to others that can foster the conditions for social justice. In short, Butler's conceptualization of the *ek-static* helps to localize some of the broader ideas I outlined earlier in this section for the collective and their specific practices.

In Chapter 4, I trace how emotion in the collective was an important aspect of forming different kinds of 'activist' identity. The formation of identity included a consideration of our emotional relationship to victims of gendered violence. The ensuing analysis is structured in three sections which explores the relationships between intense emotions, activist identity, and organizing practices in a community organization. The first section explores how emotion, organizing, and the sense of self as (or not as) an activist played out in a particular event. The second section, 'ties that bind', explores how passion, grief, and rage formed ties to others by pushing us outside ourselves. 'Ties that break', the third section, looks at the ways in which emotion both encouraged movement by breaking normative ties, as well as sometimes reifying exclusionary boundaries between 'us and them'. Ultimately, I draw the analysis together and consider how emotion as world making is useful to activism and academic activism.

4

Passionate, Sad, Angry People

Some four months into my voluntary work with the collective, I found out that all staff members were to attend a series of workshops together to help us work better as a team. I was almost absurdly enthusiastic about the workshops and the possibility of getting to see all my colleagues discuss the purpose of their work together. My eagerness for attending this event was rather unusual for me, given that under any other circumstances I would have been mutinous if someone had tried to get me to attend one of these events. My colleagues were slightly sickened at my enthusiasm; at lunch the day before the event, it turned out I was the only one excited at the prospect of the afternoon. Emily was appalled she had to attend and was desperately attempting to come up with excuses not to go. Even Ava, who usually took these sorts of things seriously, expressed to me that she was apathetic about attending because she didn't see the purpose behind it. I assumed this was being driven by Jen, but when I chatted to her about it, she didn't seem to want to attend either. The impetus behind this event therefore remained a bit of a mystery.

At 11 o'clock we piled into hired vans to be taken to our destination. I climbed into the back seat with Gracie, Kimberley, and Zoey. Gracie was carrying a giant A3 notebook; an accidentally humorous contrast to my tiny ethnographer's notebook which I was holding in my hands. Gracie told me that the coordinators of these workshops had tried to charge her an extra $30 to supply one. This was not something our organization could afford, and felt like an irresponsible use of our funds. After about 20 minutes in the van joking together, watching silly pet videos on YouTube, and listening to music, we arrived at our destination. Almost immediately Anika and Tia went looking for the smokers' area. The rest of us filed into the room marked 'café' and settled to an early lunch together before the workshop started. Emily and I grabbed the vegetarian option and went to sit with Jen and Riley in the sunshine outside.

The session coordinator, Christine, was a lithe, little woman in smart business dress. She had a habit of rocking backwards onto her heels while clasping her hands in front of her. We were introduced to her one by one and shook hands. Christine had a firm handshake and made a point of looking directly into your eyes for a few seconds before releasing you and repeating your name. The room had been altered in our absence at lunch. The large notebook that Gracie had taken with her had been used by Christine to write inspirational quotes. These were now stuck up around the room. They said things like 'be yourself because everyone else is taken' and 'courage is not the absence of fear but the admittance of fear'. Anika really liked the courage quote and wondered what the translation into Te Reo would be. The one in the front and centre of the room read:

> Welcome to your team session …
> Why we're here …
> What we'll do … and how!
> Who are you are and what you'd like to achieve.
> 'Be yourself, everyone else is taken'

Anika opened our session with a *karakia* (prayer), standing above her seat, head slightly bowed, and speaking in rapid Te Reo. At the conclusion, we all echoed with a *kia ora* (affirmation). Jen then gave a short introduction about why we were there, again standing by her chair, but facing out to the room. She said that she struggled to explain why we're here but felt we didn't have enough events for the whole team. In conclusion, Jen notes, she wanted to get a sense of how everyone understands our work. Finally, Christine took her turn to give an introduction. She stood upfront, under the inspirational banner, and said we were here to decide 'what is important to "me" and "we"'. Christine suggested that first we needed to reflexively examine ourselves before we could understand what we contribute to the 'me and we'. We are here, she said, to "build a space of trust" so that we didn't feel that "no one sees me, includes me, understands me, or accepts me".

After a coffee break, we were given a new task: discuss in our groups what we wanted out of these workshops. I found it surprising it took us this long to get to this point. In the earlier session, we spent a lot of time setting 'ground rules' and thinking about our individual identities. Now we were focusing on ourselves as a whole; as a collective. We had been rearranged into new groups so now I was sitting with Hayley, Gracie, and Esther. The room felt slightly more uneasy after being moved out of our regular teams. There was still a buzz of conversation and several of my colleagues were expressing their discontent about not working together as a whole group and a desire to have a "shared end goal" and "clarity of vision". Christine took the floor and explained that we were now going to come to the crux of the first session. We were to move on to discussing: "the question of the overarching purpose of the organization" and explain to our group: "how does your role fit into that". We were to bring the 'me' into the 'we'.

Hayley immediately turned to me, Gracie, and Esther, and zealously said to the group that she thought that the role of our organization was "to support [those who worked with clients directly] in succeeding in eliminating family violence". Gracie nodded her head vigorously at this. Hayley animatedly went on to explain that this meant doing things that frontline staff didn't have time for, like securing funding and running stakeholder education programmes. Gracie agreed with Hayley and added that she thought that it was this way because our organization was "not a top-down structure" and that our team was also charged with making policies or making sure that Māori women had equal voice and access to resources. I talked about my role and Emily's role in researching violence to provide an evidence base for our advocacy. Esther explained how her role in communications was about reaching out to the public, garnering their support, and helping them connect with women and children in abusive relationships.

We were then asked to share our thoughts about our purpose with the room. Echoing Hayley, most of my colleagues said that our team was working at a national level to promote change for women experiencing domestic violence. Emily added that our job was to "make sure that we are one of the leaders in that" and Jen re-joined humorously: "What do you mean one of?" Hayley then added her mission statement that she had given to us and then added that this was "deeply felt". Other people added that we were providing "social commentary and informing the public" and "demonstrating a commitment to [feminism, Tangata Whenua, and LGBT+ women]". The discussion also seemed particularly affirming as all my colleagues were sitting up, paying attention, and nodding in agreement with each other. Even Tia, who up until this point had kept her head down to avoid notice, had turned her whole body to the centre of the room and muttered "hard out" when Hayley offered her definition.

Suddenly, Jen halted the conversation and turned to the room and asked firmly: "Is this really what you think? I really want to know. Is this what gets you out of bed in the morning? Serious question: is that why you come to work?" Hayley said it absolutely was. Several other people around the room nodded in agreement. Two comments were then made simultaneously. Gracie said to Jen: "Do you know how cool it is to be able to say that you work for [our organization]?" but Gracie's comment was drowned out when Riley concurrently said loudly: "That isn't why I come to work. I'm contributing my skill set to an organization that needs it." Riley went on to say that for her it wasn't about domestic violence; it was the use of her personal talents. Jen went on to say firmly that "[promoting change] is not actually what [our team] is charged with doing", it was about "protecting and strengthening the frontline workers". Kimberley chimed in: "And keeping them out of the news." Abruptly, the language of our discussion changed. A more sombre discussion ensued. Other words started sneaking into the conversation: "accountability", "funding", "meeting our compliance obligations" and giving "hard lines to the frontline workers".

The atmosphere in the room seemed to shift during this discussion. The discussion had petered out and an awkward silence was developing. Around the room people were avoiding making eye contact. They seemed anxious and uncomfortable. Christine decided to end the session. To wrap it up Christine made some half-hearted resolutions that we were doing to do before we next saw her. Christine finished with a quote about change and how we could make change happen. With the session wrapped up we headed back to our office. We filed back into the van and sat in silence on the journey. Back at our office people shuffled back to their desks to finish off some of their work. I grabbed my things and left.

Part of my ethnographic enthusiasm for attending the 'working well workshop' was my interest in listening to my colleagues discuss what working for the collective meant and how they conceptualized their sense of self within that. In the tale, my colleagues offer two very different versions of what it means to work for the collective and 'who we are' as community activists or professionals. The story also illustrates the ways in which the familiar tale of the community sector plays out in a localized context. Conversations about 'who we are and should be' were not ordinarily so explicit, but still subtly informed everyday working life in the collective. On the one hand, my colleagues understood their passion for supporting victims of violence and anger at institutions which perpetuate that violence as informing their explicit activist role. On the other hand, there was a push from Jen to changing the emotional orientation to victims of violence and redirecting their identity so as to ensure professional service in line with government requirements. This incident encapsulates the movement of emotional relationships and associated circles of identity as the objects of emotion change.

In my observations of my colleagues talking about their work, I was struck by the intense emotion they articulated, in particular, their claims to a "deeply felt" passion. In Chapter 3, I demonstrated that my participants from the sector likewise perceived that passion was foundational to community organizations and activism. In the 'working well' tale, my colleagues start by understanding their role as activists through a collective sense of passion. In being asked to share how we understood our role in the organization, the description my colleagues gave was oriented around this 'sticking point' of their passion. For example, Hayley understood herself as serving the frontline workers in a way that best supported victims, and Esther understood herself as engaging in transformative dialogues with the public. In general, my colleagues perceived that what activist work was done, how it was to be done, and their relationships with others in the organization came from their intense passion for ending gendered violence. This certain kind of intense emotion, therefore, informed how my colleagues understood their identity as activists and helped to create shared assumptions of how we ought to work with one another.

Gracie highlighted how the passion was perceived to inform daily practice. The passion, she argued, influenced how the collective is structured and that because of their passion the members give priority to engaging with victims, social workers, the public, and government. The 'bottom–up' structure Gracie refers to is born from the collectives' commitment to practising collectivism. My team of colleagues generally understood themselves to be working *for* as well as *with* their frontline counterparts; the "for and of" the community value Adam talked about in the familiar tale. The process of endowing their work with passion helped my colleagues to trace the lines of an activist identity, embedded in the values of the collective including empowerment, transformation, and *aroha tētahi ki tētahi*. Although in daily life my colleagues were more sceptical of the successes of collective organizing than they appear in this tale, their collective structure is an object of passion and, interconnectedly, hierarchy was an object of aversion. The process of emotion, then, influenced the way that they organized.

Passion was also connected to my colleagues' conceptualization of their activist identities. Hayley, Gracie, and Esther took great pains to articulate that their passion shaped how they understood their identity and responsibility to others. The identities of my colleagues were shaped by centring of passion; framing their identities as community workers as 'servers' of a social justice cause. Their construction of activist identity as a 'server' can be seen as a subversive alternative to the pressures of neoliberal ideologies to act as 'service providers' to clients. Esther, for instance, sees her passion as foundational to her construction of her identity as an anti–violence activist and serving the victims of violence through public education. Seeing herself in this way, she argues, is important for ending gendered violence. The 'server' activist identity thereby operated to increase the intensity of my colleagues' sense of responsibility to victims of gendered violence.

There is a clear disruption of these lines of activist identity as Jen and Riley question the relevance of passion for the work of the collective. The neoliberal–like position put forward by Jen and Riley dislocates emotions like passion and the explicit lines of passion to the object of victims of violence. Alternatively, they both propose that the purpose of their team in the collective is to ensure an efficient, effective, and responsive organization. This different orientation of victims, the collective, and other organizations, puts more emphasis on my colleagues acting as 'managers' and 'service providers' to keep the frontline workers 'in–line' and to meet compliance obligations. The longevity of the collective, and efficient and effective organizational governance become the objects of emotion. There is still a sense that these goals and the associated identities continue to be done in service of victims of violence. The shared assumptions of how we work together and the type of emotional responsibility we hold for victims are, however, different from Gracie and Hayley's earlier account.

The debate between my colleagues illustrates the ways in which different interpretations of objects and different emotional orientations to those objects alters how we construct our identity. Both constructions of identity were in response to the imperative of the collective to support victims of violence but offered significantly different pathways to that goal. My colleagues, however, more explicitly discussed their identity as activists at the outset and identified their responsibility to victims of violence. The intense emotion of passion was connected to victims of violence and an ethical responsibility to serve these victims as part of their activism. The dislocation of intense emotions, and the promotion of other emotional orientations, highlighted that it was difficult to organize alternatively; particularly when the 'familiar tale' formed the frame of understanding the community sector. There was a tangible sense of deflation at the end of the tale, which underscores what is lost when we focus on our individual, tangible skill sets alone. Overall, the story of the 'working well workshop' underlines that intense emotions shape identity and the shared assumptions of how we should work together. The tensions between different approaches to social change was palpable. I now turn to drawing out some other intense emotions in greater depth, to explore the ways in which intense emotions increased my colleagues' feelings of responsibility to catalyse change for victims of gendered violence.

Ties that bind: emotional attachments

Intense emotions, like passion, shape our sense of self, our connection to others, and the shared assumptions of how we can work with one another. In this section, I look more closely at a variety of examples of emotion which shifted the boundaries between what was considered activism and what was not and proposed different kinds of emotional relations between us. Before I move to this exploration, I wish to pause to again acknowledge that these emotional relations can be harmful as well as helpful. As I noted in Chapter 3, emotions can operate to exclude as well as include, and emotions can operate to 'fix' us/them relations rather than open them. As I go on to look at how the specific emotions of grief, passion, and rage in my colleagues work, I explore the lines of inclusion and exclusion as well as how these emotions fixed or moved our connection with others. I also draw attention to the 'sticking point' of emotion and the importance of the sticking point in activism. In particular, this section focuses on how these strong emotions operated to increase the intensity of responsibility towards victims of violence in a way that opened up, rather than closed down, new constellations of relationships.

Effectively sharing the intensity of the emotions my colleagues oriented their work around is difficult, and I have opted to illustrate the emotions I discuss here through poetry. Other scholars and activists have used poetry as a method of presentation of material as it can offer a deeper sense of emotion because 'poetry is felt as well as read' and 'poems concertize emotions, feelings, and moods, and thus recreate experience itself to another person' (Sayers and Jones, 2015: 107). Writing through poetry offers a way to explore events without reducing them to rationality and can aid in communicating, with simple force, how the self is constructed. Additionally, I wanted to avoid offering 'thick descriptions' of emotions that privileged breadth over depth (Rosaldo, 1989). The emotion I discuss here was felt and interpreted in a variety of ways, but the intensity of grief and anger I observed lends itself to communicating the 'simple force', as the 'deeply felt' attachment to ending gendered violence was usually expressed by my colleagues simply and directly.

My first poem was written after an interview with Emily. She explained the intensity of her commitment to her activism, particularly in her role which involved writing policy submissions and conducting research, for victims of violence:

'I write.'
Emily tells me. 'I write from the position of
Anger
And sadness
And passion.
What is the injustice here? What makes me most angry about
    this bill?'

She pauses. Contemplates.

'Great. That makes us sound like a happy bunch.
We are passionate, sad, angry people.'
She looks at me. I laugh.
'Is this the point where I am supposed to deny that?' I ask.

Here, Emily highlights how she perceives a collection of intense emotions, namely anger, sadness, and passion as inextricable from her social justice activism. She describes the emotion as a 'position', an occupied space through which she carries out her activism, specifically in this case engaging in activism critical of institutions. Importantly, Emily doesn't see her position or emotions as static, but as a kind of moving investment in victims of gendered violence which make change possible (Ahmed, 2014). The intense emotions seem to make her activist identity malleable, as she notes there are different orientations that shift her relationships with victims of violence. All the lines of her emotions intersect with injustice; for her the 'sticking point' of emotion in her work. Emotion is implicated in creating change and unpicking institutional norms which condone injustice. The social and political effects of Emily's emotional orientation to victims of violence, help her to orient her activism towards transformation and *aroha tētahi ki tētahi*. In other words, passion, grief, and anger are used as starting points for her activism and allow Emily to look at exclusion of victims of violence and, subsequently, propose how we could safeguard victims by altering the 'value' codified in legislation.

From Emily's perspective, these emotions are collectively felt. She refers to a 'we'; implying that her emotional orientation to victims is shared with her 'bunch of passionate, sad, angry colleagues. Emily's emphasis that the emotions are collectively experienced, indicates that she sees those intense emotions as fundamental to activist identity as part of the collective. Importantly, the emotions of passion, grief, and anger shape Emily's assumptions about how she works with her colleagues and what action they collectively undertake. And these emotions were frequently returned to in everyday life in the collective. At the lunch table Gracie would share her disdain of the framing of gendered violence in the media; Esther would passionately protect the safety of women and gendered minorities from verbal abuse on our social media; Hayley channelled her anger at landlords who evicted victims into creating safe homes for victims and their children. As with Emily, my other colleagues also emotionally identified harmful social norms and exclusion of women's experiences, and through these experiences strengthened their actions to challenge those power relations.

Feelings of anger or rage were commonly circulated by my colleagues in everyday working life. I remember one particularly striking instance of expressed anger, which came from Ava who otherwise was a soft-spoken woman:

> Ava seems to me like a fine bone china
> Delicate and smooth
> I handle with care
>
> But when we talk of abuse
> Women and children
> Broken, smashed, fractured

'Militant', she tells me, 'really *militant*'
'I would march for the cause.'
She is unbendable iron.

Intense anger was particularly salient in our organization. Anger was 'stuck' to social norms which devalued women and gender minorities thereby making them more likely to be subjected to gendered violence. Notably, the emotion of anger shaped my colleagues' consideration of what one should *not* do (Ahmed, 2014); namely be violent (physically or symbolically) to women and gender minorities under any circumstances. Ava, as an example, highlights how deeply felt the anger was in the collective. Ava's articulation of her anger rests on several key interlinked points. She implies that anger involves movement ('marching'), solidarity ('the cause'), and the need for organized, efficient, and fierce opposition to gendered violence ('militant'). The movement evoked, being 'stuck' to (hetero)sexist norms and practices, implicates the need for collective action, tied to one another by an anger against gendered violence (Butler, 2006b). In short, shaping her understanding of her work through anger aided Ava in conceptualizing activism in relation to democratic cooperation and radical, public demands for social justice.

Anger also shaped the relationships between members of the collective. The work was primarily framed as 'the cause' (as noted by Ava). (Hetero)sexism, and intersecting inequalities such as racism, were understood by my colleagues to preclude women and gender minorities from living full lives and an additional risk of gendered violence. Accordingly, my colleagues' enacted daily practices were constructed in opposition to marginalizing social norms. In other words, anger about gendered violence and norms which reified that violence shaped my colleagues' shared assumptions of organizing in relation to they should *not* do to groups of marginalized people. Anger, therefore, encouraged my colleagues to (re)consider which identities were marginalized by oppressive systems, and consider 'the other' compassionately both in general and as individuals (Brewis, 2017). My colleagues, for example, made sure that half of their resources and leadership positions went to Māori *kaimahi* (workers); provided flexibility for members with children, such as allowing children to come to work regularly and having a room in the office dedicated to children; or regularly promoting discussions throughout the collective on the impacts of homophobia and its irrevocable interconnection with gendered violence. As with Ava, generally anger aided my colleagues to conceptualize their activist identities in relation to democratic cooperation, interlocking inequalities, the spirit of *aroha tētahi ki tētahi*, and towards a future without gendered violence.

One striking emotion that was not raised in my conversations with other members of the community sector, but suffused daily life in the collective, was grief:

Kim reads about the women and the children and the details of
Tearing, throwing, starving, hitting, raping, spitting, slapping,
  beating, battering, bruising
Daily in the database she so passionately maintains.
One day when I'm standing next to her desk, she tells me a
  number, a black and white number
Of women and children and details.

I try to make this number real.
I think about every woman I've walked by on the street, stood
  behind in line, or have ever seen.
And when I fly above my city and see the tiny homes stretch
  from coastline to coastline
I imagine that every single one of those houses and buildings
  and cars
Which I'm trying to hold in my view are filled with women and
  children and details.

Bringing myself back onto the solid ground
I see Esther standing in our office tentatively asking us to confirm
That she isn't crazy,
She is not crazy when men keep emailing her saying 'wrong'
  and telling her
To listen, that she needs to get her facts straight, that she is
  spreading lies.
Just another woman violently spreading lies about men.
'And I just think' Esther tells us,
'if those men are right, where are the bodies? There would be
  a body count to match.'
Like all of those bodies of women and children and details.

In my poem about Kim and Esther, grief shapes the ways we organize and our identity as anti-violence activists. In everyday working life, grief was commonly interpreted as 'stuck' to the abused bodies of women and gender minorities. The emotion was outwardly inflected, in that it sought to unite people in a condemnation of violence as a collective responsibility, rather than individualizing this responsibility (as would be the case with neoliberal organizing). Kim, in her work with the records and databases of victims of violence, explained her intense devotion to her work through feelings of grief over the sheer volume of records. For her, grief furnished a sense of political community (Butler, 2006b); the work of the collective was focused on reducing the need for grieving because of the destruction of so many lives. Similarly, Esther, in her media and public engagement work, focused on fostering a sense of political community through grief; frequently engaging in discussions with the public through our social media that emphasized the relational ties between abused women, gender minorities, and our communities. She would engage the public in discussions about sexism in judicial decision making, the deaths of women and gender minorities at the hands of abusive partners, and the devastating impacts of prejudice against victims of violence in our communities. Activism, then, was conceptualized as an attachment to victims of violence and a dedication to publicly mourn those victims, whose lives were minimalized or marginalized. Importantly, grief also fostered a sense of community and aided my colleagues in conceptualization of their activism in relation to *aroha tētahi ki tētahi* and social transformation.

Although grief for another person, or for groups of people, can bind us together and show us the ways in which we are implicated to others (Butler, 2006b), there is also the risk of 'fixing' some bodies as the object of grief. There was a risk, for example, that a fixed line between members of the collective (the activists) and their clients (the victims) would result in 'othering' victims as objects of grief. This fixed orientation could result in minimalizing victims of violence as experts in their own reality, and the associated embodied knowledge and agency. To 'unfix' these lines, grief would need to be endowed to victims of violence in a way that emphasized our interconnection in systems of inequality and valued victims' expert knowledge. I generally observed, however, that grief was moving rather than fixing.

Grief, as expressed by my colleagues, usually carried a sense of interconnection. We grieved for abused women and gender minorities because violence had been launched at our own bodies, and the bodies of our close friends and family. We also grieved because violence had happened to us and our community. Grief was then connected to lived experience and a recognition that victims and activists were both parts of the social fabric. It was common practice to situate the stories of victims in relation to the grief of our own stories of domestic violence, rape, or sexual assault, as well as less (physically) violent stories of sexism or demands of emotional labour. The stories of victims were endowed with the most meaning but were situated within the larger tapestry of violence. Grief for the bodies of women and gender minorities, including our own, thus shaped my colleagues' perceptions of their activism for victims of violence. We were not free until all of us were free.

Emotion accentuates our connections with one another in ways that recognize the need to value and protect those who are marginalized (Butler, 2006b). In the collective, the intense emotions of passion, grief, and anger informed how my colleagues decided to organize and how they understood their identities as anti-violence activists. I illustrated how the intense emotions of anger, grief, and passion tied my colleagues together in a way that helped them to embody values of democratic cooperation and *aroha tētahi ki tētahi*. Passion, grief, and anger were all outwardly inflected, implicating my colleagues in the lives of others. Intense emotions also shaped how my colleagues understood their identities. Rather than fixing identities of themselves as 'activists' and others as 'victims', my colleagues sought to bring forward the ever-shifting lines of our connection. Their activist identities, then, were not fixed or static. Significantly, my colleagues were continually questioning their emotions as they were aware that our emotional orientation to victims had political and social effects. Emotions were not simple responses to inequality. Through emotion, my colleagues thought as much about what they *should* do as what they should *not* do as they crafted their activist identity within systems of inequality.

Ties that break: being beside oneself

Although emotions can bind us together, they also involve a 'breaking' and a 'boundary setting'. Along those lines, Ahmed highlights that emotion can involve a moving away, as well as a moving towards, thereby involving a reifying of boundaries between groups of people (Ahmed, 2014). Emotion can be exclusionary. These exclusions are not necessarily negative; anger stuck on White supremacy, for example, can lead to the exclusion of White supremacist identities. The processes of moving away, therefore, could be affirmative. A dislocation from identities that were perceived as contributing to oppression. Likewise, Butler argues that this 'breaking', being beside oneself, is essential for moving away from normative identities and fostering the conditions that make it possible for marginalized people to flourish (Butler, 2006b). Focusing on ties that break also helps me to explore more fully how emotion can remake our identities in ways that encourage the creation of new patterns of social relationships. This potential must be considered alongside the harms of 'breaking ties'. Breaking ties with others can also result in the exclusion of groups of people and the maintenance of social norms that condone physical or symbolic violence targeted at marginalized people. In this section, therefore, I want to draw out the processes of breaking as it related to how emotion moved my colleagues, particularly focusing on how their identity as anti-violence activists was shaped by how they perceived their ties to abused women. I begin with a story about Indian migrant women that illustrates how emotion moves us but can also operate to fix identity in exclusionary and possibly harmful ways:

I entered the presentation slightly late and the speaker – a young Indian woman called Disha – had already begun her talk. There were only a few empty chairs, but in the middle of the room, so I sat on a doorstep at the edge of the dim space. Disha was telling the audience about her experiences growing up in India, highlighting the static gender roles through the story of her first marriage to an older man who refused her many freedoms, including preventing her from eating until all the men had finished their meal. After divorcing her first husband (to the shame of her family), Disha became free to work and travel. Her new-found freedoms made her even more aware of the extent of abuse against women in India. In a particularly striking anecdote, she started telling us about the 'burning brides'. They are newly-wed women who are doused in kerosene and set on fire by their husbands, so that the man can take control of the dowry and marry another woman for her money. The deaths are labelled 'kitchen accidents'. At one hospital where Disha worked, there were over 100 women in one month who died this way.

Disha then moved to telling us about her work with India migrant women in Aotearoa New Zealand. She told us that although 'burning brides' were less common, they still occurred in Indian communities in this country. The more common types of abuse, Disha told us, were emotional and economic abuse by in-laws – a dynamic seldom considered in anti-violence work in this country – and the impact of Indian community leaders who encouraged women to stay with their abusive husbands, so as not to bring shame to their community. The women sitting around me had intense responses to Disha's stories. Several women were openly crying in grief, and throughout the presentation there had been repeated, pained gasps around the room.

Disha took a few questions from the room. The first question came from an older Pākehā woman who wanted to know how Disha had "escaped the cycle" that Indian women were trapped in. The next woman simply stood up and told Disha: "you are an amazing woman of courage and strength" and explained that she was shocked at the extent of violence that Indian women suffered. The final question came from a Māori frontline worker who told Disha that her eyes had been opened, particularly because there was a large Indian community near their centre. This woman explained how she now felt better equipped to engage with Indian women. Zoey, from my team, said to me while we were applauding Disha: "I know it sounds bad, but it is because I've travelled a lot, but I don't find it [the abuse of Indian women] that surprising." She told me she thought it strange that activists who work with abuse everyday should be so shocked by Disha's stories and didn't know the types of abuse Indian women were subjected to.

Grief was the most salient emotion attached to the migrant women in Disha's stories. The revelations of her stories about Indian migrant women involved challenging our understanding of domestic abuse and our affective relationships to those who are targeted with extreme, lethal violence. The intense emotion of grief implicated the people in the room with the lives of Indian migrant women. The final questioner, in particular, highlights the 'breaking' she experienced through grief. Her now 'opened eyes' have involved movement; from a state of being unaware of our indebtedness to Indian women, to a recognition of Indian women in her community as victims of a particular kind of violence. The movement grief invokes in this case – attaching the grief to Indian women – makes our fundamental dependency and ethical responsibility to the lives of each other salient. Feeling this responsibility, through grief, shaped how the people in the room set boundaries around their anti-violence activist identity. In this case, the boundaries were moved, which demonstrates how attaching the emotion to the suffering of others can translate into physical support for our lives (Butler, 2006b). Here the intense emotion of grief that makes us beside ourselves opens up the possibilities of forming different kinds of attachments with others, thereby helping to organize alternatively for *aroha tētahi ki tētahi*.

The mobilization of emotion through Disha's talk is, however, problematic. In order for grief to move the boundaries of activist identity and alternative organizing, grief must encourage movement to undo normative relations. In this context, however, grief appears to be unidirectional, passed from privileged subjects and fixed on 'third world' practices in a way that reifies contemporary geopolitical hierarches (Pedwell, 2013). Unlike earlier examples I gave where grief was localized and personalized, as well as outwardly inflected, here the 'breaking' seems to both involve a movement towards responsibility for Indian women, but also fixes Indian women as objects of grief in a way that they, and the violence they suffer, is othered. Disha herself is understood as an object of compassion by two of the questioners – someone who suffered based on her Indian identity. In this way Disha is separated from others in the room who experienced violence, her identity as *Indian* is the 'sticking point' to grief. Nevertheless, the final questioner highlights how grieving for Indian women must involve a change in practices to include and engage with the community.

Disha's presentation was an example in which she directly set out to challenge our practices as activists and the identity of activists working with the community. She attempts to promote a reorientation of our activism through emotion to form different patterns of engagement and responsibility with 'other' women. Although presentations like Disha's were fairly common events (I observed a number of other similar presentations over my time with the collective), being moved and moving with emotion were also common features of daily life in the collective. My colleagues frequently shared personal stories related to 'breaking', linking these moments to their identity as anti-violence activists, and to their work dismantling harmful social norms and practices. One of Tia's moments of 'breaking' occurred in her first months of working for the collective. I was talking with about how she felt about becoming involved in anti-violence activism, and I asked her if anything stood out for her in her first few months. Initially, she told me about how she felt out of her depth, not having the business skills to efficiently do the reporting side of the work. Then she paused, reflected, and told me a story that changed her:

> 'Violence and abuse, we knew it growing up, there were times that we were exposed to it and felt the impact of it and stuff like that. But as an adult coming face-to-face with that first woman lying in a hospital bed. It's just ... fuck. That stands out. Anyone who works in this field, or anybody who has that first experience, can't say that it doesn't stick. It did. I was just fucking standing at the bottom of the bed and didn't know whether to walk out or just ... I just thought that actually I was waiting for her eyes to open. But they were already open. But I just couldn't see them because they were so fucking bruised and shit. That was something that stood out.'

The grief that Tia brings attention to in her story involves movement. The grief that she feels is interpreted as 'sticking' to that first moment in the hospital where Tia was confronted with the extremity of violence. The 'sticking' involves a movement from her understanding of childhood violence, to the victims of abuse she works with in her anti-violence activism. Dislocated from her original understanding of violence, Tia became beside herself with grief. That moment fostered a transformation rather than dissociation, as Butler puts it: from the 'experience of loss and fragility, however, the possibility of making different kinds of ties emerges' (Butler, 2006b: 28). Tia comes to form her identity as an anti-violence activist through grief and becomes implicated in the lives of abused women. Notably, Tia insists that 'anyone' supporting victims is moved by grief. The movement invoked by Tia implies that all our colleagues who work with victims have been pushed beside themselves through this grief, and that through circulating these experiences others can also be moved. Tia's movement also alters how she understands her anti-violence activist identity. For her, the boundaries shifted, and she reimagined her responsibility to victims of violence.

Tia also explicitly connected her 'breaking moment' to how she thought about her identity as an anti-violence activist within the context of the community sector. Tia felt that the community sector was the best place for victims of violence to engage with social support and for activists to fight for change. She contrasts our open and autonomous work with the "bureaucratic bullshit that every [government] client has to go through to either access their [services] or have their services imposed upon them" and that she is proud that "[community organizations] are not dictated to by legislation and/or government policy". Her anger in this instance is 'stuck' on harmful institutional norms which compromise women's autonomy or empowerment. Her arguments here reflected a wider attitude in the collective: that victims of violence often then have subsequent symbolic violence of the state or other institutions imposed on their bodies when they seek support. This was particularly important for our Māori *kaimahi* who carried the intergenerational harms of colonization. Tia thereby positions anti-violence activist identity outside of the boundaries of the state and consequently establishes an imperative for the collective to organize alternatively to safeguard victims from further violence. Through the grief 'stuck' on the bodies of victims of violence, Tia thereby created shared assumptions for our relation to each other in the collective and what we must *exclude* from our organizing practices.

Personal stories from my colleagues also demonstrated that intense emotion could result in exclusionary practices and the harmful 'fixing' of certain identities. Evelyn, for example, was becoming increasingly disillusioned with the approach of some members of the collective towards Tangata Whenua. One story she told me illustrated how she became beside herself with anger, being moved to break ties with some of her colleagues and shift the 'sticking point' of anger to the collective rather than to systems of racism and colonization. She told me about how she felt some members were not respecting *kaupapa* Māori processes:

'[Some members of our team] went to a meeting [with other members] uninvited and it caused a lot of shit. With *kaupapa* Māori services it has to be in agreement before hand and let them know. That is respect regardless. They took offence to it, and all sorts of other things. Anyway, it was my turn to go up there and do an audit and Michelle [a Pākehā colleague] was coming with me. [The members] wanted to clear the air of all the stuff that had happened and wanted to do a *mihi whakatau* – a kind of ceremonial blessing of her as a manager and me as worker going on there, onto their space. Levelling out the energy around [the incident] is a good way to explain it. Going in to talk to Michelle about it, her door was closed, and she suggested that we should go out and get pissed the night before because she doesn't give a fuck about their *mihi whakatau*. Didn't care if we went there smelling like alcohol. I was pissed off because this is them holding out an olive branch; you don't shit on that. But that is the attitude that it was. I lost so much respect.'

This story illustrates how Evelyn was moved by anger to breaking ties with colleagues and how through Michelle's anger she drew racist lines between Pākehā and Māori activists in the collective. Michelle had remarked to me before how angry she was at what she felt were discriminatory or racist practices towards Pākehā organizational members. The anger, for Michelle, was stuck on Māori members of the collective. The lines she drew had serious social and political implications. Māori continue to struggle against the ongoing harms of colonization which has attempted to erase the culture and language of Tangata Whenua (Walker, 2004). In Michelle's view, the work of the collective gave unnecessary priority to Māori and activists should treat all races 'equally'. Michelle's construction of activism through anger devalues Māori practices and interprets Pākehā ideas as universally beneficial. She thereby draws a strong boundary around fixed Pākehā and Māori identities. Anger that fixes identity in this way is harmful and exclusionary. For those seeking social justice, such a construction is contrary to changing power relations as it reifies extant social and political norms which underpin inequality.

Evelyn's anger moved from being 'stuck' on systems of racism and colonization to being stuck on the collective. The story she told me was illustrative of her anger at how some members of the collective treated Tangata Whenua. Evelyn is frustrated that her colleague would ignore the effort of Māori members to repair the divide and position their rituals as carrying no value. For Evelyn, the *mihi whakatau* was a practice of the collective which attempted to reset the power imbalance between Pākehā and Māori. The moment of 'breaking' for Evelyn, unlike for Tia, involved a moving away from the collective and their exclusionary practices. She felt that these practices were reifying racism in our collective; and her colleague's actions were a form of symbolic violence that excluded and devalued Māori identity; including her own. In a different way to Michelle, Evelyn also gets 'stuck' with her anger. The switch of focus from systems to the collective, altered the meaning attached to the collective by Evelyn. Through her anger, she no longer interpreted the collective as a place which supported all victims and *kaimahi* in recognition of interlocking systems of inequality. Alternatively, the boundary of her activist identity moved through her anger to exclude some of her Pākehā colleagues.

Redrawing the boundaries: emotion, activism, and academia

That activism and emotion are connected is hardly a contentious claim. My focus, however, has been on the social and political effects of intense emotions, how intense emotions inform activist identity, and the tensions that arise from the boundaries we repeatedly (re)draw around our activism through emotion. My colleagues and participants from the community sector had compelling, and diverse, ideas about the emotions which informed their work and how those emotions were shaped by ideologies like neoliberalism or systems of social inequality such as sexism or racism. For me, the most significant thing I learnt from my community sector participants was that the values we want to organize by require us to remake our emotional connections. For social justice, we need to move and be moved. My interest in emotion, activism, and alternative organizing was also from a position where I wished to understand how these lines connected to and could be (re)drawn to academia. The way my colleagues regularly reimaged the boundaries of their activist identity through emotion, showed me both the fluidity of activist identity and the need to examine where we draw boundaries of activism in relation to inequality.

Activist identities were not pure or unchanging. On the contrary, my discussion of the working well day illustrated how the community sector context in Aotearoa New Zealand compelled my colleagues to draw and redraw the boundaries of their activist identity and, interrelatedly, their role and practices as a collective. The different lines they drew had social and political effects. At the end of the working well day, my colleagues had (pretty unhappily) oriented their activist identities towards service provision and high-quality professional service. Although this shift may have had benefits for the efficiency or proficiency of our team, the political effects of a more neoliberal approach could pull my colleagues away from their feminist, collectivist, and decolonizing values. The role of the collective, then, would move away from Tia's vision of a space where victims could avoid the "bureaucratic bullshit" and layers of institutional violence. The tension between these two roles is similar to the pressure on other community organizations to formalize and adopt business-like practices in favour of community-oriented approaches. At stake is the feeling of our responsibility to people subjected to inequality and the emotional connection between us.

As I argued early in Chapter 3, however, the either/or of community or neoliberalism is an unhelpful binary which directs our focus away from ideas or practices that grow and spread in new directions. Emotion, as my colleagues understood, can both form the fabric of oppression as much as it can move us to connect with those subjected to inequality. In order to dismantle harmful and exclusionary social norms, activist identity must tie to forms of action that help undo power relations and retie our connections to each other. Grief and anger, for instance, could operate to reinforce harmful boundaries between 'us and them', as well as moving us beside ourselves in a way that expanded or deepened our responsibility for one another. Through binding and breaking practices, my colleagues aimed to create new patterns of relationships between members of the collective and between the collective and victims of violence. As my discussion has aimed to illustrate, breaking and binding were an intricate and ongoing drawing of lines between community and neoliberalism as well as between other layers of identity such as gender and race.

Intense emotions informed the shared assumptions of activist work. These emotions were part of deciding how we *did not* want to relate to each other as well as how we *did*. My colleagues' anger, passion, or grief in relation to victims of gendered violence, for instance, were connected to collective organizing. The collective structure was a form of action that directly opposed bureaucracy and hierarchy (again, noted by Tia) and attempted to change the power relations between victims of gendered violence and institutions. The 'sticking points' of emotion were outwardly inflected in those instances, reinforcing a sense of collective responsibility. I additionally focused on the intense emotions of a couple of my colleagues, to explore the felt tensions of alternative organizing. The story that Evelyn tells is a powerful example of how emotion can operate to reinforce harmful stereotypes or categorizations of activist work. Michelle and Evelyn had a shared experience of anger, but this anger had very different political and social effects. Michelle reinforced harmful (racist) categorizations of Māori, drew a clear boundary between 'us' and 'them', and excluded Māori from her activist work. Evelyn, on the other hand, was moved by anger in relation to our team. Her anger was 'stuck' on the practices which allowed racist views to be part of the collective and thereby reinforce the ongoing exclusion of Māori.

As part of the collective, I was likewise drawing and redrawing lines around my activist identity, my academic identity, the emotions of anti-violence work, the emotions of ethnographic work, and how I connected those lines to social change. My lines had social and political effects in my volunteer work as well as different social and political effects in my academic work. I experienced many tensions between those lines. Should I contribute as a volunteer in the working well workshop and offer my opinion on the role of the collective? Or should I merely observe the conflict unfolding around me? Our boundaries around what 'counts' as academic work and activist work can cause us to feel uncomfortable and unsettled if we spill over those lines. But, as my participants from the community sector and my colleagues showed me, those lines are always tangled. Our boundaries pulse broad and narrow. We must understand the lines we draw in relation to our social context and examine the radiating effects of the lines we draw.

The lines I can now draw between academia, activism, emotion, and social change are radically different from those initial boundary lines I discussed in Part I. There are not simple, clear lines that fix academics' or activists' natural emotions and responses to injustice. On the contrary the relationship(s) between academics and activists is permeated by intense emotions which are politically and socially bound. These complexities overspill. The boundary of my academic identity expanded as I felt grief which deepened my responsibility to victims of violence and anger at the struggles of the community sector to maintain our social fabric. These intense emotions were interconnected with changes in how I organized my research. My academic work and activist work became tangled as the ties that bound me to my research and the ties that bound me to my colleagues were undone and redone. Ultimately, I understood that thinking and feeling were intimately interconnected. As Karen Ashcraft says of academics: 'the more we feel what we do, the better we know what we do; and the more we know by feeling what we do, the more we have to offer' (2012: 621).

PART III

Vulnerable Bodies

5

Gendered Bodies

Kimberley and I were chatting together one lunch time, sitting on opposite sides of the lunch table. She was buoyantly explicating her views on the relationships between gender identity and violence, and I was listening intently, intrigued to hear her latest opinions on the subject. I had the opportunity to work closely with Kim during my time volunteering – assisting her in her work and talking with her regularly in our breaks. She's a young, educated, self-proclaimed 'urban Māori' who loves debating with her colleagues, myself included, about gender identity, violence, race, and politics. Our lunchtime conversation today has been about whether or not it is actually possible to end gendered violence. Kim argues that it isn't possible, not with contemporary gender identity dualisms. She tells me that until we can imagine a third possible gender, consistently and coherently, there is always going to be a violent fight for the masculine to be dominant over the feminine. She laughs and summarizes: "Basically, every time I think about gender equality, I just think it's never going to happen."

Kim then asks me what I've been working on recently. I explain that I've been doing some reading about violence, particularly thinking about the necessities of violence for forming identities (Bergin and Westwood, 2003) and I've been particularly interested in the idea that becoming something involves violently foreclosing the possibilities of other ways of being. Kim is particularly enthusiastic about the idea, linking it to her interests in how making some aspects of violence visible – 'hypering' she calls it – invisibilizes other kinds of violence. Hypering the idea that it is possible to end gendered violence invisibilizes the ways that gender inequality perpetuates, she argues. Kim has been interested in the notion of the 'undertow' of gendered violence; all the complex and subtle ways that people unconsciously revert back to harmful gendered norms.

My lunchtime conversation with Kim left me, as it usually did, unsettled in my ideas about the relationships between gender and violence, and the relationships between gender identity and the possibilities of achieving social change for victims of gendered violence. I didn't agree with Kim that it was impossible to end gendered violence, but my conversations with her were helping me to expand

and challenge my own thoughts on the relationships between gender identity and domestic violence work.

The interest in gender identity was widespread in the collective, with all of my colleagues, like Kim, keen on regularly discussing what it meant to be a woman, and what specifically it meant to be a woman undertaking anti-violence activism. My colleagues, generally, perceived women to be marginalized and targeted with many forms of violence in a society that perpetuated gender inequality by devaluing and attempting to control women. Moreover, my colleagues were, to differing degrees, also aware of how this violence was unevenly distributed among women. Jen, for instance was keenly aware of violence against lesbian women, Emily was fighting for violence against trans-women to gain more recognition in our anti-violence activism, and Evelyn was deeply committed to ending the violence against Māori men and women which she understood as embedded in colonial violence. Nevertheless, my colleagues also frequently attempted to celebrate 'being women', by encouraging and supporting each other to openly discuss their bodies and their experiences as women and to use these experiences as the foundations for their activism.

In starting to think about the connections between the body, identity, violence, and social change in anti-violence activism, I came to realize that I had not reflected deeply on how I was implicated in systems of violence. The more I engaged I became with my colleagues' questioning of their own bodies and identities, however, the more acutely I felt how I was likewise becoming unsettled in my own understanding of my body and gendered identities. My reflections on the ways I was implicated in systems of violence was very much in the vein of autoethnography (Coffey, 1999): I was using my own experiences to deepen my understanding of how anti-violence activism can operate through the body and gendered identity. In several confronting moments inside and outside the field, I came to deeply feel what my colleagues were trying to get all of us to understand through their activism: violence is unevenly distributed, but all of us are vulnerable to violence at the hands of those who are supposed to love us most. I learnt from my colleagues how becoming vulnerable to violence marks your body. And most importantly, I learnt how our bodily vulnerability is important for ending gendered violence.

My commitment in Part III is to explore three different approaches to anti-violence activism used by my colleagues which focus on the body, gendered identities, and violence. Some of these approaches have been discussed and shared by social workers, anti-violence activists, and scholars and others are unique approaches I learnt from my colleagues. In tracing these different approaches, I have used the work of Judith Butler on the body, gendered identities, and violence to think through some of the possibilities and limitations of each of these approaches. Overall, I reflect on what I learnt from my colleagues about celebrating, examining, and remaking our identities related to the body as fundamental to anti-violence activism and how these lessons could inform academic activism.

The body, identity, and violence

Before I move to considering the different approaches used by my colleagues, it is worth outlining the ways academics and activists have thought about how the body and identity are impacted by domestic violence. My outline provides a framework for understanding how my colleagues' approaches are indebted to years of activist and scholarly consideration on the social and cultural aspects of domestic violence. Any work that intersects with domestic violence can be emotionally and cognitively challenging in a number of ways. Violence has a way of getting under your skin. Many different professions who work with domestic violence including social workers (Goldblatt and Buchbinder, 2003), therapists (Tyagi, 2006), police officers (Johnson et al, 2005), nurses (Goldblatt, 2009), GPs (Kohler et al, 2013), as well as activists themselves (Nichols, 2013), have acknowledged and discussed the impacts of working with violence. Some of the impacts, like vicarious trauma or compassion fatigue, alter the capacity of someone to work with violence. Other impacts can stimulate more fundamental changes about how workers who are repeatedly exposed to domestic violence understand their identity (Seymour, 2009). Domestic violence is known to 'flood' the lives of those who work with victims of domestic violence and invoke a re-examination of gender identity (Goldblatt et al, 2009; Seymour, 2009). But why gender identity in particular?

Women who work with victims of domestic violence have described feeling particularly unsettled, and even disempowered, in their gender identities when repeatedly exposed to domestic violence (Goldblatt and Buchbinder, 2003; Tyagi, 2006; Seymour, 2009). It can be difficult to feel comfortable in your own skin when you consistently see others like you abused. As a telling contrast, domestic violence workers who identify as men tend to find domestic violence work empowering and affirmative (Seymour, 2009; Bailey et al, 2011). Men tend to find that working with domestic violence affirms their own life choices but causes them to re-examine their understanding of masculinity (Bailey et al, 2011). Scholars have noted that questioning gender identity seems to be particularly prominent in organizations, like my collective, where domestic violence is understood to be a gendered problem (Iliffe and Steed, 2000; Nichols, 2013). Understanding domestic violence as a societal gendered problem recognizes that domestic violence is a dimension of the systemic devaluation and objectification of women in education, the home, the workplace, and social life (Nichols, 2014). Women who work with domestic violence and are aware of the systemic nature of the problem can feel overburdened, overwhelmed, and devalued in their sense of self (Seymour, 2009). My colleagues who generally did understand domestic violence to be a gendered social problem and all self-identified as (cis)women, likewise felt the impacts of domestic violence work on their gender identities although in more complex ways than has typically been depicted by scholars.

Although academics have generally acknowledged the impact of domestic violence work on identity, as well as the capacity to carry out work or activism, research tends to presume that those who work with domestic violence are not simultaneously victims of violence (for example, Tyagi, 2006; Goldblatt et al, 2009; Bailey et al, 2011). There has been much less written by academics about workers or activists who consider themselves as victims of violence at the same time as working with violence (Ben-Ari, 2008). Research that has taken an explicitly feminist approach in this area (for example, Seymour, 2009; Nichols, 2011, 2013), however, strongly makes the case that women who work in domestic violence are, in fact, simultaneously advocates for ending gendered violence *and* are victims of societal structures of gendered violence. Additionally, research about identity and domestic violence tends not to investigate *how* identity is constructed. Identity categories such as 'woman' tend to be assumed rather than analysed, and the connections between being 'female' and having a 'feminine identity' or being 'male' and having a 'masculine identity' tend to be naturalized. As many feminist and queer scholars and activists have pointed out, however, 'gender' is not a natural category but is constructed through social and cultural norms (Butler, 2006a). To understand how the body, identity, and violence are connected, it is important to understand the socio-cultural construction of gender identities and the implications for violence.

Research of victims' identities and the identities of non-professional helpers (for example, victims' mothers) has more thoroughly followed this latter route and explored the construction of gendered identities in relation to domestic violence (Peled and Dekel, 2010; Gueta et al, 2016). For instance, constructions of victims' mothers' identities are negatively impacted by social ideas of what makes a 'good mother' (Gueta et al, 2016). A mother whose daughter is subjected to domestic violence is often depicted as having 'failed' to protect her daughter. Research has argued that the perception of the 'good mother' has implications for the type and extent of help victims of violence receive, and thereby hinders social change by excluding, marginalizing, and devaluing mothers that do not adhere to social norms of the 'good' mother (Peled and Dekel, 2010). Importantly, therefore, the research that has actively examined *how* gendered identities are constructed in relation to violence, highlights that as well as unsettling identities, the body, identity, and violence are connected in a way that has impacts for creating social change.

The implications of the construction of gender have long been a concern for anti-violence activists (Arnold and Ake, 2013). Anti-violence activists have often been foundational in developing sophisticated approaches to understanding the body, gender identity, and violence in ways that foster social change (Ferree and Martin, 1995; McMillan, 2007). My colleagues, for instance, were particularly cognisant of how domestic violence also impacted other identities, such as lesbian identities, a point on which research is very limited (see Ristock, 2002, 2011 for notable exceptions). One important concern for my colleagues, which had been embedded in the organization since it was founded in the 1960s, was ensuring that they were fostering change for all those impacted by gendered violence; including LGBT+ women and non-binary folk. LGBT+ women and non-binary folk have been a consistent presence and influence in domestic violence activism in the West and challenged how all anti-violence activists thought about gendered identities (Ristock, 2002; Arnold and Ake, 2013). Yet, in spite of these developments in activism, research on domestic violence and identity remains heteronormative and there has been little exploration of LGBT+ identities and domestic violence work. Research typically assumes that people who work with domestic violence are heterosexual and assume that exposure to domestic violence is so unsettling *because* of the reflection it causes on (hetero) intimate partnerships external to the workplace. Nevertheless, queer scholarship more broadly has extensively considered the relationships between the body, gender identity, sexuality, and violence.

My colleagues' approach to their activism was, then, informed by the knowledge that the body and gendered identities were important to anti-violence activism. In particular, having a 'woman's body' was an intimate point of concern for my colleagues; marked because of the daily exposure to physical and symbolic violence on women's bodies in our activism. How we understood our bodies, the vulnerability of those bodies, and how our bodies contributed to our gendered identities was therefore salient in everyday activist work. Research on victim identity has argued that the perceived 'closeness' of women to their bodies has significant impacts on how domestic violence victims understand their identities as women (Wesely et al, 2000). Despite the centricity of the body in domestic violence and the importance of the body to anti-violence activism generally, research has overlooked how gendered identities are constructed through the body by anti-violence activists.

Yet, how activists understand their own identity and *how* it is constructed in relation to domestic violence has implications for how anti-violence activism achieves social change for victims of violence. First, it has implications for the activists themselves. Understanding *how* being a woman is experienced and constituted through the body when working with domestic violence can help us all to better care for activists who are unsettled by work with violence. Supporting activists themselves is foundational to doing activist work. Second, how activists understand the body and gender identity in relation to domestic violence has implications for whose bodies are seen as worthy of protecting, valuing, and celebrating in anti-violence activist work. Thirdly, when activists make political claims condemning 'violence against women', understanding how the body is implicated helps us to understand on behalf of which bodies those claims are being made. These three core questions also have implications for academic activism. There is a lot to learn from my colleagues about the role of the body in academic activism. Specifically, academic activism must reflexively consider whose bodies are positioned as worthy of protecting, valuing, and celebrating, and who is excluded from the political claims being made. How we understand our own bodies (through gender, race, or sexuality for instance) is fundamental to how we relate to others we desire to support in academic engagement with social movements.

The three approaches I consider as examples of these issues are all related to the way in which the body and gendered identity was significant in daily activist work. I present all three approaches as viable ways of doing anti-violence activist work but advocate for the final one as a powerful way of doing anti-violence activism as well as academic activism. I respectively discuss how the identity of 'woman' was constituted through the body, and how experiences of unsettled gender identities in anti-violence activist work were both liberating and constraining for my colleagues. I then move to exploring how LGBT+ women were constructed in the collective in relation to the gendered body in Chapter 6. I look at how some of the practices of the collective reinforced heteronormativity which meant that LGBT+ bodies were sometimes positioned as less worthy of protection from violence. Finally, in Chapter 7, I offer a striking formulation of the body that my colleagues shared with me: women *as* vulnerable bodies. It is from this third approach – vulnerability – that I then take the discussion into how reimagining academic activism can take the lead from a place of ethical vulnerability.

In the lunchroom: the body and gender identity

Lunchtimes were always a particularly interesting time for me as an ethnographer, as I was able to get to know my colleagues more informally and hear about their lives. Life in the collective often rotated around this daily ritual. In particular, conversations over lunch seemed to provide a platform to discuss common interests and, importantly, to discuss issues related to gendered violence and activism. A common focus of discussion around the table connected to both issues was an interest in the body. On my very first day with my colleagues, I remember hurrying back to my desk to write about the conversation:

> two of the younger staff members – Gracie and Kimberley – were already sitting chatting about TV shows when Emily and I joined the table. It seemed to be normal to have lunch together, particularly for the younger staff members. There were then four of us at the table, and all of us were under 30. A large number of topics were covered in the hour [including] a discussion of menstruation, abortion, sexual partners, sexual health related drugs, [medical disorders] related to the womb or ovaries, marriage, dieting, mood swings, recreational drugs, and flatmates.

I continued to be fascinated by the extensive attention given by my colleagues to describing bodily experiences and discussing topics related to the body. Research indicates that many experiences related to women's bodies continue to be marginalized or hidden in organizations including miscarriage (Porschitz and Siler, 2017), pregnancy (Gatrell, 2011), menstruation (Sayers and Jones, 2015), and motherhood (Riad, 2007). Contrariwise, my colleagues appeared to be making a conscious effort to actively include women's bodies in everyday working life, and frequently discussed and celebrated those bodily experiences. Moreover, the body seemed foundational for my colleagues in understanding their identities as women and their activism on behalf of women subjected to gendered violence. There was a preoccupation, however, with ways in which bodies could be harmed or were sites of political debate. As research about domestic violence and identity elucidates, gendered identities are frequently unsettled when anti–violence workers are repeatedly confronted with domestic violence (Seymour, 2009). My colleagues' identities as women did, indeed, seem to be unsettled. Specifically, being unsettled seemed to be invoked through feelings of powerlessness, related to a lack of bodily control. The perpetual concern of the abuse of women's bodies by institutions or individuals and the constraints of social norms on what women could do with their bodies, was indicative of being unsettled.

Feminist research on the body has highlighted how experiences of the body in organizations are gendered (Jeanes et al, 2011). In particular, feminist scholars have argued that how people understand their body is shaped and disciplined by normative expectations of which bodies can successfully or even legitimately 'belong' in organizations (Jeanes et al, 2011). The norms about which bodies belong in organizations have been linked to the perpetuation of gender inequality as well as other forms of inequality related to the body (such as racial inequality) (Acker, 1990, 2006). Feminist scholarship on the gendered body, on the whole, has ascertained that women continue to be closely associated with their bodies, in ways that are both positive and negative, and framed as either needing to be controlled or repressed (Kenny and Bell, 2011), or as disruptive and less valuable than men's bodies (Sayers and Jones, 2015). In short, feminist scholars have demonstrated that despite the increased participation of women in the workplace, the prevailing notion that men can transcend the constraints imposed by their gendered bodies and that women continue to be constrained by their bodies, remains embedded in organizations (Sinclair, 2011). Women's efforts to disrupt the perception that their bodies are deviant or shameful, therefore, continues to be important for activist efforts to achieve gender equality (Pullen, 2018; Vachhani and Pullen, 2019). Around the lunch table, then, although my colleagues often felt acutely constrained by their bodies, they were determined to shift the societal devaluation of women's bodies as part of their activist work towards gender equality.

Given that I found my colleagues' interest in the body to be a significant part of their anti-violence activism, I wanted to deepen my understanding of their efforts through exploring this approach to activism with additional theories. To understand how the gendered body was significant for my colleagues and for their activist work, I draw on Judith Butler's understanding of the relationship between gendered identity, the body, and disrupting social norms. Butler has been particularly influential in feminist scholarship around the gendered body and has developed an extensive and rigorous post-structuralist informed approach to gender identity (Butler, 1993, 2006a). Her fundamental premise about gender identity is that 'identity is performatively constituted by the very "expressions" that are said to be its results' (Butler, 2006a: 25). In other words, our actions, language, gestures, clothing choices, and narratives do not express some underlying reality of gender identity. Instead our day-to-day embodiment of these things *is* our gender identity. An important claim about the body embedded in this perspective is that the body is itself produced through discourse and our day-to-day embodiment, rather than being a passive and neutral foundation upon which gendered identities are built (Butler, 2004a. For activism around gender, Butler's approach highlights that our (gender) identities and bodies are limited by culturally sanctioned social norms. These norms are powerful and restrict which identities are considered liveable and valuable (Butler, 2004a, 2004b).

Butler's arguments about the body are in contrast to a popular body of feminist work that has permeated public consciousness which argues that 'sex' and 'gender' are separate and that gender is socially constructed but sex is determined by biology. Butler, alternatively, argues that a gender identity is grounded in a social construction of the body and that gender identity is therefore 'a repeated stylization of the body, a set of repeated acts within a highly rigid and regulatory frame' (Butler, 2006a: 45); in other words, gender is performative. And because we are impelled to repeatedly stylize our body, therein lies the potential for social change. Through changing how bodies are stylized at both an individual and a collective level, the social norms which sanction particular identities can be said to be 'troubled' and this opens up the possibility of doing identities in different ways (Butler, 2004a). For achieving social change through activism, then, Butler's understanding of the gendered body speaks to the centricity of the body and also underscores how the body itself is understood socially and therefore a potential site of activism and change.

Feminist scholars who have utilized Butler's work to explore gendered bodies in organizations have illustrated that her work helps to draw strong attention to how the body is thought about in particular cultural settings as valuable and legitimate (Tyler and Cohen, 2010; Johansson et al, 2017). Such scholars have also highlighted how Butler's work can be used to understand the transformation of gender relations through remaking the gendered body (de Souza et al, 2016). This activist potential is felt particularly along two lines. First, Butler highlights the significance of social norms for recognition. In order to make collective claims on behalf of others – say, for instance, women – there needs to be an identity sufficiently bounded in order to be recognized by the law or for groups of individuals to rally behind (Butler, 2006b, 2015). At the same time, however, the radical potential of gendered identity lies in the multiple possible iterations of such identity. There is, therefore, a need to unsettle and remake our gendered identities in ways that open up the possibilities for novel and non-normative identities to be recognized as valuable and legitimate (Butler, 2004a, 2006a). For understanding my colleagues' attempts to use the body as a possible site of activism, Butler's work helps me to develop the tensions at the heart of this activity. My colleagues' conversations around the lunch table follow both the trajectories of Butler's work: the need to rally behind an identity to make collective anti-violence claims and the need to disrupt the devaluation of certain bodies through remaking gender identity.

Activist work in the anti-violence space centres the body as an important site for the negotiation of gender identity. Everyday anti-violence work always involves some form of exposure to violence perpetrated against (cis)women's bodies and non-binary bodies. There was a poster hanging behind my desk which was my early morning reminder of such violence. The top of the poster was in the shape of a roof with two sloping sides (indicating the domestic setting), and beneath the roof was a clutter of bold text words about men's violence against women written in the second person, including: beating you, raping you, spitting on you, burning you. As well as a reminder of why we undertook anti-violence activism, the second person emphasized that this violence was also violence against me and my body. The ever-present spectre of violence was unsettling. Moreover, the feminist analysis of domestic violence that my colleagues and I (on the whole) shared, meant that the concern about individual violence against women's bodies was tied up with the perception that there were reinforcing institutional and societal norms that devalued women and their bodies. To feel confident and secure in our identities as women was, therefore, a difficult task when engaging in anti-violence activism.

Our discussions around the lunch table were an important space for picking up on these concerns about women's bodies and negotiating them together. Members of our office would gather around two wooden tables in the small kitchen at the back of the office almost every day around midday. Attendance at lunch was usually indicative of stress levels around the office; at times when we were all busy most of my colleagues would eat their lunch at their desks. Lunches where at least four or five members of our office gathered together were usually animated affairs. My colleagues would laugh, joke, debate, complain, and challenge each other on a variety of topics. Interestingly, the topics that I noted on my first day in the office turned out to be a common set of themes related to the body which my colleagues returned to frequently. Personal bodily experiences, and the connection of these experiences to broader patterns of gender inequality, were positioned as inextricable from daily anti-violence work.

The majority of the focus around our gender identities at the lunch table was linked to the notion of women lacking bodily control. Around the lunch table my colleagues demonstrated an intimate concern with the ways in which women's bodies were violently limited by institutions, the law, individuals, or social norms. Gender identity, then, was not only thought about in relation to the body; it was also unsettled in relation to the body. The unsettling of gendered identities through the body appeared to have significant impacts on my colleagues' wellbeing and shaped how they approached their anti-violence work. A large part of the discussion about the body oscillated between the personal and the social, drawing links between practices that limited personal bodily freedom and that were seen to oppress women socially. Reproductive rights and capabilities – including abortion, pregnancy, menstruation, and menopause – were often central themes that proved particularly unsettling. Such reproductive themes were constructed by my colleagues as particularly salient women's issues related to women's bodies and archetypal of institutional and individual violence against women:

Gracie was reading an opinion piece in the paper, from a writer arguing that the number of women who experience mental health problems after abortion negated the number who said they would suffer mental health problems if they didn't have an abortion. Gracie immediately started swearing, muttering about violations of women's rights, and told the rest of us at the table, "the only reason that women have to claim to have mental health issues is because abortion is still listed under the Crimes Act! And unlike sticking a huge needle in your stomach and removing some of the embryonic fluid, mental health issues require no invasive medical tests!" Kimberley agreed passionately, saying that the mental health issues were caused by "absolutely ridiculous bureaucratic system that made women suffer". Kimberley went on to argue that there was a "war between the dichotomies [of men and women]" and that one, men, would always try to keep dominance over the other, women. One way for men to retain dominance over women, Kim pointed out, was to control the body and what it could do.

In this lunchtime conversation, Gracie draws attention to the notion that our gendered identities of women are tied up with our bodies and how the law, institutions, and social norms shape the possibilities of being a woman. The issues related to the body (specifically reproductive capabilities) are linked specifically to the identity of 'woman', positioning the body as an important dimension of this identity and emphasizing it as a site of political struggle. For Gracie and Kimberley, understanding what it means to be a woman involves both a grounding in a (constrained) body, and as an opposite to (unconstrained) men. The topic of abortion is, for Kimberley, related to the distinctions between men and women, in which women have a bodily vulnerability that places their body outside of their control. Both Gracie and Kimberley understand women to be situated within systems of oppression which seek to gain and maintain control over their bodies. Abortion was one example of an attempt to divorce from control and gain personal freedom over the body. Kim and Gracie draw connections between the bodies of individual women and the institutional norms and regulations which constrain the possibilities of the body. Although Gracie and Kimberley are unsettled in their own gendered identity, feeling that constraint and limitation of a 'woman's' body, their discussion also forms the grounds for them in their anti-violence activism. If violence against women is attached to a lack of bodily autonomy, fighting for control is part of anti-violence activism for women.

For my colleagues, the body was, therefore, a salient and significant site of construction of gendered identities and a site for anti-violence activism. Importantly, anti-violence activism itself also shaped how the body, and consequently gendered identities, were understood. In particular, working with domestic violence made me and my colleagues acutely aware of the lack of bodily autonomy felt by women subjected to gendered violence. One of the defining features of domestic violence, from my colleagues' understanding, was that violence was perpetrated against women because they were seen in society as 'objects' to be controlled. It was unsettling to be consistently reminded that our bodies were vulnerable to oppression and seemed to represent the limits on our freedom and self-determination. As Lloyd (2015: 169) argues: 'one cannot live one's life as one chooses if someone or something else – another person or institution or state – controls one's body, including both what is done by it and to it'. Around the lunch table my colleagues would regularly draw links between their own gendered identities and the institutional and social controls that constrained women's freedom to make decisions about their own bodies:

> One lunch time, Emily was looking at her phone and came across a news item that she wanted to share with all of us around the table. The article was about contraception; about the negative impacts which taking 'the pill' has on women's bodies. Emily said that the article showed that medical practitioners had completely different standards when it came to men's and women's bodies in terms of reproductive rights. The article – Emily read us snippets – argued that the negative side effects of taking the pill, including emotional instability, pain, and weight gain, were enormous, and that when men were exposed to similar effects they struggled to cope with the experience. Gracie responded in a sarcastic and irritated tone: "Oh poor men can't handle it, boo hoo hoo" and drew tear marks down her face with her fingers. She went on to say that the article confirms her theory that "men are happy to dick around with women's bodies in a way that they wouldn't try with [other] men". Emily fervently agreed, saying that men needed to consider the humanity of their treatment of women when making the medication. Michelle added drily: "That's two words I haven't heard together for a while: 'men' and 'humanity'."

Emily and Gracie strongly draw attention to the divisions they perceive between the treatment of women by medical institutions, and the treatment of men by medical institutions. The concern about the treatment of women centres on the (violent) misuse of women's bodies. Gracie, in particular, highlights that she understands institutions as placing less value on women's bodies; that somehow women were seen as more disposable, less worthy of protection and care, and more responsible for altering their bodies. Gracie and Michelle both draw distinctions between men and women. Men are positioned as lacking awareness and compassion while in a position of power. On the other hand, women are positioned as suffering, aware, and subjugated. The distinctions are grounded in a sense of control; who has the power to mark another's body. Women, in my colleagues' construction, lack control over their bodies; both in the sense that institutions preclude women from making their own decisions and in the sense that the individual's body becomes uncontrollable. Gracie and Emily both agree that men have power over women's bodies and abuse them in ways that they would not do to their own bodies or those of other men. This power is primarily understood as embedded in institutions, rather than directly attributable to individual men. Around the lunch table, then, gendered identities were shaped by a perception of a lack of bodily control and institutions that unevenly distribute value to different kinds of bodies.

My colleagues' construction of gendered identities in relation to the body is notable because of the legitimatization of bodily experience in the norms of our organization. The salience of violence towards women in anti-violence activism shaped my colleagues' experiences as women in the workplace and positioned the body as central to our gendered identities. As feminist research on the body and gendered identities in organizations has established, women are often aware of (and can feel deeply) how their bodies are perceived as a constraint in organizations. In anti-violence activism, my colleagues' awareness of the constraints of their gendered bodies seemed particularly complex because of the salience of bodily constraints in the context of violence and the simultaneous organizational norms that legitimated, and even celebrated, the body as focal to activism. Although my colleagues were unsettled in their gendered identities due to the repetitive exposure of violence, there were also almost paradoxical impacts for understanding gender identities and fighting for change. The unsettling of my colleagues' (and my own) gendered identities through the body also opened up the possibilities of establishing a political agenda for change through celebrating identities as women.

In both vignettes, my colleagues demonstrate an awareness of the constraints of their gendered bodies and the institutional norms which preclude their freedom of choice. Being unsettled, however, opened up the possibilities to remake the meanings attached to the body. In both vignettes the discussion of women's bodies both consolidates my colleagues' understanding of their gendered identity and provides a basis from which to make political claims and engage in activism. Drawing connections between personal bodily autonomy and social/institutional norms that constrain the body helped my colleagues to negotiate the context of violence within which they worked. Around the lunch table, meanings that were attached to the body were remade: from a position of subjugation, to a position of political change. The themes of the two vignettes were repeated in many other situations. For example, in discussing the 'women's march' of 2017 over the lunch table, Kim, Gracie, Evelyn, and Emily agreed that it was necessary to unite together as women against institutional control over women's bodies.

Additionally, a repositioning of gender identity and the construction of a site of activism were attached to other topics related to the body such as food or sex. The body, then, was a salient site for anti-violence activism that helped my colleagues draw connections between personal and systematic change.

Although my colleagues did at times feel overburdened or disempowered in their gendered identities, the unsettling of gender identities also opened up the possibilities for them to be remade. Constructing our identities through the body over the lunch table provided the grounds to negotiate a political agenda for reducing gendered violence through the body. My colleagues were therefore also to celebrate their identities for women and organize for change, even while feeling constrained. Although the gendered body did provide this potential and was often foundational to anti-violence work, the ways in which my colleagues constructed gendered identities and coordinated their anti-violence work through the body was problematic. As Judith Butler (2006a) highlights in her book *Gender Trouble*, the construction of gender identity often rests on the presumption that women have a mimetic relationship between gender identity and their sex. My colleagues' lunchtime conversations and coordination of the body as a site of activism often tended to reproduce their mimetic relationship as natural and even unquestionable. As I move to the next section, and the next configuration of anti-violence activism through the body, I explore the negative effects of these assumptions for other aspects of our gendered identities: namely sexuality.

6

LGBT+ Bodies

Recognition and celebration of lesbian identities had been part of the collective since its inception; a trend similar to other long running anti-violence organizations around the world (Arnold and Ake, 2013). The salience of lesbian identities in anti-violence activism, Tia explained to me, was partly due to the positioning of anti-violence activists as "tree-hugging, bra-burning, man-hating lesbians" by hostile communities in the 1970s. The public backlash, however, resulted in the creation of a political space in which the collective was determined to break down discriminatory social norms which limited the full participation of lesbian women in Aotearoa New Zealand. Jen, who had been part of the organization for nearly 30 years, felt liberated by the attention to lesbian identities. Before she became involved in the collective, she told me she knew that she was:

> 'Attracted to girls ... but my understanding of what a lesbian was, was this hairy, big, truck driver, butchy jeans and boots ... and I knew that wasn't the sort of woman that I wanted to be. Therefore, if I was a lesbian, and I didn't want to be one of those, then I didn't know what I was.'

Many years later, Jen was exposed to the possibilities of being a lesbian like she wanted when she joined the collective as a volunteer. She described it as extremely emancipatory, telling me: "I came out as a lesbian about the same time [as I started volunteering]. That was really quite cool because being a lesbian in [the organization] in those days was a very ... recognized and celebrated thing."

Like Jen, I experienced that emancipatory feeling when I joined an organization that openly and actively attempted to celebrate and include LGBT+ identities. Not only was my identity as a queer woman recognized by my colleagues, but was celebrated as bringing a unique perspective to how we could best support LGBT+ women in our anti-violence activism.

The contrast to the compulsive sexual and gender 'neutralization' of the business school environment (Rumens, 2016) in which I was spending the other half of my time was stark. The more accustomed I became to the norms surrounding the enactment of sexual orientation in the collective, however, the more acutely I felt my exclusion from aspects of anti-violence activism. As I swirled in the uneasy cocktail of the limitations, abjections, and celebrations of LGBT+ identities in daily anti-violence activism, I started to think about the importance of LGBT+ identities for expanding our understanding of how anti-violence activism can respond to violence against LGBT+ women and women who felt their 'difference' as marked in other ways through their bodies, such as indigenous women. The imperative of dislocating heteronormativity which shaped the way gendered violence impacted the lives of victims became central, for me, to protecting the lives of *all* women and gender minorities subjected to gendered violence. A focus on the dimensions of gendered identity related to sexual orientation also altered how I was thinking about anti-violence activism, the body, and social change.

Despite three decades of research about LGBT+ identities in organizing, the experience and understanding of sexual orientation in organizations has been slow to gain traction in some areas of scholarship; including my own field of critical organization studies (Ng and Rumens, 2017). The case for the need to pay attention to LGBT+ identities in organizations and in research is, however, clear and compelling. Even in organizations perceived as 'gay friendly' (such as the collective!), research has shown that LGBT+ people continue to feel that their identities are ignored, silenced, or marginalized (Bowring and Brewis, 2009; Giddings and Pringle, 2011). LGBT+ people also continue to face open discrimination from colleagues or third parties (Köllen, 2013; Rumens, 2016). Accordingly, LGBT+ identities are important to activist organizing, and activists need to understand the unique social, cultural, political factors that influence how we protect LGBT+ people from violence (Quesada et al, 2015; Matebeni et al, 2018; Buyantueva and Shevtsova, 2020).

The collective had long been aware of the importance of LGBT+ women for anti-violence work. When I started my volunteer role, a few of my colleagues – Jen and Emily particularly – were beginning the process of changing the collective's approach from focusing on lesbian women specifically, to all LGBT+ women and non-binary folk. The need to move away from lesbian identities specifically was also important in the postcolonial context of Aotearoa New Zealand. There was a concern that Māori, in particular, were excluded from Westernized conceptualizations of LGBT+ identities (Kerekere, 2015). The intersection of identities has also been a feature of broader discussions of LGBT+ activism (Quesada et al, 2015; Matebeni et al, 2018). In order to effectively carry out anti-violence activism, it was important for my colleagues to unpack how different groups were subjected to violence in different ways. Yet, while my colleagues espoused their support for engaging in activism on behalf of LGBT+ women, the notion that lesbian women were to be treated no differently to heterosexual women continued to be pervasive. Tia, for example, told me when I asked her about anti-violence activism with lesbian women: "what about it? They are everywhere. Who people choose to go to bed with is their fucking business. It is not illegal, so what is the problem?" Kimberley had a similar opinion:

> 'I find it fascinating that a women's organization has [an explicit activist agenda] that is solely around sexuality. I really think that it brings to the forefront of identity that somehow sexuality is a massive part of our identity as [anti-violence activists] ... Really it shouldn't matter what sexuality anyone is.'

The perspectives offered by Kim and Tia (both straight cis-women) were regularly expressed by my colleagues who identified as heterosexual. These perspectives were, however, problematic and vocally opposed by LGBT+ members of our organization:

In the second week of my voluntary work, Jen was keen for me to attend a series of talks hosted by members of the collective, held in a sort of conference like environment. My ethnographic enthusiasm was abounding, and I attended excited to see what the anti-violence activists talked about together. I decided to go and see one activist, Sara, talk about something titled 'heterosexual visibility', partly because Emily had repeatedly told me that Sara was a fantastic human being and a great speaker. The room was small and slightly dark, and there were about 30 plastic chairs facing a projector screen. The room was fairly full by the time I arrived, and I took a seat near the back where I could see most people. Emily came and sat down next to me, and I saw Jen hovering in the doorway.

Sara started off by welcoming us and saying how nice it was to see all the heterosexual women here. Immediately, there was a loud comment from a woman just to my left: "You are making assumptions!" Sara laughed and put her hand across her heart and replied: "Oh I know. I know everyone in this room isn't heterosexual – myself included!" Sara then started her presentation by showing us a video about the 'heterosexual quiz' in which she went around young people asking them questions like: "When did you first know that you were heterosexual?", "When did you come out as heterosexual to your parents?", and "What do you think made you straight?" There was a great deal of laughter from all of us in the room and from the participants in the video. Most of their responses were just 'common sense' like "I just knew", "Um ... when I first took my boyfriend home?", and "You could tell I was straight by the music I listened to" (underneath that particular comment on the video Sara had posted 'what???' in bold red text).

After the video ended and the laughter had stopped, Sara said "I'm going to get more serious now." Sara added an apology that she was going to be focusing on the church. She started talking about the continuing violence against the rainbow community, even though, she added, this was less widespread in Aotearoa New Zealand than overseas. "A transgender woman is murdered every three days" she told the now quiet audience, "a statistic which does not include self-harm or suicide rates". Sara then played another video. It was full of very violent images and violence language; often from members of the church. The violent images included a transgender woman being attacked on the street, gay men being forced to rape themselves with glass bottles, and police brutality against peaceful LGBT+ rights activists. The violent language included speeches from priests saying that boys who 'act like girls' need to be abused and beaten in order to ensure they 'act like men', emails from priests urging gay men to commit suicide, and slurs against LGBT+ people in everyday situations. During this video, many of the women in the room made small exclamations at the violence and several started crying.

No one made a sound after the video ended. Sara paused a moment, as if breathing in the effect, and then went on to explain why it was so essential to foster an inclusive society and why it was so important for anti-violence activism to address the specific forms of violence targeting the rainbow community. Sara then told her own story and explained how when she was abused by her partner the police classed the incident as 'between friends', and when she left her abusive partner she had no legal access to the (non-biological) children she had raised from birth because there was no legislation to support her custody claims. She said how difficult it was for her to get help from anyone, and how many anti-violence activists didn't recognize the violence she experienced. She told us: "people think violence between women is less dangerous because we are about the same physical size. But it can be much worse than violence between men and women". At the end of the presentation Jen added, from the doorway, that she knew how powerful Sara's presentation was and concluded: "How can anyone think that [a focus on LGBT+ women in anti-violence activism] is not relevant?"

Sara's presentation effectively drew the link between heteronormativity and the violent material implications for LGBT+ women and non-binary folk. Furthermore, the stories that Sara shared underscored the impacts of heteronormativity on the body. Sara dedicated a lot of her presentation to unpacking the meanings people in her tales ascribed to bodies and the violence perpetrated against bodies. Importantly, Sara highlighted that anti-violence activism is often saturated by the binary assumptions that a 'female body' will have a 'female heterosexual identity'. Sara's arguments echo broader sentiments in research related to LGBT+ identities in organizations: restrictive social norms surrounding LGBT+ identities are enmeshed in widely accepted binary models of woman/man and feminine/masculine (Jagose, 1996). Judith Butler's work developing the concept of the 'heterosexual matrix' has been influential in understanding how heterosexuality is normalized in many aspects of life, including in activist organizing (Quesada et al, 2015). Butler's heterosexual matrix articulates how a 'female body' is naturalized as the complementary opposite of a 'male body', thereby making heterosexual relationships appear self-evident and natural (Butler, 1993, 2004a). Heterosexuality is positioned as the norm and homosexuality is the 'other', that is, heterosexuality is 'natural' and homosexuality is 'abnormal'. Through the enactment of heteronormativity in institutions, social norms, and some activist practices, heterosexuality is made to seem coherent and is privileged by being accepted and included in daily organizational practice (Berlant and Warner, 1998; Colgan and Rumens, 2015).

The body is therefore central to how LGBT+ identities are understood. As well as other constraints on women's bodies I've discussed earlier in this chapter, 'female' bodies are also constrained by social norms which posit a 'natural' heterosexuality thereby marginalizing women who perform their sexual orientation differently (Butler, 2004a, 2006a). For example, lesbian women can articulate identities which break with the heterosexual matrix but at the risk of abjection, non-recognition, and violence for breaking with powerful social norms. Additionally, lesbian identities are often normatively constructed to uphold some of the sex/gender binary and are often expected to fit within narrow legitimated frames of reference, such as butch lesbian identities (Bowring and Brewis, 2009). As Jen indicated in her story about not seeing herself in a 'masculinized' or butch lesbian identity, there are often limited subject positions for lesbian women, making it difficult to reconcile their identities as lesbian *and* as a woman. Nevertheless, as with all Butler's work around identity, she emphasizes that the performativity of identities opens up the possibilities for the remaking of identities which, while difficult, can help to displace restrictive social norms. The rest of Jen's story about feeling emancipated in the collective, which accepted women enacting their lesbian identities in a range of ways, underscores this potential.

In relation to anti-violence activism, the heterosexual matrix has significant implications for both anti-violence activists and women and non-binary folk subjected to violence. Implicit in compulsive heterosexuality is that a 'weaker' female body is seen as vulnerable to a 'stronger' male body, thereby assuming that gendered violence results in women being vulnerable to violence from men, but not from other women (Ristock, 2002, 2011). Consequently, as Sara highlights, the severity and seriousness of violence in LGBT+ relationships is often downplayed by institutions and anti-violence activists, which means that victims often face additional barriers to receiving assistance to attenuate the violence (Shelton, 2017). Research has demonstrated that LGBT+ victims may not even be aware that their experience constitutes abuse (Shelton, 2017) because of the heteronormativity pervasive in public conceptualizations of intimate partner violence (Ristock, 2011). They may also be reluctant to seek assistance from anti-violence activists (Bornstein et al, 2006) and may even be excluded from receiving adequate or any assistance from anti-violence organizations (Ristock, 2011). The impacts of heteronormativity, as Sara demonstrated through her own story of her abuse at the hands of her partner, is that only certain heterosexual identities are legitimated as the objects of organizational inclusion and the subjects of anti-violence activism. Accordingly, one important aspect of activism that includes and celebrates LGBT+ identities is to destabilize restrictive social norms that preclude LGBT+ identities and experiences from recognition in activism and in society more broadly. Recognizing LGBT+ identities in anti-violence activism is important for protecting the lives of LGBT+ women and non-binary folk.

I now move to exploring how LGBT+ identities were understood by my colleagues in their activist work by drawing on Butler's understanding of the heterosexual matrix. To begin, I offer a story of an ordinary lunchtime conversation:

Lunchtime banter about colleagues' sexual activities was commonplace; with some of my colleagues more enthusiastically sharing stories of their experiences than others. Their excitement about discussing these experiences openly seemed related to other discussion around the body and women's experiences of the world. It was a way of politicizing their own experiences and relating them to social norms about women's lives and bodies. Having no interest in sexual relationships and no stories to add to these conversations, my primary interest was ethnographic because of my awareness of sexual orientation as fundamental to my colleagues' identities as women. Increasingly, however, I felt that some stories about sex seemed to be more acceptable to tell; particularly as my LGBT+ colleagues like Gracie, Jen, and Esther appeared to be less engaged in these conversations or only seemed to be comfortable sharing limited aspects of their experience. I felt that there were two options available: engage in detailed, humorous stories about sex with men, or remain silent. Today started off in the usual way.

Riley was really shocked by Emily's admission that she hadn't had sex in six months and said very loudly to the table: "Why don't you just get drunk and get your hussy on?" I hate when people get so shocked about this, it makes me feel like my life isn't worth living. It didn't bother Emily as much, and she immediately shared horror stories of the last time she tried to have sex with men. One of the stories was the time Emily had sex with a man who had a foot fetish, which she didn't discover until halfway through and he started telling her that he was imagining her dominating other women with her feet. Riley howled with laughter and asked where on earth Emily found these men. She happily explained that she had sex with many different men but had never come across anything as crazy as that. Riley said all you needed to know was that the men had sheets on their beds. Evelyn piped up trying to claim that they at least needed clean sheets, but Riley reassured the table with a wave of her hand that any sheets would suffice.

Several of my other colleagues decided that they would help Emily to find a man to have sex with; despite her protestations on the contrary. Esther held out her hand, demanding Emily's phone so that she could 'work' on her profile on social media. Esther claimed that "My friends call me the Tinder whisperer … The key is to be really bitchy, because men really like that". She looked over the profile, sized up Emily with a quick glance, and said that her personal description should be "probably taller and smarter than you". Kimberley laughed and agreed that men really like women being 'bitchy' for some reason. She told the story of how she met her boyfriend on Tinder; where she had a quote from Taylor Swift that read "a nightmare dressed like a daydream". Riley and Esther asked Emily several times if she was looking for a relationship or if she just wanted to "root some dude". These appeared to be the only two acceptable options.

Gracie came to join us at the table just as Riley was telling Emily that she should go out and "hump randoms that you meet in bars. It is tried and true". Riley turned to Gracie and asked when the last time she got laid was. Gracie laughed off the question, and so Riley ignored her. Emily was now adamant that she wanted her Tinder profile that she was only interested in sex if she was able to change her mind halfway through. Riley was sceptical about this because it might put men off, but told us stories of telling various sexual partners to 'get out' (of her and subsequently the house) in the middle of sex if it "wasn't working for her". Esther said that she had done that as well, spreading her legs and making shooing gestures around her crotch to indicate how she dismissed unworthy sexual partners. Gracie suggested that Emily should write that she was after "hot consensual respectful dicking" on her profile and joke that Emily should buy a squirty gun to get men out of her bed. My sense was that by this point Emily was extremely uncomfortable. Ava joined in the conversation saying she didn't understand all this modern dating and asked what had happened to emailing men. That was how she met her husband.

The banter surrounding sex with men was very commonplace in daily organizational life, as illustrated in this story, and a central aspect of identity for many of my colleagues. Within this vignette, however, there are only limited possibilities of sexual behaviour normatively condoned or celebrated. In this instance, the normative sexual orientation is governed by an engagement in sex with men, limited to a position of desirable and desiring woman, or a woman in a heterosexual, monogamous partnership. Emily, a heterosexual woman, is being policed in her (lack of) sexual activity, and is repeatedly encouraged to embody and enact her sexuality in a particular way by our colleagues around the table. The conversation here is heteronormative; encouraging each other to engage in detailed descriptions of the use of bodies in sexual interactions with men but marginalizing or silencing voices that do not adhere to the social norms. Gracie, for example, was actively excluded when she didn't meet expectations by avoiding an answer to Riley's question and was only included again when she engaged in heteronormative banter. Esther and Gracie, who both identified as bisexual, only contributed some of their experiences. In instances where Gracie did share stories about her relationships with women, or explicitly talked about her bisexuality, there was a noticeably less enthusiastic response, and even an awkward silence to the point where her (occasional) stories were only acknowledged by a nod of the head and a subsequent change in topic of conversation.

The conversation over lunch highlights the ways in which heterosexuality was embedded in daily organizational life and encouraged by the majority of my colleagues. The whole conversation appears to be premised on a (supposedly) mutual recognition of a female bodily desire for the 'male body'. The confines of heterosexuality were, moreover, particularly limited. Riley, Esther, and Kimberley constructed quite limited categories of behaviour expected from a heterosexual woman, tied to the way in which a female body was supposed to look and act. Kimberley, for instance, proposes that women need to make themselves look sexually desirable for men; proposed as something stylized women need to achieve. Esther also expresses normative expectations for the appearance of a 'desirable' female body by drawing attention to Emily's height, noting that she is 'probably taller' than male bodies. Esther's formulation posits that Emily might pose a challenge to a male body, suggesting that men might like to have the opportunity to reassert their place in a female/male relationship by proving that they are indeed 'taller and smarter' than Emily. Gracie and Esther also make reference to the expected bodily characteristics that 'male' and 'female' bodies should align with, through their gestures and reference to 'dicking'. Male and female bodies are, thereby, naturalized around the lunch table as complementary opposites. The process of naturalization marginalizes or invisibilizes the possibilities of bodies having different physical characteristics, or that 'female' bodies could desire other female bodies; or not desire at all.

The silence around LGBT+ identities, even when several people involved in the lunchtime conversation openly identified as LGBT+, echoes the findings of other research about LGBT+ identities in organizing. Silence, in other research, has been found as the predominant mode of marginalization of LGBT+ women (Bowring and Brewis, 2009; Giddings and Pringle, 2011). As Tia and Kimberley note in their conversations to me, lesbian and other LGBT+ experiences were often classed as "their fucking business" or something that "shouldn't matter". But these expressions contrast with the heterosexuality prevalent in everyday conversations between colleagues. As well as lunchtime conversations there were many other examples of 'small' exclusions of LGBT+ women. For example, Gracie was told by Jen that as a bisexual woman, she would be considered 'not gay enough' by other lesbian members of the collective to attend a meeting of lesbian women in the organization; corroborating other research which has found that bisexual women face discrimination from both their heterosexual and lesbian counterparts (Köllen, 2013).

As well as posing problems for the wellbeing of LGBT+ organizational members, particularly in relation to sharing their experiences of violence, heteronormativity became embedded in the activist work of the collective. Heteronormativity was problematic as it normalized only certain women as legitimate beneficiaries of activism. For example, Zoey, in writing the policy for guests visiting women in emergency housing, noted that women were not allowed visitors who were men but were allowed women who were visitors between the hours of 9am and 9pm. This policy is founded on the heterosexist assumption that women will have been in a violent relationship with men but not with another woman, and that victims of violence are in danger of violence from *men* but not from other women. The formulation in the policy accentuates that the concept of 'violence against women' or even 'gendered violence' is often constructed as only a particular form of violence from men to women; excluding and marginalizing LGBT+ women and non-binary folk and their experiences. Heteronormative practices thus have serious impacts on which bodies anti-violence activists perceived as legitimate victims of violence and worthy of institutional protection. I would add, however, that it was acceptable to challenge these heteronormative assumptions. After my raising the issue with the policy, it was changed to reflect the experiences of LGBT+ women and non-binary folk. That this policy and other similar policies could be negotiated was testament to the possibilities of inclusion and the long-standing work of LGBT+ anti-violence activists to ensure their experiences were included in anti-violence activism.

Consequently, although there were examples of heteronormative practices in the organization's activist work, to paint a portrait of my anti-violence colleagues as unaware of the dangers of heteronormativity or actively exclusionary of LGBT+ women would present a one-sided view of their efforts. There was a long history of celebrating LGBT+ women, as Jen's story highlights, and there was space to challenge heteronormative assumptions and open up the possibilities for LGBT+ women to be liberated in self-expression. Therefore, I now want to focus on the practices and experiences of my colleagues that did challenge heteronormativity in anti-violence work. I want to highlight how LGBT+ women were included and celebrated in a way that attempted to shift heteronormativity in and beyond the organization in their anti-violence work, explore two examples of how LGBT+ identities were unsettled through repeated exposure to domestic violence, and finally offer a detailed example of how challenging heteronormativity expanded (rather than constricted) activist work and the possibilities of who was perceived as a beneficiary of anti-violence activism.

My LGBT+ colleagues were open and reflective about the ways in which working with domestic violence had unsettled the way they thought about their identity. Jules, for instance, explained that working with violence had unsettled her sense of self as a lesbian partner; telling a group of us one day how after working in domestic violence for several months she had started to worry that her practices of slamming doors and refusing to talk to her partner constituted abuse. When she raised this with her partner, however, she had laughed and promised Jules that her behaviour lacked a crucial part of violence: causing fear as a means of control. Nevertheless, Jules still found that experiences of working in anti-violence activism had prompted her to reflect on and alter her behaviours and attitudes towards her partner. Interestingly, her concern about her own relationship was mixed together with a worry that she was being a 'bad' representative for the lesbian community. With the regular discrimination that LGBT+ women face in society, Jules was concerned that if she was seen as violent then there would be repercussions for the LGBT+ community; seeing them as defective or immoral. Another woman who openly discussed her experience of her sexual orientation and violence was Lesley, who worked directly with the LGBT+ community. Lesley came to talk with our collective about her experiences of violence as a bisexual woman and being a victim of domestic violence from one her partners. She explained some of the forms of symbolic violence she experienced that she considered unique to LGBT+ women. For example, as a bisexual woman she was coerced by her partner into changing her self-definition of her sexual orientation (that is, from bisexual to lesbian). As with Jules, this prompted a reflection and reconsideration of her own sexual identity.

LGBT+ women experienced an unsettling of their gendered identities, with some similar dynamics (such as the reflection on partnerships) and some different dynamics (such as concern about repercussions for the wider community) to heterosexual women. What both Jules and Lesley identified, however, was that they felt they had unique perspectives to add about domestic violence. They both remarked that their identities had been unsettled in a way that made them better partners and better anti-violence activists. Additionally, their experiences were enmeshed in broader issues for the LGBT+ community such as violent and negative stereotypes about LGBT+ relationships and the importance of self-identifying labels.

Anti-violence activism, then, is shaped by multiple aspects of gendered identities. Legitimating and recognizing the multiple ways that women and non-binary folk may have their gendered identities unsettled in anti-violence activism is essential for ending all forms of gendered violence. Jules and Lesley were able to give voice to the ways that the complexity and multiplicity of gendered identities shapes anti-violence work and helped to identify particular areas where anti-violence activism was needed in order to dismantle harmful social norms.

Including and celebrating LGBT+ identities within our organization was therefore important for the ways in which our collective activism recognized LGBT+ experiences as legitimate and worthy of protection. Emily, Jen, and I were, in particular, concerned with ensuring that everyone in our collective perceived LGBT+ women and non-binary folk as an indispensable part of anti-violence activism. One aspect of our activism that I was heavily involved in alongside Jen and Emily was researching the experiences of our clients in order to improve our activism and engagement for victims of violence. Jen adamantly maintained that: "We are not founding our research on heterosexist assumptions." All research conducted by our collective attempted to be inclusive of LGBT+ experiences by removing gender specific wording of victimization (that is, changing 'was *he* physically violent' to 'was your *partner* physically violent') and by asking for the gender identity of the abusive partner rather than assuming them to be a man. These attempts by Jen, Emily, and me had implications for which bodies were perceived as legitimate of recognition and protection from violence.

Naturalizing heterosexual relationships as the 'norm' of gendered violence has significant implications for both anti-violence activisms and for who anti-violence activisms consider to be the focus of activism. The embedded heteronormativity surrounding anti-violence activism has grave consequences for the inclusion or exclusion of LGBT+ women as activists and the recognition of all victims of gendered violence. If activists can better understand how heteronormativity marginalizes LGBT+ women in anti-violence activism, we gain a stronger understanding of the contours of gendered violence and therefore the 'sticking points' in which to dismantle harmful social norms. Which bodies are considered worthy of protecting, valuing, and celebrating is impacted by heteronormative practices (Butler, 2004a), and this is an issue for activists that expands beyond anti-violence activism. Activists frequently advocate for the protection of different bodies. The Black Lives Matter movement is exemplary of an awareness of the differences in how bodies are valued and protected by institutions. Black Lives Matter aims to challenge the social construction of Black bodies in order to ensure that they are considered worthy of protection. Other social movements, such as protections for non-human animals, also echo these reimaginings of the body and draw attention to how social norms and institutions perpetuate violence against certain bodies but not others.

In any activist work, then, it is imperative to understand how activists are constructing certain bodies as worthy of protection and to continue to challenge social norms both internal to the activist movements and in the activists' work influencing others, to ensure that our activism benefits all those affected by an issue, not just a subset. In the case of my collective, opening up the space for LGBT+ organizational members to share their opinions and experiences related to the body was crucial. Although my colleagues did make substantive efforts to be inclusive of LGBT+ women, heteronormative practices operated to silence and marginalize LGBT+ women and non-binary folk on multiple occasions. Nonetheless, when the experiences of LGBT+ women were recognized in anti-violence activism, we gained a richer understanding of the contours of gendered violence and consequently how to end gendered violence for all women and non-binary folk.

7

Radically Unsettled Bodies

In my discussion of two of the ways we can understand the role of the body in anti-violence activism, I have highlighted that a heightened awareness of our bodily vulnerability unsettles our gendered identities. I now want to explore how the unsettling of identities was taken in a radical direction by my colleagues: understanding women *as* vulnerable bodies. The formulation of women as vulnerable bodies, characterized by an inherent corporeal vulnerability to violence, proved to be an extremely unsettling formulation, not only for me and my colleagues, but for other women and non-binary folk who came into contact with this formulation when I shared early iterations of this work with the collective, at conferences and in other academic settings. In particular, this formulation seemed unsettling as it appeared to run counter to the decades of activism that emphasized women's empowerment and work towards the celebration of women's bodies as powerful and agentic. The centricity of bodily vulnerability to anti-violence activism for the women I worked with, however, was a striking and salient theme and one that reverberated with activists working on other issues.

In my attempts to come to terms with the implications of my colleagues' formulation of women as vulnerable bodies and the importance of this formulation for anti-violence activism, I found Butler's conceptualization of vulnerability insightful. Butler (2011b: 200) outlines vulnerability as having a twofold meaning:

> Vulnerability includes all the various ways in which we are moved, entered, touched, or ways that ideas and others make an impression upon us … [vulnerability] is also a way of indicating one's dependency on another, a set of institutions, or a circumambient world to be well, to be safe, to be acknowledged.

Drawing on Butler's conceptualization of vulnerability, I interpreted my colleagues as not only trying to recognize women's physical vulnerability to others, but also that they were attempting to underscore that we needed to cultivate the capacity to be moved or impressed on by women subjected to violence. Positioning women as vulnerable bodies accentuated the pressing need to promote institutional and domestic protection of women. Throughout my time with the collective, I too was moved by my own exposure to my colleagues and our activism with victims, and eventually came to understand women's dependency on one another and the social conditions that produced women as vulnerable bodies. I also came to understand the importance of embracing and working through vulnerability as a way of engaging in activism.

In this section I draw on a series of vignettes from my time working with my anti-violence colleagues. In these vignettes I parallel my experience in the collective with the experiences of my colleagues. I track my understanding of the formulation of women *as* vulnerable bodies across my time volunteering with the collective. An important aspect of understanding women as vulnerable bodies was the recognition that we were all vulnerable to violence at the hands of those who are supposed to love us most. The deep feeling of corporeal precarity as forming our identities unsettled the boundaries between 'victim' and 'non-victim' in radical ways. Although I learnt from my colleagues the value of understanding women as vulnerable bodies, I also felt the limitations of this formulation; particularly because of the ways certain groups of women, such as women of colour, disabled women, or trans-women, are subjected to more intense violence or different kinds of violence than their white, cis, able-bodied counterparts. Nevertheless, I argue that vulnerability can, and should, play an important role in different types of activism.

Emily and I are indulging in our Monday morning tradition of chatting about our weekends over an early morning cup of tea. We're standing in the small kitchen at the back of the office. I'm leaning against one cupboard, my hands clasped around the warmth of the cup, listening to Emily talk while watching her bob her tea bag in and out of the mug. Emily suffers from insomnia. In the little sleep she managed to get last night, she tells me that she has been having vivid dreams about guns. People keep threatening her, telling her that if she doesn't comply with what they want her to do that they would kill everyone she loved. And then shoot her. Emily explained that she had been working recently with a lot of young women forced into sex work. One story she was told was about a young woman whose boyfriend drove her to the middle of nowhere with his friends, took out a gun, pointed it into the small of her back, and told her that she had to have sex with everyone in the car, otherwise he would kill her. Emily throws her tea bag into the bin, smiles tiredly at me, and asks if we should get back to work.

--

I've just started having these dreams. These dreams are mainly about being beaten by other people, and usually occur while doing some sort of mundane activity. My dream last night was about playing netball. Whenever I did something wrong, or was seen as too competitive, I was beaten (typically punched) by someone on the opposing team. The aggressors never had a solid form. It was almost like getting beaten by your own shadow. Something I had read the other day had been haunting me and seems to have slipped into my subconscious. It was a quote from someone on Facebook who was pushing for a domestic violence law to be changed. She had written: 'You don't understand that feeling when someone you love punches you in the face for the first time.' My dreams were not scary, and I felt neither fear nor pain, and so they don't disturb me. I don't understand that pain yet. But so many do.

Before engaging in anti-violence activism, I had not given extensive consideration to how vulnerability contributed to constituting my own and other women's identities as women. I was aware that as a woman in Aotearoa New Zealand I was more likely to experience physical and sexual violence. As a researcher interested in theories of the self, I'd also been interested in the idea that our physical and symbolic vulnerability to violence from others is part of constructing and understanding our identities. In forming our identities, we necessarily make violent divisions between who we consider to be 'us' and who we consider to be 'them', and what belongs to 'our' experience and what does not (Bergin and Westwood, 2003). Although I was aware that we all share a fundamental corporeal vulnerability, this did not lead to a reciprocal recognition of the communities who are more regularly subjected to violence (Butler, 2011a). I had experienced some sexual violence, but I felt as an educated, middle-class, Pākehā woman, however, such violence had not been central to my constitution of identity as a woman. I maintained a sense of separation between myself and victims of violence; a separation which proposes that there *must* be something that separates us from someone who has been a victim of certain kinds of violence when we have not been (Campbell, 2013).

My first two vignettes contrast my feeling of separation from violence to Emily's recognition of her body as a body vulnerable to violence. In her dream Emily's body *is* the body of the women with whom she works as an activist. She appears to share a fundamental sense of vulnerability with her clients, understanding her own body as vulnerable to the same physical and sexual violence. Emily frames her body in contrast to the 'other' in the dream, the violent men who threaten her. The identity of 'woman' is situated by Emily in relation to being a victim of violence, and in contrast to the men as perpetrators of violence. There seems to be no separation for Emily between her clients as victims of violence and her own sense of self. Emily *is* the women with whom she works; in both her dreamscapes and her waking life.

My dream does not illustrate the same connection. Those who attack me are 'shadows' rather than a definable contrast to my own body; the shadows lack corporeal form. Although I express sympathy with victims of violence, I am not seeing myself as radically connected to victims of violence in the way that Emily does. My lack of connection is reflected in the way that I describe how I do not understand their pain and suffering. I am, literally, undisturbed by the violence; it has not unsettled my sense of self and I maintain the boundary between my sense of self as a woman and 'other' women who are victims of violence. The dreams I started having in my work were not nightmares in a traditional sense – I did not wake feeling unsettled or scared. It was an apprehension of violence and corporeal vulnerability but not a recognition. At this stage of my research and engagement in anti-violence activism, I have apprehended some of the possibilities of violence, but a deep sense of vulnerability has not unsettled the way I think about my sense of self in the way that Emily expresses.

The longer I engaged in anti-violence activism, the more my understanding of bodies and vulnerability began to shift. I remember one particularly intense moment where I was utterly unsettled in my understanding of what it meant to be a woman. I was sitting in our office, talking with Emily about how she was a victim of a recent sexual assault. She turned her whole body to face me, spreading out her arms, palms facing up, as she remarked: "it'll probably happen again, it is what being a woman *is*". For Emily, her identity as a woman was dependent on the actions of others which limited her corporeal autonomy and, she felt, constructed her body as inevitably vulnerable to violence. Central to much of Butler's work around the body's place in social justice is the claim that some bodies are made to be more precariously vulnerable to violence in a way that (in part) constitutes their identity. Emily is pushing this theoretical claim to its far limits by suggesting that the identity of woman is collapsible into a state of perpetual vulnerability. Ultimately, Emily claims that to be 'woman' is to be vulnerable to physical and sexual violence.

Evelyn has a remarkably quiet voice. I'm always surprised that whenever she speaks, she doesn't do so with more force. We are having coffee after work, sitting in the back corner of our local restaurant, and Evelyn is telling me why she had to take so much time off working for our collective in the last two years.

She holds out her light brown, rounded forearm to me for examination. It is marked with a long, thick, white scar. The scare was caused by snapping the bone through her skin as she aggressively defended herself when her ex-partner tried to kill her about a year ago. She is calm as she tells me: "I think I've done alright considering they thought I would never get the use of my hand back. I've had to relearn to use it, relearn to write, relearn to feed myself with it. It's still swollen now, a year later." Four months off work, another three months part-time, she finds it hard to catch up on the work she missed. But still, she reflects in her quiet voice, she feels okay when she remembers what the doctor said to her: "Don't underestimate the damage that you did. You are very lucky to still have a hand."

--

My thoughts are preoccupied today and I walk home with my arms tightly folded across my chest. I always seem to do this whenever work has been particularly overwhelming or stressful. I must look the grim and grave figure; eyebrows furrowed and legs swiftly moving around slower walkers. All of a sudden, a figure comes out of the edge of my vision and hops onto the pavement next to me. I panic. I half jump sideways, as if to avoid being tackled by this man. My arms instinctively stretch out as if to push him away. He moves in front of me, probably not even registering my movement. I shake my head, as if I'm being ridiculous. Refolding my arms, I cross the street, just as the man walks around the corner and out of my life.

Evelyn, in particular, helped me to unsettle my normative distinctions between who I perceived as a victim of violence and who was not, and thereby to understand the formulation of women *as* vulnerable bodies. During one of our interviews about identity in the workplace, Evelyn and I had a long conversation about her experiences as a simultaneous victim of domestic violence and working as an anti-violence activist. As I discussed in Chapter 5, research about anti-violence workers tends to assume that they do not perceive themselves as victims of violence; even when those distinctions are blurred (Goldblatt et al, 2009; Seymour, 2009), they are rarely collapsed. In their anti-violence activism, however, my colleagues appeared to be marked by a deep feeling of corporeal precarity that unsettled the boundaries between 'victim' and 'non-victim' in radical ways. Evelyn is a clear example, being subjected to physical violence by an intimate partner while working as anti-violence activist. My colleagues more generally, however, appeared to take it for granted that all women were victims of systemic violence (albeit to differing degrees) that attempted to control and subjugate their bodies in private as well as in public. The stories of victimization my colleagues shared with one another prompted outrage at the mistreatment of women, but never surprise at the victimization.

All women were positioned by my colleagues as vulnerable to violence, inclusive of anti-violence activists.

In my vignette, I describe an instance which, in reflection, I see myself in the uneven process of unsettling my distinctions between victim and non-victim. My initial comfort in the notion that I was somehow distinct from victims of violence was radically unsettled in the moment when I recognized my body, as a gendered body, as vulnerable to violence. Reflecting on moments such as the one exemplified in my vignette helped me to understand that for my colleagues, understanding women as vulnerable bodies embedded in systems of violence was essential for recognizing violence, demanding institutional protection, and thereby supporting one another as victims of violence. For Evelyn, she took the claims about bodies as vulnerable further than the rest of her colleagues. She argued that men were just as vulnerable to violence, albeit differing forms of violence, as women. Therefore, she claimed, we should recognize our collective vulnerability embedded in systems of violence and work to dismantle "both ends of the spectrum", that is, the different kinds of violence men and women experience because of gendered norms and institutional structures. For most of my colleagues, however, it was only women who were constructed as vulnerable bodies. Recognition of our precarity to this violence is unsettling, but, as Evelyn highlighted, can help dismantle normative distinctions between victim and non-victim that engenders a responsibility to work together to alter harmful norms, institutional structures, and, ultimately, protect one another.

I am at our regular Sunday family dinner; a tradition since my siblings and I moved out of home. My family is all gathered around our large dining room table; every seat is occupied. My father sits opposite me at the far end of the table, my sister's partner and my sister on my right, my brother and my mother on the left. We are laughing at something, although I don't know what exactly. In all honesty, I am rather preoccupied by the piece of cake that my mother has placed in front of me. A bowl of fruit sits in the middle of the table and my brother reaches to grab something to add to his dessert. I turn and laugh at something that my father says. Out of the corner of my eye I see my brother pick up his knife and I choke on my heart. I am frozen in panic. For a painful, paralysing moment I am convinced that he is going to stab me. I can see the sharp point of the knife glint and I jerk away so quickly I almost upset my glass. No one seems to notice this movement, and my heartbeat slows again. My brother slices his fruit in half. A moment later everyone, except me, laughs a something my mother says, all around the table.

--

The table in Jen's office is large and solid. The three of us – Jen, Emily, and me – only seem to occupy a very small space at the end; a long unoccupied expanse stretching before us. We're talking about the results of recent research we did about perpetrators who abuse women by precluding access to their money. It's all about control, we conclude. It is no wonder that some women attack their abusers. Emily asks us if we heard the story about the woman who after 20 years of horrific abuse, snuck into her husband's room one night and stabbed him with a knife in the chest over 30 times. The woman had been kept under lock and key, Emily explained. In the court system, she couldn't claim self-defence because the abuser hadn't been attacking her at that moment. But, Emily said, "when you're in a constant state of hyper-anxiety, you always feel like you're being attacked". Jen followed up with a story of a client of hers that had threatened her abuser with a knife. He impaled himself upon it – "as you do," Jen adds sarcastically. She was arrested for assault. The table stretches before us.

Repeat exposure to gendered violence is unsettling for women who work with domestic violence, particularly when they position this violence in relation to powerful social norms and institutional structures that systematically devalue women. Frequently, my colleagues understood themselves as vulnerable bodies. There was no professional/personal 'split' as often characterized in research. Alternatively, as women, they considered themselves as victims of violence – whether personal, institutional, or societal – as well as anti-violence activists. My colleagues recognized themselves as constituted as women through the same norms of gendered violence that marked their clients' lives. The formulation of women as vulnerable bodies provoked a recognition that helps us to understand our indebtedness to one another, rather than an apprehension of violence which maintained the boundaries of separation. Over my time working in anti-violence work, I felt how I too came to collapse the professional/personal distinction and (at least temporarily) understand my identity as a woman constituted through corporeal vulnerability. My final two vignettes respectively tell the story of one moment where I deeply felt my bodily vulnerability and a moment where I felt the political potential of understanding women as vulnerable bodies.

The vignette with my family highlights a moment where I felt the full force of my bodily vulnerability. The gathering of my family was, at least at the outset of the evening, an easy reproduction of embedded norms of my safety as a sister and daughter. The intense shock of the realization of my bodily vulnerability to my brother made the dependency of my safety on the norms protecting my gendered identity as a sister suddenly salient to me. Reflecting on this moment, I felt that I had understood the formulation of women as vulnerable bodies. My identity as a woman had been radically unsettled and for the first time I experienced the acute force of the possibilities of violence in a domestic setting normatively constructed as a 'safe space'. That the feeling of security could be so easily undone illuminated the social conditions on which I was dependent and the precarity of my dependence on others. I felt myself connected to the bodies of other women vulnerable to violence in domestic settings. For me, however, this moment passed and I was left with my shock and panic; separate in this moment from my family.

The formulation of women as vulnerable bodies seemed both an attempt to come to terms with the impacts of repeat exposure to violence on identity and a political position that attempted to catalyse a recognition of the vulnerability of women to domestic violence. Importantly, through the formulation of women as vulnerable bodies, my colleagues understood themselves as making claims on behalf of one another through a sense of shared vulnerability. Butler's sociality of ontology is again useful here for understanding that "the body does not belong to itself and it never can" (Butler, 2011c: 385). In her work she outlines that we are constituted through similar discourses and embodied experiences (Butler, 2011c), dependent on each other for recognition and for physical survival (Butler, 2006b), and any claim we make on behalf of our own bodies also resonates with claims for other bodies (Butler, 2011a, 2015). Recognizing that our bodies are interdependent in a precariousness to violence "binds us to those whom we may well not know, and whom we have never chosen" (Butler, 2011c: 384). Formulating women as vulnerable bodies appeared to be an attempt to find that 'common ground' from which to make claims for ending gendered violence.

The vignette in which I am sitting at the empty table with Jen and Emily highlights how we are bound to those we do not know through a sense of shared vulnerability to violence. In this final vignette I am not, as we are not, making clear distinctions between victim and non-victim, or activist and victim. Instead, in this moment alongside Jen and Emily, I was understanding all women as vulnerable to violence. In fact, the stories of the women centred around the object of a knife which is imbued with the possibilities of violence; just as my story was. Although we do not share an embodied experience of violence (and I am in no way claiming that I understand their experiences of physical violence) I can understand the embodied experience of the *possibilities* of violence. And in turn this gives me an embodied understanding of how gendered violence is shaped by social norms and institutional structures. This depth of feeling and the connection to other bodies I am bound to forms the foundations of activism. Around the table, Jen, Emily, and I go on to make claims for the need to protect women from physical and institutional violence on the basis of a shared sense of vulnerability; that women are vulnerable bodies and we should all be moved by their stories.

That to be woman is to be a vulnerable body, however, can be a problematic formulation. It could be taken to propose a deterministic chain which posits that the norms and institutional structures which unevenly distribute corporeal vulnerability are concrete and indiscriminate. Although the proposition could be taken this way, I argue that this formulation has relevance to the specific area of anti-violence activism and has useful effects. There are two important points I think that activists can take from understanding women as vulnerable bodies in the context of domestic violence. First, domestic violence can radically unsettle gendered identities of anti-violence activists to the point where women can feel too disempowered to effectively respond to gendered violence. Women as vulnerable bodies underscores the need to consider *how* our identities are constructed in relation to activist work. An understanding of how activists are intertwined with the work that they do can help us better understand the 'sticking points' where their activism can be helped or hindered. Second, the distinctions between victim and non-victim can be usefully collapsed to break down our normative expectations of who is perceived as a victim of violence. Activists breaking down victim/non-victims can aid us in recognizing that violence perpetrated against other bodies also impacts us, and that we have an interdependent responsibility for those bodies.

Vulnerability, academia, and anti-violence activism

At the outset of Part III, I outlined how research has highlighted that there is something unsettling about repeated exposure to domestic violence. The unsettling impacts how those who work with victims think about their gender identities and bodies. This unsettling can be uncomfortable, painful, and even cause serious psychological effects such as secondary traumatic distress. At the same time, however, this unsettling also has political potential for anti-violence activism. In this final section I want to offer some reflections on what I learnt from my colleagues, and discuss the implications of my discussion for the relationships between academia and activism:

To begin, I share one final vignette:

A couple of months into joining the collective, I was invited to join a training session designed to introduce new members to the work and practices of anti-violence activism. Our training was run by two activists who worked primarily with victims of violence – one Samoan, heterosexual woman, Sefina, and one older Māori, lesbian woman, Jules. A number of us from my team – Emily, Diane,

Esther, and me – as well as and two academics from a nearby university – Helen and Lucy – were participating. We all gathered together in a small room, sitting around in a semi-circle on old but comfy couches. Sefina is one of the warmest women I've ever met. She has a comforting way of bobbing her head gently and saying 'totally' that makes you feel like she truly understands everything you've been through. Jules is an utter contrast; emitting a tough, down-to-earth persona, bursting with dark humour.

We are sharing stories about clients and thinking about their experiences in relation to gender. Sefina and Jules have been using the popular model of a 'gingerbread person' to illustrate some of the different ways in which we might think about the construction of our gendered identities. Categories of composition include biological sex (male, female, intersex), gender identity (man–woman), gender expression (masculine–feminine), sexual orientation (hetero-bi-homosexuality), and romantic orientation (women–men). These are depicted as incremental continuums. Although it is a useful teaching tool and helps us to understand that gender and sexuality are complex, Sefina acknowledges the difficulties with these categorizing ways of thinking. To illustrate what she means, she tells us a story.

She tells us about a client who had come to our collective looking for help. Sefina was the client's first contact and suggested that the client would really benefit from participating in a 'women's programme' that the organization runs to empower clients to celebrate their identities as women. The client looked quite uncomfortable and suggested that perhaps the programme wouldn't be the right fit. Sefina was adamant, explaining that it was a really wonderful experience, and the client would get to sit with a group of women to talk through her experiences. Clearly still uncomfortable, this client clarified for Sefina that they were hesitant because they didn't identify as a woman, but as genderqueer. Sefina wasn't sure how to act. She was partly confused because the client had come to an organization explicitly defined by its 'woman-ness' in the first place. But something in Sefina told her that it didn't matter that she didn't identify with the category of 'woman'; this programme which discussed and celebrated gender identity was still right for the client.

Sefina turned to the group and asked us what we thought. Emily immediately has an answer. She explained how in her previous workplace, they had accepted anyone as a client who 'currently or previously identified as a woman'. Basically, this aimed to include everyone but those who were cis-men. The important defining feature of a client of our organization, the group agreed, was the experience of vulnerability and oppression. Labels and definitions were important for our work, but they weren't the fundamental factors for deciding who should have access to our services or who we should engage in activism with. The idea was strongly received by the room. My colleagues were keen on the idea, particularly as it helped us explain to others why gender minorities should have full access our services.

Throughout Part III, I have argued that gendered identities become unsettled when engaging in anti-violence activism. The body is fundamental to this work. Although becoming unsettled can have negative impacts on the wellbeing of activists, remaking our identities is also important for social change. Importantly, unsettling our gendered identities is essential for remaking who anti-violence activists consider to be a credible victim of violence worthy of institutional protection. Examining our gendered identities, as Sefina encourages us to do here, involves a challenging of normative assumptions of who we perceive to be the beneficiaries of our activism. That 'women' are the beneficiaries of our collective is challenged for Sefina by the genderqueer client. Her case that we should provide support for gender minorities is significant. When our institutional networks fail to care for and protect certain lives, we can lose them; both materially and discursively (Butler, 2017). As a potential solution Emily draws on the perspective that women and gender minorities are both 'vulnerable bodies' to argue for who she perceives as a beneficiary of our activism.

The lessons from my anti-violence colleagues have significant implications for academics and activists. Examination of which bodies are considered to be beneficiaries of our activism is fundamental to who will receive care and protection. The Black Lives Matter movement, the disability-rights movement, the #MeToo movement, the animal rights movement, and many other social movements all situate the body as a site of political action. There are norms within all these movements related to which bodies are constructed as the beneficiaries of the movement and which bodies need additional institutional protection. We can identify the 'sticking points' attached to certain bodies and consider, from this basis, how activism is helped or hindered through these constructions. Moreover, the ways in which social movements position certain bodies as vulnerable to particular kinds of violence can also act as a point from which to advocate for our interdependent responsibility for these bodies. Again, the Black Lives Matter movement is exemplary in this regard as the vulnerability of Black bodies to police violence is a 'sticking point' which can help all of us to understand our interdependent responsibility for challenging systemic racism.

The traditional conceptualization of academic activism has attributed the body (as opposed to 'the mind') to activism. Consequently, there has been minimal consideration within academic scholarship on the role of the body in academic activism and how an examination of the situation of the body can disrupt that harmful binary. As part of this work, I have explored the importance of my own body in relation to anti-violence activism and how my body is made (in)visible in academic work. I underscored that my understanding of myself as a 'non-victim' was deeply unsettled through my time with the collective, which helped me to understand the notion of women and gender minorities as vulnerable bodies. Furthermore, my sexual orientation (understood through the body) was significant in how I understood the norms which sometimes marginalized LGBT+ women and non-binary folk within the collective. These insights came from understanding my own body as a site of political action and myself as an embodied researcher. In short: paying attention to my embodied experience as I worked with the collective shaped my theoretical insights.

All forms of academic and activist work must grapple with vulnerability. Social justice focused research often constitutes certain bodies as sites of political action which therefore has material implications for the protection of bodies from violence. Academic and activist work can therefore both encourage us to 'be moved' by engaging with vulnerable bodies and highlight the social norms which need to be changed to ensure all bodies are safe from (material or symbolic) violence. These dual objectives take the lead of my colleagues' conceptualization of women and gender minorities as vulnerable bodies. As my colleagues underscore, recognizing a shared bodily vulnerability and dependency on each other is important for dismantling 'victim'/ 'non-victim' distinctions. Additionally, academics and activists must consider how they are part of systems of violence and consider how their practices challenge or reify these systems. In Part III, I have illustrated how this work can be done, highlighting how I was moved by my colleagues to reconsider my own relation to the body. A state of vulnerability can be unsettling, but it can also move us to connect to others.

Perhaps most importantly, the conceptualization of 'vulnerable bodies' offers insight into how the relationship between academics and activists could be reimagined. The dual meaning of vulnerability I have discussed in this chapter directs our attention to the interconnection of how we are simultaneously moved by and dependent on one another. In a sense, this entire book is an account of how I was moved by my colleagues and examined how my situation as an academic was connected to institutionalized inequality. Part III gives insight into how I was unsettled and the political effects of that undoing. An important part of that process was my examination of academic activism as embodied work. My colleagues were already acutely aware of their embodied vulnerability and their dual position as victims of sexism and activists against sexism. Nevertheless, the final vignette demonstrated that our appraisal of our vulnerability must be ongoing. Sefina, for instance, had to be moved by her client before she recognized the way in which gender minorities could be failed by institutions and excluded from protection. Vulnerability, then, involves ongoing deliberation of our identities (such as academic/activist) and how we can protect each other, materially and discursively. Vulnerability breaks down the barriers between 'us' and 'them' so that, between us, new things grow.

PART IV

A Story Like Mine

8

An Account of Ourselves

It took me a long time to comprehend the sheer force of will and bravery it took my colleagues to stake a claim to a feminist activist identity in the collective. This revelation came as somewhat of a surprise given that the collective defined itself by a feminist anti-violence standpoint. Like many anti-domestic and sexual violence activist groups that grew out of the women's liberation movements in Aotearoa New Zealand in the 1960s and 1970s, the collective was founded on a second wave feminist approach to gendered violence (Else, 1993; Connolly, 2004). This history was still influential, and the collective continued to express a commitment to feminism in their everyday activism. The collective was also understood to be feminist by our communities and other community sector organizations. As my voluntary work brought me into contact with a wider range of stakeholders, however, I became increasingly aware of the complexities of identifying as a feminist activist in the context of the community sector. There was the possibility of having our charitable status revoked (Elliott, 2016) as well as the fear of losing government funding for claiming a political status of agenda (Grey and Sedgwick, 2013b). Additionally, my colleagues told me stories of other people and organizations not wanting to associate with us on the basis of our political commitments. For example, a private sector organization refused to work with us as we were 'those bloody feminists' and we received regular backlash online for our feminist stance. For our aim as a group of anti-violence activists to end gendered violence, productive relationships, access to funding, and influence with the government were important; but so too were our feminist politics and principles.

At the same time as I was becoming more aware of the complexities of feminism in our various relationships in the community sector, I was engaged in formal interviews with some of my colleagues. In all the interviews my colleagues shared stories with me about their identities as feminist activists. I was struck by the difficulties they expressed in being recognized by their colleagues as feminist activists. Within the collective, as well as with stakeholders, it appeared that being a feminist activist was permeated by complexity. As I got to know my colleagues more intimately, I recognized that struggle over shared politics was a prominent feature of everyday life in the collective. In fact, my colleagues frequently disagreed over their different understandings of what it meant to be a feminist activist. Jen, for example, frequently came into conflict with Esther over their different perspectives of feminism. Jen described herself as a liberal feminist who worked within systems for change, whereas Esther's feminist politics were embedded in stories of sex-positive feminism and radical emancipation from patriarchal values.

The conflict around the variances within feminism is hardly new. In fact, many feminist scholars have argued that feminism cannot be understood as a singular emancipatory project, but only as an (occasionally) overlapping, evolving, and diverse collection of politics that ultimately aim for gendered equality (Beasley, 1999; Evans, 2015). Moreover, feminism is only one way of thinking about women's empowerment and equality that has variably been taken up by women from different geopolitical locations, backgrounds, and socioeconomic status (Ferree and Tripp, 2006; Green, 2007; Roces and Edwards, 2010). The Western origins of feminism as a movement was particularly important for my Māori colleagues, who grappled with collective's commitment to feminism and their own identity as Tangata Whenua (Huygens, 2001; Simmonds, 2011). These complexities and nuances of feminist identity were significant for how activism was undertaken in the collective.

Nevertheless, the vast majority of my colleagues remained adamant that feminism (in whatever form it took) was both important to their sense of self and fundamental to their activism. Such views are reiterated in research about domestic violence, which argues that a feminist approach is crucial to achieving social change which will end gendered violence (McMillan, 2007; Nichols, 2014). Even with the disagreement over feminisms there remained a sense among my colleagues of a shared responsibility for the lives of abused women and an imperative to catalyse social change to end gendered violence. Rather than asking how we could unite ourselves under a common understanding of feminism, however, my colleagues were more committed to organizing *through* difference to achieve change for abused women. Undeniably there was conflict and contestation between my colleagues over what was 'feminist' and what was not, but there was also a desire for solidarity and celebration of different understandings of feminism. In the context of the community sector, my colleagues recognized that there were added complexities in organizing for and with feminist solidarity. Which feminist activist identities were understood as legitimate or beneficial shifted and changed as my colleagues came into contact with multiple stakeholders.

My colleagues' desire for feminist solidarity (Cornwall, 2007) forms the basis of my discussion throughout Part IV. I focus on the relationship between feminist activist identities and change in the context of the community sector. In this chapter, I discuss the research which has thought about social justice-based identities and change in different organizational contexts. This provides a foundation for me to explore how my colleagues' feminist activist identities were important in the context of the community sector and for anti-violence activism. The construction and negotiation of feminist activist identities for my colleagues, I argue in the subsequent chapter, has implications for how activist work gets carried out in other contexts; including academia. Importantly, I connect activist identities to solidarity and take solidarity as a basis for how others can engage in activism through differences between their political position and context.

Activist identities in organizations

Activism and activist identities have been explored in many different contexts, but particularly in relation to social movements and other spaces where activism is traditionally seen as 'getting done'. There has been less attention to how activism happens within and through formalized organizations (such as community organizations) and institutions. When research has explored social justice activist identities in organizations, it is often in contexts where there is an overt division between activist and organizational identities of change agents. Creed et al (2010), for example, explore how LGBT+ priests negotiation the contradictions between being LGBT+ activists and their institutional role in the church. In a different context, but along similar lines, Wright et al (2012) explore how environmentalist activists in corporate contexts struggle to reconcile their activism and their organizational role. This kind of research has also looked at the academic context where Meyerson and Scully (1995) and Parsons and Priola (2013) argue that social justice or activist identities and their academic identities need to be reconciled to achieve change in and through the academy. The achievement of change is usually framed through resistance to organizational practices or managerial ideologies (Swan and Fox, 2010); often by positioning activist identities as oppositional to institutional contexts. Nevertheless, researchers of social change or activism in and through organizations have often recognized that organizational subjectivities are not necessarily contradictory to change initiatives. Organizational subjectivities can be understood as important to identities, and even positively in sync with social justice change initiatives (Swan and Fox, 2010; Maclean et al, 2015). In order to achieve social change, this research argues, there needs to be more alignment between the organizational and the political within organizations.

In contrast, research about activist identities in the community context has generally considered activist identity and organizational identity to be aligned (for example, Sanders and McClellan, 2014; Maclean et al, 2015; King, 2017). The constraints on achieving change through community organizations and the limits on activist identities are usually positioned as *external* to community organizations, that is, are constrained by ideologies like neoliberalism or the demands of external stakeholders such as government funders (Laurie and Bondi, 2005; Sanders and McClellan, 2014). In the context of anti-violence activist organizations specifically, there is usually assumed to be no division between feminist and organizational identities (for example, Rodriguez, 1988; Reinelt, 1994; Hughes, 2017). As well as the coherence of such identities, there is often an unexplored belief that there is a stable organizational feminist politics with which organizational members align. The coherence is considered to be beneficial for victims of domestic violence and to increase the potential of achieving social change (Nichols, 2011, 2014). The constraints on achieving change are also positioned as external to the organization (Reinelt, 1994; Nichols, 2014), echoing sentiments in research about the community sector more broadly. In light of these claims, research in the community sector context makes a robust case that unpacking the relationships between the context and activist identity is central to understanding both internal and external constraints on achieving social change.

Assuming both a coherent organizational politics and uncomplicated alignment of members with those politics is, however, problematic. Feminist researchers and activists have documented decades of complexity and contention over feminist politics (Arnold and Ake, 2013). And this contention has been productive. Feminists of colour and non-Western feminists, in particular, have argued that a universal politics marginalizes the differences of experiences of oppression *between* women (hooks, 1986; Irwin, 1990; Mohanty, 2003). The differing experiences of women as a result of their class, geographical location, gender identity, sexuality, ethnicity, or physical or mental ability shape their political position (Moraga and Anzaldúa, 2015). If feminist activists do not acknowledge or embrace differences between women, they can only address a narrow set of concerns and can perpetuate multiple kinds of social inequality, such as racism or classism (Lorde, 2007). Accordingly, it is important to acknowledge and even embrace the continual struggle over a 'shared politics' in daily activism. Activist identities are shaped and constrained by norms within social movements, not just norms positioned as external. When exploring the possibilities of change related to activist identities in community contexts, it would therefore be problematic to assume that all constraints to achieving social justice come external to the organization. Even when organizational identities are intimately interwoven with activist identities, struggle over fostering a 'shared politics' occurs at multiple intersections.

For activists creating change in and through community organizations, then, the reality of negotiating a shared politics with fellow activists is immensely complex. There are widely acknowledged constraints on activism in the community sector context that are material, social, and ideological (Eikenberry et al, 2019). These 'external' constraints shape how activists understand their identity and how their identity is shaped by interactions with different institutions, such as the state or corporations, and individuals, such as funders or the community. Additionally, there are organizational norms which shape activist identity. These norms are often shaped by political ideologies, such as feminism. Individual activists grapple with these norms in relation to their own experiences. Research about activism in and through organizations has often underemphasized these complexities. The fractures and fluidity of activist identity, however, are significant for activism. In Part IV, therefore, I focus on two key threads: the complexities of feminist identities in the community sector context in relation to the individual, organizational, and social; and how these fractures and fluidities in identity are still important, and even essential, to feminist anti-violence activism. At the end of Part IV, I then turn to the lessons from anti-violence activism and how these might inform academic activism.

A micro-political approach to activist identity in the community context

Given the complexity of the intersections between individual identity, the organization, and the community sector context, I decided to approach my colleagues' and my own feminist identities from a theoretical perspective that allows for a varied and detailed analysis of the nuances of identities and change: the micro-politics of identity. As Thomas and Davies (2005: 120) explain, a micro-politics of identity focuses on 'the small-scale changes that can have incremental effects, and that can make differences to how women live their lives, and live with themselves'. Rather than thinking about change in terms of a 'meta-narrative of emancipation'– which can be overwhelming and unhelpful for social issues – a micro-politics of identities alternatively involves emphasizing the struggles and tensions played out in individual identity texts. The micro-politics of identity is extremely useful for understanding change in complex contexts as it provides a model that accounts for the different shades of engagement with organizational practices and norms (Wright et al, 2012), the generative and proactive possibilities of identities (Parsons and Priola, 2013), and the variegated ways in which organizational members can catalyse change or inadvertently reinforce regimes of control (Swan and Fox, 2010). Overall, it provides a frame to explore how individual identity texts open up spaces that enable alternative subjectivities and meanings to form within organizational contexts and thereby catalyse change.

Typically, the micro-politics of identity has been applied in contexts where there is an overt division between activist identities and organizational identities. For example, Wright et al (2012) look at the micro-politics of environmentalist identities in corporate contexts and Parsons and Priola (2013) look at feminist identities in a hierarchical and masculine academic context. The aim of scholars who use a micro-politics approach to change is to destabilize and weaken forms of domination, with a long-term view of opening up spaces for challenging and changing oppressive practices and subjectivities (Davies and Thomas, 2004; Thomas and Davies, 2005). In applying a micro-politics of identity in the community sector context, I aim to understand how a micro-political approach might contribute to our understanding of the relationships between social justice identities and change in contexts of assumed organizational/political alignment. This, I propose, can help us to better understand the nuances of activist identities and the complexities of achieving change in and through organizations.

As I noted earlier, a micro-political approach to identities typically applies these ideas to specific individual identity texts (Thomas and Davies, 2005). In the collective, there was a distinctive cultural practice of storytelling about feminism. We would share stories with each other that interwove the personal and the political and connect these stories to the project of feminism (Weatherall, 2020). For example, Kimberley would tell us how at university she was told that women were 'too irrational' to work in finance, and Esther would tell us how becoming a sex worker had helped her to understand the power and worth of her sexuality. As well as the cultural practices of telling stories about our personal and political beliefs, there were organizational practices that compelled us to tell stories about our identities as feminist. The mandatory introductory training, for example, involved a half-day session on feminism and its importance to domestic violence work, during which we were directly asked to give an account of ourselves as feminist. We were asked to share personal stories of our experiences of being a woman, and then were asked to consider these personal stories in relation to feminism. In my exploration of the micro-politics of feminist activist identities, I therefore focus on the micro-politics of my colleagues' narratives that construct feminist activist identities.

As well as being a significant cultural practice in the collective, the telling of stories about our sense of self has been argued by academics to be effective for creating change in numerous ways. In my field of critical management studies, scholars have claimed that stories about our sense of self are important for stimulating personal transformation (Maclean et al,

2015), creating new ways of being (Murgia and Poggio, 2009), raising awareness of how we can think about ourselves differently (Parsons and Priola, 2013), developing new meanings (Lapointe, 2013), and giving voice to marginalized people (Gherardi and Poggio, 2007). In other words: stories do things to ourselves and to others. Generally, in anti-violence activism, stories are seen as a powerful mechanism to empower victims (Lester-Smith, 2013) and to alter public perceptions of domestic violence (Hill, 2019). Stories can be persuasive. They can inspire. They can reinforce what we already knew or open our minds to other possibilities. Stories can call us to action and provide us with a point around which to rally. The stories we tell about ourselves are also important for articulating and creating our own set of politics and our connections to others. But stories are also shaped by relations of power. They can reinforce harmful stereotypes about others. They can present very different versions of reality based on our position within the social hierarchy. Stories can cement our fear of the other or our sense of separation between 'us' and 'them'. In short: the stories we tell are important and it is important for activists to deeply consider the material effects these stories can have on others.

In Part IV, I also draw on Judith Butler's understanding of narrative identities. Butler's understanding of narrative is framed within the particular context of giving an account of oneself (Butler, 2001, 2005). From her perspective, narrative is not just telling a story about our selves, but a response to requests or allegations which ask us to account for our identities. Significantly, giving an account of oneself is related to the desire for recognition and persuasion that one is a viable subject: 'Giving an account thus takes a narrative form, which not only depends upon the ability to relay a set of sequential events with plausible transitions but also draws upon narrative voice and authority, being directed toward an audience with the aim of persuasion' (Butler, 2005: 12). My colleagues were frequently asked to give an account of their identities, conspicuously in relation to their feminist activist identity. Additionally, Butler offers an understanding of how narrative identities can simultaneously challenge and maintain social norms. For activists, where the aim is not to disrupt the movement but to support some norms while questioning others, Butler's perspective on narrative can be especially productive.

Giving an account of feminist activist identities

I begin by (re)telling the narrative accounts of my colleagues' feminist activist identities. As part of my ethnographic fieldwork, I arranged to formally interview some of my colleagues in order to deeply discuss various questions about activist identity and change at the heart of my research. I engaged in three sets of interviews with six of my colleagues during which we discussed different aspects of their experience engaging in activism on behalf of the collective. The stories I share include aspects of each of these interviews but primarily recount our conversations in the second interview when I asked my colleagues to give an account of their feminist activist identities. In sharing these narratives here, I have opted to place these accounts one after another, in order to accentuate the multiple feminist activist identities constructed by my colleagues. After sharing the narrative identities of my colleagues, I explore three dimensions of their accounts that build on the concepts of the micro-politics of identities and of 'giving an account of oneself' in relation to activism for social justice.

Jen

Jen's involvement with our organization stretched over nearly 30 years. Throughout her narrative Jen offered multiple, shifting accounts of her feminist activist identity at different points in her life and at different times of engagement with the collective. Overall, her narrative emphasized that she saw her feminist activism as evolving as she gained a deeper understanding of the intricacies of achieving social justice for women. During her study at university, Jen found that she could never "get a decent, solid feminist theory ... at times [she] could be a Marxist feminist. Then a post-structuralist. Then [she] could be liberal".[1] Different pieces of feminism, Jen noted, seemed to capture different aspects of her experience:

> 'I was in women's studies. I was a lesbian. And in those days if you were a lesbian in women's studies [radical feminism] was your politics ... [but my understanding evolved]. I was vicious actually [during my university study] in my critique of some feminist theory that I thought did just as much to damage women as it did anything. Feminism has always been like that. I get really annoyed at feminism when they use the great big capital letters and talk about *Feminism*. For you just can't do that. You can talk about *feminisms*. But they are everywhere. They are huge. It goes on forever.'

Establishing the fluidity of her feminist activist identity was essential to Jen's account of her sense of self, particularly as it became significant in her narrative as a foundation for negotiating the complexities of maintaining a feminist activist identity at various intersections within the community sector.

Jen was involved from the early days of the collective, when they were a loose collection of volunteers rather than a formalized workforce. Jen frames her feminist activist identity at this time as coherent with radical feminist politics. She found the collective to be an open, accepting space that was aligned with this radical feminism. She felt that: "we [the volunteers] were doing something that was really, really *good* and useful. Like we were on the side of the angels. The real staunch feminist angels nonetheless." Jen considers that volunteering with the collective had immensely positive impacts on her feminist activist identity and that she saw these radical feminist politics as fundamental to achieving social justice for abused women. She was supportive of the way in which frontline work was embedded in a radical feminism and Jen felt that it was "all coming from that basic place that women deserve just as much as men".

After years of participation in frontline work, however, Jen felt the toll from sustained exposure to domestic violence and decided to take a break from working with the collective. On her return she went into a managerial role instead of working on the frontline. This experience changed her view on the collective:

'We had full-time staff. We had a manager. We had a budget of a quarter of a million dollars a year ... the governance members were all employed people who really didn't want to put, and didn't have much time to put, much effort into [the organization] ... It was a totally different way of looking at things because the organization was totally different. In some ways, it was much better. It was much safer for the staff and the volunteers.'

In Jen's narrative, we can see that when she comes into contact with different aspects of organizational life her account of her identity also shifts. At the interface between the 'backstage' work, rather than frontline work, the relationship between Jen's organizational identity and her feminist activist identity changes. Rather than expressing feelings of being 'useful' or being a 'staunch feminist angel', Jen now positions her organizational identity as a risk-aware governance member. The orientation of her activism shifts from a sole focus on justice for abused women, to incorporating the safety of the staff and the longevity of the collective. In Jen's narrative we can see how she reframes her social justice identity:

'I discovered what I had known all along: that our reputation with government was very poor. That was largely a result of an oppositional and stridently aggressive form of politics that we had been engaging in. I made it my mission to make friends with our stakeholders and work towards developing a partnering approach, if you like, with our funders. I figured that our life was going to be quite limited if we didn't do that. I have done that and I think we have a far more respected place with government. However! That has come at an extreme cost in terms of our position within the sector, shall we say.'

The 'extreme cost' that Jen notes here was that she perceived that other members of our collective and other community sector organizations thought that Jen was a "sell-out" who had "lost [her] ability to speak for women" and was "in the government's pocket". Jen resists this conceptualization of her identity and is compelled to give an account of her shifting feminist activist identity. Jen emphasizes that tempering her radical politics was not something that she necessarily wanted: "It [working closely with stakeholders] has been compromising in a number of ways because I find myself having to put aside, on occasion, personal politics and convictions in the interest of something that is bigger." She narrates the change in her activist identity away from the "screaming activist place" by framing it as harmful to sustaining change for women subjected to violence. Instead, she proposes her feminist activist identity is in line with liberal feminism which seeks incremental change involving taking a "nibble at the hand that feeds you" rather than to "start barking and tear it off".

In her narrative, Jen stresses that she is not completely comfortable in the shift in her feminist activist identity, noting that it became "very compromised". In fact, there were times during which "the only way [she] can hold on to the notion of being a feminist is that [our organization] is inherently doing good things for women". In challenging the 'screaming activist' form of feminist identity in the collective, Jen maintains that: "I am possibly not as much as a one-eyed supporter of the notion that 'all things feminist are good' as I was." She emphasizes the necessity of temperance of feminism in order to effectively achieve change in the community sector because "[government] consider the NGO sector to be lesser, to be inferior" and "regardless of what any idealist might like to think, when you are dependent on the public purse for your very existence, yelling and screaming is just not going to help with your funding negotiations". In order to negotiate the tensions between the community sector, the government, and her own personal politics, Jen (re)narrates her feminist activist identity, explaining: "I would probably [be] a liberal [feminist] because I work very much within systems to achieve change." Although her challenging of the systematic perpetuation of domestic violence does involve constructing a feminist activist identity, at the same time Jen also underscores her temperance, so securing her place within the system.

Jen's narrative offers an account of shifting feminist identities at multiple intersections in the context of the community sector. She underlines that at times the most difficult intersection to maintain her feminist activist identity was within the organization. Jen is cognisant of the contradictions and complexities of her feminist identity and she negotiates this by emphasizing the variance and fluidity of her feminism early in her narrative. In doing so, Jen attempts to make her organizational identity coherent with her feminist identity. For Jen, this is a struggle, particularly when she comes into contact with external stakeholders. For example, with government Jen constructs a liberal feminist identity in order to maintain her feminist identity while ensuring the longevity of the organization. Jen maintains that this is to the benefit of the organization: "we do have a politically and philosophically informed place from which we provide services [to abused women and children]" but "we could be more politically active, we could agitate, we could do all of those sorts of things, but to do that we would have to be non-government funded".

Tia

When I asked Tia if she identified as a feminist she scoffed and replied, "No. Cos feminism is quite a Western concept. Which I am not." Tia alternatively carved out an activism embedded in her identity as Māori, which was a fundamental way in which she understood her sense of self. She explained to me that all her work reflected her identity as "*mana wāhine* [and] *wāhine toa*".[2] *Mana wāhine* is often referred to as a form of Māori feminism. Essentially, *mana wāhine* seeks to make visible the diverse experiences of all Māori women with a distinct focus on stories and lived experiences. *Wāhine toa* literally translates to 'strong women'. This was a term Tia used to describe herself and her activism that supported abused women. Tia was aware that other people, especially her colleagues, might try to position her as feminist, telling me:

'Like you can probably say, "yeah, you are a feminist", but no. I don't carry that mantle. [I am] absolutely independent. [I am] not scared to give my opinion if I think it matters. Those are probably all traits that Western concepts say "yeah that's feminism" but to me, nah, I don't like the term.'

Tia embedded her claim to a *mana wāhine* identity in her broader orientation of her self around her Māori identity. Her identity as Māori was grounded in a sense of her cultural heritage, ancestors, and language. Being Māori was central to Tia's understanding of her identity, telling me: "It's who you are ... [being Māori] is right for me. It is my identity."

Mana wāhine was understood by Tia to involve ensuring that every woman had a voice, and that different life experiences were taken into account.

Additionally, *mana wāhine* was embedded in a weaving together of personal and political stories, as Tia explained to me:

'Everybody is political. I believe everybody is, especially if it impacts on them personally. The personal is political, the political is personal. You form a political opinion based on something that happens to you … You don't have to be talking to a politician. You could be talking to a mate in a café and have different opinions but they are political opinions.'

Mana wāhine, independence, and opinions embedded in personal experience were the locus points of Tia's activist identity.

Tia had, like Jen, worked for the collective for a long time, but had only moved into backstage work in the last few years. Since the shift, Tia had increasingly struggled to negotiate her *mana wāhine* activist identity and the different organizational identity she was expected to occupy. Tia constructed distinctions between frontline work and backstage work in order to understand her organizational identity. Her description of her work on the frontline emphasized its multiplicity and fragmentation:

'With [our organization] you can't just be data input person. Or "she who does advocacy" because that is just bullshit and it just doesn't exist. You are forever wearing several caps. You can be the toilet cleaner one minute and then sitting at WINZ[3] supporting and advocating another lady in the next hour. It's always changing.'

In contrast, backstage work was described by her as straightforward, simple, and managerial. In fact, Tia saw this backstage work as a hiatus from frontline work, emphasizing that since moving into backstage work she felt that she was now able to build a sense of self outside of the collective.

In her work, Tia was acutely conscious of the need to balance the careful examination of your own identity and the women you are working with:

'[Training] is like a preparation sort of space where you have to prepare yourself in order to help and work with other people. That means unpacking your shit and having a good look at it, and trying to sort it out. And/or getting the help to help you sort it in order to be in a better space to help other people.'

Although Tia loved her work, explaining: "It's a lifestyle eh? It's not a job", she felt that "the whole *kaupapa* consumes you." The work took a toll on her *mana wāhine* identity. These are the reasons she offered for making the change from frontline work: "You become [almost unrecognizable], when you are in it for so long. I found myself getting quite cynical. And not feeling. I remember wanting to say to someone [a client] who I was sitting in front of: 'Can you just shut up? I can finish your story'." At the intersection between her identity and her work with clients, Tia felt her *mana wāhine* identity shifting in ways that she didn't resonate with.

Tia moved into backstage work but continued to work closely with frontline staff. Even after coming to work backstage Tia continued to frame her work in a practical way refusing to respond to "fluffy directions" or "bureaucratic bullshit". Tia's described her new role in the organization for me:

'Assisting the [frontline] to develop their services and to be bloody good practitioners, deliver good services, be compliant in whatever fucking standards of practice MSD[4] and shit they need to do in order for them to do what they want to do: which is working with our *whānau* [extended family].'[5]

The movement between the different intersections of frontline work with clients and backstage work with external stakeholders resulted in tensions in maintaining coherency in her *mana wāhine* identity and her new organizational identity. Tia knew "from talking with my sisters in [on the frontline] the perception was that [backstage workers were] sitting in [their] little ivory tower watching all [their] little peasants so to speak". The tension caused from her shift from frontline to backstage meant she spent a lot of time:

'Trying to debunk those myths. It looks all this and that but it really is not. Professionally working with the [frontline] they are like "can we talk to you about this and stuff" and I'm like "not really … it's sort of above my pay grade", they're like "tell us what you think anyway", and I'm like "okay but it isn't [professional Tia] telling you. If you want my own personal opinion, then I am happy to give it to you".'

For her "it is keeping really clear boundaries" between the different intersections of her work, and her *mana wāhine* identity.

Kimberley

Kimberley's narrative clearly distinguished between two distinct understandings of her identity as a feminist activist. She separated her identity into a 'non-feminist pre-rape' self, and her feminist activist self after she was raped. Until Kim was raped at university, she told me: "My identity was tied up in some Catholic ideal of purity and that women do certain things." These 'certain things' involved living "in a realm of anxiety and ticking boxes" of "married, babies, houses". Kim positions her self during those years as a naïve non-feminist. After being raped, however, Kim felt she became a feminist activist. Kimberley explained to me that this shifted her identity:

> 'I think that, unfortunately, I had to become a feminist after I got raped. I think before I wasn't really a feminist, back when I was quite slut-shamed[6] and I was quite green.[7] Then I got raped and I was like "fuck. This is a really massive injustice. What the fuck?". Then, of course, I think dealing with the patriarchal type structure like a university and just their stupid bureaucratic non-process around rape, I was just like this is so unfair!'

Kimberley positions being raped as an awakening; a consciousness-raising experience through which she became aware of gender inequality. Recognizing and fighting injustice against women became central aspects of Kim's feminist activist identity. She perceives feminism as based on equality between men and women, on the grounds that "I think that you should value women for the things that make them a woman". Essentially, Kimberley is highlighting that she believes that feminism should work to increase the perceived value of the feminine.

Kimberley struggled to maintain a coherent feminist activist identity, however, as she felt that some of her preferences and lifestyle choices were frowned upon by other feminists:

> 'I do like Justin Bieber, and I do like Kim Kardashian,[8] and I do listen to Chris Brown[9] music. I don't consider myself any less of a feminist. Some social justice warriors[10] would say that I'm not a feminist. I don't like post-wave feminism. What do you mean we are done with it? We are not. [I am] probably more of a third wave feminist. Probably within that realm. Probably intersectionalist.[11] I don't have to be a social justice warrior. I'm allowed to like things that are inherently "not feminist" and still be a feminist.'

Through her narrative, Kimberley is integrating different aspects of herself in an attempt to make her feminist activist identity coherent. Kim distances herself from a 'social justice warrior' feminism, invoking a negative stereotype of people who disavow women as feminist on the basis of (what Kim sees as) non-essential attributes. In her arguments against post-wave feminism, Kim also distances people who believe we have no more need for feminist activism. Kimberley attempts to balance what she perceives as the contradictions in her feminist identity of liking things "*inherently* not feminist" and still wanting to construct her activist identity through the term. In her doing so, we can see how the construction of a feminist activist identity can resist some subject positions while being generative of alternative ones.

Kimberley argued that her feminist activist identity was important to her work in the collective. Unlike Tia and Jen, Kimberley was fairly new to the collective. As a young Māori woman, Kimberley had only worked for one other organization before joining ours. Kim often felt out of place within the collective because she felt she didn't quite fit the expectations placed on her. Particularly, she felt she was viewed by the colleagues who had worked on the frontline as 'too soft for this work'. The tension between Kim's construction of feminism as valuing women for what makes them women (the feminine) and her feeling she was positioned as 'too weak' in her work, cause a contradiction in her activist identity which Kimberley struggled to make coherent.

In her narrative, Kim was often critical about what she understood as discriminatory practices against women in the collective. She explained to me that "for an organization that is trying to free women and children from violence they have a really great way of controlling, [which is] almost violent". At times she has:

> 'Just been finding work ruthless. It's been *ruthless*. So ruthless … it is patternistic. It comes in waves … it does feel a bit like you are waiting for a beating or something, you know, from an abusive partner. You can sense it in the waters. I have to keep reminding myself that it is nothing I'm doing. They can't be stopped. I always just relate it to an abusive relationship. There is no understanding it.'

Kimberley comments that this has impacted her understanding of feminism: "One thing it has taught me actually is that the patriarchy can be within women … just because I work for an all-female organization doesn't mean that it is not discriminatory against women". Kimberley is referring to the ways in which she understands the collective as exploiting the emotional labour of their workers, valuing and promoting masculinity over femininity in their workers, and the lateral violence between women. She uses her own construction of a feminist activist identity as focused on patriarchal structures to critique and challenge organizational practices and open up feminist subjectivities for herself in the workplace.

In response to the patriarchal type of violence Kim perceived as embedded in the workplace, she drew on her feminist activist identity to advocate for change. She told me: "I try very hard to build up other women, particularly [the frontline workers]. I try to be very positive with them, I try to highlight

their strong points … I try and allow for equal opportunities for everyone."
Additionally, Kim retained a focus on dismantling patriarchal structures,
but directed her gaze internally. She explained to me that in all her work:

'I also keep in the back of my mind that the patriarchy is everywhere.
It isn't just men … Like when I was [at university], so many girls were
like "I want to work for an all-female organization". You all think it
is going to [be great]. Doesn't matter. The patriarchy is there.'

Ava

Ava had worked backstage in the collective as her first permanent job
in Aotearoa New Zealand after her immigration from another country
in the later stages of her life. She had worked for the collective for a
number of years, through some substantial changes to the operation of
the collective. Overall, Ava felt her work had opened her eyes to the
realities of domestic violence against women and also had expanded her
awareness of "different personalities" and ways of being a woman: "I've
been exposed to a very liberal society here, that was very different from a
very Calvinistic, narrow-minded, restricted environment in [my country
of origin]. I love it."

When I asked Ava if she identified with the term feminist in her activism,
however, she didn't provide a definitive answer, instead replying: "I have
become more aware of feminism as a way of viewing the world and being."
As Ava began to unpack her statement, her narrative developed a conflicted
position between different aspects of her identity as a wife and mother, and
her construction of feminist activism. Ava explained her introduction to
feminism in her childhood:

'It was very much that my mother wore the trousers in the house
always. I always looked at my father and thought why don't you stand
up to her? … That was my model of the world. [My mother] was
more feminist than I actually gave her credit for. A lot of that rubbed
off on me. I feel strongly that I don't need a man to survive in this
world. But I do like having a man in my life.'

Importantly, Ava's text positions feminism and being a feminist activist
relative to a women's position on the role of men within her life, and within
the family unit. In Ava's description, feminism is linked to dominance or
assertiveness, and the capabilities to be successful in life without the support of
men. Ava described women as being "more passive … in their relationships,
or in the home through their father". From the perspective that feminism

is related to assertiveness and independence Ava explained why she was unwilling to identify with the term:

'I'm not a staunch feminist, but I do have some ideas, shall we say, about being a feminist. I do believe that I have a special role in our marriage and I'm happy to fill that. I also believe that he has a role that he needs to fill. I like to feel secure with him. I'm not that much of a feminist.'

In the text we see Ava's negotiation of feminist activist identity as she initially constructs herself as 'within' the category, holding 'ideas' about being a feminist, and finally as outside the boundaries of feminist activist identity. Again, we can see how Ava attributes feminism to roles within relationships and when she positions herself as having a 'special role' in her marriage as a wife, the role conflicts with the construction of feminism, and consequently Ava positions herself as outside of the boundaries of the category.

Nonetheless, Ava argued that she is "very passionate about what happens to women in the world". I asked her why she wanted to work with women:

'I guess to liberate them ... Liberation and empowerment of women. I guess what I saw were those women who get stuck in a rut, who often later in life, or need to make a life change, and then they don't believe in themselves. Empowering them to self-actualize and to be more what they think they are. We all have limiting beliefs around ourselves ... Women are no different. More so than men. Men have got huge egos generally and believe a lot more in themselves overall then women do ... That is why I wanted to work with women.'

Contrary to most of my other colleagues, Ava did not see the principles of liberation and empowerment as the defining features of feminism. She centres these within her activism, but for Ava she still does not want to identify with the term feminist because of the conflict she perceives it as causing with other aspects of her identity. For Ava, a feminist activist is someone who is completely independent of men and rejects traditional gender roles. As Ava feels comfortable in traditional gender roles, she is unable to reconcile a feminist identity with her roles as a wife and mother.

Although Ava does not construct her identity through her understanding of feminism, she demonstrates an awareness that in order to be a recognizable organizational subject, she must give an account of her relationship and beliefs about women. Once Ava had managed to construct an activist identity around assisting women – and not feminism – she became more confident and articulate in expressing her politics surrounding women. In her narrative she notes that women have difficulties in being empowered. She interweaves the difficulties of empowerment within her own personal experiences of divorce, reshaping her life by learning to be a life coach and training in self-actualization, and her 'breaking of the rut' by immigrating to Aotearoa New Zealand later in her life. Ava thus interweaves her life-history narrative and her politics of the liberation and empowerment of women.

Ava's narrative demonstrates an acute awareness that her positioning as non-feminist is a minority position in the organization. Ava attributes the tensions with colleagues as stemming from a contrast between her positioning as a woman as 'soft' and 'relational' to other (feminist) women in the organization who are 'dismissive and hard'. Nonetheless, Ava draws on the locus of empowerment and liberation of women to explain her organizational subjectivities and frames her approach to work in similar relational terms:

> 'I'm often the buffer zone. When people find it really tough they talk to me … I see myself as supporting women in our office in that way. It is about them coming in, in an unresourceful state, they can't function, they are crying or whatever. And then they'd tell me that they feel heaps better.'

Evelyn

Evelyn was relatively new to the collective but had several years of experience volunteering with other domestic violence organizations throughout Aotearoa New Zealand. Otherwise, Evelyn had spent most of her working life outside of the community sector and not involved with domestic violence activism. Evelyn had recently managed to leave her abusive partner. Being subjected to abuse was one of the primary reasons she had become involved in anti-violence activism. The lived-experience of violence formed an important locus for understanding feminist activist identity.

For Evelyn, the most significant attribute of her activist identity was that things had to come from 'life experience' or from the grassroots. Her narrative is peppered with references to being 'opened up' to 'people from different walks of life'. Evelyn's narrative follows her perception of her transition from a narrow-minded Christian upbringing, through exposure to 'different backgrounds and lifestyles', to a revised, open-minded perspective embedded in lived experience. Anti-violence activism had also opened up Evelyn's feminist identity: "my political spectrum has changed and my political understanding has changed." Most significantly, her work as a volunteer with a different anti-violence community organization shifted her perspective on men:

'[Working for a different domestic violence NGO alongside men] introduced me to this different scene that I hadn't known before and it kind of re-established my faith in men a bit; that there is change possible. That they can do this, that they can be trustworthy. That with the right kinds of supports, things can happen. They've been living proof of it for me and I still am really passionate about that. I believe that the change in men is going to be a huge part of the societal change that will eventually, and hopefully, see the demise of [our organization] as we can reach those younger generations coming up and that we can de-glorify the violence towards women.'

Evelyn embeds her narrative in her personal experiences, telling me that even in her "personal life" she is "very into equality" and that "I live, breath, eat, shit, and dream about it [anti-violence activism]". Evelyn thus weaves together her personal experience and feminist activist identity. In fact, Evelyn situates the boundaries of 'good work' around lived experiences, telling me that her biggest frustration is with her colleagues who value 'business' skills over people skills. In her working life Evelyn felt her sense of self was at odds with her colleagues: "I definitely see things differently to other people and even with my close teammates we have different filters on things."

Evelyn constructs part of her difference from her colleagues as related to her perspective on feminist activism, and she sees her approach as a counter-narrative to "some of the man-blaming ways" that she feels other members of the collective propagate. Importantly, Evelyn contends that: "I would like [our organization] to include the whole family. I think the feminism [approach of the collective] needs to be equality. Once you exclude a member of the family it just makes everything worse." Evelyn here constructs 'feminism' as an ideology exclusive of men, which violates what she understands as the core tenets of equality; the fundamental attribute of a feminist activist in her view. In her account of herself as a feminist activist, therefore, Evelyn constructs her feminism as bounded by the notions of balance, voice, and inclusivity:

'I identify with feminism being equality. I know there are different perceptions out there about what [feminism] is. To me that is equality. That is why, as a feminist, I am very passionate about men and all the changes and stuff that they have, and the equality issues that they face. It is not just women that face stuff, there is also an opposite spectrum of what men face. The perceptions of what a man has to be, versus how downtrodden women are. There is also a bit of a misbalance, obviously, which is where the equality comes in. I'm just as passionate for both. I know there are two sides to every story and I know that women can be just as violent as men.'

Evelyn's narrative conveys that she has increased her efforts to insert men into the story of feminism and position them as partners for achieving social justice for victims of domestic violence. For Evelyn, it was essential that feminist activists were inclusive of "people who have beaten their own demons, created their own change, sustainable in that change, their families have qualified them. Those are the people we need. Not the ones who fit 'the box'". However, resisting the narrative of feminism in domestic violence that focuses on women, makes it difficult for her to feel recognized as a feminist activist in the collective. Evelyn explained that she was "disenchanted with the attitude from [some of her colleagues]" and, in a similar way to Kimberley, found that the "patriarchal, the hierarchical, the white privilege, the putdowns, [and] the disempowerment" were prevalent in her experience with the collective. Nonetheless, Evelyn argued that: "There needs to be way more support for men to be able to change. Way more. That is the biggest gap. Everything that creates a perpetrator needs to be addressed."

Emily

When Emily was 17 and her sister told her that feminism was important for women in achieving equality, she responded flippantly: "Oh for fucks sake, we [women] have equal rights and feminism is just [for] hairy legged lesbians." Emily now laughs at her "shit view" of feminism which she describes as having "fully changed" now that she had gone through social worker training and "learnt about power and structural stuff". Once she moved into sexual violence activism, and then into domestic violence activism she said that she "became really feminist". For Emily this involved "rejecting a lot of expectations that were otherwise placed on me as a woman, but also recognized the tension between others". Recognizing the tensions involved taking a structural view of gender equality, as Emily explained that she saw people "as products of their experiences and their upbringing rather than people just making bad decisions".

In narrating her transition, Emily draws a distinction between attributes she considers 'feminist' and those that do not fall within the boundary. For Emily, feminism involves rejecting gendered expectations, recognizing structural inequalities, and focusing on the "intersectionality and a sense of sexual orientation and gender orientation", which she contrasts with her "shit view" of individualist perspectives on choices, and ignoring the role of sexual orientation as an important intersection.

Emily had only worked for the collective for a short time before I started my voluntary work and was primarily working at the intersection between our organization, government, and other domestic violence agencies. For Emily, the construction of the collective as feminist was a significant point of difference in her work:

'We are a really strong feminist organization. A lot of [domestic violence] organizations aren't. Or they say they are but they only really pay lip-service to the principles of empowerment; I guess [we recognize that] … every woman [is] doing the best that they can and not being instrumental in their own victimization. Whereas other organizations get really, really invested in the woman's role in stopping violence. That is something that we try really hard not to do.'

Through Emily's critique of other organizations which pay 'lip-service' to feminism, Emily indicates that she understands feminism as attached to organizational practices. Emily positions our collective as having practices which acknowledge the fundamental agency of women. Agency and emancipation from oppressive social structures are central to Emily's construction of her feminist activist identity. Emily weaves the organization's practices together with her own desires and beliefs: "[I have] passion about not having violence against women … Women blaming really, really pisses me off." Emily engages with organizational norms to construct her feminist activist self by weaving together organizational practices and personal beliefs.

As well as emphasizing the value of the organization as feminist, Emily describes how working for the collective has shaped her construction of her feminist activist self:

'[Working for our organization] has made me really aware of aspects of intersectional feminism. Particularly when it comes to things like [the intersection of gender and race] or grassroots activism, that I'm often not involved in. Working here hasn't made me any less feminist, but it has made me aware of the flaws in my feminism.'

Emily positions herself as particularly mindful of the flaws in her own conceptualization of feminism, particularly in regard to her tendency to overlook the intersection of gender and race. She attributes the flaws to the difficulties in deconstructing her lived experience as a Pākehā woman which she sees as privileged in Aotearoa New Zealand. Emily maintains, nonetheless, that her feminist activist identity also aids in challenging some of the norms around feminism in the collective:

'I think in the sense of sexual and gender orientation, I've been aware of how, even within [our organization] that really values [diversity], that really hasn't been emphasized as much as it could have been. That has been kind of reductionist in its way of thinking. So, in a way it has made me really aware of the fact that I do hold that really important perspective … and how easy it is to invisibilize that, even within my advocacy with government.'

Importantly, Emily draws a link between her own feminist activist identity and the possibilities of change at the intersection with government. She highlights that the tensions between her feminist activist identity and organizational norms are significant because: "my voice is the one that goes to parliament. It really needs to be reflecting the needs of our [diverse] clients and workers". Being aware of the strengths of other feminisms is important for Emily at the multiple intersections with external stakeholders.

One particular point of tension within Emily's narrative is the positioning of men within feminism. Emily explains that:

'Working with [our organization] has made me innately suspicious of heterosexual relationships because it [domestic violence] appears so prevalent that it is difficult to imagine any relationship not having elements of that now. It is really difficult not to recognize that in my friends' relationships now, and that is a real pain in the arse.'

Emily is again weaving together the personal and political, noting that her experiences with the collective shape her personal relationships and role in those relationships. However, in Emily's narrative there is a dissatisfaction with how her feminist activist self has been constituted through anti-violence activism to be suspicious of men's place within feminism. Emily further narrates her tension:

'As a feminist it's difficult because you really want to embrace the perception of men being equal partners and as having the capacity to be amazing partners. At the same time, you are so surrounded and immersed in work where men are the perpetrators of violence. And just casual sexism that you begin to notice in men more so than in women, that you begin to treat that with suspicion.'

Emily argues that there is an imbalance between men and women. As this underpins the construction of her feminist activist identity, and simultaneously her construction of the collective's feminist politics, Emily opts to leave open the possibility of men's participation in our activism without making it a priority. Nonetheless, Emily maintains:

'I would like to change our beliefs around masculinity, first and foremost … Then obviously violence against women would have a nice flow on effect from the erosion of harmful hyper-masculinity and we could reconstruct gender as being a non-binary thing and also without the gender roles associated with it and then we would be really happy and healthy.'

9

Through Difference

The sheer multiplicity of positions, tensions, debates, concerns, and complexities of my colleagues' accounts of their feminist activist identities underscores the absence of a singular 'feminist activism'. As well as offering a multiplicity of feminisms, my colleagues' narratives illustrate the complexity of establishing and maintaining their activist identity in the context of the community sector. Not only were my colleagues grappling with constraints on their activist identities deriving from their intersection with the government, other funders, and institutions (such as the police) but they were also negotiating constraints on their feminist activist identities as part of their interactions with their colleagues. From their accounts, it is evident that the almost utopian ideal of feminist activism grappling predominantly with *external* constraints (Reinelt, 1994; Nichols, 2011; D'Enbeau and Buzzanell, 2013) overlooks the complexity of organizing through a multiplicity of feminisms within feminist organizations. The micro-politics, the small negotiations within these discussions I had with my colleagues are therefore important to how we can effectively practice solidarity in social movements, particularly when these movements have become increasingly formalized.

In the following sections, I draw together some of the elements of my colleagues' accounts of their feminist activist identities to explore the constraints and possibilities of engaging in activism *through* difference. The remainder of Part IV is structured like a spiral: starting at the widest point of intersection with external stakeholders, narrowing the focus to within the collective, and finally looking at the stories of my colleagues specifically. I first attend to the context of the community sector to unpack how feminist activist identities shift and change at various intersections between the collective and stakeholders. As I noted in Part I, the increased formalization of community sector activism has led to a concern among scholars and community sector members that activism 'has lost its bite'. Second, I look at the negotiation of 'shared politics' within the collective and explore how my colleagues maintained some organizational norms but challenged others.

In particular, my colleagues' narratives frequently asked the listener to direct their attention *within* emancipatory projects. Third, I look specifically at the cultural practices of telling stories about personal and political identities from the perspective of 'giving an account of oneself'. Ultimately, I draw these sections together to discuss what I learnt from my colleagues about organizing activism through difference in the context of the community sector and what academic activists could learn from these practices.

At the intersection of self and organized activism: competing claims for legitimacy

A point of considerable tension evident in the narratives of my colleagues was the intersection between the construction of feminist activism and the multiple accountabilities of the collective. In community based activism there is often substantial pressure to construct an identity, often through narrative, which is considered legitimate at multiple intersections of accountability with external stakeholders (Herrmann, 2011; Gilpin and Miller, 2013). For example, King (2017) shows that conflicting demands for accountability operate to transform community organization members from 'idealistic dreamers' to 'nonprofit professionals' and Sanders (2015) notes that tensions between pursuing social justice and meeting accountability demands interdependently produce identities of organizational members in complex ways. Although some scholars advocate for embracing the tension and finding ways to make it productive (Tomlinson and Schwabenland, 2010; Dey and Teasdale, 2016), others share concern that conflicting demands make achieving social justice difficult and can damage social causes (Reinelt, 1994; Eikenberry, 2009; Eikenberry et al, 2019). My colleagues likewise faced multiple, conflicting demands at the interface between their activist identities and their accountabilities to external stakeholders.

The narratives of Jen, Tia, and Emily, in particular, foreground the intersection between their activist identity and the multiple accountabilities to external stakeholders. Importantly, the construction of their activist identities was tied to the social justice goals of the organization. Not only did my colleagues have to negotiate multiple accountabilities and conflicting discourses in order to construct a feminist/*mana wāhine* activist identity; but they wanted to do so in order to achieve social justice. As King (2017) underlines, although conflicting accountabilities can orient identities of members away from social justice, a desire to promote social change is always important to constructing personal and organizational identities in social justice community organizations. My colleagues experienced similar pressures.

Jen's account of her feminist activist identity emphasizes the incremental changes in her sense of self as she changed her role in the collective. On the frontline she was a 'staunch feminist', in backstage work she constructed 'multiple feminisms', and at the interface between the collective and government she was a 'liberal feminist'. Jen constructs each feminist activist identity in relation to the social justice mission of the collective. 'Staunch feminist' is positioned in relation to doing 'good work' on the 'side of the angels'; at the interface of government and the collective a 'liberal feminist' identity is positioned in relation to ensuring the longevity of our collective and providing clients with 'the best service'. Jen frames the negotiation of her feminist activist identity in response to the shifting demands of accountability. On the frontline, Jen's primary accountability was to victims she personally supported. At the interface between the collective and government, however, Jen's primary accountability has shifted to ensuring the collective has a good reputation and a sustainable source of funding. These shifts are significant.

At the heart of Jen's narrative of her feminist activist identity is her desire to achieve social justice for women and children subjected to gendered violence. Her feminist activist identity is, however, constrained by the pressures to construct a legitimate identity from the perspective of various external stakeholders. As her position in the collective changes to a governance role, for example, Jen constructs a liberal feminist identity which she argues was a way to maintain their legitimacy as a collective. The imbalanced power relationship between the community sector and government, Jen notes, is influential in her construction of her feminist activist identity. In order to continue to help victims of violence, Jen sees a need to engage in a more temperate politics in their relationship with government. In positioning herself as a liberal feminist activist, therefore, Jen seeks to maintain a personal connection to social justice while securing influence with government in order to increase the collective's sway over policy and legislative decisions. Parsons and Priola (2013) and Meyerson and Scully (1995) both argue that achieving change within systems can be easier from an insider position. Thus, although Jen's position as a liberal feminist is constrained, there are still benefits she sees from her orientation as an insider.

Tia was caught between the frontline and the backstage work of the collective. Like Jen, therefore, Tia has experienced an alternation of her accountabilities from victims of violence she personally supports, to more complex accountabilities to both frontline activists, victims of violence, and the state. In frontline activist work, Tia emphasizes that she was unable to distinguish a sense of self from her activist self; she was consumed by the *kaupapa*. Rather than framing this as positive for social justice, however, Tia argues that being too immersed in activism was actually damaging for maintaining her *mana wāhine* activist identity. The shift to backstage activism affords Tia the opportunity to separate her sense of self from her activism, allowing her the ability to disconnect from her work. In her backstage activism, Tia consciously constructs dual identity positions of *mana wāhine* activist and organizational member in order to negotiate both her interactions with her frontline counterparts and her accountabilities to the state. Tia positions these boundaries as necessary divisions to meet both sets of expectations.

Nonetheless, Tia carried over some of her embedded practices from frontline activism to continue to construct a *mana wāhine* activist identity in her new role in the collective. Tia's construction of *mana wāhine* as opposing bureaucracy sits within a legacy of anti-violence activism that identified, and opposed, bureaucratic processes as patriarchal structures that contradict egalitarian social justice goals (Rodriguez, 1988). In fact, Tia links non-bureaucratic practices directly to outcomes for clients, arguing that unlike the government who damages clients by making them 'jump through hoops' for service, our collective offers accessible support. Tia links her *mana wāhine* activist identity with challenging organizational practices that she understands to perpetuate the conditions which prevent abused women – particularly Māori women – from receiving support. Additionally, the construction of a *mana wāhine* identity challenges the organization practices which embed 'feminism' (in the singular) as offering the 'best' approach to achieving social justice for women. Tia's construction of her *mana wāhine* identity questions the focus on the 'Western' concept of feminism embedded in the collective. The small changes she offers in her account of her *mana wāhine* activist identity demonstrate the value of non-Western activist identities being integrated into the collective.

Emily connects her feminist activist identity to challenging "harmful hyper-masculinity" and recognizing "gender as a non-binary thing without gender roles associated". For her, constructing a feminist activist identity that breaks gender stereotypes is essential for achieving the social justice goals of the collective. Emily understands gendered violence as connected to societal expectations that women should fill certain roles in the home, with children, and in the workforce. Unsettling gender stereotypes through non-binary constructions of gender, Emily argues, will aid in achieving social justice for women and gender minorities. Emily argues that it is essential for her to maintain a "strong feminist" stance in her activism in order to unsettle these stereotypes. Emily uses other anti-violence organizations as a point of difference in order to construct what is a 'feminist organization' and 'what is not'. For Emily, the practices that sit at the heart of feminist activism are empowerment and ensuring women are not positioned as responsible for the violence. Emily is therefore able to draw on the intersection between the self and the collective to provide foundations to her feminist activism and the direction of social justice.

Emily is determined to "retain [her] idealism" and maintain a coherent feminist activist identity in her work with difference stakeholders. In contrast to Tia and Jen who produce multiple activist identities to negotiate conflicting accountabilities, Emily sees it as important to maintain a coherent sense of self. She argues that she is aware "how easy it is to invisibilize [the intersection of race and gender], even within my advocacy with government". The recognition of differences between women is therefore important to her feminist activism. Continually reflecting on differences between women is difficult for Emily, but she frames it as necessary to recognize the marginalization associated with race and other intersecting identities. Emily emphasizes that this work is crucial in order to be truly accountable to all victims of violence. Thus, we can see that Emily has been shaped by organizational norms of feminism, as she explains how they made her aware of her limitations, but also challenges other norms within the collective. The tension between her feminist activist identity and the diversity of victims of violence is seen as fundamental by Emily because her "voice is the one that goes to parliament". The small and continuous changes Emily makes to her feminist activist identity are testimony to the fluidity of activism which aims to be inclusive.

The discussion of the feminist identities of Jen, Tia, and Emily emphasize that activist identity shifts and changes in relation to the context. Some of this negotiation of feminist activist identity was conscious, such as Emily's reflection on the limitations of her feminist identity in relation to indigenous women. At other times, feminist activist identities were shaped by the expectations of stakeholders. Jen's narrative, for example, demonstrated how her need to work with government for certain policy and legislative changes shaped her understanding of her feminist activist identity. The small and incremental negotiations of feminist activist identity underscore that activism in and through community organizations is too complex to warrant a broad-brush approach to social justice. Alternatively, carefully considering the small changes to feminist activist identity in relation to the complex demands of the socio-political context can illuminate how to continue to fight for social justice even in difficult circumstances.

Jen, Tia, and Emily all insisted that the 'heart' of their feminist activism remained consistent in the complex context. In fact, feminist activism provided a point of consistency in their narrative identities which helped them to negotiate the competing demands for accountability in the community sector. Jen, for instance, was able to push for small, incremental changes within the system as an 'insider' liberal feminist activist. Nonetheless, Jen herself notes that this is a constrained position and may not effectively challenge wider systemic issues related to gendered violence. The diversity of approaches Tia, Jen, and Emily took to their feminist activism with government also indicates that a micro-political focus on community sector activism is essential. Although Jen is exemplary of the activism 'with gloves on' approach to government (Onyx et al, 2010), Tia and Emily were more radical in their approach. While it is important to put the micro-politics of activist identities in the context of broad emancipatory projects, the everyday negotiation of these identities shows the range of possibilities. External organizations do constrain activism, but activists work hard to maintain their focus on social justice, even in these complex contexts. Even if they only achieved 'small wins' within the system (Meyerson and Scully, 1995), their narratives continued to circulate the value of feminist approaches to anti-violence activism and maintained their focus on the broad emancipatory project of ending violence against women.

Feminist activism within the collective

In the previous section, I focused on the complexities of constructing and maintaining a feminist activist identity at the shifting intersections between the collective and various external stakeholders (particularly the government). As I argued in Chapter 8, the focus in research on activism in the community sector has tended to either overlook or underemphasize the importance of negotiating activist identity *within* community organizations (for a few notable exceptions see: Dempsey, 2009; Kenny, 2010; Kirby et al, 2012). Strikingly, my colleagues' narratives give extensive attention to explicating the complexities of having their feminist activist identity recognized by their colleagues. Whereas the struggle with external stakeholders was usually about organizational legitimacy and longevity, struggle within the collective focused on deconstructing harmful norms within organizational practice.

Feminist research on dismantling oppressive social norms has often stressed that even practices which are supposed to be empowering or transcend power relations can become vehicles of oppression (hooks, 1986; Ellsworth, 1989). It is therefore important to consistently question how feminist activism is situated within power relations. Feminists of colour, in particular, have argued that it is important to understand the power relations *between* women as a necessary element of social justice (hooks, 1986; Moraga and Anzaldúa, 2015). If solidarity is to be achieved among activists, they must engage in the (often painful) work of questioning their own roles in perpetuating harmful social norms. This is a necessary pain if activists are to deconstruct social norms which perpetuate violence against women. Such violence, as I have argued in Part III, is unequally distributed between women based on their other intersecting identities such as race or sexuality. In their narratives, my colleagues were consistently questioning the norms of the collective which they felt were harmful. These norms were seen to negatively impact women of colour, indigenous women, queer women and non-binary folk, and feminine women. I draw out several examples from my colleagues' narratives of negotiation of what was 'feminist activism' and what was 'non-feminist' to illustrate.

To differing degrees, all of my colleagues' narratives gave an account of the time they felt that their feminist activist identities were questioned or rejected by their colleagues. They also all highlighted times when they drew on their lived experience to question or challenge the feminist activist identities of their colleagues or their perceptions of harmful norms within the collective. The simultaneous challenging and being challenged was played out in the micro-politics of their stories and is particularly evident in Kim, Ava, and Evelyn's narratives.

Kimberley argued in her story that in order to challenge the social norms which perpetuate violence against women, feminist activism needs to reimagine the value placed on the feminine. Within the collective, however, Kim found it difficult to gain recognition as a 'feminine' feminist activist, arguing that she was positioned as 'too soft' or 'too weak' for anti-violence activism by her 'staunch feminist' colleagues. Kim argues that the devaluation of the feminine in the collective's activism was a part of women's socialization within the patriarchy and the 'internalization' of harmful norms which devalue the feminine (and by association women). In a similar way, in Ava's narrative she highlights her discomfort with the notion of a 'staunch feminism' which she feels is incompatible with her more feminine roles as a wife and as a mother. Like Kim, Ava thinks that her nurturing or caring roles in the collective are perceived as less valuable than hard-line externally facing activism. Other scholars have also noted similar difficulties in ensuring that feminine practices are seen as valuable in organizing as these are continually positioned as less valuable than masculine practices (Jeanes et al, 2011). Without challenging the devaluation of the feminine, however, Kim and Ava argue that it is difficult to empower women and end gendered violence.

Ava challenges the devaluation of the feminine in her narrative through positioning her dedication to empowerment of women as compatible with cultivating a nurturing role in her relationships with other women in the collective. Along the same lines, Kimberley argues that her practices of "building up women" also revolve around "valuing women for what makes them women", that is, supporting other women through feminized practices of nurture and care. Both Ava and Kim understand the feminine to be sidelined in the collective's activism. Kim, in particular, links the devaluation of the feminine to women's socialization within patriarchal discourses. In order to dismantle the devaluation of women which contributes to gendered violence, Kim argues that it is necessary to foster nurturing relationships between women which increase the value attributed to the feminine and to create sustained bonds necessary for feminist activism. Through positioning the patriarchy within the collective as well as external to it, Kim is able to identify and challenge the collective's practices which inadvertently devalue the feminine. While Kim and Ava do challenge the devaluation, they also (inadvertently) reify harmful assumptions about the inherent connection between women and the feminine (as discussed in Part III). Thus while challenging some norms through their construction of feminist activism, they simultaneously reify others.

Evelyn also constructed the patriarchy and other marginalizing social norms (including colonization) as within the boundaries of the collective. She argued that the collective engaged in practices saturated with "the patriarchal, the hierarchical, the white privilege, the putdowns, [and] the disempowerment". In order to foster the necessary solidarity for the activism to dismantle these complex and intersecting forms of oppression, Evelyn suggested a different approach to that of Kim and Ava. Evelyn was intent that the collective should be more inclusive of men and their activism should dismantle how both women *and* men (overlooking non-binary folk) were negatively impacted by the patriarchy, hierarchy, and White supremacy. From Evelyn's perspective, her colleagues often excluded men from the narrative of domestic violence; positioning them as disembodied 'perpetrators' rather than as men likewise 'created' through the negative implications of patriarchy, hierarchy, and White supremacy. Evelyn connects the exclusion of men from some of my colleagues' feminist activist identities to a White feminist[1] narrative on domestic violence. Evelyn argues that an anti-violence activism that excludes men, overlooks the importance of the Māori view that wellbeing, safety, and healing must involve the whole community.

Evelyn argues that our collective would benefit from rethinking our understanding of 'equality' along the lines of the Māori perspective on gender equality and gender roles. Mikaere (1994: 125) explains that in traditional Māori society: 'Both men and women were essential parts of the collective whole, both formed of the *whakapapa*[2] (genealogy) that linked Māori people back to the beginning of the world, and women in particular played a key role in linking the past with the present and the future.' Evelyn's understanding of equality was imbued with a similar understanding; that our efforts as feminist activists needed to pay attention to the 'collective whole' and the intergenerational inheritance of our gendered roles in society. Through this construction of her feminist activist identity as being for equality, Evelyn argues that permeating our collective's practices with a recognition of parallel harmful social norms that affect men will help to holistically dismantle the social conditions of patriarchy, hierarchy, and White supremacy. Positioning these intersecting oppressions within the collective, Evelyn suggests that feminist domestic violence organizations need to challenge feminism which excludes or disembodies men within their narratives of violence. In doing so, she contends, we can more effectively catalyse change that will end gendered violence for our communities in Aotearoa New Zealand. Like with Ava and Kim, however, Evelyn's narrative of feminist activism overlooks the heterosexual matrix and includes only two gender identities, excluding non-binary folk and queer relationships. Once again, Evelyn challenges some norms while reinforcing others.

Although the process of questioning feminist activist identities was often painful and unsettling for my colleagues, it was also necessary. If we are to dismantle the complex social processes which sustain gender inequalities, we must question normative feminist identities in feminist activism. At times, my colleagues were challenged by other activists to reconsider their own feminist identity and at other times my colleagues drew on their feminist activist identity to challenge their colleagues and the collective's practices. The dissent among my colleagues was not in search of a singular approach to ending violence, but instead with the aim of solidarity to engaging in multidirectional approaches to dismantling our patriarchal, hierarchical, and White supremacist constructions of feminist identities. My own position as a queer feminist made me aware of the exclusions of non-binary folk and queer women from much of the collective's activism. These layers of activism, grounded in lived experience, highlight that contesting how we understand our activist identities is necessary if activists are to find alternatives to oppressive social norms.

Weaving together the personal and political: giving an account of the feminist activist

I now turn to examining the form of the narratives themselves. The specific cultural practices of the collective asked activists to give an account of themselves. These practices had interesting effects that are important for fostering social change. I look particularly at the accounts of Ava and Tia to examine how accounts of feminist identity drew on the notion of 'the personal is political' and were compelled to give an account in relation to feminism, even when refusing the term. In many anti-violence community organizations that developed in the 1960s and 1970s – particularly those that claimed the feminist mantle (to borrow Tia's term) – the link between the personal and the work of the organization was considered essential, as personal experiences of oppression were argued to form the foundations of organizing differently in ways that were more empowering to women (Rodriguez, 1988). Weaving together the personal and political has a long history in feminism, with Hanisch (1970) using the term 'the personal is political' to describe how consciousness raising groups in the women's liberation movement made connections between personal experiences of being a woman and the need to take collective political action.

The stories that my colleagues considered appropriate to be shared were shaped by organizational norms, which, as discussed, constrained the possibilities of being understood as a viable subject (Butler, 2005). The narrative accounts offered by my colleagues also demonstrate the weaving together of the personal and the political. Kimberley, for instance, directly relates her becoming a feminist activist with being raped; thereby offering a sequential transition from 'non-feminist' to 'feminist' through her personal stories aimed at persuading the audience that she is a viable feminist subject (Butler, 2005). The use of the personal as a basis for feminist organizing is contentious, however, as it can commodify experience, and 'the personal' is always constructed through power relations which unevenly distribute social value to experiences (Phipps, 2016). At the same time, however, in giving an account of oneself you have the possibility of reflecting, and thereby reconsidering, moral and political norms (Butler, 2005). In other words, each time my colleagues gave an account of their feminist activist identity they were offered the possibilities of (re)considering how they understood the importance of feminism for our collective and creating new, non-violent, ways of relating with one another.

The personal stories woven into the narrative accounts of feminist identity by my colleagues share some similar themes. Most prominently, the accounts contain stories that emphasize gendered socialization and suffering. Socialization as women takes the form of stories of upbringing that were perceived to shape my colleagues' political perspectives. Ava highlights her "Calvinistic narrow-minded" upbringing, and Tia shares stories about being raised to be proud of being Māori. Stories of suffering – particularly in relation to violence from men including sexual abuse, sexual assualt, domestic violence, and abandonment – were also often a centre point of accounts of feminist activism. Ava told the story of her husband abandoning her and Tia shared stories about her childhood exposure to domestic violence. The privileging of these two dimensions can be seen to be related to the norms in the collective. For example, in the compulsory training sessions we were asked to give an account of our upbringing in the form of a *mihimihi*[3] (introduction) and stories of our *tūrangawaewae*[4] (standing place), followed by an account of the 'worst things' and the 'best things' about being a woman, and concluded by an account of our understanding and (possible) commitment to feminist activism in relation to those other things. Organizational practices thus established links between our personal stories and our relationship to feminist activism, and put the emphasis on certain kinds of stories.

Ava's account exemplifies these storytelling norms. Early in Ava's account she emphasizes that because of her "very Calvinistic, narrow-minded" upbringing, the move into our collective involved unsettling various embedded aspects of her identity. She compares this early mindset to the "very liberal society" she engages with in our collective. In this way Ava establishes both a plausible transition towards a feminist politics but establishes what she perceives as a legitimate reason for feeling uncomfortable with those politics. Her story thus provides the grounds for her to refuse to adopt a 'feminist activist identity'. Nonetheless, Ava is still compelled to give an account of her identity in relation to feminism in order to retain legitimacy as an organizational subject. Instead of positioning herself as a feminist, Ava more hesitantly concludes that she has "become more aware of feminism as a way of viewing the world and being". As Butler (2005: 8) argues: 'the "I" has no story of its own that is not also the story of a relation – or set of relations – to a set of norms'. In order to establish an activist identity in the collective, Ava must position her self in relation to feminism – even if that position involves rejecting the norms. Her hesistation is indicative that she is aware that her discomfort with feminism is not widely accepted by her colleauges.

From the basis of this sequential transition, Ava weaves together 'personal' stories to establish her political position in the collective; not in relation to feminism, but in relation to the empowerment of women. In her narrative account, Ava explains that in her activism she seeks to liberate and empower women. She embeds this position within her personal experiences. Ava explains that she saw "those women who get stuck in a rut, who often later in life need to make a life change, and they don't believe in themselves". She relates this imperative to her own life history, in which she tells the story of her husband abandoning her and her children, compelling her to make a substantial change in her life. This story of how to break away from the 'rut' forms the grounds of her political commitments to the liberation and empowerment of women. Through her account Ava establishes that in her activism she will engage with women in a way that will help them to "believe in themselves" and "feel better" about their work in the collective. Although Ava doesn't explicitly construct a feminist identity she is still able to construct an identity as a legitimate organizational subject by adopting a 'feminist analysis' which seeks to empower women.

In a similar way, Tia also negotiated the storytelling norms in her account to reject the term 'feminist'. Tia told me explicity that she belives that "the personal is political and the political is personal. You form a political opinion based on something that happens to you". The 'personal' for Tia was rooted in her Māori identity. Tia told me that growing up:

'We knew exactly where we were from and who our ancestors were … we would go home and feel like we owned it because we were part of it … our dialect in Te Reo was important … it has always been important for us to keep in touch with our cultural identity.'

The importance of her Māori identity was something that Tia was adamant that she passed on to her children. The account that Tia gives of her personal identity as Māori is woven into her political position. She explained to me that although "[I] don't believe that what is right for Māori is right for everybody" that she was "becoming aware of Māori issues" and in her practice she would use "Māori models of practice as opposed to Western [models]".

The stories of her Māori identity in Tia's account formed the grounds for the rejection of the term 'feminist' as a "Western concept". Tia weaves the personal stories of learning about the importance of being Māori in her childhood to her current identification with *mana wāhine* activist identity. Through her account Tia also links stories of her childhood to her feeling out of place or limited as a young Māori woman. In this way Tia's account draws on the collective's norms to offer a viable account of her identity as a *mana wāhine* activist in relation to feminism. She thereby establishes new assumptions for how we should interact with one another from the perspective of *mana wāhine*. She acknowledges that her position is one among many different positions one could take to promote change for victims of violence, but through her account establishes *mana wāhine* as a legitimate identity from which to engage in activism for social change. The contrast of *mana wāhine* activism to feminist activism also challenges the exclusions of indigenous ways of being from conventional feminist identity in the collective.

Even in narratives where my colleagues did not identify as feminist, my colleauges were still compelled to give an account of their activist identity in relation to feminism. In doing so, my colleauges *had* to reflect on the value of feminist identity for activism with their colleagues and for broader anti-violence activism. In this way, colleauges who did not express alignment with 'feminism' still considered their own political position in relation to parts of the project of feminism; such as empowerment of women. The storytelling norms of the collective promoted the understanding that in some way our socialization as women was linked to suffering, and that the opposition of suffering through activism was connected to the project of feminism. In this way organizational norms established a mechanism for feminist activist identity to be seen as a legitimate political position for opposing harmful social norms and for reducing suffering. Feminist activist identity was therefore associated with assumptions about how we should act to reduce suffering; including dismantling harmful social norms that perpetuated violence against women.

The shape of these accounts thereby promoted feminist solidarity. The personal stories accentuated that members of our collective were marked by their differences. In the collective it was considered important to share these stories and connect them to how we intended to undertake our activism. My colleagues thus marked how their stories were similar or different to others in the collective. The exploration of personal differences was seen as fundamental to the political positions my colleagues occupied for activism. Lived experience was highly prized and the collective's storytelling norms encouraged, and even compelled, members to give an account of their life experiences in relation to feminist activism. As the accounts of Ava and Tia demonstrate, however, these norms could also be exclusive. For those who identified other than feminist, a plausible account of their 'non' feminism had to be given. Although this was a painful process for those who felt uncomfortable or out of place in feminist activism, it was a vital process for fostering solidarity. The storytelling practices also gave an account of which women they incorporated into their feminist activism. Jen and Emily highlighted the importance of queer women, Tia and Evelyn of indigenous women, Ava and Kim of feminine women. The micro-politics of their individual stories were foundational to their activist work as a collective.

The micro-politics of academia, activism, and storytelling

At the outset of Part IV, I explained that my inspiration for focusing on the micro-politics of activist identity had come from my colleagues' desire to organize *through* their difference. Anti-violence activism in the community sector aiming for a singular, coherent 'feminist activism' – as many studies of anti-violence community organizations either problematically presume, or advocate – was not only impossible, but undesirable. Singular, often utopian social justice projects can overlook the complexities and nuances of power relations which make any emancipatory project necessarily local, contextual, and contested. We should not, however, abandon political projects, such as feminism, which underpin social movements. Instead, we must acknowledge the contradictions and challenges within these projects. Differences must not be erased, but must, as Audrey Lorde (1983) argues, 'be seen as a fund of necessary polarities between which our creativity can spark a dialectic'. In testament to embracing and working through those differences, my colleagues expressed a desire and carried out the work necessary to organize through their differences for feminist solidarity.

In the context of the community sector, my colleagues' narratives demonstrated the difficulty of maintaining a feminist activist identity in their work with the state, other community organizations, victims of violence, and funders. The pressures of constructing 'professional' identities instead of activist identities are intense for community workers, and these pressures constrain the possibilities of social justice in the community sector context. Nonetheless, maintaining activist identities is essential so that members of community organizations can establish and pursue their agenda for social justice. My colleagues' narratives emphasized, however, that pressure to embody certain types of activist identity often came from within community organizations, as well as from external partners. Such pressures are therefore essential to understanding how social justice is pursued by individual members.

A micro-political approach to the stories told by my colleagues proved to be extremely fruitful for my analysis of how they constructed their feminist activist identity. In the context of the collective, my colleagues supported the mission and were, by and large, supportive of the collective's practice which did often align with their ideas about social justice. However, my colleagues also articulated how they perceived their own feminist (or non-feminist) activist identity to challenge certain harmful norms in the collective. Through these challenges, my colleagues aimed to create ways of doing activism that were intersectional and non-violent. This process was sometimes painful for my colleagues, but it was a necessary pain in order to foster activism that incorporated a multidirectional approach to social justice. The storytelling norms of the collective, which compelled members to tell stories about their activist identity in relation to feminism, were important for linking lived experience to the broad emancipatory project of feminism. The practice of giving an account of feminist identity thereby created shared assumptions about how we should interact with one another, what practices we should engage in, and how we understood these to be beneficial for ending gendered violence. This promoted solidarity among my colleagues as it accentuated our differences and how our lived experience could contribute to the project of feminism.

Although the layers of self, organization, and social context have been usefully analytically separated throughout Part IV, they are, of course, concurrent. At the same time as being compelled to give an account of feminist activist identity, my colleagues were attempting to deconstruct their own harmful practices and were also under pressure to construct an identity perceived as legitimate by external stakeholders. The micro-politics of my colleagues' stories are, therefore, essential for understanding the complex negotiations of the multiple layers of activism. In the context of the community sector, constructing and maintaining activist identity is a messy endeavour. The community sector literature has primarily turned its gaze 'outwards' (that is, the social environment), but as I've demonstrated in this part, also turning the gaze 'internally' to community organizations can highlight important practices of constructing and maintaining activist identities. Uniting under a shared politics seems unfeasible in the context of the community sector where multiple accountabilities mean that it may be useful, and even necessary, to engage in a multidirectional approach to social justice.

There are many lessons here for reimagining the relationship between academia and activism. The multiple layered approach I have taken here resonates with the diversity of approaches to academic activism that I outlined in Part I. Academic activism has been argued to take place within social justice movements, within the university, and with university students. Each of the layers of academic activism compels the construction of multifaceted academic identities in accordance with the context. In their work with social movements, for instance, academics are pressured to draw on aspects of social justice while maintaining the 'usefulness' of their research. At the same time, academics are compelled to give (entrepreneurial) accounts of their selves, and in their teaching work are asked to educate critically, engagingly, and (increasingly) on mass. A micro-political approach to these multiple layers can therefore be very helpful for looking at how the negotiation of all these different layers creates an 'academic activist' account of their sense of self. Importantly, my colleagues demonstrate that it is often necessary to have differing identities across these intersections. The layers of this kind of identity work often result in a fractured sense of self, which may be productive even while it causes tension between different parts of the work.

My colleagues' storytelling norms emphasize the importance of connecting the personal to the political through 'giving an account' of oneself. Academics are likewise frequently compelled to give an account of themselves across teaching, research, and community engagement. These accounts have political dimensions. Such accounts can, for example, connect personal experience to emancipatory projects and thereby foster stronger connections to social justice movements. These accounts can be undertaken informally – such as in the classroom – or formally – such as through the writing of research. Importantly, however, these accounts can equally reinforce harmful assumptions about 'academic' versus 'activist' work and may marginalize the complex and dynamic collaboration with communities. As Judith Butler emphasizes, each account is an opportunity to redraw the lines of our identity. Although we will reinforce some harmful categories, we can also expand the boundaries of who, or what, counts. Our orientations to emancipatory projects and our relations to others can shift and change over time through these accounts.

The telling of these stories, as my colleagues demonstrate, can be done to promote solidarity and connection *through* difference. The work needed to share, challenge, and (re)tell stories can be as painful as it is productive. But there is no denying that it is *work*. Although I have presented the formal stories my colleagues shared with me here, they undertook this work on a regular basis when debating the role of the collective or their social justice practices. Significantly, my colleagues underscored that these stories are constrained within, as well as beyond, the collective. There was not a single anti-violence agenda in the collective. We had to follow multiple lines of identity and examine their interconnection. When we share stories of academia, activism, and the tangled relationship between them, what emerges will need to be frequently (re)told. The work of drawing stories together is ongoing, and these stories will never be singular. Our layers of accountability, our identities, and our political positions are important because they are entangled with the stories of others. Telling stories can connect academia and activism in many ways and value what we share as well as how we are different.

Conclusion:
Our Words Must Spill

I have written of those who seek to bring justice to abused women. I have written in anger, and in grief, and in hope. I have written of the one in three women in my homeland of Aotearoa New Zealand who are subjected to violence. I have written of those whose lives and deaths are violently excluded from such statistics. I have written of those who lived and died at the margins of normative ideas of 'victim' and 'woman'. I have written of those who experience layers of injustice from colonization to racism to heterosexism. I have written of the long-standing efforts of feminist anti-violence activists. I have written of those who recognize the institutional failure to protect vulnerable bodies from violence and organize to oppose such injustice. I have written of those women who dedicate their waking hours to creating deep emotional bonds between us. I have written of those women who tell stories of the abused, the dead, the discarded. I have written of those women who are the best of humanity consistently confronted by the worst. I have written of women in all of their glorious complexity.

I am undone by those women.

Core to this book has been my experience working alongside my colleagues in a feminist anti-violence collective. My colleagues were dedicated to supporting those subjected to gendered violence and changing the social conditions which underpin that violence. Although my colleagues had variable relationships with the idea of activism (as I discuss in Parts II and IV), they were, nevertheless, proud bearers of four ongoing commitments to collectivism, feminism, decolonization, and LGBT+ pride. These commitments were foundational to their effort to identify and dismantle harmful social and institutional practices and to foster new, more equitable, ones. My colleagues' efforts can be understood in reference to Black feminist Audre Lorde's famous sentiment: 'the Master's tools will never dismantle the Master's House. They may allow us temporarily to beat him at his own game, but they will never enable us to bring about genuine change' (Lorde, 1983). My colleagues were creating new tools. My colleagues were building a new house. This book has been an account of those tools.

The tools taken up by my colleagues were consistently refined in relation to an ever-shifting socio-political context. Politicians go in and out of office, businesses become more or less interested in supporting employees subjected to violence, benefit entitlements change, high profile cases of violence come to light, vigils are held for dead women, pandemics drastically alter pathways to safety. The four commitments had guided the work of the collective since the 1960s. To continue this legacy, however, my colleagues were required to reimagine how to embody those commitments and pick up those tools in a vastly different context. My colleagues were compelled to repeatedly negotiate their identity as feminists (Part IV), debate the role of the collective (Part II), and to (re)examine the connection between gender identity and violence (Part III). The words of Clifford are again relevant here: 'We ground things, now, on a moving earth.'

A moving earth necessitates a rich variety of tools to till the soil and allow us to flourish. The dynamic integration of theory and practice undertaken by my colleagues underscores that social change is less about having the 'right' tools, and more about what happens when we practice our commitments to justice in different terrains. As Deleuze and Guattari put it: 'tools exist only in relation to the interminglings they make possible or that make them possible' (1987: 105). My colleagues took ideas about intersectional feminism to government negotiations; ideas of gender fluidity to their work with victims of violence; ideas of emotion and ethical responsibility to their work with businesses. Each part of this book offered insight into the fluctuating landscape and the wide variety of tools that are taken up or put away in the fight against gendered violence. Activism is never singular. It is never static. Alternatively, my colleagues substantiate that we must develop our imaginative capacity for identifying and dismantling injustice and share tools to (re)build a more just world. May the tools delineated here resonate with those working on other social justice issues, in other countries, or in other traditions. May we develop solidarity by sharing our tools and learning from the tools of others; even when those struggles are not our own.

The feminist solidarity my colleagues fostered, as I discussed in Part IV, was grounded in a recognition that our differences are intimately and irrevocably tied to collective struggle. My colleagues explored their differences with an intent to understand how our identities shape experiences of injustice and access to tools for opposing that injustice. In other words, they aimed to organize and create tools that worked *through* our differences, rather than in spite of that difference. To again quote Audre Lorde (1983: 99): 'difference must not merely be tolerated but seen as a fund of necessary polarities between which our creativity can spark like a dialectic'. Our differences are not, however, fixed. In Part III, I looked at the shifting margins of gender identity and sexuality. In Part II I explored the evolving idea of the community sector activist. In Part IV, I traced the many lines of feminism, race, and indigeneity. To understand difference, we have to follow the lines of our identity which are connected to innumerable other lines, and then to yet more lines in other directions. We must understand how our difference continues to spill.

As I illustrated throughout the book, feminist collective organizing is far from some utopian ideal of cooperation free from conflict. Feminist anti-violence activism was unsettling, complex, and sometimes contradictory *work*. My colleagues worked to feel an ethical responsibility for victims. They worked to understand how our bodies were marked by institutional violence. My colleagues worked to embody a feminist politic. And at times this work was not successful. Sometimes my colleagues were excluded as LGBT+ women and/or as indigenous women. Sometimes they were excluded because of their conceptualization of feminism. Sometimes my colleagues embraced neoliberal ideas of individual responsibility over ideas of collective responsibility. We do ourselves a disservice, however, if we try to erase complexity or struggle. I have focused on the mess, the contradictions, the exclusions, and the conflicts because these are *productive* tensions. Such tensions are not a sign of failure, but indicative of the ongoing, necessary struggle to confront inequality and violence within, as well as beyond, activist organizing.

And in turn, I have brought the tools I learnt from my colleagues into my own terrain. At the outset of this book, I posed questions about the relationship between activist work and academic work, as well as questioning how we draw lines between what 'counts' as academic/activist. By bringing my colleagues' tools to these questions, I have sought to reimagine this relationship and explore novel opportunities for social change. This reflective process invited the reader to follow the multiple lines of connection (or divergence) between activist work and academic work. My rhizomatic narrative has spilled over those lines. I have traced and retraced lines of academic *and* activist, body *and* mind, theory *and* practice, and emotion *and* reason (to name a few). The 'and' is indispensable. It is the middle from which new ideas, tools, and connections grow or overspill (Deleuze and Guattari, 1987: 22). Accordingly, through my focus on the '*and*', I have explored what grows from the middle of my research work *and* my colleagues' anti-violence work.

Tracing these lines, I offer (necessarily) incomplete answers to my initial questions. 'Academic' and 'activist' are not fixed identities, but multifaceted and evolving ideas about how we contribute to society and (ideally) social justice. For my colleagues, it was the '*and*' of: activist *and* professional, cis-woman *and* activist, researcher *and* activist, feminist *and* activist, activist *and* Māori which expanded and deepened the boundaries of 'activist'. The nuanced portraits of my colleagues have moved away from reductive or rigid ideas of the activist and towards the singularity of their '*ands*'. The lines of academic identity are equally as nuanced. I have explored my own 'ands' throughout this book: academic *and* activist, academic *and* queer, academic *and* feminist. These lines are made and remade. A move away from the deadlock of the singular allows us more insight into the infinite variety of our intersecting identities and their potential connection to social justice.

Crucially, the '*ands*' of activist *and* academic must be examined in relation to interlocking systems of inequality. Our lives are threaded with power. My colleagues were expert at understanding power in relation to gendered violence. They had intricate knowledge of how powerful institutional norms shape who is trusted, who is protected, who holds knowledge, who is considered emotional, who has control over the distribution of resources, and so on. Moreover, the collective was founded in recognition that interlocking violence of racism, colonization, heterosexism, and sexism mean that the experience of violence differs *between* women as well as between gender minorities. In the same intricate fashion, the lines of academic/activist must be examined in relation to the powerful institutional norms I discussed in Part I and intersecting lines of identity which shape social recognition and access to resources.

The examination of our place, and the place of others, within interlocking systems of inequality requires vulnerability (Part III). We are collectively dependent on institutions for safety and recognition, but, as I have discussed, that safety and acknowledgement is not evenly distributed among us. We must come to (re)know those lines of inequality. Whereas some are protected because of their race; others are at risk. Whereas some are protected because of their gender identity; others are exposed to violence. For us to understand those lines, we must cultivate a capacity to be moved by others. Our knowledge of lines and our capacity to be moved across lines are interconnected. I came to know my connection to victims of violence through understanding the (fragile) norms that protected me from violence. Knowledge of interlocking systems of inequality, then, involves unsettling the lines between 'us' and 'them', of 'academic' and 'activist', and understanding how we are connected, in power and fragility, to institutional norms. These lines are ever changing. We must regularly reflect and ask ourselves: What are my lines? What lines can I draw, and at what price for myself or others? How could those lines be rearranged to redistribute resources? How could those lines be redrawn to recognize others?

The relationship between academia and activism, then, is dynamic, complex, and necessarily infused with power. My reimagination of this relationship asks us to follow lines of interconnection where our thinking and our doing are inescapably intertwined. I advocate for this position not as a prescriptive approach to academic activism, but as a framework for how we *could* reimagine the many ways academia and activism are interconnected. The identities of 'activist' and 'academic' can be meaningful and powerful. But they are never singular. A focus on the 'and' helps us to understand that these identities overlap in interesting and thought-provoking ways. The tools, ideas, and interconnections that emerge from that middle, that '*and*', offer novel insights into how we can collectively achieve social justice. It is not just those insights, however. To reiterate the words of my participant Shiner: "It isn't just the 'doing good' factor, it is [about] what you might become."

I am a different scholar from the one who started this project. In part, this book has been an account of my personal transformation. I have woven my experience throughout this book because I consider it important to know how I changed as a researcher, in order to understand how anti-violence work can change us. To reiterate the words of Karen Ashcraft (2018: 621): 'the more we feel what we do, the better we know what we do; and the more we know by feeling what we do, the more we have to offer.' What I learnt from my feminist anti-violence colleagues has changed how I approach my work and how I think of my role(s) in contributing to social justice. This approach can be messy. This approach asks us to be vulnerable and emotional. This approach asks us to challenge our thinking. This approach asks us to follow lines in all directions. And then follow them again. In the tradition of scholars and activists who offer holistic reimaginings of the role of the academic, activist, theory, and practice (see Part I), the approach presented in this book develops our imaginative capacity to create novel ways of organizing for social justice. And I consider this work far from over. This book is the middle from which things grow.

Ultimately, I have told a story of my feminist anti-violence colleagues and my experience working with them. I have told a story of academics and activists. I have told a story of how my colleagues' anti-violence work inspired me to reimagine what I knew about academia and activism. This story is embedded in a history of inequality, a community traumatized by gendered violence, and a society whose institutions fail to protect vulnerable bodies from violence. But this is also a story which honours the transformative work of those who seek justice for victims of gendered violence. Through this work, I have explored new ways of thinking about academia, activism, and collaborative work for social justice. The conclusions I have offered here are not neat or total. Instead, these conclusions refract the many lines of feminist anti-violence work. We are made of those lines. We must share stories of the lines that connect us and the lines that diverge. We must trace what happens between those lines.

Our words must spill.

Notes

Preface

[1] I refer specifically to women as at the time I volunteered with the collective, all members were cis-women. On either side of my official nine months' volunteer work, however, gender minorities and cis-men were also members. Importantly, the knowledge of the LGBT+ community is woven into the practices and theories of the collective I discuss in this book. I acknowledge and explore their work throughout this book, but specifically in Part III.

Chapter 1

[1] Māori are the indigenous people of Aotearoa New Zealand; Pākehā are white New Zealanders of European decent.

[2] Tauiwi is a word for 'non-Māori' and literally translates to foreigner or outsider.

Chapter 2

[1] Tangata Whenua literally translates to 'people of the land' and can refer to a specific area or to Māori as the indigenous people of Aotearoa New Zealand.

[2] Iwi means people or nation and is the largest form of social group.

Chapter 8

[1] Jen was particularly cognisant of the debates over the features and values of feminism. Beasley (1999) gives an overview of the different positions 'within' feminism that Jen covers and positions herself as, at various times.

[2] Māori concepts about women and their power. See Simmonds (2011) for an overview of the concepts of *mana wāhine* and *wāhine toa*.

[3] Work and Income New Zealand. They provide employment services and financial assistance.

[4] The Ministry of Social Development. They are a primary funder of social services.

[5] The Māori concept *whānau* refers to: extended family, family group, a familiar term of address to a number of people. *Whānau* is the primary economic unit of traditional Māori society. In the modern context, the term is sometimes used to include friends who may not have any kinship ties to other members. It is commonly used by Pākehā as well as Māori.

[6] Being 'slut-shamed' refers to the activity of criticizing women for their real or perceived promiscuity. See Attwood (2007) for an overview of the use of the term 'slut' and its relevance to feminism.

[7] Inexperienced, naïve, and lacking a critical awareness of politics.

[8] Kimberley's reference to Kim Kardashian and feminism is a significant one. Kim Kardashian is a controversial figure within feminism (Jones, 2014; Martin, 2017; Ruekgauer, 2017), but some argue that she is an important figure for promoting feminism because of her status on empowerment through sexuality and her entrepreneurial attitude to beauty and fashion (Jacobs, 2016). Kimberley uses Kim Kardashian to contrast her earlier position on 'slut-shaming'.

[9] The singer Chris Brown was convicted of domestic violence again his ex-partner Rihanna (Bowes, 2009). The case was particularly high profile, and anti-domestic violence campaigners regularly make use of the case in protests (Ryan, 2015).

[10] Social justice warrior is a colloquial term for a range of positions (often feminist) that are variably claimed to damage social causes by being overly dogmatic in their beliefs about social justice causes (Sarkar, 2016; Young, 2016).

[11] Kimberley references several feminist bodies of thought here: post-wave feminism, intersectional feminism, and third wave feminism. Post-wave feminism is used to mark a rejection of feminism on the grounds that success in equality is achieved and now must be maintained. Intersectional feminism refers to feminisms that take the intersection of various oppressions (such as race and gender) as their focus. Third wave feminism is a collection of approaches including these two, but also refers to the need to not present feminism as monolithic. See Evans (2015) for an overview of third wave feminisms.

Chapter 9

[1] 'White feminism' has received substantive criticism by anti-racist scholars (hooks, 1986; Lorde, 2007; Applebaum, 2010; Swan, 2017). As a form of feminist identity, White feminism is seen to focus on dismantling the struggles of White women while simultaneously failing to recognize the distinctive intersectional oppressions of women of colour.

[2] *Whakapapa* is a scared and significant concept for Māori. It refers to genealogy (and the recitation of genealogy) and is foundational to a sense of cultural connection and wellbeing.

[3] A *mihimihi* is an informal introduction. Many different styles are used but usually a *mihimihi* includes an account of where you are from and your *whakapapa*.

[4] *Tūrangawaewae* is most commonly translated as 'a place to stand'. It refers to places where we feel at home in the world and connected to the land.

References

Acker J (1990) Hierarchies, jobs, bodies: A theory of gendered organizations. *Gender and Society* 4(2): 139–158.

Acker J (2006) Inequality regimes: Gender, class, and race in organizations. *Gender and Society* 20(4): 441–464.

Ahmed S (2012) *On being included: Racism and diversity in institutional life.* London: Duke University Press.

Ahmed S (2014) *The cultural politics of emotion.* Edinburgh: Edinburgh University Press.

Ahmed S (2017) *Living a feminist life.* Durham, NC: Duke University Press.

Ali PA and Naylor PB (2013) Intimate partner violence: A narrative review of the feminist, social and ecological explanations for its causation. *Aggression and Violent Behavior* 18(6): 611–619.

Alvesson M and Gabriel Y (2013) Beyond formulaic research: In praise of greater diversity in organizational research and publications. *Academy of Management Learning & Education* 12(2): 245–263.

Alvesson M and Willmott H (1992) *Critical management studies.* London: SAGE Publications.

Alvesson M, Bridgman T and Willmott H (2011) *The Oxford handbook of critical management studies.* Oxford: Oxford University Press.

Anzaldúa G (2012) *Borderlands: La frontera: The new mestiza.* San Francisco: Aunt Lute Books.

Applebaum B (2010) *Being white, being good: White complicity, white moral responsibility, and social justice pedagogy.* Lanham: Lexington Books.

Arnold G and Ake J (2013) Reframing the narrative of the battered women's movement. *Violence Against Women* 19(5): 557–578.

Ashcraft KL (2018) Critical complicity: The feel of difference at work in home and field. *Management Learning* 49(5): 613–623.

Ashkanasy N and Cooper C (2008) *Research companion to emotion in organizations.* Cheltenham: Edward Elgar.

Attwood F (2007) Sluts and Riot Grrrls: Female identity and sexual agency. *Journal of Gender Studies* 16(3): 233–247.

Bailey B, Buchbinder E and Eisikovits Z (2011) Male social workers working with men who batter: Dilemmas in gender identity. *Journal of Interpersonal Violence* 26(9): 1741–1762.

Barrett BJ, Almanssori S, Kwan DL and Waddick E (2016) Feminism within domestic violence coalitions. *Affilia* 31(3): 359–371.

Beasley C (1999) *What is feminism? An introduction to feminist theory.* London: SAGE Publications.

Behar R (1996) *The vulnerable observer: Anthropology that breaks your heart.* Boston: Beacon Press.

Bell A (2006) Bifurcation or entanglement? Settler identity and biculturalism in Aotearoa New Zealand. *Continuum* 20(2): 253–268.

Ben-Ari A (2008) Splitting and integrating: The enabling narratives of mental health professionals who lived with domestic and intimate violence. *Qualitative Inquiry* 14(8): 1425–1443.

Bergin J and Westwood R (2003) The necessities of violence. *Culture and Organization* 9(4): 211–223.

Berlant L and Warner M (1998) Sex in public. *Critical Inquiry* 24(2): 547–566.

Bernal V and Grewal I (2014) *Theorizing NGOs: States, feminisms, and neoliberalism.* Durham, NC: Duke University Press.

Bordt R (1997) How alternative ideas become institutions: The case of feminist collectives. *Nonprofit and Voluntary Sector Quarterly* 26(2): 132–155.

Bornstein DR, Fawcett J, Sullivan M, Senturia KD and Shiu-Thornton S (2006) Understanding the experiences of lesbian, bisexual and trans survivors of domestic violence: A qualitative study. *Journal of Homosexuality* 51(1): 159–181.

Bowes M (2009) Chris Brown to get domestic-violence counselling. *McClatchy – Tribune Business News*, 27 August.

Bowring M and Brewis J (2009) Truth and consequences: Managing lesbian and gay identity in the Canadian workplace. *Equal Opportunities International* 28(5): 361–377.

Brennan M (2019) Scholarly activism in and for renewed Australian universities. *Social Alternatives* 38(3): 56–62.

Brewis DN (2017) Social justice 'lite'? Using emotion for moral reasoning in diversity practice. *Gender, Work & Organization* 24(5): 519–532.

Burstow B (1992) *Radical feminist therapy: Working in the context of violence.* Newbury Park: SAGE Publications.

Butler J (1993) *Bodies that matter: On the discursive limits of 'sex'.* New York: Routledge.

Butler J (1997) *The psychic life of power: Theories in subjection.* Palo Alto: Stanford University Press.

Butler J (2001) Giving an account of oneself. *Diacritics* 31(4): 22–40.

Butler J (2004a) *Undoing gender.* New York: Routledge.

Butler J (2004b) Violence, mourning, politics. In *Precarious life*. London: Verso, pp 19–49.

Butler J (2005) *Giving an account of oneself.* New York: Fordham University Press.

Butler J (2006a) *Gender trouble: Feminism and the subversion of identity.* New York: Routledge.

Butler J (2006b) *Precarious life: The powers of mourning and violence.* London: Verso.

Butler J (2011a) Bodies in alliance and the politics of the street. In Sholette G and Ressler O (eds) *It's the political economy, stupid: The global financial crisis in art and theory*. London: Pluto Press, pp 118–124.

Butler J (2011b) 'Confessing a passionate state …': Judith Butler in interview. In Hark S and Villa P-I (eds) *Feministische Studien*. pp 196–205. www. degruyter.com/document/doi/10.1515/fs-2011-0204/html

Butler J (2011c) Remarks on 'queer bonds'. *GLQ: A Journal of Lesbian and Gay Studies* 17(2): 381–387.

Butler J (2015) *Notes toward a performative theory of assembly.* Cambridge, MA: Harvard University Press.

Butler J (2017) We are wordless without one another: An interview with Judith Butler. In Berbec S (ed) *The Other Journal: An intersection of theology & culture: The Seattle school of theology & psychology* 27.

Buyantueva R and Shevtsova M (2020) *LGBTQ+ activism in Central and Eastern Europe: Resistance, representation and identity*. Cham: Palgrave Macmillan.

Campbell R (2013) *Emotionally involved: The impact of researching rape.* Abingdon: Taylor & Francis.

Cheney G, Santa Cruz I, Peredo AM and Cheney G (2014) Worker cooperatives as an organizational alternative: Challenges, achievements and promise in business governance and ownership. *Organization* 21(5): 591–603.

Choudry A (2020) Reflections on academia, activism, and the politics of knowledge and learning. *The International Journal of Human Rights: Activist Scholarship in Human Rights* 24(1): 28–45.

Clifford J and Marcus GE (2011) *Writing culture: The poetics and politics of ethnography*. Berkeley: University of California Press.

Coffey A (1999) *The ethnographic self.* Thousand Oaks: SAGE Publications.

Colgan F and Rumens N (2015) *Sexual orientation at work: Contemporary issues and perspectives*. New York: Routledge.

Connell R (2019) New maps of struggle for gender justice: Rethinking feminist research on organizations and work. *Gender, Work & Organization* 26(1): 54–63.

Connolly M (2004) *Violence in society: New Zealand perspectives.* Christchurch: Te Awatea Press.

Connor M and Yerbury H (2017) Small worlds and active citizenship: Interactions between an NGO and its Facebook community. *Third Sector Review* 23(2): 109–129.

Cornwall A (2007) Myths to live by? Female solidarity and female autonomy reconsidered. *Development and Change* 38(1): 149–168.

Corry O (2010) Defining and theorizing the third sector. In Taylor R (ed) *Third sector research*. New York: Springer, pp 11–20.

Couture S (2017) Activist scholarship: The complicated entanglements of activism and research work. *Canadian Journal of Communication* 42(1): 143–147.

Creed WED, DeJordy R and Lok J (2010) Being the change: Resolving institutional contradiction through identity work. *The Academy of Management Journal* 53(6): 1336–1364.

D'Enbeau S and Buzzanell PM (2013) Constructing a feminist organization's identity in a competitive marketplace: The intersection of ideology, image, and culture. *Human Relations* 66(11): 1447–1470.

Dale A and Onyx J (2005) *A dynamic balance: Social capital and sustainable community development*. Vancouver: UBC Press.

Davies A and Thomas R (2004) Gendered identities and micro-political resistance in public service organisations. In Thomas R, Mills AJ and Mills JH (eds) *Identity politics at work: Resisting gender, gendering resistance*. London: Routledge, pp 105–122.

de Souza EM, Brewis J and Rumens N (2016) Gender, the body and organization studies: Que(e)rying empirical research. *Gender, Work & Organization* 23(6): 600–613.

Deleuze G and Guattari F (1987) *A thousand plateaus: Capitalism and schizophrenia*. Minneapolis: University of Minnesota Press.

Dempsey SE (2009) NGOs, communicative labor, and the work of grassroots representation. *Communication and Critical/Cultural Studies* 6(4): 328–345.

Denicolo P (2014) *Achieving impact in research*. London: SAGE Publications.

Dey P and Teasdale S (2016) The tactical mimicry of social enterprise strategies: Acting 'as if' in the everyday life of third sector organizations. *Organization* 23(4): 485–504.

Dickson S (2016) Hohou Te Rongo Kahukura – Outing Violence: Building Rainbow communities free of partner and sexual violence. www.kahukura. co.nz/wp-content/uploads/2015/07/Building-Rainbow-Communities-Free-of-Partner-and-Sexual-Violence-2016.pdf

Dodge J and Ospina SM (2016) Nonprofits as 'schools of democracy'. *Nonprofit and Voluntary Sector Quarterly* 45(3): 478–499.

Douglas H (2015) Embracing hybridity: A review of social entrepreneurship and enterprise in Australia and New Zealand. *Third Sector Review* 21(1): 5–30.

Eikenberry AM (2009) Refusing the market. *Nonprofit and Voluntary Sector Quarterly* 38(4): 582–596.

Eikenberry AM, Mirabella RM and Sandberg B (2019) *Reframing nonprofit organizations: Democracy, inclusion, and social change.* Irvine: Melvin & Leigh.

Elliott M (2016) Unravelling charities' ability to do good. *New Zealand Herald,* 16 August.

Elliott S and Haigh D (2013) Advocacy in the New Zealand not-for-profit sector: 'Nothing stands by itself'. *Third Sector Review* 18(2): 157–178.

Ellsworth E (1989) Why doesn't this feel empowering? Working through the repressive myths of critical pedagogy. *Harvard Educational Review* 59(3): 297–324.

Else A (1993) *Women together: A history of women's organisations in New Zealand/ Nga ropu wahine o te motu.* Wellington: Historical Branch, Dept. of Internal Affairs and Daphne Brasell Associates Press.

Erakovic L and McMorland J (2009) Perceptions of 'good governance' in New Zealand non-profit organisations. *Third Sector Review* 15(2): 125–147.

Eschle C and Maiguashca B (2006) Bridging the academic/activist divide: Feminist activism and the teaching of global politics. *Millennium* 35(1): 119–137.

Evans E (2015) *The politics of third wave feminisms: Neoliberalism, intersectionality, and the state in Britain and the US.* London: Palgrave Macmillan.

Fanslow JL and Robinson EM (2011) Sticks, stones, or words? Counting the prevalence of different types of intimate partner violence reported by New Zealand women. *Journal of Aggression, Maltreatment & Trauma* 20(7): 741–759.

Ferree MM and Martin PY (1995) *Feminist organizations: Harvest of the new women's movement.* Philadelphia: Temple University Press.

Ferree MM and Tripp AM (2006) *Global feminism: Transnational women's activism, organizing, and human rights.* New York: New York University Press.

Fineman S (2000) *Emotion in organizations.* 2nd ed. London: SAGE Publications.

Flood M, Martin B and Dreher T (2013) Combining academia and activism: Common obstacles and useful tools. *The Australian Universities' Review* 55(1): 17–26.

Foucault M (1977) *Language, counter-memory, practice: Selected essays and interviews by Michel Foucault.* New York: Cornell University Press.

Fung A (2003) Associations and democracy: Between theories, hopes, and realities. *Annual Review of Sociology* 29(1): 515–539.

Gatrell C (2011) Policy and the pregnant body at work: Strategies of secrecy, silence and supra-performance. *Gender, Work & Organization* 18(2): 158–181.

Ghatak M (2020) Economic theories of the social sector: From nonprofits to social enterprise. In Powell WW and Bromley P (eds) *The nonprofit sector: A research handbook*. 3rd ed. Stanford: Stanford University Press, pp 319–332.

Gherardi S and Poggio B (2007) *Gendertelling in organizations: Narratives from male-dominated environments*. Frederiksberg: Samfundslitteratur.

Giddings LS and Pringle JK (2011) Heteronormativity at work: Stories from two lesbian academics. *Women's Studies Journal* 25(2): 91–100.

Gilpin DR and Miller NK (2013) Identity brokerage and nonprofit community building. *Journal of Nonprofit & Public Sector Marketing* 25(4): 354–373.

Goldblatt H (2009) Caring for abused women: Impact on nurses' professional and personal life experiences. *Journal of Advanced Nursing* 65(8): 1645–1654.

Goldblatt H and Buchbinder E (2003) Challenging gender roles: The impact on female social work students of working with abused women. *Journal of Social Work Education* 39(2): 255–275.

Goldblatt H, Buchbinder E, Eisikovits Z and Arizon-Mesinger I (2009) Between the professional and the private: The meaning of working with intimate partner violence in social workers' private lives. *Violence Against Women* 15(3): 362–384.

Goodwin J, Jasper JM and Polletta F (2001) *Passionate politics, emotions, and social movements*. Chicago: University of Chicago Press.

Grace G (2010) Reflection on the university and the academic as 'critic and conscience of society'. *New Zealand Journal of Educational Studies* 45(2): 89–92.

Green JA (2007) *Making space for Indigenous feminism*. Black Point, Canada: Fernwood Publishing.

Grey S and Sedgwick C (2013a) The contract state and constrained democracy: The community and voluntary sector under threat. *Policy Quarterly* 9(3): 3–10.

Grey S and Sedgwick C (2013b) Fears, constraints and contracts: The democratic reality for New Zealand's community and voluntary sector. Report presented at the Community and Voluntary Sector Forum, Victoria University of Wellington, 26 March. www.wgtn.ac.nz/sacs/pdf-files/Fears-constraints-and-contracts-Grey-and-Sedgwick-2014.pdf

Grey S and Sedgwick C (2015) Constraining the community voice: The impact of the neoliberal contract state on democracy. *New Zealand Sociology* 30(1): 88–110.

Gueta K, Peled E and Sander-Almoznino N (2016) 'I used to be an ordinary mom': The maternal identity of mothers of women abused by an intimate partner. *American Journal of Orthopsychiatry* 86(4): 456–466.

Hale CR (2019) *Engaging contradictions: Theory, politics, and methods of activist scholarship*. Berkeley: University of California Press.

Hanisch C (1970) The personal is political. In AK Shulamith (ed) *Notes from the second year: Women's liberation 1970*. New York: Radical Feminist, pp 76–77.

Herrmann A (2011) Narrative as an organizing process: Identity and story in a new nonprofit. *Qualitative Research in Organizations and Management: An International Journal* 6(3): 246–264.

Hill J (2019) *See what you made me do: Power, control and domestic abuse*. Carlton: Black Inc.

Hochschild AR (1979) Emotion work, feeling rules, and social structure. *American Journal of Sociology* 85(3): 551–575.

Hochschild AR (2012) *The managed heart: Commercialization of human feeling*. Berkeley: University of California Press.

hooks b (1986) Sisterhood: Political solidarity between women. *Feminist Review* 23(1): 293–315.

Hughes J (2017) Women's advocates and shelter residents: Describing experiences of working and living in domestic violence shelters. *Journal of Interpersonal Violence* 15(16): 1–20.

Hull R, Gibbon J, Branzei O et al (2011) The third sector. In Gilmore S (ed) *Dialogues in critical management studies: Volume 1*. Bingley: Emerald.

Huygens I (2001) Feminist attempts at power sharing in Aotearoa: Embracing herstory or significant learning towards treaty-based structures. *Feminism & Psychology* 11(3): 393–400.

Huygens I (2011) Developing a decolonisation practice for settler colonisers: A case study from Aotearoa New Zealand. *Settler Colonial Studies* 1(2): 53–81.

Iliffe G and Steed LG (2000) Exploring the counselor's experience of working with perpetrators and survivors of domestic violence. *Journal of Interpersonal Violence* 15(4): 393–412.

Irwin K (1990) 'Challenges' to Maori feminists. *Broadsheet*, 182: 20–24.

Jacobs L (2016) The face of the modern feminist: Kim Kardashian. *UWIRE Text*, 10 February, p 1.

Jagose AR (1996) *Queer theory*. Carlton: Melbourne University Press.

Jeanes E, Knights D and Martin PY (2011) *Handbook of gender, work and organization*. Chichester: Wiley.

Jensen PR (2017) 'People can't believe we exist!': Social sustainability and alternative nonprofit organizing. *Critical Sociology* 44(2): 1–14.

Jensen PR and Meisenbach RJ (2015) Alternative organizing and (in)visibility. *Management Communication Quarterly* 29(4): 564–589.

Johansson J, Tienari J and Valtonen A (2017) The body, identity and gender in managerial athleticism. *Human Relations* 70(9): 1141–1167.

Johnson L, Todd M and Subramanian G (2005) Violence in police families: Work-family spillover. *Journal of Family Violence* 20(1): 3–12.

Jones A (2014) In an age when a woman's bottom can break the internet, feminism is a term we cannot do without. *The Independent*, 15 November, p 37.

Kenny K (2010) Beyond ourselves: Passion and the dark side of identification in an ethical organization. *Human Relations* 63(6): 857–873.

Kenny K and Bell E (2011) Representing the successful managerial body. In Jeanes E, Knights D and Martin P (eds) *Handbook of gender, work and organization*. Chichester: Wiley, pp 163–177.

Kerekere E (2015) *Takatāpui: Part of the whānau*. Auckland: Tiwhanawhana Trust and Mental Health Foundation.

Khasnabish A and Haiven M (2015) Outside but along-side: Stumbling with social movements as academic activists. *Studies in Social Justice* 9(1): 18–33.

King D (2017) Becoming business-like. *Nonprofit and Voluntary Sector Quarterly* 46(2): 241–260.

King D and Learmonth M (2015) Can critical management studies ever be 'practical'? A case study in engaged scholarship. *Human Relations* 68(3): 353–375.

Kirby EL, Koschmann MA and Dempsey SE (2012) Nonprofits as political actors. *Management Communication Quarterly* 26(1): 147–151.

Kohler S, Höhne A, Ehrhardt M et al (2013) General practitioners and managing domestic violence: Results of a qualitative study in Germany. *Journal of Forensic and Legal Medicine* 20(6): 732–735.

Köllen T (2013) Bisexuality and diversity management: Addressing the 'B' in LGBT as a relevant 'sexual orientation' in the workplace. *Journal of Bisexuality* 13(1): 122–137.

Kondo D (1990) *Crafting selves: Power, gender, and discourses of identity in a Japanese workplace*. London: University of Chicago Press.

Land C and King D (2014) Organizing otherwise: Translating anarchism in a voluntary sector organization. *ephemera* 14(4): 923–950.

Lapointe K (2013) Heroic career changers? Gendered identity work in career transitions. *Gender, Work & Organization* 20(2): 133–146.

Larner W and Butler M (2005) Governmentalities of local partnerships: The rise of a 'partnering' state in New Zealand. *Studies in Political Economy* 75(1): 79–102.

Larner W and Craig D (2005) After neoliberalism? Community activism and local partnerships in Aotearoa New Zealand. *Antipode* 37(3): 402–424.

Laurie N and Bondi L (2005) *Working the spaces of neoliberalism: Activism, professionalisation and incorporation*. Oxford: Blackwell.

Lester-Smith D (2013) Healing Aboriginal family violence through Aboriginal storytelling. *AlterNative: An International Journal of Indigenous Peoples* 9(4): 309–321.

Lloyd M (2015) The ethics and politics of vulnerable bodies. In Lloyd M (ed) *Butler and ethics*. Edinburgh: Edinburgh University Press, pp 167–192.

Lorde A (1983) The master's tools will never dismantle the master's house. In Moraga C and Anzaldúa G (eds) *This bridge called my back: Writings by radical women of colour*. New York: Kitchen Table: Women of Colour Press, pp 98–101.

Lorde A (2007) *Sister outsider: Essays and speeches*. Berkeley: Crossing Press.

Love TR (2019) *Indigenous organization studies: Exploring management, business and community*. Cham: Springer International.

Maclean M, Harvey C, Gordon J and Shaw E (2015) Identity, storytelling and the philanthropic journey. *Human Relations* 68(10): 1623–1652.

Martin A (2017) Sharon Osbourne on Kim Kardashian's sexy selfies: 'That's not feminism!'. *UPI News Current*, 5 September.

Mason DE (1996) *Leading and managing the expressive dimension: Harnessing the hidden power source of the nonprofit sector*. San Francisco: Jossey–Bass.

Matebeni Z, Monro S and Reddy V (2018) *Queer in Africa: LGBTQI identities, citizenship, and activism*. London: Routledge.

McLeod J (2017) The New Zealand cause report: Shape of the charity sector. JBWere, March. www.philanthropy.org.au/images/site/blog/FINAL_127046581_The_NZCause_Report_0217-V7-DIGITAL.pdf

McMillan L (2007) *Feminists organising against gendered violence*. New York: Palgrave Macmillan.

Meyerson DE and Scully MA (1995) Tempered radicalism and the politics of ambivalence and change. *Organization Science* 6(5): 585–600.

Mikaere A (1994) Māori women: Caught in the contradictions of a colonised reality. *Waikato Law Review* 2(1): 125–149.

Mohanty CT (2003) 'Under Western Eyes' revisited: Feminist solidarity through anticapitalist struggles. *Signs* 28(2): 499–535.

Molisa P (2010) White business education. *Critical Perspectives on Accounting* 21(6): 525–528.

Moraga C and Anzaldúa G (2015) *This bridge called my back: Writings by radical women of color*. 4th ed. Albany: SUNY Press.

Murgia A and Poggio B (2009) Challenging hegemonic masculinities: Men's stories on gender culture in organizations. *Organization* 16(3): 407–423.

Naples NA (2003) *Feminism and method: Ethnography, discourse analysis, and activist research*. New York: Taylor & Francis.

Naples NA (2010) Borderlands studies and border theory: Linking activism and scholarship for social justice. *Sociology Compass* 4(7): 505–518.

Neilson B, Sedgwick C and Grey S (2015) Outcomes plus: The added value provided by community social services. Report, New Zealand Council of Christian Social Services. https://nzccss.org.nz/library/research-analysis/Outcomes%20Plus%2025%20May.pdf

Ng ES and Rumens N (2017) Diversity and inclusion for LGBT workers: Current issues and new horizons for research. *Canadian Journal of Administrative Sciences / Revue Canadienne des Sciences de l'Administration* 34(2): 109–120.

Nichols AJ (2011) Gendered organizations: Challenges for domestic violence victim advocates and feminist advocacy. *Feminist Criminology* 6(2): 111–131.

Nichols AJ (2013) Meaning-making and domestic violence victim advocacy. *Feminist Criminology* 8(3): 177–201.

Nichols AJ (2014) *Feminist advocacy: Gendered organizations in community-based responses to domestic violence.* Lanham: Lexington Books.

Nowland-Foreman G (2016) Crushed or just bruised? Voluntary organisations – 25 years under the bear hug of government funding in Aotearoa New Zealand. *Third Sector Review* 22(2): 53–69.

Onyx J, Armitage L, Dalton B, Melville R, Casey J and Bank R (2010) Advocacy with gloves on: The 'manners' of strategy used by some third sector organizations undertaking advocacy in NSW and Queensland. *VOLUNTAS: International Journal of Voluntary and Nonprofit Organizations* 21(1): 41–61.

Parker M (2013) 'What is to be done?' CMS as a political party. In Malin V, Murphy J and Siltaoja M (eds) *Getting things done.* London: Emerald, pp 165–181.

Parker M (2018) *Shut down the business school: What's wrong with management education.* London: Pluto Press.

Parker M, Cheney G, Fournier V and Land C (2014a) The question of organization: A manifesto for alternatives. *ephemera* 14(4): 623–638.

Parker M, Cheney G, Fournier V and Land C (2014b) *The Routledge companion to alternative organization.* Abingdon: Routledge.

Parsons E and Priola V (2013) Agents for change and changed agents: The micro-politics of change and feminism in the academy. *Gender, Work & Organization* 20(5): 580–598.

Pedwell C (2012) Affective (self-) transformations: Empathy, neoliberalism and international development. *Feminist Theory* 13(2): 163–179.

Pedwell C (2013) Affect at the margins: Alternative empathies in a small place. *Emotion, Space and Society* 8: 18–26.

Peled E and Dekel R (2010) Excusable deficiency: Staff perceptions of mothering at shelters for abused women. *Violence Against Women* 16(11): 1224–1241.

Petray TL (2012) A walk in the park: Political emotions and ethnographic vacillation in activist research. *Qualitative Research* 12(5): 554–564.

Phipps A (2016) Whose personal is more political? Experience in contemporary feminist politics. *Feminist Theory* 17(3): 303–321.

Porschitz ET and Siler EA (2017) Miscarriage in the workplace: An authoethnography. *Gender, Work & Organization* 24(6): 565–578.

Pullen A (2018) Writing as labiaplasty. *Organization* 25(1): 123–130.

Pullen A, Harding N and Phillips M (2017) *Feminists and queer theorists debate the future of critical management studies.* London: Emerald.

Quesada U, Gomez L and Vidal-Ortiz S (2015) *Queer brown voices: Personal narratives of Latina/o LGBT activism.* Austin: University of Texas Press.

Ranis P (2016) *Cooperatives confront capitalism: Challenging the neoliberal economy.* London: Zed Books.

Rawiri Waretini K (2012) Takitoru: From parallel to partnership – a ritual of engagement based on Te Tiriti o Waitangi for implementing safe cultural practice in Māori counselling and social science. *MAI Journal (Online)* 1(1): 61–75.

Reedy PC and King DR (2019) Critical performativity in the field: Methodological principles for activist ethnographers. *Organizational Research Methods* 22(2): 564–589.

Reedy P, King D and Coupland C (2016) Organizing for individuation: Alternative organizing, politics and new identities. *Organization Studies* 37(11): 1553–1573.

Reinelt C (1994) Fostering empowerment, building community: The challenge for state-funded feminist organizations. *Human Relations* 47(6): 685–705.

Reiter B and Oslender U (2014) *Bridging scholarship and activism: Reflections from the frontlines of collaborative research.* Ann Arbor: Michigan State University Press.

Riad S (2007) Under the desk: On becoming a mother in the workplace. *Culture and Organization* 13(3): 205–222.

Ristock JL (2002) *No more secrets: Violence in lesbian relationships.* New York: Routledge.

Ristock JL (2011) *Intimate partner violence in LGBTQ lives.* Florence, SC: Taylor & Francis.

Roces M and Edwards L (2010) *Women's movements in Asia: Feminisms and transnational activism.* New York: Routledge.

Rodriguez NM (1988) Transcending bureaucracy: Feminist politics at a shelter for battered women. *Gender & Society* 2(2): 214–227.

Rosaldo R (1989) *Culture & truth: The remaking of social analysis.* Boston: Beacon Press.

Ruekgauer A (2017) Kim Kardashian and feminism. *UWIRE Text,* 16 March, p 1.

Rumens N (2016) On the violence of heteronormativity within business schools. In Köllen T (ed) *Sexual orientation and transgender issues in organizations: Global perspectives on LGBT workforce diversity.* Cham: Springer International, pp 389–404.

Ryan S (2015) 'Not enough evidence' to show Chris Brown reformed. *New Zealand Herald*, 30 September.

Sanders J, O'Brien M, Sokolowiski S and Salamon LM (2008) The New Zealand non-profit sector in comparative perspective.

Sanders ML (2015) Being nonprofit-like in a market economy. *Nonprofit and Voluntary Sector Quarterly* 44(2): 205–222.

Sanders ML and McClellan JG (2014) Being business-like while pursuing a social mission: Acknowledging the inherent tensions in US nonprofit organizing. *Organization* 21(1): 68–89.

Sarkar S (2016) Why I hate the term 'SJW'. *Huffington Post*, 12 April.

Sayers JG and Jones D (2015) Truth scribbled in blood: Women's work, menstruation and poetry. *Gender, Work & Organization* 22(2): 94–111.

Sedgwick E (1994) *Tendencies*. Abingdon: Taylor & Francis.

Seymour K (2009) Women, gendered work and gendered violence: So much more than a job. *Gender, Work & Organization* 16(2): 238–265.

Shaw S and Allen JB (2006) 'We actually trust the community': Examining the dynamics of a nonprofit funding relationship in New Zealand. *VOLUNTAS: International Journal of Voluntary and Nonprofit Organizations* 17(3): 211–220.

Shayne JD (2014) *Taking risks: Feminist activism and research in the Americas*. Albany: State University of New York Press.

Shelton SZ (2017) A queer theorist's critique of online domestic violence advocacy: Critically responding to the National Coalition Against Domestic Violence website. *Journal of Homosexuality*. DOI: 10.1080/00918369.2017.1374060.

Sieben B and Wettergren Å (2010) Emotionalizing organizations and organizing emotions: Our research agenda. In Sieben B and Wettergren Å (eds) *Emotionalizing organizations and organizing emotions*. London: Palgrave Macmillan, pp 1–22.

Simmonds N (2011) *Mana wahine*: Decolonising politics. *Women's Studies Journal* 25(2): 11–25.

Sinclair A (2011) Leading with body. In Jeanes E, Knights D and Martin P (eds) *Handbook of gender, work & organization*. Chichester: Wiley, pp 117–130.

Smith LT (2012) *Decolonizing methodologies: Research and indigenous peoples*. London: Zed Books.

Smithies C and Lather PA (1997) *Troubling the angels: Women living with HIV*. Boulder, CO: Westview Press.

Speed S (2006) At the crossroads of human rights and anthropology: Toward a critically engaged activist research. *American Anthropologist* 108(1): 66–76.

Sudbury J and Okazawa-Rey M (2009) *Activist scholarship: Antiracism, feminism, and social change*. Boulder: Paradigm.

Sutherland N, Land C and Böhm S (2014) Anti-leaders(hip) in social movement organizations: The case of autonomous grassroots groups. *Organization* 21(6): 759–781.

Swan E (2017) What are white people to do? Listening, challenging ignorance, generous encounters and the 'not yet' as diversity research praxis. *Gender, Work & Organization* 24(5): 547–563.

Swan E and Fox S (2010) Playing the game: Strategies of resistance and co-optation in diversity work. *Gender, Work & Organization* 17(5): 567–589.

Te Puni Kōkiri (2010) *Arotake tūkino whānau: Literature review on family violence*. Te Puni Kōkiri.

Tennant M (1989) *Paupers and providers: Charitable aid in New Zealand*. Wellington: Allen & Unwin.

Tennant M (2005) Welfare interactions: Māori, government and the voluntary sector in New Zealand. *History Australia* 2(3): 1–15.

Tennant M (2006) *Defining the nonprofit sector: New Zealand*. Baltimore: Johns Hopkins University Center for Civil Society Studies.

Tennant M, O'Brien M and Sanders J (2008) The history of the non-profit sector in New Zealand. Wellington: Office for the Community and Voluntary Sector.

Thomas R (2018) *Questioning the assessment of research impact: Illusions, myths and marginal sectors*. Cham: Springer International.

Thomas R and Davies A (2005) Theorizing the micro-politics of resistance: New public management and managerial identities in the UK public services. *Organization Studies* 26(5): 683–706.

Tomlinson F and Schwabenland C (2010) Reconciling competing discourses of diversity? The UK non-profit sector between social justice and the business case. *Organization* 17(1): 101–121.

The Trapese Collective (2014) Education: By the people, for the people. In Parker M, Cheney G, Fournier V and Land C (eds) *The Routledge companion to alternative organization*. Abingdon: Routledge, pp 329–344.

Troth AC, Lawrence SA, Jordan PJ and Ashkanasy N (2017) Interpersonal emotion regulation in the workplace: A conceptual and operational review and future research agenda. *International Journal of Management Reviews* 20(2): 523–543.

Tyagi SV (2006) Female counselors and male perpetrators of violence against women. *Women & Therapy* 29(1–2): 1–22.

Tyler M and Cohen L (2010) Spaces that matter: Gender performativity and organizational space. *Organization Studies* 31(2): 175–198.

Ulus E and Gabriel Y (2018) Bridging the contradictions of social constructionism and psychoanalysis in a study of workplace emotions in India. *Culture and Organization* 24(3): 221–243.

UNODC (United Nations Office on Drugs and Crime) (2018) *Global study of homicide: Gender related killing of women and girls*. Vienna: United Nations Office on Drugs and Crime.

Vachhani SJ and Pullen A (2019) Ethics, politics, and feminist organizing: Writing feminist infrapolitics and affective solidarity into everyday sexism. *Human Relations* 72(1): 23–47.

Varkarolis O and King D (2017) Voicing researched activists with responsive action research. *Qualitative Research in Organizations and Management: An International Journal* 12(4): 315–334.

Walker R (2004) *Ka whawhai tonu mātou: Struggle without end*. Auckland: Penguin.

Weatherall R (2020) Even when those struggles are not our own: Storytelling and solidarity in a feminist social justice organization. *Gender, Work & Organization* 27(4): 471–486.

Weatherall R, Gavin M and Thorburn N (2021) Safeguarding women at work? Lessons from Aotearoa New Zealand toward effectively implementing domestic violence policies. *Journal of Industrial Relations*. https://doi.org/10.1177/0022185621996766

Wesely JK, Allison MT and Schneider IE (2000) The lived body experience of domestic violence survivors: An interrogation of female identity. *Women's Studies International Forum* 23(2): 211–222.

Wilkinson E (2009) The emotions least relevant to politics? Queering autonomous activism. *Emotion, Space and Society* 2(1): 36–43.

Wilson D, Jackson D and Herd R (2016) Confidence and connectedness: Indigenous Māori women's views on personal safety in the context of intimate partner violence. *Health Care for Women International* 37(7): 707–720.

Woodside AG (2016) *Bad to good: Achieving high quality and impact in your research*. Bingley: Emerald Group.

Woolford A and Curran A (2013) Community positions, neoliberal dispositions: Managing nonprofit social services within the bureaucratic field. *Critical Sociology* 39(1): 45–63.

Wright C, Nyberg D and Grant D (2012) 'Hippies on the third floor': Climate change, narrative identity and the micro-politics of corporate environmentalism. *Organization Studies* 33(11): 1451–1475.

Yerbury H and Burridge N (2013) The activist professional: Advocacy and scholarship. *Third Sector Review* 19(2): 119–134.

Young C (2016) The totalitarian doctrine of 'social justice warriors'. *The Observer*, 2 February.

Index

References to endnotes show both the
page number and the note number (231n3).